Bilingualism in the USA

Studies in Bilingualism (SiBil)

The focus of this series is on psycholinguistic and sociolinguistic aspects of bilingualism. This entails topics such as childhood bilingualism, psychological models of bilingual language users, language contact and bilingualism, maintenance and shift of minority languages, and socio-political aspects of bilingualism.

For an overview of all books published in this series, please see
http://benjamins.com/catalog/sibil

Volume 44

Bilingualism in the USA. The case of the Chicano-Latino community
by Fredric Field

Bilingualism in the USA

The case of the Chicano-Latino community

Fredric Field

California State University, Northridge

John Benjamins Publishing Company

Amsterdam / Philadelphia

TM The paper used in this publication meets the minimum requirements of American National Standard for Information Sciences – Permanence of Paper for Printed Library Materials, ANSI z39.48-1984.

Library of Congress Cataloging-in-Publication Data

Bilingualism in the USA : the case of the Chicano-Latino community / Fredric Field.
      p.   cm. (Studies in Bilingualism, ISSN 0928-1533 ; v. 44)
Includes bibliographical references and index.
1. Education, Bilingual--United States. 2. Bilingualism--United States. 3. Hispanic Americans--
      Education. 4. Mexican Americans--Education 5. Language acquisition.
LC3731.B575   2011
370.117'50973--dc23   2011018543
ISBN 978 90 272 4183 2   (Hb ; alk. paper)
ISBN 978 90 272 4184 9   (Pb ; alk. paper)
ISBN 978 90 272 8509 6   (Eb)

John Benjamins Publishing Co. · P.O. Box 36224 · 1020 ME Amsterdam · The Netherlands
John Benjamins North America · P.O. Box 27519 · Philadelphia PA 19118-0519 · USA

Table of contents

Acknowledgments

I would like to express gratitude to all those who have had a role in the writing of this book, above all to Kees Vaes, the editor at John Benjamins who has seen this project through from front to finish. I would also like to thank the administrators of California State University, Northridge (CSUN), for granting me a sabbatical leave in the Fall of 2008 to put notes for several chapters into (relatively) coherent form, and the colleagues who helped guide me through the proposal process. I have benefitted much from the support of the Dean of Humanities, Elizabeth Say, and from the confidence expressed in me by George Uba, department chair, and my colleagues in the English Department. I would be remiss if I neglected to mention Margie Seagoe, currently secretary for Graduate Studies in the English Department at CSUN; I am very grateful for her continual words of wisdom and encouragement.

In addition, I would like to express thanks to the Linguistics Department at the Max Planck Institute for Evolutionary Anthropology in Leipzig, Germany, particularly, to the chair, Bernard Comrie, and fellow researchers, for providing support for my work on language contact during my visits there. Also thanks go to the administrative staff, e.g., Julia Cissewski, Claudia Büchel, and all the others, for their thoughtful support.

I would also like to thank Professor Thom Huebner (San Jose State) and Professor Juana Mora (CSUN), both who painstakingly reviewed various drafts of the manuscript. I have tried to incorporate their comments and criticisms into my work to the best of my abilities. Of course, all errors of commission and omission that have survived the editorial process are solely mine.

Special thanks go to members of my family, particularly to my wife, Cathy, who has endured my traveling and seclusion (in the cluttered space I call my office), and to my extended family, the Verdugos, y familias Arrañaga, Monge, Ramos, y Caubet (y Sanchez). You may never know how much you have shaped my life and views of the world (and our places in it).

List of figures

List of tables

Preface

The topic of bilingualism in the U.S. is extraordinarily complex, and, as a consequence, it is difficult to make generalizations about almost anything. The thing that makes it complex is the sheer number and magnitude of issues: *race* (and various views of the evolutionary nature of humankind), *immigration* (and the social and economic impact of huge, largely unplanned population movements), *national identity* (patriotism, social responsibility, and culture), the *civil rights* of human beings (to be treated fairly and justly), *education* (and the socialization of children), and *human cognition* (how we "know" things like language), just to name a few. All of these major issues are interconnected, and, hence, dynamic. Yet, we all know that they can be broken down into much smaller units, into particulars that can be juxtaposed as contrasts – as the saying goes, the devil is in the details.

For example, on the side of national identity, there are highly charged definitions of what it means to be a law-abiding American *citizen* (responsible taxpayer, voter, participant in U.S. political processes, English speaker) in contrast with *alien* (permanent resident, undocumented worker, speaker of a "foreign" language) and all their connotations. The U.S., in reality, is a multilingual society, always has been, so it can be surprising, perhaps even puzzling, particularly to linguists, that there are still heated debates over bi- and multilingualism and the social and psychological benefits of knowing more than one language. In the Western world, people today agree that discrimination and the restriction of a person's rights based on nationality or race are simply unacceptable or morally wrong. (The U.S. is still dealing with fallout from past injustices; some things cannot be swept under the rug of selective memory.) But, how is a *national* identity forged in the face of the incredible social, cultural, and linguistic diversity one finds in the U.S.? Is it even possible?

Education, by itself, is no less complicated, especially in light of both population growth and international migration. On the one hand, a little less than two centuries ago, well before education was universal and mandatory in the U.S., local schools dealt with local issues. Children went about the business of learning their ABCs and the three "Rs" as we would expect them to do, or so goes the impression one gets from many perhaps idealized versions of past American life. On the other hand, in today's world, the realities seem stark and foreboding. Massive population movements have changed the rules, and national educational systems are required to deal with *national* issues. In some quarters, national interests give way to globalization. Those who have their eye on a global economy and an integrated international community may find national allegiances limiting and counter-productive. Where is the ideal citizen of the world when it comes to international competition for natural resources, survival, and the role of all nations in such key matters as global climate change?

While these very general issues provide a place to start, this book has a goal and a focus, and that is to lay some groundwork for a relatively informed view of bi- and multilingualism. The Chicano-Latino community in the U.S. is a case study. While this community has indeed experienced many of the fortunes and misfortunes of other minority groups in the U.S., it is also unique. Some things that have held true for some earlier immigrant groups do not seem to hold for this community. And, of course, this begs the question "How come?" What is it about so-called Hispanics that Anglo Americans want to lump them into one huge super-category? As a group, they are the largest *ethnic* minority in the U.S. But, what is an ethnic group? Latinos in the U.S. are a heterogeneous lot, embracing varying nationalities, races, cultures, and lifestyles.

Understanding of Latinos as a diverse sub-set of American society cannot be reached by flinging stereotypes, no matter how benevolent their motivations (e.g., in the educational practice called tracking or streaming). Within this putative ethnic minority, there is a *language minority*, the Spanish-English bilingual community. Hence, we need to confront topics that range beyond merely the social (immigration, citizenship, and civil rights) to purely linguistic ones. What happens in *all* bilingual communities when social relationships among language groups are *not* equal, and instead, we find asymmetrical relations of dominance? In this respect, the consequences are well-documented and predictable. There is isolation. There are bilingual, contact phenomena. Languages will be mixed in various ways, with ramifications reaching from home to school, from the classrooms to the boardrooms of international businesses, and from the front page of the *Los Angeles Times* to the window paintings of a shop or cafe.

It is the nature of case studies, as illustrations, to bring the reader back to general principles. Many language minority groups may be able to see the same patterns of success and failure in school, of teacher prejudices, and community discrimination. It is safe to say that Punjabis in the U.K. experience many of the same difficulties as Chicanos in Southern California (and the reverse). So, while the focus may seem narrow and individual at times, it is hoped that, through a similar kind of multifaceted analysis, the application will be wide and informative to the many, particularly for the Latino population in the U.S. in general.

Chapter 1

Introduction

Bilingualism as a worldwide phenomenon

Not too long ago, the common perception of "national" languages may have been that in Germany, Germans speak German; in Italy, Italians speak Italian; in Spain, Spaniards speak Spanish; and in the United States of America, Americans speak English. However, this perception is undeniably simplistic. Thinking in terms of one language-one country certainly doesn't capture the diverse linguistic landscape of Europe and the Americas today. Not only are there various *kinds* of German spoken in almost every major region of Germany, there are other languages indigenous to what is now the political entity of Germany (e.g., the Slavic language known as *Sorbian*) in addition to the myriad of languages spoken by millions of immigrants and former "guest workers" in that country.[1]

Italy is no different with many languages spoken within its national borders (e.g., the language varieties of Tuscany, Milan, Venice, and Florence). Many of these are commonly assumed to be dialects of a single language; therefore, they have been traditionally put under one general umbrella known as Italian. But, they are all unique. Every variety has its own grammatical rules and pronunciation patterns, standards, literatures, and cultures. With respect to Spain, after the Barcelona Olympics of 1992,

---

1. Guest workers, or *Gastarbeiter* in German, were foreign nationals allowed into the country to fill general, low-wage blue-collar types of jobs in industry during the labor shortage following WWII. Among these were Italians, Turks, Spaniards, Greeks, and Yugoslavs. Many reunited with family members and have become permanent residents.

most informed people understood that the language Americans call "Spanish" is actually named Castilian (*castellano*) and that it is only one of the several languages of that nation. They include Galician (*Gallego*), Catalán, the language of Barcelona and some nearby regions (e.g., Majorca and Valencia), and Basque (a linguistic *isolate*, apparently unrelated to any other European language), not to mention dialects of all of these. In each of these three nations (Germany, Italy, and Spain), one can find speakers of dozens of languages, from Vietnamese to Russian, and from Quechua to Amharic.

The U.S. is a nation of immigrants; most people expect to hear that the number of languages spoken in the U.S. are in the hundreds, and rightfully so. In every case, various immigrant groups brought their languages with them. They included the original settlers from the Southeast of England and their particular variety of English, along with settlers from other areas of Britain, e.g., from the North and West of England, and from Ireland, Scotland, and Wales. The latter three groups also brought their ancestral languages with them, related forms of Gaelic spoken in their homelands before English took root (Irish, Scottish, and Welsh, respectively). Their original countries had been incorporated into the United Kingdom (U.K.). Waves of immigrants flowed into the so-called New World, among them speakers of several European languages (e.g., French, Spanish, Swedish, and Dutch).

Over time, German-speaking people settled into areas now known as the Mid-Atlantic states, the so-called Pennsylvania Dutch, who were not really Dutch (from Holland); they were mostly from lowland areas of what is now known as Germany.[2] Scandinavians (Danes, Swedes, and Norwegians) came in great numbers, eventually settling in the Midwest states (Minnesota, Illinois, the Dakotas, etc.). Later, Italians started coming to East Coast cities. French folks had their own French colonies (Quebec, Acadia, and Louisiana). As early as the 17th Century, among the very first of these imported languages were a number of West African varieties (e.g., Ewe, Hausa, and Yoruba), brought by the predecessors of those who would become slaves. African-origin people were brought to the fledgling colonies almost from the beginning. They have lived mostly in the American South, and eventually began moving north after the Civil War of the 1860s, later to the Midwest, and finally westward, particularly after World War I.

In the case of Spanish, many speakers were already "here," occupying land that would later be taken over by the U.S. The Southwestern states (e.g., Texas, New Mexico, Colorado, Arizona, Nevada, and California) were under Spanish rule for three centuries, and then, briefly, under Mexican rule (after Mexico declared independence from

---

2. There was no political entity known as Germany when the British colonies were first being settled; there was a loose collection of German speaking states such as Hesse (where Hessians came from), Saxony (where Saxons came from), and Prussia (where Prussians came from). They spoke their own varieties, or dialects, of German.

Spain in 1810 and, following the War of Independence, achieved complete autonomy in 1821). From the middle of the 20th century, immigration into various parts of the U.S. from other Latin American (Spanish-speaking) countries has escalated considerably as the immigration laws in the U.S. changed.

Importantly, every single immigrant group has had its own unique history. Each has brought its own language, and at times, its own system of education, in many cases, heritage language education (e.g., Germans, Scandinavians, and more recently Asian groups such as the Japanese). Migrants come to the U.S. today from over a hundred countries, from Albania to Zimbabwe. They, too, bring with them their languages, customs, and views of culture.

It is also true that the first settlers from the British Isles met speakers of non-European languages as soon as their feet touched land, speakers of a host of indigenous, Native American languages, often called *Amerindian* (from a blending of the words American and Indian) or *First Nation* languages, the Canadian preference for referring to the original inhabitants of the North American continent and their tongues. As the new inhabitants – interlopers – learned the languages of their indigenous neighbors, they became bilingual (if they weren't already), which did happen in the early days of settlement. As the original inhabitants learned English (Spanish or French), they, too, became bilingual (if not already so in other local language varieties). In other words, from its inception, people in the part of the world that became the United States of America have spoken many languages: there has never been a time in history on this continent, as far as anyone knows, when the inhabitants spoke only one language.

1.   The roots of multilingualism

In common terms, *bilingualism* means having the ability to use two languages. Many of today's specialists link bilingualism with *multilingualism* because in either case, a person speaks more than one language (e.g., see Myers-Scotton 2006: 2; Bhatia and Ritchie 2006: 1). On the societal level, a community is multilingual when a number of languages are commonly used, regardless of how many individuals are multilingual. In fact, in most recent studies, the two terms are often used interchangeably because to know more than one language is to know multiple languages.[3] The opposite of multilingualism is probably more clearly *monolingualism*, that is, being able to speak one language, presumably one's first (or *native*) and only language. In nations like the U.S. and the U.K., where a large international language such as English is used as the

---

3.   There is also the issue of speaking varieties of a single language based on the situations of speech, or *registers*. It is safe to say that even proficient speakers of only one language are familiar with registers and/or dialects of that language that may be socially or regionally distinguished.

principal medium of social discourse, there may be large segments of society that are indeed restricted to the use of that one language, and are, therefore, monolingual, or *unilingual*. As a consequence, bilingualism is often viewed in such societies as knowing the predominant language along with another, lesser-used variety, although it could very well involve any combination of language varieties. Throughout the world, however, it is not uncommon to find clusters of people who speak several languages, and on a daily basis. There are entire communities that use three, four…seven languages to conduct business and to communicate among social groups.

In a general sense, there are two principal reasons for the development of extensive cultural contact and multilingualism on a world scale: (a) expansionism – the growth and expansion of political entities beyond their traditional borders through military or political conquest (e.g., imperialism along with its byproduct colonialism), and (b) cooperation (or, in the case of political and economic domination, exploitation) – the responses of sorts by other equally powerful or, economically weaker nations (groups or individuals) to the successes of large, political and commercial entities, as they engage in economic cooperation. This can occur through immigrant or resident minorities or through multinational businesses/corporations.[4] In either case (conquest or cooperation), where wealth is generated, there is the opportunity, at least in principle, for enterprising people to participate in the economic machinery, in labor (production and distribution of goods), buying, and selling. These processes over time have contributed to global trends toward industrialization, urbanization, multilingualism, and, ultimately, to globalization, forging multilevel links among governments and businesses, in technology, education (official versus lesser-used languages), and mass communication.

For example, in the world today, it is easy to see how financial markets react to political and social events worldwide. Stock prices rise and fall on the failures or successes of multinational corporations. The U.S., while reeling from its own internal national debt (and individual state budget crises), still lends large amounts of money to foreign nations ostensibly to ensure that markets stay open, particularly concerning the international supply of oil. Food supplies are equally important, and the effects of national disasters (tsunamis, earthquakes, and floods, for example) have international repercussions.

In the "Old World" (including Europe, Asia, and Africa), many cities developed into centers of commerce along trade routes, at international crossroads that linked East and West, North and South, even though human migration certainly predates the development of any kind of urban center. These magnets of commerce were centers of

---

4. European powers in the so-called New World pursued their own strategies of colonialism. In the case of the Spanish Conquest, the military played the principal role in the establishment of administrative capitals and population centers. The British in North America originally created economic enterprises through charters to exploit the natural resources of claimed lands. They then began to carve out workable land for those who came to live in the colonies. In the final analysis, either strategy came from expansionism.

opportunity, and many languages were typically spoken. In many cases, one language or another would emerge as a *lingua franca* of sorts, a language variety that by virtue of its usefulness and accessibility for intergroup dealings would become valuable as a medium for all the forms of communication necessary for trade, various kinds of cooperation, and in forging an economy.

Today, on a much grander scale in terms of size and scope, a number of languages have evolved into so-called *superlanguages*, for example, English, Spanish, Mandarin (Chinese), Russian, and Arabic, that cross national boundaries, reaching international and/or world status. They are the results of similar linguistic processes (the emergence of a lingua franca) and the need for a language with wide commercial, social, and political appeal. In the current economy, trade centers are linked in increasingly complex ways. The exchange of information is accomplished in split seconds whereas, in the "old days," runners may have gone from village to village forming the only communication system available (then came telegraphs, telephones, etc.). In the same ways, behind every kind of globalization effort is language as the medium through which information is represented and passed. And, of course, a global economy has now emerged that is becoming more like a living, natural entity with physical properties (metaphors) like "life blood" (capital) subject to breakdowns and natural disasters (e.g., financial *tsunamis*). It is becoming increasingly clear how vital the superlanguages have become, especially English which has become so interwoven worldwide with technology, the Internet, international finance, the stock markets, politics, and international media/news agencies.[5]

In our contemporary world, migration motivated by powerful social, political, and economic factors has changed the face of Europe (East and West), the Americas (North and South), Asia, Africa, and Oceania, and will continue to do so. In fact, the history of the United States can probably be characterized more by tremendous population shifts than almost anything else, from the very first English settlement in Jamestown, Virginia, in 1607 to the continuing in-migration of "foreigners" in the 21st century. The westward expansion of English speakers during the emergence of the U.S. as a nation involved a gradual, but systematic, process of conquest and settlement, along with the establishment and spread of Anglo-Saxon language and culture via institutions of government, education, and the economy. Seemingly against all odds, and out of an astonishing mélange of elements, a nation was forged.

---

5.   Linguists sometimes refer to the "biggest army theory," that is, that the spread of English throughout the globe was a result of the military might and the political ascendency of Great Britain in the 16th through 19th centuries. There was a well-known expression, "The sun never sets on the British Empire." This was because, literally, the sun at any point in time was shining on a part of this global empire. The U.S., in similar fashion, has contributed much to the spread of English in the 20th century and beyond through its own brand of imperialism.

The impartial observer (if there is such a thing) certainly could say that the steady march of the British Colonial power was not without its excesses. We do know that the problems that ensued are in many cases still with us. So-called Indian reservations (and now, gaming casinos) are still operating; indigenous languages are still dying (in terms of the numbers of speakers); and issues of minority languages, minority rights, and so on will be with us for some time.[6] One of the benefits of revisiting history, without its gilded edges and somewhat rosy hue, has been the creation of a lot of newfound interest in ethnic studies, women's studies, and the like. The cultural milieu today, particularly in educational circles, suggests that we look beyond what appears to be the celebration of British colonialism and the spread of Anglo-Saxon culture and look again at the history of this great country, only this time through the eyes of those who bore the brunt of it: through the eyes of Native Americans, African Americans, Mexicans, women, and all the other various ethnic, religious, and linguistic groups that make up what could be the most diverse society the world has ever known.

Immigration and the displacement of the original populations has been constant, sometimes taking place in more extensive and intensive waves, but constant nonetheless. Right from the beginning, it is important to emphasize that each and every significant area, state, county, city, or village, has had its own unique settlement history, geographical characteristics (and, therefore, economy), and population demographics – its own face, so to speak. As a consequence, despite what may appear to be a relatively homogeneous culture, or the impression of a homogeneous, Anglo Saxon society, we are extraordinarily diverse. New Yorkers are not San Franciscans, and folks from the San Fernando Valley in Southern California may have very little in common with people from Daytona Beach, Florida. Pittsburg, California, is not Pittsburg, Kansas, and neither of these is Pittsburgh, Pennsylvania.

2.   Language contact

The migration of social groups has always been an inherent part of our human character. As a result of natural disasters (flooding, droughts, famines, etc.), conflict among peoples (e.g., the apparently human urge to conquer, dominate, and expand ethnic or national frontiers), a quest for better living conditions, and perhaps merely a sense of wanderlust, major population shifts all around the globe have created situations in

---

6. Languages are not living organisms that can die; obviously, so-called dead languages are those whose *speakers* have died out. Of the original indigenous languages of North America, few remain living (in this sense). An "endangered" language is one that has fewer than 1,000 speakers (Edwards 1994: 22). And, in an age of superlanguages, such groups may dwindle to the point that their original languages become extinct.

which groups of people come into close physical proximity, or *areal* contact, with other groups. In most, if not all cases, they will develop and maintain somewhat permanent social and economic ties with one another, alliances of a sort. Even when situations of contact are not so friendly, knowing another group's language can be of strategic importance. In peaceful times, individual groups may share the same or neighboring territories and natural resources, conduct regular business or trade, and eventually build social ties via intergroup marriage, joint commercial enterprises, and cultural exchanges of many types. In the process, people learn each other's languages and customs. As a result, bi- and multilingualism have undoubtedly existed since the dawn of civilization. It is the normal state of human society, as it is today in Europe, Africa, Asia, Australia, and the Americas.

The movement of peoples in the Old World (the New World has been no different) has also meant the *spread* of languages. Probably the most known in European history was the emergence of the Roman Empire that stretched along the northern shores of the Mediterranean Sea from modern-day Portugal in the west to Italy and further into Romania and Slovenia in the east, and the spread of its language, Latin – one of the first superlanguages (Brosnahan 1973: 41). Each distinct region of Imperial Rome had its original inhabitants who were colonized and who learned a colonial language, and, therefore, its own unique underlying social and linguistic foundation, or *substrate*, for the culture, language, and nation that would eventually emerge. In the process of spread, there were the initial effects of *language contact*, degrees of bilingualism, and so on. But, one would expect other bilingual phenomena to occur, as well, phenomena such as linguistic borrowing (speakers of local languages would use words from Latin in their original languages, and the reverse, Latin speakers would use indigenous words for novel cultural items), code-switching (switching from one language to another in conversation), and so on. Simply put, languages are in contact when they are shared by members of a single community; two languages "live" in the head of one speaker. It is axiomatic in linguistics that languages in contact will influence each other.

It is also true that every language has its *dialects*, regional and social varieties of the language proper, and Latin was certainly no exception. All languages change through time; they may change gradually as a consequence of internal forces (e.g., as a result of physical processes involved in pronunciation like the loss of certain sounds as a result of variation) or as a consequence of external forces via contact.[7] So, dialects of Latin

---

7. One noticeable example of internal change in English would be the Great Vowel Shift, whereby the vowel system shifted from its earlier somewhat "normal" European system to present-day *systems* represented by various national, regional, and social forms in England, the U.S., Australia, and so on. Another would be how a shift in stress led to the loss of inflectional morphology in Old English (Anglo-Saxon) and the drift of English from a typically Germanic grammatical system to a simpler one (Fennel 2001: 6, 161).

evolved over time into separate national and regional languages with their own histories, traditions, and literatures. These language varieties stretch throughout Southern
Europe, forming a *continuum of dialects* – a gradual shading of the original language,
Latin, across former colonial possessions (Chambers and Trudgill 1980: 6–8). It has
been said that, if a traveler were to walk from village to village west to east convers-
ing with people as he or she went along, starting, say, in Portugal and hiking through
Spain, France, Italy, and so on, that the differences are so gradual that our traveler
would be able to understand with little difficulty the dialect of the next village.

There are areas, linguistic islands in a sense, where non-Latin languages were and
are still spoken, where understanding during a transcontinental walk would be next
to zero. But, at their borders, various forms of bilingualism were sure to develop, one
reason why Europe has been multilingual for millennia. Similar situations occurred in
Central Europe with speakers of Germanic languages as they migrated eastward into
Slavic speaking areas of modern-day Poland and Russia, perhaps one-time parts of a
greater Slavic homeland (and one of the historical land issues of the two World Wars).
Slavic peoples to the East migrated in nearly all directions, into the Balkans (the former
Yugoslavia) and further eastward into Asia. So, one would expect pockets of languages
to exist as remnants of earlier communities, e.g., the Basque in Spain and France, or as
intrusions of sorts by migrating groups, e.g., German in Russian territories.

It is not always clear, however, exactly where the boundary between dialect and
language is, even to the trained linguist. In simple terms, a *dialect* is a version of a
language that shows some kind of regular, systematic differences from other versions
or dialects of the same language. There may be variation in lexicon (vocabulary and
choice of words), phonology (how words are pronounced), morphology (how words
take shape in their grammatical contexts), or syntax (the order in which certain classes
of words can occur). The variation may be very slight or quite noticeable, depending
on point of view. In addition, there might be very different *cultures* represented by the
same language so that the patterns of discourse (the *ways* people express themselves)
will vary, reflecting specific views of culture (e.g., what may be interpreted by society
as learned or *cultured* behavior) and personal interaction. There is also some discussion of when a dialect may become a separate language. For instance, the continuum
of Romance varieties in Europe involves former dialects of Latin that are now considered independent languages. Evidently, language status is a result of shifting political
borders and the emergence of nationalities based on the political landscape. From a
linguistic perspective, this begs the question of what constitutes a language, and there
is no simple, cut and dried answer.

3.   Bilingualism in the U.S.: A first look

The first issue confronting bilingualism in the U.S. is a clear idea of English. It is the de facto national language, and no one seriously questions that. Nevertheless, English itself is not monolithic in the sense that it has always been the same everywhere one goes. It consists of various dialects, always has. Indian English (spoken in India) varies quite a bit from American English. British English differs from American English, but most of the forms and structures in each are considered to be at the core of this thing we call English (Lehmann 1992: 114–125).

As English spread throughout North America, the processes of change have been similar to what happened to Latin. Indigenous languages did leave their marks on the colonial language, but only minimally in the accumulation of isolated vocabulary words (e.g., *moccasin*, *bayou*, and other regional words) and place names (valleys, mountains, rivers). Even before the Revolutionary War (1775–1783), writers in England had noted the emergence of a unique form of English, with numerous words and expressions that appeared in reports of the colonies.

To illustrate the power of politics, after the revolution, leaders of the new republic deliberately emphasized the differences with a bit of linguistic engineering, with innovations made to distance American usage from its colonial past. There was a vibrant spirit of national pride in the new republican system of government that had replaced the old monarchy. The new system was even linked to the evolution of human society, to a Utopian ideal, that was a step up from previous, feudal types of government. (The French Revolution, beginning in 1789, was not far behind.) Some familiar historical figures were involved in this self-conscious attempt at a specifically American kind of English: Thomas Jefferson was known for coining words (e.g., *belittle*); Benjamin Franklin pushed for a separate spelling system; and Noah Webster, lexicographer, influential author, and dictionary writer, led spelling reforms that tried to reflect spoken language more closely. Older British spellings were changed to American ones (e.g., *colour* became *color*, *centre* became *center*, *tyre* became *tire*, and *waggon* became *wagon*).

There are, of course, significant borderland areas in North America around the southern part of Quebec in Canada, especially in the metropolitan area of Montréal where French and English are in close social and linguistic contact, and in huge borderland communities on either side of the U.S.-Mexico border from Texas to California, areas once colonized by Spain (hence, the earlier spread of Spanish), e.g., near the San Diego, California/Tijuana, Baja California area. Particularly relevant to this book, within the Spanish-English bilingual population broadly defined, there are important sub-groupings distinguishing among U.S. and foreign-born, citizens and non-citizens, with their own particular histories and ethnic identities. Bilingual communities of various kinds have resulted from both (a) the incorporation of lands previously inhabited by indigenous peoples or claimed by other colonial powers, and (b) massive immigration, that together represent a vast, often untapped reservoir of heritage languages.

4.   Languages of the U.S.

Estimates of the number of languages and numbers of speakers of each language vary according to the period of American history. Most often U.S. decennial census figures are cited; however, even within that relatively short ten-year period, there is considerable change from census to census. In the interim period, occasional surveys are taken by the Census Bureau and other agencies (e.g., the Modern Language Association) concerning the expansion (or reduction) of various linguistic groups. The following chart is based on figures from the 2007 U.S. Census Bureau, Language Use in the United States, American Community Survey Reports, issued in April 2010.

Rank (Language)	Number of speakers	Percent of total
1. English (only)	225,505,953	80.27
2. Spanish	34,547,077	12.30
3. Chinese	2,464,572	0.88
4. Tagalog	1,480,429	0.52
5. French	1,355,806	0.48
6. Vietnamese	1,207,004	0.43
7. German	1,104,354	0.39
8. Korean	1,062,337	0.38
9. Russian	851,174	0.30
10. Italian	798,801	0.28
11. Arabic	767,319	0.27
12. Portuguese	687,126	0.24
13. Polish	638,059	0.23
14. French Creole	629,019	0.22
15. Hindi	532,911	0.19
16. Japanese	458,717	0.16
17. Persian (Farsi)	349,686	0.12
18. Urdu	344,942	0.12
19. Greek	329,825	0.12
20. Gujarati	287,367	0.10

Figure 1.1 Languages of the U.S. in terms of numbers of speakers

This chart gives us two valuable insights: English is by far the undisputed leader, and Spanish outnumbers all other minority languages put together. What the chart does not depict is the number of non-native speakers of English (bilinguals) that exist among these non-English speakers. According to the 2007 census data, 19.7% of the U.S. population spoke a language other than English at home. Well over half of them speak English very well. That is, 55.9% (30,975,474) of those reported that they spoke English very well, and only 8.1% (4,494,991) did not speak English at all.[8] All in all, less than 1.6% of the total population of 280,950,438 did not speak English, demonstrating the overwhelming dominance of English nationwide.

According to the National Virtual Translation Center (NVTC), a federal organization established in 2003 to work with and support intelligence gathering agencies and coordinate various professional translation services nationally, only 9% of Americans speak their native language plus an additional language compared with 53% of Europeans (http://www.nvtc.gov/lotw/languageStudy.html). As a consequence, there is a shortage of proficient translators and other language professionals in the U.S. diplomatic corps, the military, and other intelligence gathering agencies, possibly compromising U.S. security and its business interests abroad and at home. The NVTC states that there are 311 languages spoken in the U.S., 162 indigenous (or *autochthonous*) varieties plus an additional 149 immigrant languages (which includes English). The NVTC also reports that, of those who study languages other than English in U.S. schools and universities, about 90% choose Spanish, French, German, and Italian, with only around 10% dedicated to Less Commonly Taught Languages (LCTLs) such as Pashto, Farsi (Persian), Arabic, Chinese, and Russian. This seems to show the U.S. is following the old expression, "cutting off its nose to spite its face," discouraging the development of proficient multilinguals so that it can promote English to the exclusion of all other languages.

America's apparent disdain for multilingualism certainly seems to discourage learning additional languages. Perhaps, it even helps instill fear that "exotic" languages (those unlike the narrow range of familiar European languages traditionally taught) are too difficult to learn. It obviously ignores the fact that children learn their native languages regardless of type *plus* English as a matter of course in the U.S. Moreover, those who speak LCTLs natively may be discouraged from attaining high levels of proficiency by the subtractive practices and policies of the U.S. educational system and as a result of the national push for *Americanization* of all students – to demonstrate loyalty to the U.S. by abandoning their native languages and adopting an English-only view. Worldwide, bilingualism includes nearly every conceivable combination of languages and dialects. As just one example of a lesser known language that is nonetheless spoken

---

8. See Language Use in the United States: 2007, at www.census.gov/prod/2010pubs//acs/index.html.

in the U.S., *Gujarati*, an Indo-Aryan language spoken in India and the first language of Mohandas K. (Mahatma) Gandhi, is used by some 46 million people worldwide (Lewis 2009). According to 2000 U.S. Census Data, it was used by over 235,000 people in the U.S. (287,367 in 2007), more than 47,000 in New Jersey and 33,000 in California. A language such as this, though it may not be on the minds of most Americans, has value worldwide, and because it is also closely related to the languages of Pakistan and Bangladesh, it is of strategic importance.

The numbers provided by the Census Bureau, easily accessed over the Internet through population estimates and press releases distributed by their Newsroom, paint a dramatic portrait of a changing nation. For example, in a US Census Bureau press release dated May 17, 2007, Robert Bernstein, of the Public Information Office, writes that the nation's (ethnic) minority population had surpassed the 100 million mark. Bernstein cites Bureau Director Louis Kincannon as saying that "About one in three U.S. residents is a minority... To put this into perspective, there are more minorities in this country today than there were people in the United States in 1910. In fact, the minority population in the U.S. is larger than the total population of all but 11 countries." Another milestone reached during the period of July 1, 2005 to July 1, 2006 was that the nation's Hispanic population (the largest and fastest growing minority) had reached 44.3 million (14.8 percent of the total population), while the nation's black population had reached 40.2 million. So, it does seem that images of a homogeneous, White America are a thing of the past. Washington D.C. and four states are now "minority-majority." Hawai'i topped the list with 75 percent minority in 2006, followed by the District of Columbia at 68 percent, New Mexico at 57 percent, California at 57 percent, and Texas at 52 percent.

It is immediately noted that the term "Hispanic" is controversial to say the least (see section below). As this book progresses, one recurring theme is how *the linguistic and social categories themselves are problematic*. A particular set of statistics may reflect racial characteristics, another language status, and yet another, ethnic/cultural traits. At other times, socio-economic data are used that cross all racial, ethnic, and language lines and classifications. As a result, the reader should beware that associations are not always easy to make, especially when different politically-motivated groups choose to highlight certain educational and/or language issues and link them to race, language, or immigrant status.

5.   The term *Hispanic*

The U.S. is a complex nation with a diverse population, from the national to local levels. Proceeding from this general starting point, the main goal of this book is to take a serious look at one major subgroup, the Chicano-Latino, sometimes called *Hispanic*, community.[9] Terminology is troublesome. As an ethnonym, Hispanic was first used in the 1970 U.S. census for the purpose of classification and later expanded to *Hispanic or Latino* in the 2000 census. Hispanics are typically considered an ethnic group, but *ethnicity* is notoriously difficult to define. Based on race (e.g., color of skin, texture of hair, and facial characteristics), country of origin, culture, and social characteristics, Chicano-Latinos are extraordinarily diverse. Even if we look only at the Spanish-English bilingual community (a language minority) regardless of those factors, we are dealing with a very diverse group strictly on a linguistic basis. There are many national varieties of Spanish with regional and social variation that are reflected in immigration and settlement patterns, e.g., in New York City, Miami, El Paso, and Los Angeles. Similarly, there are multiple varieties of English in the U.S., by region, e.g., Northern, Midlands, Southern, Western, and by social grouping, e.g., Ebonics and Chicano English. Language *usage* (how and when it is used) is an integral part of everyone's social identity, but it is merely one characteristic among many.

The term Hispanic can be controversial, and not everyone called this is exactly happy with it. The word itself is highly politicized: to some it is a term of ethnic pride, a link to Spain and *European* heritage (cf. Acuña 1995: 8–10). To others who simply can't identify with a European heritage, it can signify more than five hundred years of domination and struggle. It may even come close to a "dirty" word to some in the Chicano-Latino community. It was evidently coined for political expediency, to create a coalition of sorts for increased political clout to rival that of other prominent minority groups (e.g., African-Americans who have been traditional Democrats in the South). In that respect, it has been successful. However, so-called Hispanics are not one big, happy, and cohesive family, which is not to say that they are fragmented. To be fragmented, the community had to be united in the first place, and that has never been the case, except, perhaps, in opposition to political domination of a colonial power.[10]

The term *Latino*, which is apparently a shortened form of *latinoamericano* (Latin American), has sometimes been used to include speakers of other Romance (Latin) languages, for example, speakers of Portuguese in Brazil and French in Canada, the

---

9. *Hispania*, from which the word Hispanic is derived, is apparently the Roman (Latin) word for the Iberian Peninsula, containing all the various kingdoms of historic Portugal, Spain, Andorra, and Gibraltar.

10. By analogy, one could call anyone an *Anglo* or *English* who belongs to a nation that was once under British domination. This would include Canada, the U.S., Australia, India, Pakistan, Bangladesh, Nigeria, Kenya, New Guinea, the British West Indies, and so on, regardless of race, religion, or language status. Just as those nations that were subject to British colonialism, individual nations that were part of the Spanish Empire each have their own indigenous and European-origin residents, plus, like Mexico, most likely those of African-origin and mixed heritage, each with their own unique ratios of colonizer to colonized,.

U.S., and briefly in Mexico (e.g., in the short-lived French invasion of Napoleon III in 1881).[11] Theoretically, it could be extended to include all people of distant "Latin" origin, e.g. Italians and Romanians. Nevertheless, it tends to have a more neutral connotation than its counterpart, Hispanic, in places like Southern California (Suárez-Orozco and Páez 2002). Experts, however, do not consider Hispanic and Latino to be synonymous, although they are often used interchangeably. Hispanic mainly applies to Spaniards and people of Spanish ancestry; Latino is typically restricted to Latin Americans (including Mexicans). For much of the history of the Pacific Southwest, however, the term Mexican has been used along with its hyphenated alternative, Mexican-American.

Chicano (variously spelled Chicano/a, Chican@, Xicano/a) is most likely a derivation of the Spanish *Mexicano*. It typically has an association with the Civil Rights Movement and Chicano activism, which accounts for its usage in much of the Southwest (Moore and Pachon 1985: 12; see also Peñalosa 1980: 2). In contrast to Hispanic, Chicano tends to signify social identification with the indigenous populations of Mexico and to those of mixed European and indigenous ancestry (*mestizos*). In Mexican and other similar cultures, the term *indio* (Indian) is still used as a generic term for indigenous/native peoples. For the purpose of this book (and, perhaps, clarity), the term Chicano will refer generally to U.S. born Mexican Americans (or American Mexicans), and specifically to those who reside in California. To refer to those who reside in parts of Texas (e.g., in El Paso), the term *tejano* (Texan) will be used at times (with respect for Tex-Mex culture). Despite a number of cultural and historical connections, Texas and California are indeed distinct, separated by other former Spanish and Mexican territories (Nevada, Arizona, and New Mexico), each with its own unique sociopolitical background. Note, however, that the term Chicano tends to be inclusive of any person who self-designates as one. The terminology can be confusing because there is so much variation, especially in California. Perhaps to avoid the confusion, it's best not to label people.

Terms denoting national origin call forth the strongest responses. To state the obvious, Spaniards are not Cubans, and Cubans are not Mexicans. It is insensitive, to say the least, to call a person a Mexican if he or she is a Spaniard or a Cuban (and vice versa). National rivalries (sometimes based on preconceptions of race) can be

---

11. An interesting side note is the U.S. (unofficial) holiday of Cinco de Mayo (fifth of May) which commemorates the defeat of French forces in the southern Mexican city of Puebla. In Mexico, it only has regional significance (in the state of Puebla), but it has become symbolic of Mexican independence in the U.S., particularly in California. But, of course, St. Patrick's Day is also celebrated by millions of non-Irish in the U.S.

quite fierce.[12] They all have completely different national histories and widely differing racial and social characteristics, cultures, foods, music, almost anything that can be linked to social identity (e.g., political heroes). And, each nation has its own distinctive pronunciation and local vocabulary items in addition to urban and rural versions of Spanish with their own subtle grammatical characteristics. Puerto Ricans are unique, as are Dominicans, Argentines, Colombians, Uruguayans, and all those that may have originated in or passed through what is known collectively as Latin America.

In many cases, the only things that members of these disparate groups have in common is a characteristic Spanish-sounding surname, which is the result of their common colonial status and subjugation at the hands of the Spanish, and perhaps Roman Catholic religion, but not always. And, just because a person has a last name like Sanchez or Ramos does not mean that he or she speaks Spanish; he/she may not. That person may speak only English or any of a number of indigenous languages (e.g., Náhuatl, Quechua, Aymara, Mayan, or many other possibilities, including languages of the Philippines such as Tagalog). Of course, one must not forget that speakers of other languages have settled all over Latin America, from Germans to Portuguese to Italians along with sizable Mandarin-speaking, Korean, and Japanese populations in such urban centers as São Paolo, Brazil. Almost any linguistic minority that can be found in North America can be found in South America, as well. So, last names may not say much.

One purpose of this discussion is to stress the *uniqueness* of each and every bilingual community in the U.S., particularly various Spanish-English bilingual communities. Another is to encourage students and teachers to understand both the dangers of stereotyping and the need to be aware of the complex nature of individual human beings. Time and place are significant as major determinants. The U.S. is a nation composed primarily of former immigrant populations; Americans simply can't assume that a Spaniard living in New Mexico in the 17th century had the same experience as a Puerto Rican living in Hartford, Connecticut in the 1950s. Chicanos in Southern California have had little in common with Cuban Americans and other immigrants

---

12. Even in California, where people should know better, one still hears the expression "Spanish food" used to refer to Mexican food. They are not even similar. New Yorkers often call Puerto Ricans "Spanish," perhaps connecting a language to a race or ethnicity (e.g., an area in New York City called "Spanish Harlem"). The word *Spanish* is the American English word for (a) a person from Spain (not Puerto Rico), (b) one of the many languages of the nation of Spain, specifically, Castilian (not Basque, Catalán, etc.), (c) or some item that may be associated with the nation, language, or culture (e.g., Spanish grammar, Spanish tile). Spain was the conquering, colonial power, *los conquistadores*. Puerto Rico is an island that was conquered, colonized, populated with numbers of African-origin slaves, and exploited by Spain for centuries. These are big differences.

from Central and South America or the Caribbean in Southern Florida.[13] In the literature on so-called Hispanics in the U.S., it is often noted that Puerto Ricans are citizens by virtue of the territorial status of their homeland, Puerto Rico; they are *not* immigrants. Many have migrated to the U.S. mainland, to be sure, but they are not subject to any sort of immigration laws or quotas. Cubans, in contrast, were political refugees who received aid from the federal government (see Chapter 6 and discussion of the Coral Way school).

Because of their prominent places in the literature on education and language rights (as benchmarks of sorts), the three most frequently studied groups are Cubans, Mexicans, and Puerto Ricans. A contrast between Miami Cubans and L.A. Chicanos is only one example. The individual histories of these two groups in the U.S., heterogeneous in themselves, are completely distinct – one at one time apparently advantaged, and the other consistently disadvantaged (in terms of the systematic discrimination they have faced). Language-wise, because varieties of the same languages are involved (varieties of Spanish and varieties of English), and because the individual socio-political histories of their respective homelands may have included a period of European Spanish colonization, there may be certain parallels, particularly linguistic ones. But, one must be vigilant not to overgeneralize or create stereotypes where they simply do not exist. To this end, some chapters include discussions of the specific situation in Southern California as a case study, but readers are encouraged to examine other communities for similarities (and differences).

6.   The order of this book

One of the main goals of this book is to lay some of the groundwork of a more informed view of linguistic diversity and societal bilingualism in the U.S. In order to reach that goal, there is extensive discussion of the pros and cons of bi- and multilingualism, for example, of the potential benefits of bilingualism as a national resource against a backdrop of its perceived (or imagined) negative effects. Other key points are the social costs of the ever-present national pressure to make English the *only* language of social importance (not just *primary*) and the consequent coercive pressure to minimize or suppress the usage of "other" languages, in other words, the *subtractive* nature

---

13. In recent years, there has been a growing presence of Mexican immigrants, documented and undocumented, in Florida, along with sizable populations of Nicaraguans. Nevertheless, *cubanos*, as founders of a large language minority community, have exerted influence within the community. Much of the relevant history of bilingual education is tied to them. It is into a predominantly Cuban American community that Mexicans and other Latinos are moving, which has not gone without its interethnic tensions.

of educational and language policies in the face of the tremendous growth of language minorities in the U.S. The purpose of this introductory chapter has been to bring up a number of the issues that will be covered in greater depth in the body of the work.

The rest of the book is divided into two general parts. Part I (Chapters 2 through 4) deals with general issues of bilingualism in the U.S. Chapter 2 presents various views of bilingual language acquisition (i.e., how people become bilingual), from individual to community-wide bilingualism. It deals with children who acquire two languages more or less at the same time, or *simultaneous language acquisition*, with predictable consequences, while other sections apply to older learners who learn their languages one after the other, *sequential acquisition*, e.g., as they learn English as a second or subsequent language. Discussion covers various types of bi- and multilingual families (e.g., when one parent is a native speaker of English and the other of Spanish, or when neither parent is a native speaker of English), and the linguistic consequences we can anticipate in the different types of environments. For instance, native-born Spanish-English bilinguals typically engage in conversational code-switching (the more-or-less unplanned alternation of languages) among themselves, while those who have learned their second/subsequent language as adults may find it difficult to codeswitch at all, except when the situation of speech changes, for example, when the participants change, or the topic of conversation abruptly changes.

From a more social and linguistic perspective, Chapter 3 addresses bilingual contact phenomena. Discussion includes diglossia (the compartmentalization of languages according to situations of usage), linguistic borrowing (using words from one language in another), various types of code-switching (and their social motivations and linguistic effects), and the gradual loss of community languages through shift (changing from the usage of a traditional or heritage language to a new, socially dominant one) and attrition (the gradual loss of a language in terms of numbers of speakers). Contact phenomena such as these follow predictable patterns, as the literature attests. Whether we consider code-switching normal, as the natural consequence of the asymmetrical social relationships among languages and speakers (as the experts say), or aberrant, as some kind of social misbehavior (as popular misconceptions attempt to portray), we need to have at least a basic understanding, most of all, of *who* is likely to engage in bilingual contact phenomena such as linguistic borrowing and code-switching, their likely causes and effects, and when and where they are likely to occur.

In addition, language evolution and change is a topic that requires some thought. Since languages in contact invariably affect each other, there is some discussion of so-called Hispanic (or Chicano) language varieties. For instance, since Spanish-speaking children in the American Southwest typically do not receive any kind of regular instruction in a *standard* variety of Spanish, they are pretty much left to themselves to develop their own local version of Spanish. With the history of neglect of formal instruction, there seems to be no alternative. The literature on American Spanish is replete with reports of the Spanish of young people in the *barrios* (neighborhoods or ethnic enclaves) throughout the Southwest, particularly in Texas, Arizona, New Mexico, and California, heavily interlarded with English vocabulary. Many speakers have no idea that the words they use are *anglicismos* (Anglicisms), and not "real" Spanish. As a consequence, the lack of proficiency in standard forms by Chicano speakers is often a source of ridicule from native speakers of national standards (not only European Spanish) who look down upon such speech as substandard or inferior. In fact, in view of the long history of contact and the influence of English on local varieties of Spanish, an entire educational movement has emerged: *Spanish for Native Speakers*.

Another consequence of language contact and the construction of social identity has been the emergence of a distinctive Chicano-Latino version of English, Chicano English (ChE), the topic of Chapter 4. ChE has emerged as a social dialect (or *sociolect*) with a history somewhat similar to that of African American Vernacular English (a k a AAVE, Black English or *Ebonics*). Both *dialects* function as markers of individual and group identity. They even share a number of linguistic features, as well (e.g., the so-called double negative, as in "I didn't do nothing"). This chapter describes typical pronunciation patterns and the types of grammatical characteristics that set off ChE as an ethnic, contact variety, the result of long-term contact between Spanish and English. Importantly, ChE, like AAVE, is considered *nonstandard*, so discussion centers on the nature of dialects; e.g., there is no hierarchy of varieties from superior to inferior, all prejudices to the contrary. Dialect awareness in the classroom is currently a critical component of education nationwide, particularly in urban school systems.

In the past, some linguists have lumped together so-called Hispanic varieties of English probably as a result of certain structural similarities. However, there are questions regarding the different varieties of Spanish and English that are involved, the social conditions, culture, and significant issues of language usage. (Puerto Rican Spanish is a unique Caribbean variety that differs substantially from that of the Pacific Southwest, in general. And, there are noticeable pronunciation differences among varieties of English spoken in the Northeast, Southwest, and West.) A variety similar to the ChE of Southern California associated with Tex-Mex culture in the Spanish-English bilingual community in El Paso, for example, among *tejanos*, reflects its own unique blend of Texan English, identified, perhaps, as the intersection of Southern American and lower Midlands varieties according to settlement patterns (Bailey and Tillery 2006: 37–38) with nearby regional varieties of Spanish, most notably Northern Mexican Spanish (or *norteño*). In Southern California, the English is distinctly Californian, at one time influenced greatly by the influx of English speakers from the Midwestern U.S. (and the completion of the transcontinental railroad), with the Spanish coming from multiple sources. To Chicanos in L.A., Tejanos have a characteristic accent. Traditional foods and customs in El Paso or San Antonio can differ greatly from those in Los Angeles, particularly in terms of rural Texan cultural influences versus those of urban Southern California.

Part II (5 through 8) continues the discussion into more specific areas, including a brief history of the "concept" of bilingualism in the U.S. and how changing American attitudes towards bilingualism play out in society and the political jumble of education. Chapter 5 discusses American attitudes to bilingualism. As noted above, the situation in the British American Colonies was multilingual from its inception, and it is likely that bilingualism was such a part of daily life that it was not considered a problem or even seriously debated except perhaps for a few isolated instances towards the end of the colonial period and immediately after independence. After all, many of the first American settlers came from the nations of northern Europe: they looked much like the British in physical appearance, and, in many cases, shared a similar European culture. As time went on, Anglo American attitudes towards bilingualism became somewhat ambivalent, evolving in a sense from relative tolerance and admiration for those who spoke specific European languages, say, French or German, to outright oppression, especially against speakers of specific language varieties spoken by *visible* minorities, those who don't look like the "founding fathers," drawing occasional charges of racism and ethnocentrism.

However, with the establishment of a fundamentally monolingual political structure, with English the principal and quasi official language of national institutions such as the government, economy, education, and media, linguistic competition has seldom been an issue. At least, it didn't appear seriously controversial in the first century or so after independence. It is also clear that an American version of English has been an integral part of the Americanization process and socialization into American culture, however that may be defined.[14] Since the end of WWII, as more and more different language groups have migrated into the U.S. from Southern and Eastern Europe, Asia, and Latin America, the existence of *foreign languages* and their presence in the daily lives of Americans, have become more pressing issues. The political construct of Americanization and issues of citizenship have always been linked to the English language as a unifying factor, particularly from the end of the 19th century, as immigration drew

---

14. With the common confusion of language, thought, and culture (which are indeed separate), English has been considered the key to learning how to think like an American, that is, to think like the idealized Anglo-Saxon colonists of the 17th and 18th centuries. Obviously, this ignores the contributions of non-Anglo-Saxon minorities. Nevertheless, the hegemony of English and the Anglo-Saxon culture at its base cannot be overlooked, and it is through the political institution of government and its role in education that we see this view propagated and enforced.

from a worldwide base and the allure of the American Dream reached to the ends of the earth. Again, the perception of the stereotypical American is that she/he is an English speaker, and a native one at that. Nevertheless, nowhere does one find such a complex of issues as those found in the Spanish-English bilingual community in the U.S.

Because issues of language maintenance and usage affect all levels of the bilingual community, linguistic issues will overlap with educational ones. What do we do with all of these children who speak Spanish at home, on the streets, and on the playgrounds with parents and their closest friends? What really is the best way to help them adapt to U.S. culture and society and to learn Standard American English? Is the knowledge of Standard English absolutely necessary? What sorts of factors inhibit learning? Chapter 6 confronts these issues by looking at the various programs that have emerged in the U.S., the research in bilingual language acquisition (which *should* inform our educational practices), and the politics of bilingual education. Different approaches have different roots: some are rational and based on available research, but some are politically motivated and based on social perceptions and ingrained educational biases. The research reveals that some pedagogical practices are more effective, benefiting the child learners, while others are more effective from an economic standpoint. And, of course, in times of budget crises, economics usually wins out over sound teaching practices.

Chapter 7 deals with concepts of literacy and the effects of schooling. While all children will learn to speak a native (first) language, not all children learn to read in that language. Children who are compelled to learn to read and write in a language that they have not learned yet have twice the burden of learning: they are effectively learning two things at once. Children who learn to read in their native language, therefore, are at an advantage, while children with this increased burden are clearly at a disadvantage. In addition, culture and literacy have been linked for generations; however, it is not always clear to the non-specialist how culturally-based concepts of literacy influence educational practices.

For example, it appears to be the school's job to *Americanize* students, to teach Anglo-Saxon culture and values, which is arguably necessary for the mastery of certain types (or levels) of literacy. In keeping with educational standards and required proficiency in Standard forms of English, schools require the usage of highly literate forms of the English language in student essays, forms that can take years – up to a decade – for English Language Learners (ELLs), as well as their monolingual and native bilingual peers, to master fully. Therefore, neglecting a student's native language can have long-term consequences, particularly when the lack of knowledge of Standard English and Anglo Saxon literacy practices force the child to remain behind her peers in the content areas (e.g., social studies and the sciences). Familiarity with literate concepts (which can be learned in any language) undoubtedly helps a child learn to read those concepts in English. In this instance, a prior knowledge of academic topics in a native language facilitates learning to read and write fluently and accurately in English. It does not hinder the learning process; it helps it. The educational system has always needed to formulate reasonable goals based on social and educational reality; any ill-conceived attempt may have unforeseen consequences.

The final chapter, Chapter 8, takes a look at the current situation for Chicano-Latinos in Southern California. There is discussion of numbers, specifically the numbers and percentages of students in the public school system in the State of California who are Chicano-Latino, and/or Spanish-English bilinguals, and how they fare in a system whose mission is ostensibly to educate all citizens in an equitable manner. The emphasis is not so much on solutions or quick-fixes to "problems" as they are on suggestions for ways to (a) view the persistent behaviors that are typically found in the bilingual classroom; to (b) help students and prospective teachers, administrators, and so on discern if these behaviors are truly problems in a human sense; and to (c) understand whether the difficulties that students have come from the home (cultural, linguistic, or educational background), from an unresponsive, ill-informed educational system, or all of the above. By developing insights into causes, perhaps we can recognize and develop informed methods and practices.

Each chapter concludes with a list of key terms, a summary that provides an overview of the chapter's contents, and a list of activities (topics for discussion and practice essay questions) designed to help students process and react to information that they have learned. The issues are indeed complex and multifaceted, to the point that some things may even be counter-intuitive, going against common expectations. One example of this is the assertion that bilingual contact phenomena *are truly normal*. Switching from language to language is not necessarily an indication of lack of language abilities or low intelligence. It is merely a human response to an unequal language environment in which there are costs and benefits to language usage. An informed view is a better one, especially when there are so many popular misconceptions around.

Key terms

Amerindian, *anglicismo*, Anglo American, Anglo Saxon, bilingualism, Chicano, code-switching, contact phenomena, dialect continuum, dialect, diglossia, First Nations, globalization, Hispanic, immigrant, indigenous, language contact, Latino, linguistic borrowing, migration, monolingualism, multilingualism, New World, Northeast, Old World, population shift, sociolect, Southwest, spread, standard language, superlanguage, unilingual, visible minority.

Summary

The U.S. and Great Britain have never had official, national languages, though many of the nations of the world certainly do in spite of the predominance of English. Both nations have rather large indigenous and immigrant populations. It is also true that large-scale immigration into the United States at various times in its history has caused major demographic and linguistic changes. However, it is also true that English itself is an immigrant language. Worldwide, multilingualism and multiculturalism are the results of massive population movements throughout history, so the U.S. and Great Britain are far from unique. Powerful social, political, and economic factors have changed Europe, the Americas, Asia, Africa, and Oceania. And, with change comes conflict, social and linguistic.

As English spread throughout North America, it came into contact with indigenous (Native American) languages. The initial effects of language contact typically involve degrees of bilingualism as groups establish alliances of sorts. Other consequences are linguistic borrowing (the use of words from one language in another), code-switching (switching from one language to another in conversation), and so on. As cultures and languages collide and begin to interact, they come into *contact*. Simply put, languages are in contact when they are shared by members of a single community; two languages "live" in the head of one speaker. It is also axiomatic in linguistics that languages in contact will affect each other, so some kind of change is to be expected. Another consequence of language spread is the development of dialects. For example, the expansion of the Roman Empire led to the emergence of dialects of Latin that eventually became separate languages. English is progressing along similar lines; English is not the same in England as it is in the U.S., Australia, South Africa, and other places in which English is spoken. So, it is not monolithic or static in nature. It changes just like all other "normal" languages.

One estimate states that 311 different languages are currently spoken in the U.S., 162 of which are indigenous languages – many of which are gradually disappearing (through the processes of shift and attrition). However, Spanish is by far the most widely used language other than English in the U.S. It is spoken by around 30 million people. Ethnic minorities in the U.S. continue to grow; four states are now minority-majority. The population of so-called "White Americans" has been surpassed in those states, indicating profound ethnic and linguistic change. The largest ethnic minority, so-called Hispanics, is not necessarily one big, happy family. Millions of children are classed as Hispanic in schools around the country. However, the term can be used to describe or designate people of various races, nationalities, and cultural characteristics. Each and every group under the Hispanic umbrella is unique. We all must be careful not to overgeneralize or create stereotypes where they simply do not exist.

Activities – topics for discussion

1. English is the *de facto* national language of the U.S. Should that status be official? Make a list of points that you can think of on both sides of the debate regarding the establishment of English as the (or *one*) official language that all U.S. citizens are required to know.

2. How would you defend the language rights of speakers of minority languages? Do you feel that Spanish is perceived differently from other minority languages in the U.S.? How would you defend the language rights of speakers of Spanish?

3. Is the development of English as a *superlanguage* a good thing? On the one hand, it unifies all those who speak it. On the other hand, it seems to devour every language in its path. Interestingly, the same can be said about Spanish in Latin America. Outline the costs and benefits of the spread of superlanguages.

4. English is obviously the predominant language of the U.S. What are the other languages of the "top ten" of the most frequently used languages in the U.S.? Which of these were spoken by the original immigrants to North America?

5. California's population is now a minority-majority, meaning that most of it's inhabitants are members of a group classified as an ethnic minority. What do you think are the social costs and benefits?

Practice essay questions

1. Describe cultural and linguistic contact. What are the typical consequences of language contact worldwide?

2. What are some of the causes of multilingualism in the U.S.? Discuss the social, political, and economic factors that have motivated population movement into (and in) the U.S.

3. Define indigenous (Native American) languages. Include in your response what seems to be happening to Native American languages in what is now the United States.

4. What does the controversial term *Hispanic* mean? What other terms can be used to describe a person of "Hispanic descent?"

5. How many languages are now spoken in the U.S.? Identify the top ten most frequently spoken languages. And, discuss whether the numbers of language minority members is likely to increase or decrease.

Chapter 2

Bilingual acquisition
and the bilingual individual

Most people have some sort of mental image of bilingualism, what it means to be bilingual and what a bilingual person is like. Perhaps, the most common conception of a bilingual is someone who can speak more than one language. But, how proficient must a person be in her languages to qualify? As soon as we take a careful look, we run into problems of definition. The term *bilingualism* (which includes multilingualism) can, in fact, be used to refer to a state or condition existing among members of an entire society – societal *bilingualism* (e.g., the U.S. as a bilingual nation) and to particular programs (e.g., bilingual education). It can also refer to the linguistic abilities of individual people – *individual bilingualism*, called by some *bilinguality* ("bilingualness"). English speakers who have taken a year or two of Spanish in high school or college may not feel comfortable considering themselves "really" bilingual or comparing their abilities to the fluent speakers they hear all around them, but, according to some definitions those Spanish learners are bilingual – emerging or *incipient* bilinguals.

Definitions of individual bilingualism are always relative, relative to how well the speaker knows each language, whether it's spoken, signed, and/or written. Judgments of bilingual abilities are often very subjective, as well, relying more on how the bilingual feels about his/her proficiency in each language than anything truly objective. Self-assessment is a notoriously inadequate measure of bilingualism because some people (certain personality types) will overestimate their abilities in a language, while others who may be more self-deprecating will underestimate (or understate) their actual abilities. Of course, the problem is the lack of a precise definition of what it means to be bilingual and the difficulty we have measuring bilinguality. In the case of the second-language learner, one may assume that maximum proficiency in one language, the native or "first" language, has been reached, but actual abilities in that language can still vary considerably according to age and many other social factors.

This chapter surveys different ways of viewing bi- and multilingualism in society and the often vague and possibly even misleading terms used by government agencies, political interests, the media, and educators. It examines how we as individuals learn the languages we use and the differences between the ways children acquire language(s) and the ways adults manage to learn them later in life. It looks at the various scenarios that dictate how languages develop in various bilingual communities (how and where they're used), and, importantly, how people go about trying to measure how well we know our languages, who is fluent or proficient, and who still needs more time for their languages to develop. The chapter is a little long on terminology, but the concepts presented are foundational for learning about how people become bilingual.

Perhaps the first step in understanding bilingualism, per se, is the discussion of language acquisition, how people essentially "get" their languages. First, all human beings will acquire at least one language, with the possible exception of those born with a serious genetic anomaly or brain lesion (as a result of injury or disease) that might bar or inhibit the processes of language acquisition. The ability to *do* language (the *faculty* of language) has a very special status for our species. And, it has nothing to do with intelligence or IQ. Those born with such conditions as Down's Syndrome, for example, where cognitive abilities may be severely limited, will acquire human language in more or less the usual way. It is rare that we find children with specific language impairments (SLI) whose language develops differently from the usual course of acquisition. So, we begin with the observation that human beings will acquire the language(s) to which they are exposed. From a purely linguistic perspective, the playing field starts out level.

1.   Language development

Research over the past five decades or so has produced a lot of information on language acquisition. A few fairly simple observations have led to the development of a massive body of literature, and many of the controversies that have occurred are far from settled. Noam Chomsky, a prominent linguist (and author of many books on politics, as well), and his colleagues noted that children do not merely echo back the things that their parents say. They appear to recreate their language(s) anew, from the bottom up. They acquire their native languages efficiently, effortlessly, and quickly. And, they do this in a reasonably predictable order. Their acquisition is efficient because they always make steady progress; they don't quit or fail. It is effortless in that they don't have to study hard every day or do mountains of homework. They just seem to get it as time goes by. And, it is quick because it is noticeably faster than how older people seem to learn new languages. Moreover, children acquire language without the benefit of a teacher, direct instruction, or textbook – no adult-to-baby dictionary. It is important to understand fully that children will acquire the language variety to which they are exposed in their immediate environment. Their native language will be the language variety spoken by their parents and other caregivers, whatever language or dialect that might be.

At the heart of the matter is the fact that all human beings learn to talk just like they learn to walk. Some acquisition specialists have proposed that a child's capacity to get language is *innate* or inborn – it is a biological endowment. Others may disagree in different ways and to lesser or greater extents, but it has proved difficult to explain why all normal children, regardless of race or socioeconomic background, acquire language without appealing to some sort of natural, inborn capacity. Most if not all linguists can agree – quite an accomplishment – that all human beings will acquire the language of their parents or caretakers and, therefore, that every child must have some sort of natural language-learning capacity. Evidently, we are born with the ability to "know" language. The debate usually surfaces when trying to define precisely what that capacity is. One thing is certain: learning a language is not like learning history or science. It is a skill, much like learning to play a musical instrument or sport. For the developing child, language is not acquired through conscious study and memorization like the knowledge of biology or chemistry…or linguistics.

Terminology can be a problem in any newly emerging science, and language acquisition studies are no different. So, a few definitions are in order. For example, a *native* language is generally the first one a child is exposed to. Some early studies referred to the processes of learning one's first or native language as *First Language Acquisition* or *FLA*, but because many, perhaps most, children in the world are exposed to more than one language almost from birth, a child may have *more than one native language*. As a consequence, specialists now prefer the term *native language acquisition* (NLA); it is more accurate and includes all sorts of possible childhood situations. Those of us who've tried to learn a language later in life usually don't fail to notice that the process is different. Learning a second or subsequent language is slow and tedious by comparison, and very conscious. The process is so different, in fact, that researchers give it another name, *second* or *subsequent language acquisition* (SLA). However, the terms *first* and *second* refer to chronological order. Therefore, the term *subsequent*, in the sense of "following, later," is preferred to *second* for the obvious reason that the language a person learns after her/his native languages could be the third, fourth or whatever language. SLA typically refers to how adults learn languages later in life.

1.1   Native language acquisition

NLA is most closely associated with the typically unconscious ways children acquire their languages merely through observation. For anyone who is around young children every day, it is remarkable how they just seem to pull words and expressions out of the air. With rare exceptions, they always seem to be marching towards a goal. And, what we know of NLA also helps account for the fact that we seldom if ever remember learning our native languages. We usually don't recall a point in time when we didn't speak it, and we even find it difficult to imagine *not* thinking in it. Our native languages are interwoven into all our thoughts and memories of where we come from and who we are as human beings. All native speakers of English have to take the word of experts that they went through each of the steps that all other native-speakers follow and made all the same kinds of mistakes and discoveries. We may not remember saying *pusketti* for "spaghetti," but that only underscores the fact that NLA goes on beneath our conscious grasp. People who acquire more than one "first" language as young children may not recall learning either one. We may have memories of sweating out tests in a classroom, but seldom remember learning words for "water" or "milk" in our languages.

In contrast, we usually remember (quite painfully) trying to learn a "foreign" language in high school or college. It involves conscious study, lessons or lectures, rote memorization (those little 3 × 5 cards to help us learn words), practice (the unending exercises in our textbooks at the end of the chapter), and drills according to the dictates of the foreign language teacher. Current teaching methodologies may minimize this kind of experience, but the learning process for adults appears to be different nonetheless. We think that we are progressing quite nicely until we meet our first native speaker (other than the teacher, perhaps). It can be a challenge to understand and converse with native speakers of a language that we are still learning.

It's even tougher for language learners to understand two native speakers talking rapidly to each other about familiar topics, especially those speakers who have known each other for a long time. Animated facial expressions and hand gestures don't usually help, either. Native speakers seem to know what things mean beyond just the surface definitions of words. Some of the toughest encounters involve jokes: a learner may know every single word and still miss the punch line. While the natives are laughing out loud, the poor learners may politely laugh or try to look amused. This is apparently because native speakers play with words and exploit all the possible meanings a word can have. Their usage of language is nuanced and creative. Learners, especially beginners, tend to focus on simple, literal definitions of words as their vocabularies start to grow. As proficiency in their second language develops, they can become increasingly aware of words with multiple senses, figurative meanings, and other more sophisticated connotations. Vocabulary learning is a gradual process.

Another significant population to consider at this point consists of those who have studied English as a Foreign Language (EFL) in their home countries for a considerable amount of time. Their experience may be skewed towards written language (an international form) and academic registers of English, and in the vast majority of cases, their exposure to English will have little apparent connection to the speech of native speakers in casual conversation. Their exposure to the spoken language (which is typically informal, fluent, and very rapid) may be minimal. While they may present slightly different challenges for teachers and administrators, they are simply a subset of second/subsequent language learners who may only need special attention with local speech patterns and informal usage. In contrast, those children who have been exposed to mostly informal speech as the model for SL acquisition will most likely need help with the written, formal registers of academic English.

However, the terms NLA and SLA themselves seem to lose their meaning when children learn multiple languages at the same time. For children, processes of NLA and SLA are not necessarily complete polar opposites; it may simply be a matter of degrees, with age being an important issue. As a consequence, a lot of new research has emerged on the topic of childhood language acquisition, especially the development of bilingualism, because of the many contrasting conceptions (and misconceptions) of bi- and multilingualism, particularly their effects (Meisel 2006:91).

1.2   Age and bilingual language acquisition

Age is, therefore, one of the most important developmental considerations. The age of three has been proposed as a reasonable point after which (i.e., after the fourth birthday) the acquisition process may slow or change (McLaughlin 1978). After that, children may still be able to learn to speak a subsequent language with native-like accuracy, but the roles of social and cultural factors may grow in importance. However, bilingual children who are exposed to both languages by their third year seem to undergo their own unique processes of Bilingual First Language Acquisition (BFLA) (Yip & Matthews 2007:25–27; De Houwer 2009). The term refers to the bilingual acquisition of two first or native languages.[1] It is gaining ground in the literature as ongoing work suggests that children who grow up as bilinguals constitute a special population. They have unique skill sets and may enjoy certain cognitive advantages

---

1. The opportunity to become a native bilingual is a consequence of upbringing, which includes exposure to two (or more) languages and the support of parents and educational institutions (Pearson 2002:306). As seen in the contrast between additive and subtractive bilingualism, all (or most) Chicano-Latinos have the potential to become balanced bilinguals and to enjoy the cognitive and socio-economic advantages that provides, but this raw potential may not be realized for political reasons.

in school and later in the job market. The point is that proficiency in both languages needs to be assessed, not just in English. Bilinguals are neither monolinguals nor learning a second/subsequent language. The long-range welfare of the child is at stake, not just short-term success in a language arts class. Classes designed to teach English as a second language (ESL) may not help a child who is already a native speaker. As we'll see in later chapters, some English-only programs simplify classes in content areas and slow down the presentation of knowledge. This may appeal to the biases of some educators towards certain ethnic minority groups, but it does not ensure success.

For those who are learning their languages sequentially, one after the other, establishing which language is the native or stronger language can be especially important in school settings, particularly when trying to establish fair comparisons with their monolingual peers (Romaine 1995: 181). It can be critical in estimating their potential to succeed in English-only classrooms. Consequently, the age at which children are first exposed to their various languages (and whether that exposure has been continuous) needs to be factored into any assessment of their linguistic abilities. Later in this chapter, we will discuss some of the difficulties in measuring proficiency in standardized tests, but, at this point, one important piece of information is the age at which multilingual children are first exposed to their languages.

In very broad strokes, everything in child language acquisition appears to be orderly and systematic. All children go through the same stages of development, though some will start earlier or go faster, while others will start later or proceed more slowly. Importantly, bilingual children go through the same stages as monolingual children in each of their languages. They learn individual sounds, put them together into syllables, form words, and then put those words into longer, multiword utterances. In general, within the first year or so of life, they begin learning the sounds of their language(s), its *phonology*.[2] Some time during the second year, they begin learning the basic rules or patterns of word formation, its *morphology*. The third year (between 2 and 3), they start stringing words together into longer utterances and learn about the grammatical relationships among words (e.g., nouns and verbs) and the basic order in which words appear – its *syntax*. They learn what a well-formed sentence is. Later, in the fourth year, they begin learning the more social aspects of language usage (e.g., how to take turns in speaking) and effective communication within their individual community.

Consequently, most children who are acquiring Standard American English (SAE) already know the sounds, sound patterns, word-formation rules, and how to construct meaningful sentences in that language before they reach kindergarten or hear a teacher profess, "A noun is the name of a person, place, thing, or idea." When a child correctly

---

2. Technically, *phonology* is the study of the rules of pronunciation, or how sounds function in a language to convey meaning. The term *phonetics* refers to the analysis of individual speech sounds, e.g., the vowels and consonants of a language. We can't study one without the other, so individual sounds and the rules/patterns they fit into are often included under a single term, phonology.

puts the 3psp -*s* on a verb, as in "Mommy loves ice cream," he or she already is sensitive to what a *subject* is and such grammatical characteristics as the count-mass distinction and singular versus plural – s/he knows a lot about nouns and pronouns as grammatical subjects. A conservative estimate is that by the first day of school (kindergarten), the child knows 80 percent of the structures of his/her native language and more than 90 percent of its sound system. This is a remarkable feat, particularly when considering the child does this unconsciously, naturally, and without a teacher.

Concerning childhood SLA, researchers distinguish between *early learners* and *late learners*. From a pedagogical perspective, some suggest that the children with the greatest potential for learning a second/subsequent language are preschoolers who are exposed to the second language (L2) within a week of being exposed to an L1. At that point, acquiring a subsequent language is an instance of *early second language acquisition*, and the child is an early learner. The term *late learner* is used for those who begin SLA relatively late, after puberty, when the ability to learn a language natively seems to lessen. In between, there may be a great deal of individual variation, and things change more subtly and gradually. With the possible exception of phonology, learners can still become very proficient regarding second-language grammar (e.g., morphology and syntax).

Regarding the optimal periods for native or native-like abilities, late arrivals (late learners) tend to find SL learning more challenging and time consuming. They may not have the same kind of success as early arrivals/learners. In a study of grammaticality (acceptability) judgments, Johnson and Newport (1989) reported that early English learners who had arrived in the U.S. as young children seemed to have certain advantages. However, around eight to ten years of age, they began to show a gradual decline (not a sudden drop off) in their judgments, which appeared to plateau at age 15 (Myers-Scotton 2006: 344–5; cf. Larsen-Freeman and Long 1991: 160–1).[3] This suggests that the earlier (or younger) a child is, the better, but, beginning around age eight, the capacity to learn native-like proficiency in a second/subsequent language begins to slow. Older adolescents may not fare as well as younger ones in general, implying that younger children may indeed have some kind of special ability. However, younger children may also have more opportunities to interact with native-speaking peers and other native speakers than older children, so even slight differences in social environment may influence exposure to quality input. In addition, the ability to acquire a second language doesn't appear to stop suddenly, and apparent age-related differences don't necessarily mean that older learners cannot reach high-levels of proficiency. We do not want to overgeneralize; some older children are very successful, while some

---

3.   Acceptability judgments are learners' responses to particular sentence constructions, whether or not they fit the general patterns of syntactic knowledge of a native speaker. E.g., "Is the following an example of an acceptable sentence in English…"

younger children do encounter difficulties, perhaps the long-term consequences of attitudinal and motivational factors.

Concerning teachers' expectations, K-2 students seem to have the clearest potential to achieve native or native-like skills in English. Children from grades 3 to 8 may show relative degrees of success, with the younger ones outperforming the older ones in the long run. High school students (grades 9–12) who are only beginning to acquire English (beginners) can make up for their apparent lack of ease by consciously asking questions and paying attention to form. They can exploit the knowledge of their native language(s). However, just as any other typecasting, there will be exceptions. Most of us know students who break the mold, so to speak, shatter stereotypes, and acquire superior skills out of determination and discipline. But, we should also expect some of the youngest to do poorly, perhaps for sociocultural and economic reasons. Some younger adolescents (around the age of puberty) may be highly motivated to blend in and succeed. There will also be variability in all groups. Beyond biological age and maturation, there is the issue of *aptitude* (Larsen-Freeman & Long 1991: 167–172). In a classroom of 30 students of the same socioeconomic background and age, some will just do better than others. The rate of acquisition among individuals will vary.

1.3   NLA versus SLA

Intuitively, processes of NLA and SLA are somehow different. But most of those differences are not exactly obvious. One of the first issues to be addressed is whether or not the uniquely human ability to acquire language stops completely, or merely slows down. The fact that many adults do succeed in learning subsequent languages suggests that it does not stop entirely, but the difficulties that they have suggests that something does indeed change. Evidently, the biological advantage gradually decreases, but recent research indicates that it can be restarted under the right conditions and with enough motivation. And, it doesn't seem to stop completely in all areas of language. Apart from pronunciation, grammatical aspects can continue to develop regardless of biological age. Significant vocabulary growth is also an ongoing process not restricted to childhood. Some differences in the kinds of success SL learners reach appear to be based less on biology and more on social or psychological factors (e.g., attitude).

One obvious difference is the influence that a native language can have on the learning and performance of a subsequent language. Obviously, children learning their native language(s) don't have another or "first" language to interfere with the learning of a "second." Their NL gradually develops on its own. However, in SLA, the NL, or "mother tongue," influences SL acquisition through a process called *transfer*, most noticeably in pronunciation, producing the persistent "foreign accent."[4] The term refers to how speakers unconsciously and automatically apply the rules of one variety to another. For example, SL learners typically transfer the pronunciation patterns of their native language to the *target language* (TL) of SLA. It can occur in other ways, as well, including grammar and other pragmatic aspects of language usage. The second language develops in steps or stages, just as a child's native language develops. At each stage, the speaker's internalized grammar is complete in the sense that it guides what he or she is able to produce.[5] For the SL learner, this developing competence is called a *learner's variety*. (In this sense, transfer allows the learner to produce utterances in the TL, essentially filling in any gaps.) In SLA studies, this learner's variety is called an *interlanguage* (IL). It represents a stage between zero or no knowledge of the TL and a final stage that can be extremely variable, however far that particular learner might advance towards native-like proficiency (Myers-Scotton 2006: 358; Cook 1993: 17–20; Larsen-Freeman & Long 1991: 60–61).

However, for native bilinguals, their languages can influence each other in subtle ways, through transfer in either direction. For Chicano-Latinos, Spanish can be nearly everywhere in the language-learning environment, affecting the varieties of English that serve as models of acquisition. The Spanish models they have can equally be influenced by the socially dominant and ever-present English. As a result, a child's English may show the evidence of a Spanish "accent," even though she may be a monolingual speaker of English.

Dealing with the host of issues addressed in SLA research goes beyond the scope of this book. However, it is important to note that many of the proposed answers are not always cut and dried, a simple and categorical "Yes" or "No." The current state of knowledge is still evolving, but that does not mean that teachers and administrators can afford to ignore what the researchers have to say, especially when there is a clear consensus based on an accumulation of evidence.[6] There are differences between NLA

---

4. To the linguist, an *accent* is a mark written above a letter, e.g., in the Spanish word *está* ("it is"). Colloquially, the term is used to represent a pronunciation pattern, e.g., using the pronunciation pattern of one language while using another, or applying the pronunciation patterns associated with a specific region (the "New York" accent), nation (a "British" accent), or social group (a "Chicano" accent).

5. It is the grammar that the speaker has to work with.

6. There are many excellent texts in the growing field of language acquisition that address these questions, e.g., *Language Development* by Erika Hoff and *How Languages are Learned* by Patsy Lightbown and Nina Spada. As a relatively new field of science, controversies still exist, to be sure. It is the nature of science to self-correct: when preliminary conclusions are reached, other experts set out to replicate studies to test the range of those conclusions, e.g., whether or not they are generalizable to other populations. Our intuitions may say that children have a special gift for picking up languages. That is true, but we cannot therefore conclude that older adolescents or adults *cannot* acquire languages. There may be a host of social and personal factors affecting the process.

and SLA, to be sure, but the commonalities imply that there are underlying processes that can teach us much about human language and the nature of the language learner. As indicated above, age needs to be considered, but its effect may be almost ambiguous. On the one hand, children seem to have an advantage because they can acquire languages merely through observation. On the other hand, adults have an advantage because they can use their prior experience. They can use translation dictionaries and texts (assuming they are literate in a native language).

It is somewhat axiomatic in SLA studies to say that "older is faster but, younger is better" (Larsen-Freeman & Long 1991:155). Older beginning learners may progress quickly at first, while younger learners may appear to struggle for a while. However, the younger learners will eventually pass older ones, especially when considering long-term attainment. Age, however, is not an absolute barrier. Rather than a clear dichotomy between child and adult, there is a scale between ends of a continuum, and gradations of age (and degrees of maturity). Adolescents are in the middle, but even among them, age evidently plays a role. E.g., many of the older ones start out quickly and with dedication, while some younger adolescents begin the learning process relatively slower. However, the younger ones may gradually pass their older counterparts. Reasons cited for this difference is that older learners can compensate for the apparent slowing of acquisition processes by taking advantage of books and their ability to ask questions when they run in to difficulties. They appear to get off to a quick start in the learning process. But, the outcome for younger learners is almost always better when we consider the long-range goal of complete proficiency and being able to speak and read like the native speakers do.

2. Types of bilingualism

Colloquially, the term *bilingualism* can be applied to many things. It can refer to groups, e.g., the Spanish-English bilingual community in the U.S., or to individuals, e.g., your uncle who speaks French as well as English, a bilingual person. It can also refer to institutional entities such as bilingual education or specific types of programs, methods, or materials (e.g., a bilingual class or textbook). Groups are composed of individuals, so, a particular immigrant group in the U.S., becomes bilingual as one member after another adopts English and becomes bilingual. Bilingualism spreads from person to person as the community adjusts to its newly adopted language and culture. The same can be said about particular bilingual contact phenomena. For instance, if enough individuals habitually switch from one language to the other in the phenomenon known as code-switching (or CS), then it may become widespread and a socially accepted behavior, becoming a characteristic of the community.

In the establishment of community-wide, or *societal bilingualism*, there are a number of possible scenarios, or routes to bilingualism. In each scenario, there are certain expected outcomes. The many kinds of language contact phenomena that we see within a community (e.g., code-switching and borrowing) appear to be shaped by two general factors: (a) *language history* – how the languages are acquired or learned within a community, and, consequently, levels of individual proficiency in each language; and (b) *language usage* – how the languages pattern out in the community, the where, when, and with whom of language usage. Chapter 3 discusses the latter, language usage and various bilingual phenomena. In this section, we focus mainly on the former, ways community members learn their respective languages.

The order in which languages are learned often sets the stage for how they are used within the community. Strictly speaking, there seem to be only two possibilities. Languages can be acquired one after the other, a process called *sequential*, consecutive, or successive (in succession) acquisition. Or, they can be acquired roughly at the same time, a process referred to as *simultaneous* acquisition. When the languages are acquired simultaneously, there is no obvious demarcation line between NL and SL. Both languages are learned natively, so a more accurate term for a speaker who has learned her languages in this manner may be *native bilingual*. Such a child is not an English learner (or ESL student). However, research has pointed out that children typically favor one language over another. One may be stronger or *dominant*, either socially (relative to the importance of the language in society) or psychologically (in the child's mind). The language that the child uses most often to sort through new and difficult information, regardless of its status as first or second language, is typically called her *primary* language.[7] The reasons for the apparent imbalance usually reflect the ways the languages are acquired. If one is learned in the home and the other in school, then we should expect that usage may depend on the situation of speech – the places where they are used, or the people with whom the child interacts. Levels or degrees of proficiency in either or both languages is a separate, but equally important issue.

We can also look at whether a language is added to the child's linguistic repertoire – so-called *additive bilingualism*, or if it is learned essentially at the expense of the native language, called *subtractive bilingualism*. The outcome of these two scenarios can be quite different. On the one hand, additive bilingualism is typically associated with the addition of important skills in the classroom and in society at large. On the other hand, subtractive scenarios are the norm in states like California, where voter initiatives have all but eliminated bilingual education. The acquisition of English is seen as so important for the development of the child that all other languages, including the child's native

---

7. People often mentally calculate simple arithmetic (five times five = ___) in the language in which arithmetic was first learned.

language, are devalued and neglected. But, the outcome is the loss of a native language and culture at the core of the child's identity. (Strong bilingual programs are designed to prevent this particular kind of outcome.) In today's increasingly politicized educational arena, subtractive bilingualism has its critics (cf. Moll & Ruiz 2002: 365).

2.1   Sequential and simultaneous bilingual acquisition

In sequential acquisition, the learner has been exposed to and/or achieved some degree of mastery in her native language before beginning to learn a second or subsequent language (the onset of SLA). Evidently, the younger the child is when the acquisition processes begin, the better off she will be. There is a consensus in the literature that *age of arrival* (AO), the age at which a child arrives in the country where a language is spoken and is first exposed to it, is much more significant than the *length of residence* (LOR), how long she has lived there, particularly in the long run (Larsen-Freeman & Long 1991: 154–161). Therefore, the age at which a child begins to acquire English seems to be more important than how long she has resided in the U.S., a presumably English-language environment. In contrast, many Adult ESL classes in states like California are full of those who have lived in the country for many years, yet still have difficulty with English. However, if we consider social factors, e.g., the language these apparently resistant learners use in the home, at work, and even before and after class, it becomes clear that the only exposure to English that they have is during the three-hour ESL classes they attend in the evenings. Change the social circumstances, and the outcome may change, as well.

Monolingual children begin to acquire language as soon as they are exposed to it. For them, the basic acquisition process is complete by the age of three or four. Concerning second-language acquisition, some research has indicated that if the child is seven or younger at the time of arrival into an English-speaking nation or environment, she will acquire English phonological patterns with native or near native-like skills. Her speech may conform to native-speaker norms. These pronunciation patterns consist of intonation patterns (e.g., distinguishing statements from questions), aspirated consonants and consonant clusters (the initial consonants of *top* and *stop*, respectively), and the subtle differences among vowels (distinguishing *cat* from *cot*) (Larsen-Freeman & Long 1991: 154–167).

Social conditions also play significant roles, for instance, regarding attitude and motivation for learning. If the child's native language is learned in a foreign country where it is socially dominant or the language of power (e.g., Standard Spanish in Mesoamerica or Spain), then the NL will enjoy a "high" status as the language of the dominant socio-economic group in the country of origin. When learning English in a classroom, the target will most likely be a standard, as well, so both language varieties that the child has are prestige languages. But, if a nonstandard variety is learned natively in the U.S., where it is a clear minority language, then it may be negatively stigmatized because of its stereotypical associations with minority group status, lack of education linked to specific immigrant groups, and even to poverty in specific neighborhoods (where immigrants live) – their level of income and types of jobs. U.S. Spanish is not the only language that can be perceived in this ambivalent way; similar views of heritage languages exist in the Korean-English, Japanese-English, and Chinese-English communities, as well, although socio-economic factors can be entirely different.

Other social factors can also influence long-term success in academics, particularly due to the great emphasis on language (ESL) in the U.S. and the lack of a clear distinction between (a) language learning and (b) the acquisition of academic knowledge. Some Spanish speakers who arrive in the U.S. at relatively older ages, and who have been educated in their home countries, fare better academically and in the acquisition of Standard English than their native-born counterparts in classroom situations because they bring with them transferable language and literacy skills. If they already know how to read in Spanish, they only need to learn English. They share the same alphabet (though the English spelling system can be complicated), so the job is only to transfer the same reading skills to another language. These acquired skills also allow them to use dictionaries and textbooks to speed up the initial processes of language learning. Because of prior success in school, they are also likely to have gained an intellectual basis for understanding academic references. Non-literate, undereducated children and those who are literate in other, non-alphabetic writing systems may not be able to use their prior abilities to springboard into English.

In contrast, those who lack the necessary preparation may be forced to take the time to learn English basically from scratch and wait until they've learned enough of the language to participate in content areas such as social studies, history, the sciences, and perhaps arithmetic. They are, in essence, learning to read in a language they haven't learned yet. The typical progression is to learn to speak a language, and then learn to read it. However, in the case of second-language learners, they are often forced to learn to read in a language they don't know yet – doubling their learning burden (see Chapter 7 on the acquisition of literacy). This is one of the main criticisms of monolingual ESL programs in lieu of bilingual education. Children may fall further and further behind their English-proficient counterparts as time goes on.

Age usually correlates with grade level, but this is not always the case for children who fail to progress from one grade to the next with children of the same age. Those who are allowed to pass to the next grade without actually achieving grade-level competence in content areas will always be a step behind their native English-speaking classmates. This can be discouraging for children, and it can create additional social problems. Constant failure undoubtedly contributes to higher drop-out rates among certain ethnic minority students. As for language development, it can be challenging to connect newly learned English words (labels) to complex, and typically abstract academic concepts. As stressed above, a child educated in Spanish may already have a label (a Spanish word) for a concept, knowing what that concept means. All she needs to learn is a new label. However, if she has not been exposed to the concept before, she will have to learn both concept and word.

Simultaneous acquisition is normally advantageous to the child. But it often depends on both the amount and the types of exposure to each language. However, there may be an increased likelihood of contact phenomena (code-switching and borrowing), not so much because children have a tendency to mix languages, but because the environment in which the languages are used may provide highly influential models of language mixing, particularly in the home and among close friends. Simultaneous acquisition may also lead to *diglossia*, in which the languages that the child is acquiring are assigned to specific speech situations (at home or elsewhere) or according to certain people and places. This can lead to two different results. One is that the child may acquire a wide range of registers in both languages and effectively uses either language with equal skill, in a positive sense. Or, the exposure to the different languages is restricted to specific situations of usage. Children may be limited to informal registers of the home language and formal, academic registers of English in school. This imbalance, in turn, can motivate different kinds of language contact phenomena, particularly code-switching according to the topic (academic topics are in English, close personal topics in Spanish). In families where the languages are customarily mixed, language-mixing behaviors can become the norm.[8]

2.2   Additive versus subtractive bilingualism

Another telling way to view societal bilingualism is in the contrast of additive versus subtractive bilingualism. Additive bilingualism applies to a situation in which competence in a SL is added to competence in a NL, which is the case for those who are fluent, proficient speakers of a NL before emigrating to the U.S. This is one possible scenario in acquiring different languages: an individual or group of people migrate to a new country, learn that country's language, and add it to their *linguistic repertoire* (the language or set of languages that they already know). As Spanish speakers colonized the areas now known as the American Southwest, many of the indigenous peoples adopted Spanish for utilitarian reasons, and consequently became bilinguals. The key point is that the original languages are not necessarily neglected or lost in the process. The NL still forms the basis of cultural and individual identity.

---

8.   See Chapter 3 for discussion of borrowing and code-switching.

Additive bilingualism may also refer to the *positive cognitive outcomes* of bilingualism, while subtractive bilingualism suggests "negative affective and cognitive effects of bilingualism" and an implicit lack of development of *both* languages (Baker 2006: 74). Then, too, additive bilingualism implies that bilinguals are either proficient in both languages or are becoming proficient, and, importantly, that they have positive attitudes to both languages. Research that shows positive cognitive effects for bilingualism typically involves this type of acquisition. For example, bilinguals who acquire their SLs after they've already mastered their NL in the four basic skill areas (listening, speaking, reading, and writing) demonstrate their ability to use the NL for reasoning and critical thinking. The evidence suggests that proficient bilinguals may have some sort of cognitive advantage over monolinguals, for example, in particular analytical skills and recognizing and dealing with ambiguity (Baker 2006: 157–160; Myers-Scotton 2006: 337–339). Proposed reasons (causes) for these advantages remain somewhat controversial; past research has been somewhat vague about (a) how bilingual skills and proficiencies should be classified, (b) what types of bilinguals enjoy the benefits, and (c) whether the benefits are permanent or merely transitory (e.g., during the early school years, but not necessarily lifelong).

In contrast, subtractive kinds of bilingualism typically yield very different cognitive and social effects. It involves the neglect and eventual loss of the original, heritage language. It also implies that a new, socially dominant language will be learned at a cost (the loss of a socially less important language). This cost often comes in the form of the devaluing of the child's NL (as somehow inadequate or deficient) and culture, affecting the child's self-image and self-esteem. This can certainly influence attitudes towards the dominant language (and its speakers) and the motivation to assimilate into the language and culture of education. Subtractive bilingualism may also occur in situations of rapidly advancing language shift, where an entire community is shifting from a minority, stigmatized, or culturally receding language to a majority, prestige, or culturally dominant language. This is clearly the case in many segments of the Spanish-English bilingual community in Southern California.

In a majority view, the benefits of learning the socially dominant language far outweigh the benefits of keeping an old, "foreign" language, which is clearly a subjective value judgment. Accordingly, the social stigma for lack of proficiency in English is a negative one, and to be avoided. There is also the stereotypical view that the lack of Standard English skills is caused by a corresponding lack of education, according to the so-called deficit model of education. Some teachers, whose job it is to provide educational opportunities for all regardless of ethnic or language minority status, often believe that subtractive forms of education are to the child's benefit, and with tremendous zeal, seek to Americanize students as quickly and efficiently as possible. By eradicating a minority language and culture, they think that they are lifting children "up" to the perceived standards of the majority of American students, assumed to be proficient monolingual speakers of English. They may be very well-intentioned and believe that they are performing an important service for the minority community in insisting on only English acquisition and marginalizing Spanish.

In the long run, what is at issue is not *the addition of* English to the child's linguistic repertoire. The issue is to what extent this process needs to be subtractive – the long-term educational and social costs may be considerable, to the child and to society.

2.3   Individual bilingualism – two languages, one speaker

Because communities are made of individuals, it is important to look at the various ways languages affect each other in a person's head, how the social and biological processes may interact to produce different results. Perhaps the first linguist to look at the individual bilingual and the mental or psychological representation of languages was Uriel Weinreich, who examined the possibilities of one, merged language system versus two, coexistent systems in the bilingual mind. In his classic study, he proposed three types of bilingualism: Type A, *coordinate*; Type B, *compound*; and Type C, *subordinate*. They were thought to be ways that languages are represented in the bilingual's brain, based on how they've been learned (Weinreich 1953 [1968]). The *coordinate* bilingual learns her native language at home, and the second language at school, in two distinct environments. Each language has its own set of social domains, and a separate conceptual system. It is implicit that the languages are learned more-or-less sequentially. So, for a bilingual who has learned Spanish at home and, then, English at school, a word like *libro* would have its own meaning (the object that it signifies, or referent), and the word *book* will also have its own independent meaning.

A *compound* bilingual, in contrast, acquires both languages essentially in the same social contexts, so there is the tendency for one, *fused* representational system – simultaneous acquisition is implicit. Each form, *libro* and *book*, therefore, represents the same object/referent. A single concept would have two forms or labels; thus, for the compound bilingual, the languages are interdependent, rather than independent. The compound bilingual is also a more likely candidate for language *interference*. For Weinreich, interference was bidirectional, implying transfer of characteristics from either language to the other, and that the languages affect each other in relatively unpredictable ways.[9]

---

9. In later studies, the term *interference* acquired a negative connotation because of the assumed randomness of its effects. Probably as a result of the obvious influence of a native language on the acquisition of a second language, especially in phonology (the "foreign" accent), it has more recently been thought of as unidirectional, that the language learned first leaves its mark on the one learned later. Because of its negative connotations, the term temporarily fell into disfavor among educators and other language specialists, being replaced by the more neutral term *transfer*. As will be discussed later, transfer has also accrued some negative baggage. However, some specialists choose to use

A third type of bilingualism, subordinate, is a sub-type of coordinate, with two distinct language systems. However, with the subordinate bilingual, the second (non-native) language is considerably weaker than the first, and the second language can only be accessed through the first. For example, if a native English speaker were to learn ancient Hebrew (perhaps for religious purposes) primarily from written sources (in order to study the language and not use it for interpersonal communication), then each word would have to be translated one at a time. The dominant, native language, acts as a filtering mechanism, or go between. Consequently, the word *sefer* ("book") would necessarily call up (or *evoke*) the English word *book*, but not necessarily a mental image of what a *sefer* is. In fact, the meaning would have to pop up mentally in English for it to be understood. This phenomenon is common in the early stages of SLA, when a particular SL word doesn't call up a mental image of an object, only the word form in the dominant (native) language as if on a page in a glossary or dictionary.

Recent work has neither confirmed nor denied Weinreich's insights, but what Weinreich observed can easily be linked with the different outcomes of simultaneous and subsequent (successive) language acquisition scenarios. The contexts of language acquisition/learning can lead to a variety of different results. In any case, the possible scenarios generate a lot of speculation. Given the complex and dynamic ways that languages can interact in the minds of bilinguals (lexically, phonologically, syntactically, semantically, etc.), a two- or three-way distinction is probably inadequate, particularly in view of the rapid advances in technology designed and used to measure brain activity. Today's neurolinguists and psycholinguists have much greater resources for peering into the human mind-brain.[10]

2.4   One system or two

A bilingual is obviously not a monolingual in two languages. For example, a Spanish-English bilingual is neither a monolingual Spanish speaker nor a monolingual English speaker. A child who lives with two or more languages will have a very different life experience than the child who acquires only one. Nevertheless, each language appears to develop similarly to the ways the languages develop with monolinguals of the respective languages. They follow the same steps, and there appear to be no differences in the language acquisition processes when both languages are learned simultaneously. Their

---

the term interference to describe the negative (or inhibiting) effects of the mother tongue, while reserving transfer to describe bidirectional influence (including borrowing words), particularly the positive effects of transferring literacy skills from on to the other (see, e.g., Van Coetsem 2000: 34–37 concerning contact phenomena, and especially Hornberger 2003: 17–20, in respect to biliteracy).

10. It should be interesting to note, however, that Weinreich's terminology was an excellent place to start because his observations and intuitions were based on experience, an experience that linguists of his day shared. And, as with other pioneers in language contact, his *terms* are still useful.

proficiency levels in each language may vary, however. Some bilinguals may resist the acquisition of one or the other for sociocultural reasons; the heritage language may stop being used because the number of domains in which it is used cease to exist outside the home (language attrition). Children will not acquire a language just because they are around it (Myers-Scotton 2006:327). They need to interact with speakers in meaningful ways, or the opportunity may be lost. In that event, the linguistic character of the heritage language may be affected, too, as forms and structures disappear from usage in the language.

In view of language mixing behaviors and transfer phenomena, there is continuing debate about how language systems are represented in the mind of the bilingual, whether the bilingual child has one unitary language system that essentially controls both languages, or two separate systems, one for each language. The answer to this may account for a lot of cross-linguistic influence. Research, however, has produced ambiguous results. Earlier studies suggested that the child basically formed one general language system and only gradually learned to differentiate them, teasing them apart in a three-step process. First, the child begins to (a) develop separate lexical systems, and then (b) develops a single, unitary grammatical system (e.g., word order, inflectional affixes) that encompasses both lexicons, moving on to (c) eventually separate language systems. The theoretical questions remain on how and when the child teases apart two separate grammatical systems.

The one-system view is summed up by De Houwer (2005), whose Separate Development Hypothesis suggests that "…in learning to speak, children raised with two separate languages from birth approach their languages as two distinct, closed sets" (30). In other words, for native bilinguals, learning two languages does not cause mental confusion or inhibit the acquisition of either language. Acquiring a heritage language does not inhibit or impede acquiring a socially dominant one; and the reverse, acquiring a socially dominant language does not interfere with acquiring a heritage language. The importance of this is that they do not get confused, and their languages do not randomly interfere with each other. Children may mix languages in various ways (in code-switching or borrowing), but this is not a result of their lack of control. It is more likely a result of their input and the language mixing behaviors of members of their community.

Different facets of grammar are likely to play important roles, too. For instance, there is some evidence that particular kinds of words (i.e., concrete nouns representing tangible objects) are easily and rapidly translated by proficient bilinguals from one language to the other, while other aspects of grammar can be more problematic (e.g., translating words, expressions, and grammatical strategies that only exist in one language). Thus, access to the two separate lexicons (*lexical access*) appears to correlate somewhat with word type and frequency in so-called *translation pairs*, words that have clear translation equivalents. Despite simultaneous acquisition scenarios, most children will still show a preference for one language, their dominant or stronger language. The direction of the translation (from L2 to L1, or the reverse) also appears to influence efficiency in translation. Typically, translating from a weaker variety into the psychologically dominant language is quicker than the other way around, from a stronger language into a weaker one (Kroll & de Groot 1997: 169). Nevertheless, the two separate lexicons (mental dictionaries) do appear to be connected. Children at a very young age respond with the appropriate choice of language based on the participants, despite the fact that at the one-, two-, or three-word stage, they may mix languages, perhaps drawing on their total, combined linguistic resources. Of course, in families where languages are frequently mixed, children will have mixed models; they are more likely to continue to mix languages.

Another issue concerning childhood bilingualism is whether or not their overall intellectual behavior is affected or delayed (Myers-Scotton 2006: 337–340). Based on erroneous reports and stereotypes that asserted direct correlations between bilingualism (in lower socioeconomic groups) and poor academic performance, there has been a popular belief that bilingualism is harmful to the child. These beliefs, based on current stereotypes of particular kinds of bilinguals, continue to pop up among teachers and parents. However, current research seems to suggest that bilingualism not only does not delay development, but it provides some advantages. Where there are differences in proficiency levels in each language, they are minimal. For example, in one study of Spanish-English bilinguals in Miami (Pearson, Fernandez & Oller 1993), it was reported that English dominant bilinguals did as well on vocabulary levels in English as their monolingual peers, though children who were not English-dominant scored slightly below. Differences in grammatical proficiency gradually disappeared with age, with older bilinguals catching up to their monolingual counterparts.

3.   Types of bilingual individuals

In all bilingual communities, speakers will exhibit a range of proficiencies in either or both (all) languages, from full to partial (or zero) proficiency.[11] In fact, all speakers will fall somewhere on a continuum of proficiency in each language, from completely

---

11. Proficiency is somewhat synonymous with competence, referring to a speaker's overall ability in a language. Fluency (in a flowing manner) refers to ability to speak (sign, or write) a language rapidly and on a wide range of topics. Accuracy, which is obviously independent of speed, means how well a speaker uses a language, according to native-speaker norms. A speaker of a nonstandard dialect may generate forms that diverge from the so-called standard. From a purely linguistic standpoint, the differences should not be confused with errors or mistakes. Her speech may be accurate according to native-speaker norms, just not the norms of a prescribed standard variety.

proficient in one to almost no knowledge in the other. In the community, there-fore, one expects *continua of proficiencies* (Menn 1989: 340; Romaine 1989: 371 and 1995: 72). All possible combinations may exist in some sense. That is, there will be *monolingual*, or *unilingual*, speakers of either language who may have no or only a small degree of passive knowledge in the other. In the Spanish-English community of the U.S., for example, there are those who are *fluent-proficient* in Spanish (they know it well and can use it in many different situations) and only partially proficient in English. The reverse is also true where speakers are fluent-proficient in English, but only partially so in Spanish.

There are "ideal" or *balanced* bilinguals (known also as *proficient bilinguals*) who demonstrate superior skills in both, although one language is typically stronger than the other in some subtle ways despite the apparent balance of the two. (An *ambilingual*, patterned after the word ambidextrous, is one who can use her languages interchange-ably.) The vast majority of bilinguals are less than ideal, however, with one language psychologically favored (dominant or stronger) over the other. So, one language will appear stronger than the other.

A continuing controversy, as surprising as it may sound to some, is the possible existence of *partial* bilinguals, so-called *double semilinguals*, those who demonstrate minimal proficiency in both languages (Baker 2006: 10–12). In educational circles, there are names for them – although these names may not be in print in official statistics, e.g., *limited* bilinguals, and less formally, *limited-limited* and *non-nons* (Wiley 2005: 156). This may be a small, nearly invisible minority, but it is of significant social concern. It suggests a child with no language, who pieces together two languages poorly, and implies a situation of neglect and social deprivation.

However, one of the key elements in the discussion of this controversial group is the issue of testing, and how test makers determine who is and who is not proficient in a language. The issue of relative proficiency is problematic for a number of reasons (Baker 2006: 21–41; 358–367). For example, how does one test passive comprehen-sion skills (ability to understand) without requiring active performance (giving an answer), in either spoken or written form? A child may understand an examiner perfectly well and for a variety of social or cultural reasons, not appear to respond appropriately according to the expectations of the examiner.

A second issue specifically regarding testing is the use of "standard" languages. Not every child is exposed to Standard English in the home. In cities like Los Angeles, where children are obviously exposed to local varieties of English and Spanish in the home, there is no guarantee that those children are sufficiently exposed to standard varieties of either to reach proficiency in a standard, U.S. Spanish or Standard Ameri-can English. It is not fair to hold a child responsible for knowing something she or he may not have been exposed to or expecting proficiency in formal, academic registers of a language without the benefit of instruction.[12] Many children do, however, become quite proficient in a nonstandard, local form of Spanish, and in nonstandard varieties of English such as AAVE or Chicano English.

Perhaps the most problematic issue is testing a bilingual child according to native-speaker, monolingual norms in a standard language. This will affect evaluation and placement in age-appropriate grade levels and different programs for the child who is neither monolingual nor a speaker of a standard variety.[13] One may safely assume that a child who is in the process of mastering two languages and a variety of registers in each may *appear* slow or behind his/her monolingual classmates, especially when the child is being tested in a language based on highly literate, written, and standardized forms of language associated with upper socio-economic levels of society, not the variety most often used in the child's home environment, (The consequences of political decisions, in this case, the abandonment of bilingual education, are felt on many social and linguistic levels.) Unfortunately, this can contribute to negative stereotypes of minority children as slow or behind in their work, or lead teachers to assume that their lack of response is an *unwillingness* (reticence or reluctance) to learn, study, or apply themselves to a task. When a child doesn't understand what the teacher is saying, the teacher should expect her to seem fearful of a response, sensing that she may be wrong either way, speaking or remaining silent. The child's expectations of comprehensibility may simply not match those of the teacher.

The students to whom educators should be most attentive are children who test as somehow low in either or both *standards*.[14] However, they are often assigned into

---

12. Basically, registers of speech are varieties or forms of a language appropriate for the situation of speech. We all speak one way in casual conversations with close friends and another in formal situations in institutional settings (e.g., at court, at the doctor's, or in school). See discussion of registers in Chapter 3.

13. The issue of what is standard is complicated by what may be called "regional standards." A teacher from the dominant language group will assume that he or she speaks the standard and, thereby, judge utterances of the child accordingly. When the child uses forms that deviate from the teacher's norm, her speech may be viewed as deviant or nonstandard. Regional standards are influenced by regional dialects, e.g., Northern, Southern, and so on. So, a Southern-speaking child may sound odd to a teacher from the North; rural forms may sound odd to the urban teacher; and children from lower socioeconomic strata may sound odd to the middle class instructor.

14. In essence, a standard is the language variety of a privileged social elite, the language of educated people. All school children must learn it to some extent in order to function in school. In the U.S., the standard is the variety of English used in government, the media, in education, and the economy. While it ostensibly serves as a "unifying" language, it still must be learned and taught. It stands in opposition to a *vernacular*, which is the language acquired in the home and associated with regional or social varieties. See Chapter 7 for discussion of *standardization*.

mainstream, English-only classrooms in the hopes that they will eventually learn at least one language, English (the so-called sink or swim approach). These apparently semilingual children typically, in fact, speak *something*, perhaps a nonstandard dialect (or two) or a mixed variety (conversational code-switching) which draws upon all environmental sources, e.g., the home language(s) and/or various versions of a socially dominant language, which may include learner's varieties (interlanguages) spoken by parents. All children learn to speak the language of their parents or other caretakers and other members of *their* community. Obviously, one cannot rule out proficiency in a blended or intertwined variety (see Bakker 1997). Further investigation may reveal links to lower socioeconomic status and a lack of educational opportunity (which often go together), but not to a lack of linguistic aptitude or intelligence.

Because the nature of bilingualism is dynamic, one is warned against applying static labels, especially one that is put into any type of permanent (cumulative) educational file that identifies and classifies children. But, this seems to be the nature of education, particularly in the era of the No Child Left Behind Act. It has become critical to count the number of students who have transitioned from one category to another. Head counts have become necessary to the functioning of entire schools and academic programs. Such practices are not without flaws.

Baker (2006), in his discussion of semilingualism, refers to the oft-cited, pioneering studies that investigated educational problems mistakenly associated with bilingualism (Skutnabb-Kangas & Toukomaa 1976; Skutnabb-Kangas 1981). Finnish-speaking children were found to do poorly in Swedish schools, and the suspicion was that bilingualism was to blame. "Semilingual" or other poorly masked equivalents have been used to imply the following: shows small, restricted vocabulary (inadequate) and flawed grammar (inaccurate according to monolingual norms in a standard language); has conscious and slow production of language (non-fluent); lacks creativity in both languages; has trouble thinking and expressing emotions in either language. These are very serious charges for a child who is expected to perform under pressure in a language that he or she is still in the process of learning.

Baker (2006: 10–12) cites five major problems with this concept of semilingualism:

i.   It has a disparaging connotation that implies underachievement as a kind of self-fulfilling prophesy;
ii. If languages are relatively under-developed, the causes may originate in socio-economic conditions, and not in internal linguistic processes of acquisition;
iii. Bilinguals typically use their languages according to people, places, and topics. A child may be competent in her languages in some contexts and not in others;
iv. Testing procedures may not be sensitive to what the child actually *knows*, only to what the child does not know. Deficiencies may be artifacts of tests that are biased against nonstandard dialects and nonstandard discourse patterns;

v.   In that a bilingual child is not two monolinguals in one body, it is not fair to compare a bilingual user of two languages with monolinguals of either language.

Consequently, the labels "semilingual" or "double semilingual" are discouraged, and, are rightfully no longer used. Nevertheless, children will show a range of abilities in each language that can suggest a relative lack of development. But, rather than focus on perceived deficiencies in specific skills that a child may not possess at the moment, it might be wiser to concentrate on helping the child continue to grow (establishing realistic goals and approaches) and to encourage the development of linguistic abilities that expand naturally under the appropriate conditions.

4.   Difficulties in measuring proficiency

In view of what specialists know about varying proficiency levels, in addition to testing, another controversial topic is measurement, how to determine scales of proficiency in each of the bilingual's languages objectively, impartially, and scientifically (e.g., Edwards 2006: 8–11). Obviously, schools and other institutions have a need to measure linguistic abilities and to categorize populations of people for educational and political purposes. However, it is also important for the test makers to understand the nature of the results they get and to treat the data they generate in equitable ways (*not* to foster damaging stereotypes). Simply put, there is no one, single, and clear method of generating infallible language data or ways to interpret them. Children are handed the environment in which they are raised. Their underlying natural abilities can be affected by social factors, e.g., socio-economic and ethnic minority status. Measuring the linguistic abilities of adults is no less problematic. As a result, the ability of researchers to generalize test results across age groups is highly suspect. Comparing migrant workers in Southern California (whose English skills may only develop minimally) with children in the public school system (whose skills may be rapidly evolving) is simply not valid.

If test results are used to categorize children, particularly in academic settings, then the labels themselves may create stereotypes. As studies have shown, educators, who should know better, have been just as guilty of stereotyping children as any other social group (Penfield & Ornstein-Galicia 1985: 71–73). Once tagged with a label, children may have a tendency to live up to that label, whether positive or negative. Terms such as *limited-English-proficiency* (LEP) carry negative connotations, and, even when the term is changed to *English-learner* (EL), the negative associations can remain, particularly within minority ethnic groups (cf. Baker 2006: 27). Categorizing human beings will always include fuzzy categories with blurry edges. There is an inherent danger in labeling even for ostensibly benevolent purposes.

Inherent in any testing procedure of language abilities is a scoring system (with values placed on scores), and an implicit question of the reliability of the test to yield the results that it was designed for. As a consequence, the focus needs to be a broad one inclusive of many factors, rather than one that homes in on one specific aspect of (bilingual) language acquisition. For example, if a program or study has a single focus on the development of syntax or vocabulary, it will miss other important areas of communicative competence. In testing school-age children, there are many factors that interact in dynamic ways to influence their scores.

When testing individual bilingual abilities, some of the most fundamental issues are (a) the testing situation and the effects of the child's experience (or lack thereof) in educational settings; (b) dialect status (which varieties are being tested); and (c) skill areas (spoken versus written modes) and the assumed correspondences of active and passive competence.[15] The testing situation includes how the child interacts with people based on relationships, e.g., with authority figures, parents, family, and peers. Tests may be administered in a setting by people unfamiliar to the child; she may feel threatened or uncomfortable. The physical setting may be a factor, e.g., a large room with large numbers of test-takers (and distractions caused by interactions), as well as scheduling (e.g., on a Saturday when the child has other time commitments). In the testing situation, there is also the issue of language modes, or psychological states of language activation (discussed in the next chapter). For instance a Chicano-Latino (Spanish-English) bilingual may be in a bilingual mode with both languages mentally activated (thinking bilingually) when reacting to other bilingual student test-takers. With both languages activated (she is thinking in two languages), performance on a test measuring competence in only one language, requiring a monolingual mode, English, may suffer, particularly in unfamiliar circumstances with many distractions.

Tests designed to determine competence or general proficiency may test for *fluency*, *accuracy*, or both. Fluency is typically a quantitative measure, the how much and how fast of language performance. It can be distinguished from accuracy, how well (according to native-speaker standards or norms) a child can produce the language. We've all heard English speakers who can talk "a mile a minute" who, nevertheless, make lots of "mistakes" along the way. If the test is designed to determine proficiency in SAE according to norms established by monolinguals (age and/or grade appropriate behaviors of native monolinguals), then the bilingual child is automatically at a disadvantage. Results will be biased against the bilingual child.

---

15. The term *mode* is used in two distinct ways, (a) as a means or medium of expression such as written versus oral modes, and (b) as psychological states, such as bilingual versus monolingual modes. Perhaps, adding to the potential confusion is the term *modality*, which co-occurs with *mode* in the first (a) sense (e.g., "the modality of writing", or as a grammatical term (mood and modality) when referring to subjunctive or indicative *mood* or the expression of *modality* when discussing the meanings of modals (modal verbs) such as *can, could, may, might, must*.

Obviously, tests attempt to measure proficiency in a standard variety, but the test-taker may be a native speaker of a nonstandard variety (e.g., Ebonics or Chicano English).[16] It's not likely that the test will have samples of the actual speech that the child uses in her community. As with the bilingual, the child loses the expressive power of her native language and must resort to relatively unfamiliar forms and meanings. Tests also focus on certain *registers*, e.g., formal, written, academic language, and on specific *topics* with specialized vocabulary that are not part of the child's daily speech. So, questions that might be answered correctly if posed in terms the child comprehends may go unanswered. Consequently, the test may measure specific skills in a standard variety, but it will not measure the child's overall linguistic ability. Whether oral or written, most tests neglect the child's ability to communicate in her real-world environment.

4.1   The nature of language

When discussing testing language ability on a more theoretical level, we need to define what we mean by language, and what we mean by ability. There is certainly more than one way to look at it. The concept of *competence*, itself, has a somewhat controversial history. As a term, it has been used in opposition to the concept of *performance* (Chomsky 1965). In a Chomskyan sense, competence refers to a speaker's overall knowledge of a language, her internal (symbolic) representations of grammar, akin to a mental state. Performance is the output, the speaker's external application of this inner knowledge. The distinction is a theoretical one, influenced by a host of situational factors, limitations of memory, and physical processes involved in the production of speech. The controversy has centered mainly on the obvious difficulty in assessing underlying knowledge. When we look at actual data, we are limited to performance, which is full of mistakes and not a reliable "guide to competence" (Cook 1993: 5). This is problematic enough for any testing program when trying to understand underlying competence in just one language, more so when attempting to measure competence in two or more.

Linguistic approaches often focus on the (micro level) particulars of phonology, morphology, and syntax to measure development, from the emergence of individual sounds to the development of larger units of speech. Recent research has tackled this emphasis on strictly grammatical aspects of language by looking to *culturally transmitted*

---

16. Standards are arbitrarily set by the language community itself. Regarding languages such as Spanish, French, and Italian, standards have historically been based on the speech of a prestigious group or region. With English, one might suspect the London dialect to have great influence. Standard American English, however, is not based on the speech of any city or region, though it could be argued that it is based on the speech of a socially dominant and prestigious group, those of white Anglo-Saxon heritage who have held institutionalized influence since the founding of the original British American colonies. More accurately, SAE is an ideal form of language, with identifiable features, and the forms come to us by consensus, from English teachers and authors of dictionaries and textbooks.

aspects of performance. Some models, especially those used in educational settings, divide the knowledge of language into at least three general areas: (a) a linguistic component inclusive of specific language skills such as grammar (syntax and morphology), lexicon (vocabulary), and pronunciation (individual sounds and processes); (b) a sociolinguistic/pragmatic component, including awareness of the appropriate usage of specific language forms according to situational factors (genres, registers, dialects, and strategies for interaction); and (c) a discourse component, including understanding and organizing much larger units of speech (conversations, speeches, and reading and constructing written texts) in culturally defined ways. Some researchers divide aspects of this rather broad view of human speech in more specific ways, but competence, per se, is *not* restricted to internal linguistic processes only. Behind each area of performance, there is a different kind of competence or knowledge.

An important example of language beyond grammar is the *speech act*. We not only communicate information to each other; we also communicate our desires and intentions. That is, we *do* things with speech. We make requests, ask questions, make promises, assert truth, order people around, get someone's attention, plead, cuss, inquire, ask/tell, inform, express regret, console, and so on. Speech acts typically employ so-called performative verbs such as *bequeath*, *promise*, *bet*, *wager*, and *swear* or *affirm* (under penalty of perjury). Examples are saying "I do" or "I will" during a wedding ceremony (by the correct person at the appropriate time), making a bet, and signing a check, loan document, letter of intent (to attend a specific university), or contract. Children internalize the purposes and the effects of behaviors by observing the interactions of those in their environment. In this sense, speech is a culturally determined behavior, not just an abstract mental or cognitive system; it is something that happens in the community. Socialization involves how children become members of their communities and how they acquire societal and cultural norms. Even in the most obvious sub-culture or counter-culture, there are norms of interaction and interpretation. There is the well-known expression: "There is honor among thieves." From the classroom to the street gang, there are rules that everyone who wants to belong must observe and follow.

Language can also be described in terms that refer to the development of both language and literacy, e.g., the four skills of listening, speaking, reading, and writing. In some current research, particularly in the context of bilingualism and biliteracy, the simple dichotomy between competence and performance has come under increasing scrutiny, mostly because these skills all seem to be interrelated, situated along continua of abilities, and influencing each other in various ways (O. Garcia et al 2007). In addition, there is the tension between standard language and dialects. Gee (1996: 21) refers to "socially contested" terms such as "language" and "literacy" that are interpreted by individuals according to their own internalized belief systems.

On the one hand, the linguist sees language as consisting of both a biological component (the specific ways a grammatical system is acquired) and a social one (how language is acquired from one's social surroundings). Therefore, dialects are a reality; they can diverge considerably from a standard variety. What is normal, correct usage for one child according to the norms of his/her community (those from whom language is acquired) may differ from the usage of another, and especially so when comparing nonstandard usage to the language used by teachers in the classroom – an idealized standard. On the other hand, there is the "naïve" theory that accepts the pronouncements of school and government officials that standard forms are the correct forms, and anything that veers off from that is an error – and a problem. Consequently, a child may successfully acquire grammatical competence in a nonstandard dialect and, while taking a standardized test, apply skill in her native language in performance. But, that child may achieve a low score based on the internal biases of the test and test givers.

We can also infer that testing only one ability to the exclusion of the others will yield limited results, just as we can see the limits of testing grammar only and excluding culturally transmitted facets of language. Testing specific areas of grammar in only one language in a bilingual's repertoire may not measure her ability to express herself or communicate. A student may be very adept at code-switching (a skilled behavior) or Chicano English and not test well in SAE grammar. And, if educators wish to measure a bilingual's overall abilities in either of her languages, they need a broad perspective. Within the Chicano-Latino community, a test designed only to measure linguistic competence will show nothing about the individual's ability to communicate with her peers, or with the millions of other Chicano-Latinos in Southern California. It may also fail to help the educator assess what can be done in critical areas of literacy, being able to read (critically) and write in academic registers and to participate successfully in academic discourse (which involves culturally-influenced facets of performance). While many components of language are interrelated, one does not necessarily develop automatically from the other, particularly in bilingual or bidialectal communities.

4.2   Language testing in childhood

Specialists in communicative disorders typically use standardized measures for the diagnosis of delays in language development, and for the evaluation of treatment and remediation. The methodology includes data collection of average length of a child's utterances (*mean length of utterance* or MLU) to estimate the development of syntax for a child suspected of having problems and comparing that against age-appropriate norms established by testing monolinguals.[17] Various other tests include

---

17. Mean length of utterance, typically referred to by its acronym, MLU, is a way of estimating grammatical development. It is the average length of a series of utterances based on the number of morphemes they contain. However, the length of a child's utterances does not necessarily reveal how she is mastering the grammar of her language (Elliot 1981: 102). Roger Brown (1973) proposed that

the MacArthur Communicative Development Inventories (CDIs) that consist of checklists of gestures, words, and word clusters that the children (infants 8–16 months and children/toddlers 16–30 months) are reported to understand and produce, and the Peabody Picture Vocabulary Test (locating items in pictures) for children from the age of 3 and up to adulthood.

However, most tests like these are designed to test monolingual native speakers. As mentioned above, this automatically creates problems for the bilingual. It has become axiomatic that a bilingual child is not two monolinguals in one body (Grosjean 1995: 259). One might suspect that bilinguals will lag behind their monolingual counterparts, but this is apparently not the case (Myers-Scotton 2006: 326; Genesee 2003: 204–228), with the exception of vocabulary development. Bilinguals have twice the number of words to learn. (Speakers of similar European languages often have an advantage in this regard because of cognates – words that are obviously similar, e.g., English *school* and Spanish *escuela*.) It is likely, too, that languages are compartmentalized according to domain of usage (e.g., one for the home, one for school) contributing to a mismatch of sorts (cf. Michael & Gollan 2005: 392). As a result, childhood tests measuring vocabulary in English will be biased in favor of unilingual English speakers.

4.3   Testing and placement

The following contains brief summaries of different types of tests. The list is not meant to be exhaustive, or even comprehensive of the kinds of tests being given nor of the nature of the tests, themselves. They are only intended to provide a short overview of the many ways children and adults are tested on their language abilities:

summative tests	Sum up abilities in four standard/main skills (listening, speaking, reading, and writing). They are usually given at the end of a school year to estimate progress and used for placement for the next year. Because they are given at the end of the school year, attitudes and motivations for test taking can vary greatly, and the results should only be used as very general guidelines.

---

the number of morphemes (an average based on 100 utterances) would be a better gauge because it showed the acquisition of inflections and other grammatical characteristics more clearly. Some criticisms of Brown's approach have centered on the difficulty of determining a child's utterance (when it begins or ends), and which morphemes should be counted. E.g., the irregular past was counted as a single morpheme while the irregular past (root + -ed) was counted as two; and, Brown didn't distinguish between function words and inflectional affixes.

formative tests	Give feedback during the learning process, and provide profiles of students according to progress being made (or lack thereof). These tests can assist teachers in addressing individual problem areas or areas of strength.
language background scales	Are self-rating scales to indicate *usage* of language (in the home, at work, or at school). They often project only a limited picture because they don't mention frequency of usage and because lists of possible contexts are often limited. They don't cover every conceivable situation of speech. They also do not indicate levels of proficiency, except perhaps in limited fashion.
norm-referenced tests	Compare individuals with others to establish a ranking (top 10%, percentile rankings, or number correct), usually according to national or regional scores (standings). These are typically summative and used for subsequent placement or for remediation in specific areas. (Norm referenced tests may compare a bilingual against monolingual standards.)
criterion-referenced tests	Do not overtly compare one student with a group. Instead, they highlight a list of specific skill areas. These are typically formative, but may fail to distinguish between qualitative and quantitative measures (accuracy and fluency, respectively). Ostensibly, they avoid unfair comparison with monolinguals. In practice, however, the tests can still be used for comparison, e.g., among schools within a district.

Psychometric testing to measure dominance of one language:

word association – speed	Done in a laboratory setting, these tests are designed to measure the speed of reaction on a word association task, comparing reaction times in each of the bilingual's languages to particular word forms.
word association – quantity	Tests the quantity of associations in each language in a timed task, e.g., in a one minute span, to a general noun such as *animal* or *color* and counting the number of words that can be associated.
timed reading	Measures the amount of time taken to read similar passages or lists of words in both languages. The main problem is that tests cover only one sub-set of skills and may not measure balance, how well the respective languages are known overall in all skill areas.

There are inherent problems with each of these tests. For example, one might assume that the bilingual will be quicker in a native, or dominant language (dominant in the sense of strength of the associations between form and meaning). However, it is not uncommon for an individual to have greater grammatical, sociolinguistic, and discourse knowledge in a variety that is not her native language. Greater overall competence can be gained in the language used most frequently and in the widest range of social contexts, for example, in situations where a bi- or multilingual person is educated in only one of his languages and uses that language at home, at work, and in the vast majority of institutional settings. In many African nations, there are many local and regional varieties, and the language used nationally in education and in cross-cultural, multiethnic settings is one of the various superlanguages (English, French, or Arabic). If a speaker no longer interacts with speakers of her/his native language, it may no longer be her dominant language. In the Chicano-Latino community, this is often the case. Dominance can change over time, and according to the domain of usage. One should suspect that psychometric tests (measuring psychological aspects of language), will be useful on an individual and perhaps temporary basis in measuring brain activity, but they will produce somewhat ambiguous data, yielding results that change over time.

5.   Types of bilingual families

One of the most important ways for educators to get to know the children in their classrooms is to be sensitive to and become knowledgeable about their individual family backgrounds. From the human perspective, culture is a powerful force that shapes our thinking. Our *worldviews*, the ways we view society and our places in it, will determine the kinds of assumptions we bring to the learning situation. With ethnic and language minority children, the worldview that they have may not come from the dominant culture, from the dominant Anglo-Saxon culture at the foundation of the American educational system. During their initial encounters, at least, a child's worldview will come from their heritage languages and cultures that can differ greatly from the culture of the classroom. One thing, however, that bilingual families have in common is the possibility for diversity. Under one roof, there can be members of different cultures, and each generation can have its own unique characteristics, motivations, and loyalties.

The following descriptions are adapted from a well-known survey of bilingual families, mainly in European contexts (Romaine 1995). According to Romaine, there are six types of bilingual families: Type 1 (one person – one language); Type 2 (one language – one environment); Type 3 (non-dominant home language without support); Type 4 (double non-dominant home language without support); Type 5 (non-native parents); and Type 6 (mixed languages). These types can be applied in almost any bilingual setting worldwide, but they tend to be generalizing. So, some caution is necessary to prevent overgeneralization and stereotyping. Every family situation still needs to be evaluated one at a time. The Chicano-Latino family, for example, often includes more than one type within the same household. Because of the nature of the extended family, several generations may live together, including monolinguals in either Spanish or English, and those who have learned both sequentially and/or simultaneously.

5.1 Types 1 and 2

In the Type 1 family (*one person–one language*), the parents have *different* native languages with some competence in each other's language. The native language of one parent is the dominant language of the community, while that of the other parent is not. (Children at a very early age can tell the difference between the mother's language and the father's language.) To ensure that their child has the opportunity to become bilingual, each parent speaks his or her own language to the child (hence, one person – one language). For instance, the father may speak Spanish to the child while the mother speaks English. If it is the mother who speaks Spanish and the father English, then the outcome may differ. Mothers are more likely to spend a greater amount of time with a child than fathers in the most formative stages, from birth to age three, so there is a greater likelihood that the child will acquire and maintain the heritage language. One outcome may be that the child will be sensitive to language choice among the participants. She may also have the potential to learn a wide range of registers in the heritage language, but this will also depend a great deal on influences outside the family, for example, relationships with educators who promote proficient bilingualism and biliteracy.

In the Type 2 family, similar to Type 1, the parents have different native languages with some competence in each other's languages. The native (or primary) language of one parent is the dominant language of the community, while the native language of the other is not. However, both parents speak only the non-dominant language to the child at home, particularly when the child is very young, possibly with the idea of maintaining a heritage language and passing on shared cultural values through membership in the minority language community (and to ensure bilinguality for the child). For example, in the Chicano-Latino family, the child may be exposed to Spanish at home and English outside of the home, *one language – one environment*. This can also be a strategy by parents to make sure their child learns the languages separately, and as with Type 1 families, minimize language mixing. As the child ventures away from home, she eventually comes into contact with English-speaking peers in the neighborhood and in school through interactions with teachers, aides, and administrators. In that language usage patterns according to genres (situations of speech), knowledge of the heritage language may be limited to informal registers of speech, particularly in the absence of instruction in formal registers of Spanish (or whatever the heritage language is). This is one way in which diglossia becomes part of the bilingual child's life. In the Spanish-English bilingual community of the U.S., this is very common, especially when the extended family is involved in child rearing.

For both Type 1 and Type 2 families, other social and cultural variables may enter the mix, as well, for example, family structure. For Anglo Americans and those from other similar Northern European backgrounds, the family structure tends to be very loose-knit. Because a lot of migration occurs within U.S. borders, family members may be stretched out from coast to coast and from North to South. Families of Southern (or Mediterranean) European heritage (e.g., Italians and Spaniards) tend to be very tight-knit. Many Chicano-Latino families fit this model more closely. They may be large, with many uncles and aunts (*tios y tias*) related by blood or by friendship. Grandparents are typically counted on to babysit (childcare), so *their* native language(s) are in the child's linguistic environment as possible models for acquisition.

The Spanish to which the child is exposed can be from dozens of homelands where Spanish is the principal language, from Spain to Argentina, and from Venezuela to Southern California. Therefore, children may have daily contact with family members who are (a) monolingual speakers of English (e.g., Chicano English or regional varieties spoken in parts of Texas), (b) monolingual speakers of varieties of Spanish (different national standards and regional varieties), (c) developing bilinguals at least conversant in all of the above, and (d) native bilinguals who may mix varieties together (code-switching, etc). Because of socioeconomic conditions and other relationships, children may also be exposed to varieties of English spoken by African Americans and folks of Caribbean or other origin, and, consequently, other concepts of family. The possibilities are so diverse that it is not possible to know a child's background simply from physical appearance.

5.2   Types 3 and 4

Type 3 families (*non-dominant home language without support*) involve some subtle differences. Parents share *the same* native-language, a culturally non-dominant language, and they speak it with their children. Both have learned the dominant language as a second language. They are essentially without the support of extended family members because they're still establishing residence, new communication networks, employment for themselves, and educational opportunities for their children, a lot to ask of any family. For example, both parents are native speakers of Spanish with varying degrees of education in that language, but they may be from different nations, with their own cultural attitudes towards education and language learning. In Type 1 and Type 2 families, it is likely that at least one parent is familiar with Anglo-Saxon culture and the expectations of teachers, so the child may get some help at home with homework and so on (or from older siblings). However, despite having their children's best interest at heart, this support may be lacking in the Type 3 family.

At the risk of overgeneralization, folks from some parts of Latin America may expect the teacher to be responsible for *all* aspects of education, so there is little apparent support (so-called *parental involvement*). This occurs in the Spanish-English community in Los Angeles, particularly among first-generation immigrants, e.g., when there is no history of higher education in the family and both parents work. Anglo teachers, in contrast, expect parents to be involved in all facets of the educational experience, in supervising and helping children with their homework and cooperating with the teacher's suggestions (with frequent notes home and parent-teacher meetings). Thus, one can anticipate a clash of expectations.

In the Type 4 family (*double non-dominant home language without community support*), parents have *different* native languages, and neither parent's language is the dominant community language. Each parent speaks his/her native language to the child from birth (producing a multilingual child). In urban environments, this is not unusual, especially in communities where ESL programs are offered for adults of many language backgrounds. People meet and form unions to raise families. Type 4 families in Los Angeles may include multilingual situations in which one parent speaks Spanish, and the other a range of languages from Zapotec to Tagolog to Vietnamese. The child is left to learn English in school (or in day care) or from SL-learners in the home (e.g., from older siblings). Also, because Spanish colonial domination at one time reached parts of Austronesia (the Philippines and Micronesia, where many indigenous languages are spoken) and throughout Central and South America, people from a very wide variety of backgrounds and ethnicities have Spanish-sounding surnames. In fact, the last name may give no indication at all of *country* of origin.

This may also occur in rural environments where seasonal farm labor is drawn from a pool of documented and perhaps undocumented workers. For instance, in and around Los Angeles, there are rural communities where some farm workers speak varieties of indigenous Mesoamerican languages who are not proficient in Spanish. (Many of these workers have grown up in an environment outside the reach of Spanish and the influence of formal educational practices.) Because many are somewhat familiar with Spanish, at least more so than with English, there are now programs to teach these workers to speak and become literate in *Spanish* (the quickest way to become literate in a major written language). While this may seem somewhat contradictory to current federal and state practices, and, needless to say a huge political controversy in an English-only atmosphere, local authorities have decided that it is more important that these workers learn to read safety manuals and other printed materials necessary for their jobs in a language that they may know somewhat, than to incur the expense of having documents translated into a language spoken by a relatively small group of workers.

5.3   Type 5: Non-native parents

While this situation may be rare, it is not unheard of. In this scenario, both parents are native speakers of the dominant language. However, one of the parents addresses the child in a non-native language (that is also not culturally dominant). For example, both the father and mother speak English, but the father uses another language such as German or French (or ASL) with the child, which may or may not be a heritage language of either parent (Romaine 1996: 185). With an increased interest in American Sign Language (ASL) and knowledge that learning a language natively will have a long-lasting impact, some adults teach ASL to their children. An interesting fact of ASL is that the majority of its speakers (signers) are non-natives. One reason for this is that many deaf and hard-of-hearing children are born to hearing parents and are diagnosed relatively late. Thus, NL acquisition may be slightly delayed (Barent 2006: 317). Hearing parents and siblings, in order to communicate with the new member of the family, may learn ASL as a second language. Of course, children born to deaf or hard of hearing parents who sign will be native signers.[18] In the event that their children are able to hear, deaf or hard of hearing parents may seek ways to provide an oral language environment for the child, with grandparents and/or other family members. In any case, a child who knows ASL and an oral language is bilingual.

5.4   Type 6: Mixed languages

This scenario is probably best understood in third-generation households in which both parents are proficient bilinguals and large segments of the community are proficient bilinguals, as well.[19] There is no patterned bilingualism like that of the Type 1 family, one language – one person, nor in the Type 2 family, one language – one environment. The social conditions for bilingual behaviors and language mixing are almost always present. The existence (as a cultural practice) of bilingual phenomena is accepted in the community and perhaps even encouraged and valued in certain social contexts. In Type 6 families, both parents mix languages in various ways through rapid conversational code-switching and different levels of borrowing. And, CS may occur irrespective of participants, setting, and topic. Children may engage in intrasentential CS with parents and other caregivers, even grandparents, and particularly among themselves (among siblings and close friends).

---

18. See Barent (2006) for discussion of L1 and L2 acquisition of ASL and language mixing phenomena by ASL-English bilinguals.

19. See discussion below in the following section for a definition of the Three Generation Rule.

The members of the Type 6 family are typically native bilinguals who are perpetually in a bilingual language mode.[20] In the more extreme instances, speakers may not be able to anticipate which language another speaker (or themselves) will use at any given moment. All other family types involve monolingual modes for each language by necessity, but not necessarily for the Type 6 family. Also, this type of setting creates an environment in which so-called double-semilinguals may go relatively unnoticed, particularly when children are exposed to nonstandard varieties of both English and Spanish (e.g., Chicano English and Chicano Spanish with many borrowed words from English), and everyone in their immediate family is a fluent code-switcher.

Conversational code-switching may come to symbolize a synthesis or fusion of sorts of the two languages, thus becoming a marker of an entirely new identity (see, e.g., Gumperz 1982:62–64; Zentella 2002; cf. Heller 1982). This new, mixed identity can mean that the Chicano-Latino feels some social distance from monolingual speakers of Standard Spanish and monolingual speakers of Standard English, alike, and feel a close sense of solidarity with other Chicano-Latinos. It follows that some members of Type 6 families may also have the added social and cultural dimension of being members of "in-between" social groups who don't identify with either culture (heritage country or Anglo American).

Acquisition scenarios are also important. When languages are learned sequentially, one after the other, as with many first- and second-generation immigrants, children may become bi-cultural, and equally comfortable in each language and culture. A person who grows up in Mexico, for example, will acquire cultural values and mannerisms associated with the majority culture and language, Mexican Spanish. As this native Spanish speaker acquires English (standard or nonstandard), new cultural values and mannerisms may be adopted, as well. In contrast, for some, perhaps younger Chicano-Latinos, the old culture may be stigmatized negatively as old-fashioned (particularly when it represents, e.g., the rural interior of Mexico) and very far from the pop culture they are learning from peers in school and other social settings.

Seeking a social, cultural, and political identity of their own, for those who are caught in the middle between an old culture and an entirely new one, the in-between social status may grow to mean *neither* Mexican nor American (i.e., not white Anglo-Saxon) (cf. Zentella 2002). The establishment of a new social identity may be partly a response to the institutionalized prejudices that their parents have experienced, but it is also most likely a symbol of their in-between status and not belonging to either traditional culture. The term "born here" can be very significant; it can signify being "able to cope," without the difficulties that new immigrants face on a daily basis. Chicano-Latinos, in creating their own unique blend of linguistic and cultural identity, are at no

---

20. See Chapter 3 for a more complete description of language modes.

disadvantage whatsoever (a) linguistically, as native-speakers of English; (b) socially because their friends and peers are also U.S.-born; and (c) culturally as part of popular culture. They have grown up with contemporary cultural values and cutting-edge entertainment technology, unlike their immediate ancestors from the "old-country."

In the Chicano-Latino, Spanish-English bilingual community, the two most common family types are most likely Type 3 and Type 6. Type 3 usually correlates with first-generation immigrants as they learn to cope with a new linguistic and cultural environment. Type 6 correlates generally with third-generation immigrants, who may be struggling to maintain competence in Spanish and the culture of their ancestral homeland in the face of assimilation into U.S. culture. Types 1 and 2 likely correlate with first- or second-generation bilinguals who may have formed unions (e.g., via marriage) with native speakers of English who are not necessarily proficient in Spanish. Type 4 correlates with immigrants from different language backgrounds, both minority languages; they may also be first, second, or third generations. Type 5, the rarest, is unusual for its non-native speaking parent teaching a minority language.

5.5   Type 7: Post-shift with rememberers

We can easily propose an additional type of family as an extension of Type 6, the Type 7: *post-shift with rememberers*. Throughout Southern California there are families of native bilinguals who have completed the unconscious shift to English. Their usage of one of their native languages, Spanish, has become restricted to very few social contexts. The language is not their dominant language. However, because they are familiar with Chicano English, have contacts with Spanish speakers (of various nationalities), are closely aligned with Chicano/a social values (and politics), and maintain long-distance family ties (e.g., in Mexico), they may remember certain key expressions (hence, *rememberers*), and greetings quite well. In addition, they may *sound* as if they *should* know Spanish (to a teacher or native English-speaker), and even have a Spanish-origin surname (e.g., Verdugo, Anaya, Ramos, etc.). However, high-levels of proficiency in a language entail constant usage, and access to formal, academic registers of the language clearly entail training and education in the language. There may also be relative proficiency in local, Chicano Spanish, which is typically very informal and laden with English words made "Spanish" morphologically (e.g., verbs such as *parkearse* with appropriate tense endings, etc.) and phonologically (produced with Spanish-sounding pronunciation, e.g., *troca*).

Members of this type of family, as descendants of the Type 6 family, may have had bilingual parents proficient in both dominant and non-dominant languages who failed to notice that their children were losing their heritage language and culture. The children may respond appropriately to familiar questions like "¿Qué pasó?" and

"¿Cómo estás?" with "Nada" or "Bien, gracias. ¿Y tú?" respectively (with the "correct" accent), but when the conversation goes beyond familiar greetings and expressions, the children switch to English, a normal language behavior within the Chicano-Latino community at large. Shift has progressed to the point of no return. Type 7 family members are less likely to be in-the-middle culturally, identifying with U.S. culture first and foremost, on their way to being fully assimilated members of U.S. society. For many, this is the desired goal of acculturation. For others, it implies the unnecessary loss of a valuable heritage, a language and culture, and the result of subtractive types of education.

Evidently, characteristics of each type of bilingual family correspond to, and, perhaps, influence types of bilingualism. For instance, a child may be exposed in her own household to family members going through different sequential and simultaneous acquisition scenarios, various types of social groupings (e.g., multicultural versus in-between status), additive versus subtractive bilingual acquisition and educational experiences, and the outcomes of many types of language instruction, from a parent's (or grandparent's) participation in adult ESL programs to her own exposure to bilingual classrooms or mainstream language arts classes. Nevertheless, the type of family from which a child originates can reveal the complexity of home life that she experiences and the range of linguistic influences available to her.

6. Motivation and the three generation rule

We come to some of the social and psychological factors that may help explain how different family types develop and how language shift may work within families and out into the community. As individuals face the challenges of adapting to a new language and culture, at least two major social-psychological factors will play important roles (Larsen-Freeman & Long 1991: 172–192). They are *motivation*, the psychological drive new immigrants need in order to learn a new language and new customs (to assimilate), and *attitude*, how they feel about the language and its speakers. Importantly, motivation and attitude are *relational* and depend on reasons for immigrating in the first place, the reception they receive in their newly adopted land, and any attitudes they may have acquired or inherited in their home country.

In discussions of the ESL classroom, motivation to learn English is a hot topic because educators know the difficulties some learners have. They note two types of motivation, *instrumental* and *integrative*. For example, the motivation for learning the new language may be as a means to find work, pay the bills, go to the market, and enroll children in school – the language becomes an instrument to gain employment. However, acquiring native-like skills in a new language and assimilating fully to the ways native speakers behave linguistically may seem out of reach, based on individual and community experience. Some immigrants may become pessimistic about assimilation, as well. For many Latin Americans, when first-generation bilinguals wind up residing in *colonias* established by others who came from the same region or state, the instrumental motivation can be very strong, but, the language of home and work will likely be Spanish, so social needs are sufficiently met by the heritage language and culture.

Immigrants must have much stronger motivation in order to blend in with the dominant culture of their new country. This additional degree of motivation is called integrative because it can lead to personal and family integration into the new cultural milieu. It needs to come into play if the ultimate goal is complete assimilation into American culture, to be an "American" or to blend in as thoroughly as possible, perhaps for the sake of the children. For the children of immigrants, assimilation is undoubtedly both within reach, and desirable because many of their peers are U.S. born, as well. The two types of motivation are not necessarily exclusive.

Coming to the U.S. for economic reasons, however, does not preclude the existence of some negative feelings. Attitudes toward the dominant culture and language have an obvious impact, as evidenced by other ethnic minorities in the U.S., for instance, African Americans who have experienced segregation and harassment from racists. This kind of treatment does not occur only in the American South. If a person sees (Standard) English *speakers* in a threatening way (as arrogant, prejudiced, aggressive, or resentful), then the *language* may appear threatening and undesirable by association. This may occur in addition to any anti-American feeling that the immigrant knew in her country of origin.

Many observations such as these have contributed to the formation of *the three-generation rule*. It represents the normal course of language shift and shows how native/heritage languages can fall into disuse and eventually become lost to the community (cf. Wiley 2007:27f). It still needs to be viewed as a continuum with blurry boundaries, not necessarily as an inevitable fate in every case. But, it does seem to portray the social changes that succeeding generations encounter as they adapt to new cultural and linguistic surroundings. Many early immigrants from Northern Europe (Scandinavians, Germans, and Dutch), of course, adapted to a new language, but they also shared certain physical characteristics and a basic common Western European culture. The task of assimilating into American culture and language may be different for current Latin American immigrants who, to a great extent, share neither racial stock nor a common culture with Anglo America. The motivation to assimilate can run into severe obstacles.

As a general rule, the first generation of immigrants consists of adults and older adolescents who have migrated for economic reasons. They attempt to learn the new, majority language for obvious utilitarian reasons, and the acquisition of a new language will come through processes of SLA, even if English was studied in the country of origin. (A term of more recent coinage, *generation 1.5*, refers to those who arrive in a new country in the early teens. They may have their own unique set of difficulties and issues.) For older newcomers, the process is relatively slow and tedious, and it requires time in a classroom.

The second generation is typically the first generation born in the new country, e.g., "here," in the U.S. These are the ones most acutely caught in the middle between two languages and cultures and the process of language shift (see Chapter 3). Children of first-generation parents are quite often native bilinguals, relatively fluent in both the heritage language and the more socially dominant, majority language. They may also develop stronger literacy skills in English and much less so in their heritage language due to the lack of quality bilingual education and the fact that English is the language of instruction. They are often faced with where and when it is appropriate to use either or both of their languages.[21] For second-generation Spanish-English bilinguals, there is a great deal of socio-economic mobility, and scaling the ladder of "success" can become a powerful motivator. Both languages are used for communication in the family: Spanish with parents and grandparents (who may have come to the U.S. to join the extended family) and with other family members in those age groups (uncles, aunts, cousins), and English with children, teachers, employers, and co-workers. Second-generation bilinguals may alternate usage of languages in various ways.

The third generation may have little or no memory of what it was like to live in the ancestral homeland and to be completely immersed in its language, culture, and economy. They typically choose only one language, the language of their peers and the one with the most social and economic clout. In the U.S., that is obviously English. This seems to be the case with Spanish-English bilingual families. The work of Joshua Fishman points out how, if immigration from Mexico and other Latin American countries were to cease, the Spanish-English bilingual community might be no different from Swedish-English, Czech-English, or Italian-English bilingual communities at the beginning of the 20th century (Fishman 1991:192). Spanish would shrink or disappear in the U.S. But, on-going immigration provides a fresh supply of native Spanish speakers and replenishes the numbers of first-generation bilinguals, who act as models

---

21. Loyalty to the original homeland is usually transmitted from parent to child as parents reminisce about how things used to be "back home." Nevertheless, children born in the U.S. or who arrive at an early age may feel ambivalent about their inherited language and culture, likely shaped by the attitudes of the dominant culture where they currently live. A child whose parents come from Paris or Zurich may feel differently about a faraway ancestral homeland than a child whose parents come from rural Jalisco or Michoacan, Mexico.

of proficiency in Spanish. This constant influx of native speakers affects the appearance of language maintenance (retention of a heritage language and culture).[22]

One can see that the dynamics of home-life in the Spanish-English bilingual community nationwide can indeed be influenced by a multiplicity of factors. Such is the case in Southern California, as well. There are children who are part of multi-generational households, who fall victim to problematic testing procedures (and questionable measurement of their linguistic and academic abilities), and who have gone through many types of language-acquisition scenarios. If our intention is to make their educational experience a positive (thus productive) one, then the educator's awareness of the many factors affecting student performance is important.

Key terms

additive bilingualism, age of arrival (AoA), ambilingual, balanced bilingual, bilingual first language acquisition (BFLA), bilinguality, competence, compound bilingualism, continuum of proficiency, coordinate bilingualism, criterion-referenced tests, culturally transmitted, discourse knowledge, dominant, early (v. late) SLA, English as a Second Language (ESL), English as a Foreign Language (EFL), fluent-proficient, incipient bilinguals, individual bilingualism, innate, instrumental motivation, integrative motivation, interference, interlanguage (IL), L1, L2, language acquisition, language background scales, language skills matrix, learner's variety (interlanguage), length of residence (LOR), lexical access, limited bilingual, linguistic repertoire, motivation, native bilingual, native language acquisition (NLA), native language, native-like, norm-referenced tests, performance, proficiency, proficient bilingual, psychometric, rote learning/memorization, second/subsequent language acquisition (SLA), self-assessment, semilingual (double), Separate Development Hypothesis, sequential (consecutive) acquisition, simultaneous language acquisition, societal bilingualism, sociolinguistic knowledge, specific language impairments (SLI), speech acts, standard English, subordinate bilingualism, subtractive bilingualism, summative tests, syntax, target language (TL), transfer, translation pairs, utterance.

---

22. There is also some evidence that shift is not merely from Spanish to English, but to Spanish-English bilingualism due to the prevalence of Spanish within specific communities. The Latino National Political Survey, a study done in the early 1990s, indicated that widespread bilingualism existed in Chicano, Cuban-American, and Puerto Rican subgroups. This study found that only 1% of Mexican origin population in the U.S. spoke only Spanish. For the Cuban and Puerto Rican populations, the rates were higher, but still only around 5% and 7%, respectively. On the other side, 7.4% of those of Mexican origin spoke only English while 2.2% of the Cubans and 2.8% of Puerto Ricans did so. Chicanos, therefore, were less likely to use Spanish in the household, although the majority of Latinos lived in bilingual households. These figures clearly refute claims that Latinos in general refuse to learn English, but also those that claim that Spanish is completely disappearing as a result of attrition (Wiley 2007:72).

Summary

A *native* language is generally the first one a child is exposed to. Some early studies referred to learning one's first or native language as *First Language Acquisition* (FLA), but because most children in the world are exposed to more than one language almost from birth, specialists now prefer the term *native language acquisition* (NLA). It is associated with the unconscious ways children acquire their languages merely through observation. Because it's so unconscious, we seldom if ever remember learning our native languages. In contrast, we usually remember (quite painfully) trying to learn a "foreign" language in high school or college. It involves conscious study, lessons or lectures, rote memorization, practice, and drills. Learning a subsequent language is slow and tedious by comparison, and very conscious. It is so different that researchers give it a different name, *second* or *subsequent language acquisition* (SLA).

Bilingual children who are exposed to both languages by their third year undergo their own unique processes of Bilingual First Language Acquisition (BFLA), the bilingual acquisition of two first or native languages. Ongoing work suggests that children who grow up as bilinguals have unique skill set and may enjoy certain cognitive advantages. All children go through the same stages of language development, though some start earlier or go faster, while others will start later or go more slowly. Importantly, bilingual children go through the same stages as monolingual children in their languages. They learn the sounds, put them together into syllables, form words, and then put those words into longer utterances.

Of the observed differences between NLA and SLA, the most obvious is the influence a native language can have on the learning and performance of a SL, a process called *transfer*. Transfer refers to how speakers unconsciously transfer the rules of one variety to another. Age is also an important factor, helping to distinguish the two extremes of NLA and SLA. It is axiomatic in SLA studies that "older is faster but, younger is better." Older beginning learners may go quickly at first, while younger learners may appear to struggle for a while. However, the younger learners will eventually pass older ones, especially considering long-term attainment.

The term bilingualism can refer to many things. E.g., there are different possible routes to community-wide, or *societal bilingualism*. Languages can be acquired one after the other, called *sequential*, consecutive, or successive acquisition; or, they can be acquired roughly at the same time, referred to as *simultaneous* acquisition. When a language is added to the child's linguistic repertoire, this is known as *additive bilingualism*, typically associated with the addition of important skills in the classroom and in society at large. An SL can be learned at the expense of the native language, called *subtractive bilingualism*. In the U.S., the acquisition of English is seen as so important for the child that all other languages may be devalued and neglected, and essentially subtracted or lost. Additive bilingualism may also refer to the *positive cognitive outcomes* of bilingualism, while subtractive bilingualism suggests "negative affective and cognitive effects of bilingualism" and an implicit lack of development of *both* languages. Subtractive bilingualism implies that a new, socially dominant language will be learned at a cost (the loss of a socially less important language at the heart of the child's identity). In the long run, what is at issue is not *the addition of* English to the child's linguistic repertoire; the issue is to what extent this process needs to be subtractive.

Weinreich proposed three types of bilingualism: Type A, *coordinate*; Type B, *compound*; and Type C, *subordinate*, thought to be ways that languages are represented in the bilingual's brain, based on how they've been learned. The *coordinate* bilingual learns her native language at home, and the second language at school, in two distinct environments. A *compound* bilingual, in contrast, acquires both languages essentially in the same social contexts, so there is the tendency for one, *fused* representational system. A third type of bilingualism, subordinate, is a sub-type of coordinate, with two distinct language systems. With the subordinate bilingual, the second (non-native) language is considerably weaker than the first, and the second language can only be accessed through the first. In view of language mixing behaviors and transfer phenomena, there is ongoing debate about how language systems are represented in the mind of the bilingual, whether the bilingual child has one unitary language system that essentially controls both languages, or two separate systems, one for each language. The Separate Development Hypothesis suggests that "…in learning to speak, children raised with two separate languages form birth approach their languages as two distinct, closed sets" (30). Learning two languages does not cause mental confusion or inhibit the acquisition of either language.

In a bilingual community, one expects *continua of proficiencies*. There will be *monolingual*, or *unilingual*, speakers of either language who may have no or only a small degree of passive knowledge in the other. In the Spanish-English community of the U.S., for example, there are those who are *fluent-proficient* in Spanish and only partially proficient in English. The reverse is also true where speakers are fluent-proficient in English, but only partially so in Spanish. There are "ideal" or *balanced* bilinguals who demonstrate superior skills in both. The vast majority of bilinguals are less than ideal, however, with one language psychologically favored over the other. So, one language will appear stronger than the other. A continuing controversy is the existence of *partial* bilinguals, so-called *double semilinguals*, those who demonstrate minimal proficiency in both languages. In educational circles, they may be called, e.g., *limited* bilinguals, and less formally, *limited-limited* and *non-nons*. This may be a nearly invisible minority, but it is of significant social concern. Part of the controversy is testing. Regarding bilingual skills (and diagnoses), the most fundamental issues to consider are (a) the testing situation itself and the effects of the child's experience (or lack thereof) in educational settings; (b) dialect status (which varieties are being tested); (c) skill areas (spoken versus written modes) and the assumed correspondences of active and passive competence.

The motivation for learning the new language may involve an *instrumental* motivation based on the need to find work, pay the bills, go to the market, and enroll children in school – the language becomes an instrument to gain employment. To blend in with the dominant culture of their new country requires a kind of motivation called *integrative* motivation because it can lead to personal and family integration into the new cultural milieu. Following from issues of motivation and attitude is the *three-generation rule*. First generation immigrants, generally adults and older adolescents who have migrated for economic reasons, will attempt to learn the new, majority language for obvious utilitarian reasons through processes of SLA. The second generation is typically the first generation born in the new country, e.g., "here," in the U.S. These are the ones most acutely caught in the middle between two languages and cultures and the process of language shift. The third generation may have little or no memory of what it was like to live in the ancestral homeland and to be completely immersed in its language and culture (and economy). They typically choose only one language, the language of their peers and the one with the most social and economic clout. In the U.S., that is obviously English.

Activities – topics for discussion

1. Do you remember learning your native language? What about a second/subsequent language? Discuss the differences between NLA and SLA.

2. What types of standardized testing are you familiar with? Describe them in terms such as summative, formative, and norm-referenced. Have you ever been exposed to psychometric testing (e.g., testing translation skills)? Describe the experience.

3. Are you familiar with bilingual children who don't seem to know any language (either language) very well? What do you think the causes are? Do they, in fact, communicate with others, e.g., by rapidly code-switching or by speaking a nonstandard variety?

4. Do you or any of your friends belong to a bilingual family? Discuss which type of family that is. If you don't have any bilingual friends, are there students at your school who come from bilingual families? Discuss the possibilities.

5. What are some of the problems that you see with standardized testing for bilingual children?

Practice essay questions

1. Explain the one-system view of childhood bilingualism. What is the alternative? E.g., how does the one-system view conflict with what is known of Bilingual First Language Acquisition (BFLA)?

2. Discuss the difference between additive and subtractive bilingualism. In your response, include any potentially harmful effects that subtractive forms of bilingualism can cause.

3. Compare and contrast Type A, Type B, and Type C bilinguals, and the probable limitations of such distinctions.

4. Discuss the different kinds of motivation that people can have in adopting a new language and culture. Include in your discussion some of the barriers to cultural and linguistic assimilation.

5. Explain and discuss the three generation rule.

Chapter 3

Bilingual phenomena in the U.S.

1. Language variation: Dialects and registers
2. Bilingual language contact:
   Social and linguistic change
3. Maintenance, shift, diglossia, and convergence
4. Linguistic borrowing
5. Code-switching
6. Language modes

There is hardly a community in the world that does not show the effects of cultural and social contact among people. This is one reason why the media are continually awash with stories of minority groups in Europe, in the U.S., California, and in local school districts. We can even feel a sense of urgency at times, and that the need to deal with at least some of the problems has somehow become acute. There are questions of the use (or nonuse) of minority languages in schools (e.g., the usage of Spanish or Vietnamese by teachers in U.S. schools), in the media, and in society. There is concern for the survival of minority immigrant (heritage) languages and endangered indigenous languages, two kinds of languages that may cease to be used if someone doesn't do something about it. There are two seemingly contradictory social issues: the first concerns the rights of linguistic minorities to speak their ancestral languages freely. The second is the need to speak a national language, that is, for all citizens and residents, irrespective of ethnicity, to benefit from the potential unifying force of a large majority language. But, do these two views truly need to be exclusive? Political issues range from official language policy (making English the official national or state language) to reactions to signs in shop windows and what to do about intergroup clashes, ethnic gangs, and social tensions in a multilingual, multicultural society.

Many of the changes that the world is presently experiencing have perhaps been inadvertently "engineered," in the sense that the expansion and growth of one political, national, or social entity necessarily motivates a response from other political, national, or social entities. One of the major consequences of colonial expansion (and imperialism) of different empires at various times in history has been the establishment of large national languages and the emergence of so-called *superlanguages*, e.g., Mandarin Chinese, Russian, English, and Spanish, and more recently, Arabic and perhaps Japanese. As languages and empires expand, people and languages come into various kinds of contact.

In these superlanguage environments, many of the hundreds of local, smaller indigenous languages have vanished completely, though, in most cases, the people have not. They may simply be absorbed by the dominant colonial group. Many languages have been swallowed up by an expanding giant, and the effects can still be felt today. In some ways, it has been "survival of the fittest."[1] In most cases, the smaller languages have gradually died out as speakers were pressured to learn new, national languages, and old, traditional languages were left to die, so to speak – a phenomenon sometimes referred to as *linguicide*. But, many minority languages have successfully existed for centuries alongside the expanding state languages, and bi- and multilingualism has been the norm. Perhaps the best known example is that of Switzerland, where German, French, and Italian have co-existed for centuries.[2] Over the centuries, however, the superlanguages have increasingly replaced smaller, less important ones. The *spread* of such languages as English has fit nicely into some concepts of "globalization," and a global economy.

Nevertheless, multilingualism is returning, albeit from a different direction. After centuries of trying to establish the dominance of one language in the U.S., there has been a kind of reversal of the process, perhaps with a sense of irony and poetic justice. In-migration into the U. S. has involved the creation of more than a hundred (perhaps hundreds of) new contact situations that have replaced those that were originally forged by the aggressive expansion of the nation. This time, rather than clash against the languages that were already present, or "here," people are coming from all over the world to live in the U.S., and, needless to say, bringing their languages and cultures with them. A native language isn't like a set of baggage that can be tossed aside; it is something that people can't walk away from, take off like an old dress or suit, or turn off, like an old, sentimental recording from the past.

---

1.   Popular among linguists is the "Biggest Army Theory" for the growth and spread of English as an international language. Originally a Germanic dialect spoken on the British Isles, English evolved (with the help of Norman French), and developed into the language of England and the principle language of the U.K., though it has never been the "official" language. However, backed by the British Army and the British Navy, the empire grew to the point that it covered the globe, according to the saying, "The sun never sets on the British Empire."

2.   Other examples are the different languages of modern-day European countries such as Spain and Belgium, in most African nations, and throughout Asia despite the existence of former colonial languages that became "national" languages. One cannot say that peaceful co-existence is always the rule; one can say, however, that minority languages have continued to exist despite the efforts of powerful elites to militate usage of a particular, socially or politically dominant language.

Obviously, extensive and intensive cultural and linguistic contact is no longer an isolated event or "problem" confined to ancient international crossroads or modern urban centers, especially given the kinds of population movement that now occur around the globe. However, it is axiomatic that people who come in close areal and social contact with each other typically form social, economic, and perhaps cultural ties, and subsequently learn each other's languages. One of the first consequences of contact, then, is some degree of individual bi- or multilingualism. In addition, because individuals from one speech community learn the language(s) of another, there will be the linguistic evidence of non-native, second or subsequent language acquisition (SLA) and its effects in any contact situation, for example, in a characteristic "accent" or way of speech.

Since language and cultural contact involves people, some things are almost certain to happen. People will switch from one language to another in a flowing and fluent manner, or mix the languages in various ways, children and adults, young and old. These things occur among individuals in most major cities, everywhere from the office copy machine to the checkout line at the supermarket. Public and private language behaviors like these are called *language contact phenomena*. They are social behaviors that involve (a) individual speakers and (b) groups of speakers. That is to say, (a) some processes are confined to the individual, while (b) others will directly or indirectly involve entire groups. Linguistically, an individual behavior starts with and affects only the individual who engages in that behavior, regardless of how widespread it might be. For instance, one person may alternate the use of languages in different ways or translate words and expressions from one into the other with no apparent loss or gain in either language.[3] Of course, others may do the same, but it is still an individual behavior. Other phenomena involve the behavior of groups, for instance, an aggregate of linguistic behaviors that ultimately affects the *language* of the entire community. If enough speakers adopt English words into their variety of Spanish, their Spanish will change, perhaps to the extent that speakers of other varieties of Spanish no longer understand them. *Language change* is a natural process that happens to all living languages; it can come from internal, as well as external causes. Spanish, itself, has changed over the centuries, diverging considerably from its distant parent, Latin.

[3.] Translation requires the development of certain kinds of skills. For instance, a translator must choose between a literal, word-for-word translation and a more general meaning-based one. This can be a very critical distinction in institutional settings such as courtroom proceedings. Conversational code-switching, discussed below, causes other problems for official court interpreters who have to tease apart languages and translate into one or the other (when only two languages are involved). E.g., in major urban areas in the U.S., having the ability to translate, say, Spanish into English and the reverse, English into Spanish, is not necessarily sufficient. Official interpreters need also to be able to translate rapid, on-line switches into English – when the first word is spoken in a language that is not English, all proceedings stop and an interpreter is immediately called.

Language phenomena such as *diglossia* (assigning each language to appropriate contexts, e.g., home versus school or work), *borrowing* (the use of words and other elements from one language in the other), and *code-switching* (the alternate use of languages within a single conversation) are all the consequences of various dynamic social, psychological, and linguistic factors. They are to be expected in the classroom and in the community at large, during lunch breaks or even on the telephone. Discouraging such behaviors on school playgrounds, or labeling them "problems" outside of the classroom may actually fan the fire of rebellion, so to speak, and give the behaviors additional social value as indicators of group membership. We will not eliminate them by discouraging, denigrating, or prohibiting something that was not a problem to begin with. Adding to a child's ability to cope with academic language is a reasonable goal in American education; stamping out the usage of minority languages is not.

One of the more interesting consequences of the growing prevalence of such linguistic behaviors worldwide has been the development of a relatively new branch of linguistics, *contact linguistics*, which looks at the causes and effects of language contact. The interest in these apparent linguistic oddities incorporates the many different social and psychological aspects of language. For example, there are those *sociolinguists* who look at language usage in society. Concerning contact phenomena, this entails the social histories of communities, the patterned usage of languages within bi- and multilingual communities, how languages and their speech communities evolve, and so on. But, interest in bilingual phenomena is not restricted to sociolinguists and those interested in language evolution and change. Many other specialists who investigate language as a *mental faculty* and who look at human *cognitive abilities* are taking a laboratory approach (rather than a historical or social one), to look specifically at what the human mind/brain is doing when it "does" language. Our human faculty of language is not restricted merely to knowing one language, as unique as that is among species. Our language faculty seems to have no theoretical limit regarding the number of completely distinct languages we can know and use, irrespective of the amazing diversity that languages can show.

1. Language variation: Dialects and registers

The best place to begin the discussion of bilingual phenomena is to take a look at the multifaceted nature of language: no individual language is monolithic and invariant, always spoken in the same way in every place and situation. Languages can vary according to the place or region in which they are spoken. For example, speakers of American English in two different parts of the country may have their own special words for certain things. Their pronunciation, grammatical structure, or usage (e.g., the ways speakers interact, greet each other, or order information when telling stories) may vary, as well. Varieties linked to specific areas or parts of a country are usually called *regional dialects*. The variety of American English that is spoken, for instance, in the American South is called Southern English; the variety of Mexican Spanish spoken in the expansive highlands around Mexico City is called *altiplano*, or "highlands" Spanish. There are also varieties of a language that can be associated with specific groups of people called *social dialects*, e.g., Ebonics (or African American Vernacular English/AAVE) and Chicano English (discussed in the next chapter). Every language that we know of consists of dialects of one sort or another.

Language *variation* may also depend on various social factors, as well. Our speech changes according to the *situation of speech*, the "who, what, where, and why" of speech, sometimes referred to as a *genre* (cf. Biber 1988:70–71).[4] Change just one of those situational elements, and the forms of speech, or the *register* of speech, will also change. The first thing is obviously who I am talking with (or, "...with whom I am talking") according to accepted social relationships, even if that relationship is that of a stranger. We generally talk differently and about different things with parents or school teachers than we do with our best friends. Our speech can be determined by the topic of conversation, where we are, who we are talking with, and the purpose of our conversation, whether it is just chit-chat, borrowing money, or apologizing for being late to an important interview.[5]

1.1 Factors that determine speech

Dell Hymes, a well-known sociolinguist, classified the factors that determine speech according to their social and cultural contexts (Hymes 1974). His distinctions have been models for many subsequent authors. The list is often pared down to three principal elements: (a) *Setting*; (b) *Purpose*, and (c) *Participants*. The setting is the physical location (coffee shop, library, home) and includes the emotional or psychological setting, or *scene* (college basketball game, funeral, study session). E.g., a funeral is usually at the grave site or in a church or chapel and the emotions tend to be sad or grieving.

---

4. "By *genres* are meant categories such as poem, myth, tale, proverb, riddle, curse, prayer, oration, lecture, commercial, form letter, editorial, etc. (Hymes 1974:61). There are typical patterns of speech (registers) that correspond to each and every genre. The term may be extended to include communicative activities (speech acts) that can be distinguished by external situational factors and conventionalized patterns of speech.

5. To illustrate, imagine going to the family doctor and talking about an important body part. The term you use will tend to be medical sounding. But, when you're at home, talking with family, best friends, or your spouse ("significant other"), you may use an entirely different word to describe that same body part.

Most parties are happy, noisy occasions where people tell jokes or stories, and talk about work or personal relationships. The setting includes *the topic* (e.g., favorite musical group or singer, an illness or physical condition, the War in Iraq).

The purpose (why we talk to each other) involves making a request or purchase, delivering a sermon or joke, or telling a story. Requesting help from a professor in her office would involve different language (a different register) from that used at a roast or party; asking questions of fellow students in a classroom when discussing an assignment will be different from trying to borrow money from your best friend, or asking a classmate for a date. The forms of language that you use with a girlfriend or boyfriend, husband or wife when expressing affection will differ when discussing taking out a loan for a home. The purpose can be influenced by the intentions of the speaker and how she wants things to turn out (the outcome). And, it can include the *goals* of our communication (what I'd like to see happen as a result of an encounter with someone). For instance, if we are asking for information (or money), making a request ("Can I borrow your..."), negotiating some kind of settlement or debt, asking for a raise in pay, giving an order or command, or making a complaint about something, we will have to choose conventional ways to do it, within some kind of limits. For the monolingual English speaker, this involves the choice of register. To the Spanish-English bilingual, this may mean the choice of language.

The participants (or *interlocutors*) encompass *who* the people in the event (the speaker and addressee) are and the social relationships among interlocutors. For example, we speak differently to different people out of respect or familiarity according to the roles they play in our lives (e.g., physician talking to a young mother, wife speaking to husband, classmates talking to each other). We tend to adjust our speech accordingly when we are around English professors, ministers, parents, grandparents, teammates, roommates, and so on. When we talk to our peers, our speech will differ from the ways we talk to our social superiors (which is determined by social context). Age, gender, and culture play significant roles, as well, especially in establishing degrees of respect. Those brought up speaking Spanish are typically trained to use formal address (i.e., *usted*) with adults or other social superiors. Children may use the familiar (*tú*) with other children and with family pets. Spanish has the formal, linguistic means to represent degrees of respect, although most varieties of Spanish worldwide have become less formal in practice. To express respect, English speakers must resort to monitoring the use of slang, slowing down speech for older folks (who may not share a common social context), and speaking more carefully and clearly.

These three basic factors interact in dynamic ways. For example, we speak one way to our personal physician when we are in her office and another way if we are playing tennis, at a funeral, or at a party. When we talk about spiritual matters to a minister, priest, rabbi, or other clergy, we may use special, spiritual-sounding words (and avoid colloquialisms and profanity), but that may change if we're talking about the same topics with someone on our softball team. Traditional male-female roles can complicate things, too, Men at electronics stores often talk "down" to women because women are not expected to be knowledgeable in technical matters – although times have definitely changed in this respect. Conversely, men talking with a salesperson in the lingerie section of a department store may have difficulty expressing certain concepts. When talking to the friendly, neighborhood law enforcement officer, it may depend on the location – on the highway with the driver's window rolled down or at a doughnut shop.

Hymes mentions two additional sets of factors of interest, *norms of interaction* – how we behave in particular social contexts, and their counterparts, *norms of interpretation* – how we interpret the behaviors of others, e.g., how loudly or rapidly people talk. Norms of interaction determine when and how we speak. For example, most Anglo-Americans whisper at the library, in church, or at a funeral, and they yell and scream at a professional or school sporting event. There are also customary rules for touching and body movement that we follow in certain situations; making eye contact may have several norms of interaction. We do not usually touch our professors, for example, except to shake hands. In many subcultures, these norms vary considerably, with lots of touching that may seem more appropriate between close friends. In some cultures, people never directly criticize a teacher or professor or make direct eye contact out of respect. This is not so with many Anglo Americans, who feel quite free to ask questions or express that a professor is not being clear or behaving properly. In the U.S. it is not customary for students to show deference to a professor, or to open doors for her, while in other countries, professors are held in deep respect.

Norms of interpretation, in contrast, determine how we feel about the behaviors of people, whether they belong to our own community or not. These norms define when people are being polite, aggressive, or rude. Some of us can be very critical about the ways a person eats or uses a cellphone. Many foreign students feel that Americans are very friendly, informal, somewhat noisy, and maybe nosey and too personal (we often ask personal questions when we first meet someone). Americans may view Asians and Latin Americans as quiet, polite, and very private. Our perceptions of the behaviors of members of other cultures often reveal much about our own. If one views Americans as demanding and loud, then the person doing the viewing is most likely less demanding and quiet in comparison. Californians may be viewed by residents of other states as self-absorbed and shallow. That's very likely the result of the media and portrayals of Hollywood celebrities, self-centered teenagers, and so on. People from California, who typically say, "Excuse me" when they get within two feet of each other, may think New Yorkers are pushy, rude, and aggressive, because, evidently, they can bump into each other on the street or in an elevator and don't seem to react (according to the Californian's expectations). This is the stuff of comedy routines – stereotypes are always wrong, in a sense, but often based on some grain of truth or experience. Of course, all judgments (norms of interpretation) are ultimately subjective and conditioned by one's culture.

1.2   Registers of speech

In essence, a register is a language variety similar to a dialect, but determined by the interaction among the various factors listed above. It is something like an individual style that a person uses according to the specific characteristics of the speech situation. Speech, in this sense, is not merely a thought process; it is an event. Instances of speech, or *speech events*, include term papers and other academic discourse; work related interviews, résumés, and application letters; face-to-face conversations with professors or other professionals, customers or clients, casual acquaintances, close friends and family members; and telephone conversations with various people, from medical doctors to our best friends.

The *mode* (spoken, signed, or written) may influence the register, as well.[6] For example, written discourse is usually more formal than spoken (or signed) forms, but this is not necessarily an ironclad rule. We can also write little, informal notes to our roommates and stick them on the refrigerator door ("Don't mess with my…"), and we will probably speak in a rather formal (and standard) way (our best effort) when making a presentation in class. Spoken registers may include pronunciation, word choice, and grammatical (syntactic and morphological) features. For example, when speakers of English talk informally about popular culture, they typically use certain words and structures that would not appear in formal academic writing. Pronunciation may be fast and patterned after specific, nonstandard varieties (e.g., AAVE).

Because there is a continuum in the situations of speech, there will be a continuum of registers, e.g., from the language variety used when presenting a formal paper at a conference to having a casual conversation with (or texting) your closest friend on your cellphone. Consequently, one of the most important ways sociolinguists rank registers is by comparing degrees of *formality* and degrees of *informality*. It is not just a matter of whether one sentence or phrase is categorically informal and another is its total opposite and clearly formal. (Many successful speakers, e.g., comedians, politicians, and motivational speakers, will insert little informal expressions or sayings into

---

6. This usage of the word *mode* differs from the usage of Grosjean and the subsequent discussion of language modes as psychological states.

their otherwise formal speech.) Some traditionalists, however, make the mistake of thinking that formal usage is characterized by lots of rules, and informal usage by its *lack* of rules. The fact is that there are just as many characteristic rules to both types of registers. Here, the word *rule* refers to the patterns that native speakers and writers create and adhere to as they actually use the language. Thus, speech of all kinds reflects their underlying grammatical, sociolinguistic, and discourse knowledge of their language.

Consistent with a range of situation types is a continuum of speech types (registers). There is a continuum of grammatical features that we can identify and measure that generally correlate with a continuum of genres (Biber 1988: 70–71). Every register, just like any other language variety, can be characterized by sets of linguistic features. That is, a register is determined by the sum or totality of lexical, phonological, and grammatical features with their characteristic patterns of usage. Particular linguistic features occur in relative numbers. For example, certain words go with corresponding situations of usage. Formal registers share many features, and informal registers do, as well. In between lies a continuum of features: those associated with formal registers cluster more densely at one end, and those associated with informal registers cluster more densely at the other end.

To illustrate, informal registers contain relatively short words (fewer longer, Latin-based vocabulary items, more contractions, etc.), short sentences (not so many long complex sentences with clauses introduced by subordinating conjunctions), and sentence fragments ("Because I care") (Biber 1988: 106; Finegan 1994: 368–386). Right? On the one hand, informal spoken registers are marked by (1) the use of high-frequency words and expressions (e.g., *but, from now on, I promise*); (2) relatively greater use of colloquialisms (including contractions, slang, and the so-called dirty words), (3) the use of the words *no* and *not* to indicate negation (instead of the prefixes *dis-*, *un-*, or *in*); (4) a greater proportion of Verbs to the number of Nouns; (5) usage of first- and second-person pronouns; (6) relatively fewer prepositional phrases and frequent use of simple adverbs and adjectives and other deictic expressions (e.g., pointing, and demonstratives *this* and *that*); (7) use of direct questions; (8) simple and compound sentences (and occurrence of coordinating conjunctions); and (9) frequent use of active voice (passive infrequently). Both pronunciation and grammar in casual conversation may appear nonstandard with lots of "ain'ts," so-called double negatives, and the absence of third-person, singular *-s* on verbs. It follows that informal registers happen in face-to-face encounters ("I like your new 'do'").

On the other hand, formal academic English is characterized first by the near total absence of those informal features (e.g., the lack of contractions, sentence-ending prepositions, and slang), all the things that English professors warn students not to do on exams and term papers. Speech sounds more like newscasters speaking Network

English, and the grammar will be as close to SAE as possible.[7] It can also be described by specific features, too, e.g., by the usage of third-person pronouns, academic sounding (and longer) words, compound and complex sentences (rather than short, simple sentences), and the increased usage of passive voice. Formal, typically written registers (e.g., legalese, the language of the law) are marked by (1) special words (compound adverbs such as *notwithstanding, heretofore,* and *hereby*); (2) the absence of contractions, slang, and other colloquialisms; (3) the use of suffixes (e.g., *dis-, un-,* and *in-*) for negation instead of *no* or *not*; (4) a higher ratio of Nouns relative to Verbs; (5) frequent third-person pronouns (*it* or *they*); (6) the frequent occurrence of prepositional phrases (for precision and clarity of meaning); (7) declarative sentences in place of questions; (8) indirect discourse (complex sentences and the occurrence of subordinating conjunctions); and (9) more frequent usage of the passive voice relative to active voice.

It follows that formal speech most likely occurs in writing (and speaking) about people, places, and events outside of the immediate environment, frequent topics in the realm of academics. Because formal speech needs to conform more strictly to Standard English and contains frequent third-person pronouns (*it* or *they*), there will be other grammatical consequences. For instance, sentences that have *I* or *you* as the subjects of sentences do not require an *-s* on a verb. They are thus easy for English Language Learners (ELLs) and conform to most nonstandard dialects, as well. But, speakers and writers have to remember to put the *-s* suffix on verbs in the present tense when the grammatical subject is the third-person, singular – *he, she, it, Bob,* or *the teacher* <u>says</u>. In addition, most teachers say to avoid the first person perspective when writing academic papers. By using certain forms, we can "sound" like we're being informal and carrying on a personal conversation rather than arguing a point on a classroom assignment. And, because these are identifiable features, teachers find them very easy to spot.

Another way to look at registers of speech is according to *information* versus personal *involvement*. For instance, professors give lectures that contain lots of information, definitions, explanations, and instructions. The registers they use are relatively formal, though they are known to express their opinions in informal ways. When we pass friends and acquaintances in the hall or on the street, we may simply greet them with a "Hey!" and exchange no information at all. As with degrees of formality, social relationships typically determine whether our conversations are mainly informational or more personally involved.

---

7. Network or Media English is the style of speech used in the media by news reporters and other public figures. It is generally designed to avoid colloquialisms or anything that could mark it as regional – in essence, it is the voice from "nowhere." In that we ALL speak a regional variety, there are language schools that teach this type of pronunciation as part of the training required for radio and television personalities. As a result, it is often considered "standard" pronunciation, but it may only be a compromise, and a way to make everyone sound the same.

When teachers talk to students in a classroom setting, during class, they often as-sume next to no background knowledge, unless they're reviewing material previously covered. Speech becomes very informational, and it will also be somewhat formal (to reinforce social distance in the teacher-student relationship). If an instructor meets a student somewhere else, e.g., at a basketball game or at the supermarket, he or she will adjust his or her speech accordingly. (This also may depend on how well they know each other.) If they happen to talk about linguistics, then the vocabulary will be af-fected, but when they're talking about a particular basketball player or where the pro-duce section is, expect the way they talk to change, too. When we talk to close friends, we may not be giving any new information at all. The relationship itself may be more important than any information that we are communicating. Using the wrong register can create an awkward response. E.g., close, personal friends may not react well when we become very informational and formal. They may think we're lecturing them.[8]

Different word choices and grammatical strategies are assigned to every situa-tion we can think of, from visiting a medical doctor to going to a nightclub, party, or ball game with close friends. One goal of education, therefore, should be to encour-age ELLs and emerging bilinguals to have full access to a wide variety of registers in every language they know, so that they can engage in all sorts of language activities, from casual speech to academic writing. The truly proficient bilingual will be familiar with a range of registers in both languages. As discussed above regarding subtractive bilingualism, the institutionalized neglect of a heritage language can affect both the individual's proficiency in that language and the registers available for acquisition in the community. When a minority language is restricted to home usage, access to aca-demic registers will be limited.

In reference to the rules of formal and informal speech, linguists and teachers have clashed occasionally on the nature of *rules*. Many linguists like to point out that lan-guage is *rule governed*. This refers to the internalized and unconscious knowledge of grammar that allows a native speaker to create and comprehend novel utterances, ac-cording to a mental representation of language (discussed in the previous chapter). In this context, linguists have appealed to the concept of *native speaker intuition*, which is simply what native or proficient speakers consider a "correct" or well-formed sentence in their language variety based on unconscious knowledge. We infer rules, in this sense, by observing patterns of speech in our environment, by members of our community.

Written, academic English is full of rules, but rules in a different sense. They are not rules that are part of our biological endowment that reflect the collective, unconscious

---

8.   In this context, gender can be a factor. Masculine and feminine roles, though heavily stereotyped, can influence the informational and involved character of conversations. At the risk of overgeneral-ization, masculine speech may tend to be more informational in cross-gender communication, while feminine speech tends to show more personal involvement. Obviously, whether one is better than the other is completely subjective, and a matter of personal bias.

linguistic knowledge of a community. They are rules in a punitive sense that determine the mechanics of written, formal English, e.g., spelling, punctuation, capitalization, grammar, and vocabulary choice (diction). If you break the rules, you may be penalized in the form of a lower grade or get criticized for being ignorant. On the street, so to speak, we still communicate, identify who we are, and demonstrate our knowledge of language by the ways we talk.

2.   Bilingual language contact: Social and linguistic change

People and cultures are said to be in contact when they share the same basic physical or geographical space. *Languages* are said to be in contact when they are spoken by the same group of people on a regular basis. In essence, two or more languages in contact share the same speakers, from the individual to an entire speech community.

Within nearly every known language contact situation, there is some sort of *asymmetry* or imbalance in the social relationships between or among groups that determines the social status of language varieties. One variety will be somehow *larger* (in the sense of numbers of speakers), *culturally dominant* (more useful within particular *domains*, socially defined subject areas or fields), or more prestigious (it is the language of a privileged or *superordinate* group that is somehow looked up to by other groups – or that looks down on *subordinate* groups). As a consequence, social conditions within the community tend to influence *language choice* and *usage*, and who prefers to be identified with that language of power. So-called superlanguages generally have all three characteristics, so they typically dominate in a large number of social arenas (e.g., in government, education, technology, and the media). This clearly has been the case with English in the U.S., Russian in nations formerly part of the USSR, Spanish in Latin America, and Mandarin throughout Eastern Asia. As a consequence, a minority or subordinate language may undergo a number of social and linguistic changes that reflect its status. For example, along with gradually restricted usage within a broad range of social situations, there may be a corresponding decline in the forms (registers) of speech.

A minority or subordinate language may undergo social and linguistic changes that reflect its changing status. For example, along with social contraction (the gradually restricted usage of the language to a narrow range of situations or registers of speech), there is an often noted structural and lexical contraction in the language itself (Silva-Corvalán 1994). When a minority language is used merely for, say, informal occasions, then the kind of vocabulary appropriate for more formal, educated settings may be neglected, not learned, and subsequently lost to the community. That is, as younger speakers use the non-dominant, minority language in fewer and fewer social settings, they may either forget or not learn specific (formal-sounding) vocabulary items and sentence structures (e.g., subjunctive forms in Spanish) appropriate for more formal situations. In other words, people may speak a language at home (the "home" or heritage language), and about typical family or personal matters (what's for dinner, it's somebody's birthday), but have great difficulty talking about academic topics, the news, politics, or even sports. This is commonly reported within bilingual communities in the U.S. When discussing such political issues as bilingual education and language policy with those who are affected the most, this is an important topic. A potential community resource, individuals proficient in two or more languages, shrinks simply due to the neglect of a language.

Language systems are invariably systematic and complex; therefore, *contact phenomena will be systematic in discernable ways*, irrespective of their apparent complexity. (A language system may appear very complex, but it will be systematic nonetheless.) After all, people who rapidly and seamlessly switch from English to Spanish and back again understand each other just fine, and that's easy enough to see. It's difficult to find a "problem" with this type of bilingual behavior, unless people are offended by it for some reason, according to a culturally-based bias against language mixing. It is often interesting, in this respect, to read of the history of English and how it evolved out of essentially a patchwork of Germanic dialects that came into intense contact with Norman French.

In sum, language contact phenomena are to be expected as the normal consequences of uneven social practices and policies, whether we speak about a language gradually *receding* (declining in use) in a community, or if we speak about how languages are mixed together in the early stages of bilingual acquisition (e.g., by children interacting with siblings, caregivers, and other community members). As much research has shown, going from one language to another in different ways or combining the two together can serve to express *ethnic and/or social identity* and, in some cases, to indicate social solidarity with other members of the community. We all have a tendency to talk like the people we talk with, thereby reflecting the social groups to which we belong. Linguistically, we express who we are by the ways we talk, and this is true if you are a university professor, school teacher, sports fan, gang member, hip-hop artist, dock worker, computer expert, whatever you might be. It is not only in the things we talk about, what we choose to discuss, but in the ways we actually talk. We express our *individual identity*, where we see ourselves in the world, in our choice of words (e.g., slang, professional jargon, various "dirty" words), the way we sound (pronunciation patterns we associate with particular groups), and even the kinds of grammatical choices we make, e.g., using so-called nonstandard forms like double-negatives, which have a definite appeal in the world of hip-hop.

3.   Maintenance, shift, diglossia, and convergence

Underlying all contact phenomena is a web of interrelated and often dynamic social factors. The very existence of a bilingual community sets up the opposition of language *shift* and language *maintenance* (cf. Thomason and Kaufman 1988). Shift is a gradual process that includes the acceptance of the dominant language and a tendency to abandon a heritage language with all of its possible connotations as "foreign," "old-country," "lower socioeconomic strata," and so on.[9] It progresses from individuals and outward into the community at large. Historically, language shift may be the consequence of some sort of political conquest (e.g., conquest and colonization by major political powers) or cultural and/or socio-economic dominance (irrespective of numerical minority status). It also occurs in communities that have become linguistic minorities via migration of some kind (e.g., in-migrant groups in the U.S. and Europe).

Maintenance of a minority language, in contrast, means simply that members of the community choose to speak their ancestral tongue, their *heritage language*, and transmit that language to their descendants, from parents to their children. However, this is not always the case. It is also possible that parents will "think" that their children are learning their heritage language, but, because of advancing shift, that may not actually happen, especially when parents primarily speak the dominant language in the home. Preserving a minority language requires effort and a strong motivation to do so. Maintenance can be total, partial, minimal, or not at all. Various *bilingual phenomena* can certainly help towards keeping a language alive, at least in the short term. In a sense, shift is staved off, even if the language is used only on a relatively small number of occasions, or merely restricted to informal (familial), spoken settings (in the home, among friends, etc.). In relatively rare instances, shift can be reversed (Fishman 1991), or at least a reversal can be attempted, for example in various language revival scenarios such as Irish Gaelic.[10] But, this requires marshaling community support, which isn't always easy when there is a larger societal and socio-economic benefit in the usage of the dominant language, particularly in very small and dwindling language minority groups.

Social dominance implies that the language of a dominant group occupies (nearly) all significant social domains, e.g., education, politics, and so on, and to gain or have access to those important institutional domains, speakers of minority languages will have to use the dominant language. As Latinos become increasingly assimilated into principally Anglo-Saxon America, the importance of Spanish may diminish. For some,

---

9. See Fishman (2006) for discussion of maintenance, shift, and reversing language shift in the U.S.

10. Probably the most amazing instance of "revival" is the emergence of Modern Israeli Hebrew, though the true Semitic nature of the language is a matter of considerable controversy. It is an open question how much Polish and Yiddish have influenced its basic character.

the choice is quite simple, and given the profoundly monolingual thrust of the American educational system (and its subtractive effects), resistance seems futile. Within this cultural and linguistic milieu, one is always faced with the tension between *minority and majority language* status. *Language minorities* deal with the results of shift on a daily basis, and contact phenomena such as diglossia, borrowing, and various kinds of code-switching are typical occurrences.[11]

When people speak a language that has minority status and is essentially looked down upon by a majority, socially dominant, or socially prestigious group, we should expect some sort of reaction by the users of the minority language. In the face of advancing shift, one such reaction is to abandon the minority language altogether, or, in a sense, partially abandoning it by reserving it for usage on a minimum number of occasions. In this way, both (a) the number of speakers who use the language eventually dwindles and (b) the numbers of words and structures that are modeled (the quality of the input for acquisition) for younger speakers shrinks accordingly. These two phenomena working in concert are often referred to as *language attrition*. One by one, speakers of language X die out who are not replaced by speakers from younger generations. An increasing number of their potential replacements "fail" to acquire the ancestral language. Gradually, the language may become *lost* (no longer available) to members of that speech community. Concerning the minority language itself, an increasing number of words may be neglected (typically those used in formal settings) and unconsciously replaced by words and structures from the dominant language, possibly motivating both code-switching and borrowing, but certainly affecting language change.[12]

There may be a number of reasons why shift takes place, but mostly it is the result of social (socioeconomic) pressure from speakers of the majority, prestige, or dominant language. Skill in a dominant variety may yield tangible socioeconomic benefits, and younger members of the community may just choose to speak (shift to) that language and avoid the stigma often placed on linguistic (and/or ethnic) minority status. To be sure, there are bilingual communities in which neither/none of the languages are really "dying," in which maintenance is relatively successful. For example, portions of the bilingual Spanish-English community in Los Angeles are shifting to English, but

---

11. E.g., some members of the Vietnamese-English community in California *refuse* to speak Vietnamese with their children and, as a result of this conscious choice, speak only an interlanguage (or learner's) variety of English in the home. This may be a contributory factor in the emergence of Vietnamese-English, which has emerged as a lingua franca of sorts within a number of in-migrant Southeast Asian communities.

12. Anecdotally, there are reports of the neglected (and, therefore, inferior) state of Japanese, Korean, and other immigrant languages in the Los Angeles area, a source of consternation among those who wish to maintain these heritage language and, therefore, preserve an ethnic (or national) identity.

the Spanish language is certainly not dying. It is still a superlanguage in its own right and the language of power throughout Latin America. (The U.S. is the third largest Spanish-speaking nation after Mexico and Spain, recently surpassing Chile in numbers of speakers.) Yet, there is no official status and little or no formal instruction available to millions of native speakers in states like California (outside of Spanish as a foreign language courses in secondary schools). With little formal support, shift seems to be inescapable. It is a bit like the planned obsolescence of a minority language.

Diglossia, the sometimes conscious and planned functional split of language varieties according to the situations of speech can be another result of maintenance. For instance, one language may be chosen for use in the home, while the other is used outside the home in more official, institutional settings (e.g., in school, on the job, in government, and in the media). Deliberate *compartmentalization* (putting each language in its appropriate box or compartment) may be part of the attempt to hold on to the heritage language since it provides predictable places and events where the language is modeled and used. Diglossia certainly can be an indication of shift, impending language attrition, or, *death*, particularly when the number of social domains dwindles to zero.[13] It is at least an indication of the community's potential for or tendency towards shift. However, there are situations in so-called stable bilingual situations where attrition is perhaps slowed down or prevented. Therefore, diglossia may function as a coping mechanism in the survival of an *endangered* language.[14]

In communities where shift has become particularly evident, proficiency typically drops in the heritage language in favor of the dominant one (Campbell & Muntzel 1989:184–186). The receding language may also show a gradual loss of native vocabulary and increased borrowing (Dressler 1988:184–185; Huffines 1989:212). But, in some cases, borrowing may also indicate a desire to maintain the receding language and resistance to the steady advances of the dominant language – a sign of vitality in the face of shift (Woolard 1989:359–360; Gal 1989:330). In general, the linguistic stability of communities is significant: communities where bilingualism is relatively stable are those that tend to be additive (a dominant language is added to proficiency in the heritage

---

13. Languages are not living entities that can physically die. Death, in this sense, is merely a metaphor. As a result of attrition, a language may become extinct in the sense that it disappears from usage in a community. So-called *dead languages* are those whose speakers have died, languages such as Latin, Sanskrit, and Ancient (biblical) Hebrew. They are no longer learned as native languages by children and are no longer culturally transmitted. Hence, they can no longer change – only living languages change.

14. Note, too, that diglossia itself is easily linked to inter-sentential code-switching, so one can argue that the continuum between code-switching and borrowing consists of degrees from discourse-level switches to single-word switches to on-line borrowings and onto massive lexical and structural borrowing.

language) and diglossia is the rule (Fishman 1989: 183). Where shift is more advanced and the situation unstable, communities tend to be subtractive (the heritage language is steadily losing linguistic ground). The heritage language may shrink to a very narrow set of registers, a kind of *monostylism* (Dressler 1988: 188–189). Lines separating language usage become blurred, and code-switching becomes conversational; speakers will use both varieties with the same participants (Woolard 1989: 359). Borrowing of all types increases to fill lexical gaps (deficiencies) where words and expressions have been lost (Woolard 1989: 359–360; Tsitsipis 1989: 133; Huffines 1989: 223–225).

Another alternative to attrition that can be a byproduct of maintenance is *convergence*, a type of language change.[15] This is typically a community-wide phenomenon in which the non-dominant language takes on characteristics of the dominant language at deeper levels of grammar – that is, structural levels of grammar deeper than garden-variety borrowing of nouns and verbs (Myers-Scotton 2002: 164ff). Within a segment of the bilingual community, there may be forms of diglossia. But in other significant portions of the community, speakers may not compartmentalize their languages neatly according to the speech situation. They may even mix languages in different ways. Mougeon & Beniak (1991) refer to this as "unpatterned bilingualism." Convergence takes place as the socially dominant language makes greater and greater inroads into the linguistic patterning of the non-dominant language, to the extent that children, as native bilinguals, acquire the ways that speakers of the dominant-language group organize their lexicon and express grammatical relationships among words, and apply these principles to the non-dominant language. So, the languages become more and more similar as time goes on. This includes adopting word order patterns in phrases and clauses, and other grammatical strategies of the dominant language. This occurs in many bilingual communities in the U.S., but also in communities worldwide.

For instance, in Chicano (or local L.A.) Spanish, a person may say, "Estoy Fred," which literally (more or less) means "I am Fred." This is word-for-word the way an English-speaking person would use Spanish words when speaking some kind of learners' Spanish, but according to the English pattern. In Spanish, when one introduces oneself, one appropriate way to do this is to say, "Me llamo Fred," which literally means, "Me, I call Fred." Most people who have taken a semester or two of Spanish in school

---

15. In the literature on contact and externally motivated language change, convergence usually refers to when two (or more) languages become more alike (like streams of water whose direction or flow converge into one). This implies that both varieties give up equal degrees of autonomy, and all distinctiveness is eventually lost. However, in practice, convergence is typically one way, reflecting the asymmetrical relationships among languages and speakers. That is, only one language becomes substantially like the other even though influence may be mutual to an extent. That is, one language *drifts* towards the other and acquires characteristics of the other. This drift can reach typological proportions, as in the case of (poly)synthetic languages "becoming" more analytical.

would know the difference, but the pattern does not necessarily show ignorance of the "proper" Spanish forms. Instead, it shows that local Spanish has taken on the characteristics of English (cf. Silva-Corvalán 1994). Of course, local Spanish has a lot of English words in it, too (discussed below), but convergence is a different kind of borrowing. In other words, the basic grammar of the recipient language may be permanently altered along lines of the culturally dominant language.[16] Chicano Spanish is an example of this kind of convergence, and the result is a language variety that *sounds* like Spanish, but has so many borrowed English words and structures in it that native speakers of national standards of Spanish may not understand it.[17]

According to Myers-Scotton (2002), long-term, intensive (constant and strong) and extensive (widespread) contact may produce this kind of convergence, and quite apart from the borrowing of words like nouns and verbs (*lexical* borrowing). While the two processes, convergence and borrowing, can work in concert and in synergistic ways, their motivations appear to be distinct. Convergence seems to be a result of the intensity of bilingualism, and perhaps evidence of a conflict or tension within an ostensibly multilingual community between maintenance and shift. In addition, at deeper levels of grammar, at the level of structure rather than just words, the imitation/copying of donor grammatical strategies seems to encourage the borrowing of individual grammatical items such as conjunctions, prepositions, and so on, to occupy critical positions for indicating a phrase or clause boundary, for example. (Words like conjunctions and prepositions typically occur at the very beginning of the phrase or clause they go with.) This is, indeed, the case in Mexicano (Náhuatl), an indigenous language of Mexico, that has borrowed many prepositions and conjunctions from Spanish (Field 2002). The borrowing, or recipient, language begins to appear and function like the dominant, donor language because it has borrowed *the ways* in which phrases and clauses are constructed, and not just a lot of content words like nouns and verbs.

---

16. Matras (2000) argues that "categorial fusion," in which the grammatical categories (particularly, highly grammatical words such as prepositions and conjunctions and their associated structures) of two languages become essentially the same, is "...triggered by cognitive pressure to reduce the mental-processing load and so eliminate the choice among two competing systems" (577). This view is basically shared by Silva-Corvalán (1994). In categorial fusion, speakers "...draw on the resources of just one single system for an entire functional category," and the "non-separation" of language systems. This implies that a minority-subordinate language can become nearly identical with the superordinate language structurally with respect to word-order patterns, function words (e.g., how prepositions are used), and inflectional categories (usage of past tense). In other words, there is a one-way convergence of the minority language along lines of the dominant language.

17. See Chapter 1 for reference to the Spanish for Native Speakers movement.

4. Linguistic borrowing

The term *borrowing* itself may be a bit misleading; the borrowing language isn't really taking anything from the other language, the so-called donor, and nothing will be paid back. Because of the history of the U.S., there has been a lot of interest in linguistic borrowing over the years, especially due to a few well-known studies by Einar Haugen on varieties of American Norwegian and Swedish in the 1950s (e.g., Haugen 1950, 1953) and the penetrating studies of language contact by Uriel Weinreich (e.g., Weinreich 1953).

According to most definitions, borrowing is the use of a word, form, or structure in one language, say, in one's native language, that comes from a different language or dialect. The word *chic*, meaning fashionable or attractive, comes from French, and when you say "Gesundheit!" to someone who just sneezed, you're using a German word that means "health." These words have been borrowed into English. They have actually become permanent members of the English language *lexicon*, and they are now in English dictionaries. A borrowed word may be phonologically adapted to the pronunciation rules of English, and pronounced strictly English (*chic* pronounced as "chick"). *Adaptation* can be somewhat part way: the name of the California city, *San José* isn't pronounced exactly as it is in Standard Mexican Spanish, but it isn't pronounced completely English either (e.g., something like "san hoe zéy"). According to the Spanish pronunciation, it would be something like [san xo-sé].

The compromise pronunciation is an approximation, and some (not all) distinctive Spanish sounds are replaced by English ones. The "j" is more like an "h" sound in place of the Spanish *jota*, a velar fricative (/x/) – which sounds something like clearing your throat, and the voiceless (/s/) in *José* is replaced with a voiced *z*-sound from English. It shows an effort at "sounding Spanish," but doesn't quite make it all the way. This is true with many words in California English that originate in Spanish, for example, *frijoles* (Mexican-style refried pinto beans), *tortilla* (the round flat bread used for nearly every Mexican dish), and so on. Some words have been borrowed with minimal adaptation, e.g., *taco*. There are many humorous examples (to Spanish speakers), for example, the city names of *La Jolla* and *San Juan Capistrano* pronounced completely in English [la jalə] and [sæn juən kə-**pí**-strə-no]. (Most folks in Southern California have their own amusing examples of out-of-state, English pronunciations of place names and common foods, even the name *Los Angeles* has many different pronunciations.) It is sometimes good to remember that, when someone who comes from another country and speaks a language other than (California) English, they may pronounce words with an "accent." This door swings both ways: when an English speaker tries to pronounce a word from Spanish, it may wind up sounding distorted and very non-Spanish.

Haugen (1950) made a number of distinctions among different kinds of borrowings, focusing primarily on words. For example, there are (1) LOANWORDS, that show the importation of a word whether or not it is fully adapted to the pronunciation system of the recipient language; (2) LOANBLENDS, that are combinations of forms from two languages, typically foreign and native forms, e.g., *television* (*tele-* from Greek and *vision* from Latin); and (3) LOANSHIFTS, that have a foreign concept (meaning) that is represented by a native or recipient-language form. This last term includes *loan translations* (or *calques*); the example most often cited is the English word *superman*, which is a concept borrowed from the German compound *Übermensch*, but represented by English morphemes. Loanshifts can also include *semantic loans* (semantic extensions), where the form and meaning of a native word are stretched to include a new, perhaps related idea. For example, the meaning associated with U.S. Spanish word *grados*, literally "degrees" as in the temperature, is expanded to include the meaning of English "grades," in the sense of grades or marks received in school (Spanish *notas*) (Silva-Corvalán 1994: 170).

Linguistic borrowings can be broken down in another way into (a) ADDITIONS, those that provide labels for objects and concepts newly introduced to the culture (e.g., words such as *delicatessen*, *pizza*, and *sushi* from German, Italian, and Japanese, respectively) and (b) the much less common SUBSTITUTIONS, words for which forms are already available in the recipient language. E.g., for many Californians, the term *wrap* may be an English-derived substitute for the Spanish-derived *burrito* for a type of sandwich (which does not capture the essence of wrapping a filling in a piece of flatbread – or *tortilla*. Other examples in English may include such specialized terms as the German word *Weltanschauung* ("worldview") in philosophy, and Italian musical terms such as *lento* ("slowly"), *piano* ("softly or quietly"), and *fortissimo* ("very loud"), for which English equivalents exist. Substitutions are typically unidirectional, from dominant to non-dominant language, as is the case in both U.S. Spanish and Modern Mexicano (with many borrowings from Spanish). Substitutions get a lot of attention in articles about borrowing because there is a real question why speakers of one language would borrow a word from another language when they already have one of their own. There must be some kind of social payoff or benefit.[18]

---

18. In the literature on philosophy, some German words have been borrowed; using borrowed words such as *Angst* (vague feeling of anxiety or depression), *Weltanschauung* (worldview), and so on shows both familiarity with technical terms and with the language of great German philosophers.

4.1   Direction of borrowing

Borrowing is generally a one-way phenomenon, with the non-dominant or recessive language borrowing more words from the socially dominant language than the other way around, from recessive to dominant. And, Spanish is not alone by any means: there are many languages in the U.S., not just Spanish, that borrow words from English. In the U.S., the language of power is clearly English; in sociolinguistic terms, it's called the *High* variety (e.g., Fishman 1977, 1989). No one needs to call it the "national" language because anyone who moves to the U.S. will know how important it is. There is a saying that sums it up: "The giant knows he's big." English is dominant in almost every official sphere of communication, in government, education, the general media, and so on. All other languages in general U.S. society pale in comparison, and will be considered *Low* in some way. This does not mean that Spanish will not be dominant in some way in another situation. There are times in the Spanish-English bilingual community when proficiency in standard forms of Spanish is considered prestigious, for example in Spanish-language media (print, television, etc.), or when talking about particular topics (Mexican politics). Terms like "dominance" can be controversial, if for no other reason than they can vary in meaning from place to place and from occasion to occasion. In Mexico, the language of power and prestige is Spanish. Therefore, many indigenous languages of Mexico and other Latin American nations borrow lots of words from Spanish.

However, the dominant language may borrow a significant number of terms from a recessive language, as well. California English has borrowed terms for *cultural items* (additions) from several languages. From Spanish, there is the following list (to name only a few):

1. *burrito*
2. *cantina*
3. *chili con carne*
4. *fajita*
5. *frijoles*
6. *quesadilla*
7. *salsa*
8. *taco*
9. *tortilla*
10. *tostada*

Of course, these words come from *Mexican* Spanish. A tortilla in Spain is an egg omelet, and a burrito is a small *burro* (male donkey). Nevertheless, most Californians know what these words are, and they will use them whenever necessary.

The other way around, for English borrowings in local Spanish, there is no comparison. There are hundreds of words and phrases listed in U.S. Spanish dictionaries and recent texts, e.g., *Spanglish* by Ilan Stavans. Many of these words are used on a daily basis in the Los Angeles area. They may be words for things that don't exist in Spanish, for relatively new concepts. For example, job titles may differ in the two languages; the word *babysitter* presents a concept that is foreign to many non-U.S. cultures, so it gets borrowed relatively quickly. Borrowings may be the result of frequency and the ubiquitous nature of English. For example, in U.S. Spanish, there are many English words borrowed and adapted to Spanish phonology and morphology: *Marketa* (from English "market") stands in place of the Spanish form *mercado*; *parkearse* (from English "to park") replaces Spanish *estacionarse*; *puchar* (from English "to push") stands for *empujar*, and *troca* (English "truck") substitutes for *camion* – all substitutions. Many native speakers of U.S. Spanish are unaware that these words are not truly Spanish. They are not found in older Spanish dictionaries from nations and cultures that use Spanish as their principle language.

4.2   Social processes

There is a process to borrowing, from the time it first starts until it is completed, when a previously "foreign" word more-or-less officially becomes part of the borrowing language (variety, or dialect). Based on an analogy from the world of computers, the first steps in the process have been described as *copying* items or structures from one language (as from a file or program) and *pasting* them into another (Johanson 1992). A form from language Y (the dominant or donor language) is learned by a speaker of X (the original and borrowing language) and then reproduced (copied and pasted) in X. A speaker of Spanish (X) may borrow a word from Y (English), and adapt it to his/her own Spanish pronunciation.

However, borrowing may eventually reach into the community at large as Y forms are adopted by other speakers of X and the borrowed elements *diffuse* (spread out) into the community. Hence, forms fan out from individuals in one social network to those of other, interlocking social networks. This part of the process has been called *diffusion* or *propagation* to represent how the word is pasted into the vocabularies of more and more speakers. For a term to be acknowledged as fully borrowed, it must be *conventionalized*. That is, it is used (and pronounced) in fundamentally the same ways by a significant number of people in the community. It must be accepted (by speakers of X) as belonging to the recipient language. For example, the word *marketa* is considered Spanish in many parts of Los Angeles, in "L.A." or local Spanish, and it has pushed its way into parts of Mexico. It is not recognized as authentic Spanish in other places. In fact, some speakers of standard Spanish find it amusing, and very English, an *anglicismo* (Anglicism) – an English word made to appear Spanish.

Nevertheless, it is often noted in long-standing bilingual situations that the origins of many borrowed terms are lost, and there is often little or no awareness that a particular borrowed form was ever borrowed. This is true when examining languages such as English that have borrowed extensively from French, e.g., words such as *guarantee* and *warranty* are the same word borrowed *twice* from two different dialects of French, at different times in the history of the language. Likewise, speakers don't seem to notice borrowed words when speaking L.A. Spanish. For all intents and purposes, these Anglicisms have become Spanish, indistinguishable from indigenous Spanish words.

The literature on borrowing also mentions *where* borrowing is likely to occur. It typically happens to minority languages in contact situations, whether they're old and established situations or relatively new ones. It also occurs where people engage in code-switching of different types (see below). In the Pacific Southwest, in Arizona, Texas, Colorado, and so on, there has been a long history of contact, and the research on borrowing from English into Spanish goes back at least to Espinosa (1915).

Perhaps, particular words will be in a sense the *most attractive* to the borrowing community. For instance, French terms may be particularly attractive to perfume companies or clothing designers. They may have particular *relevance*. It is somehow important to know them in their source language, for instance, the special usage by philosophers of *Weltanschauung*, meaning basically "world view" in German (the language of many important philosophers such as Goethe). They also are very likely to be *frequent* (read on signs, heard in the streets) due to the ubiquitous nature, of, say, a prestige, majority, or otherwise culturally dominant language. For example, the term *esprey de pelo* is used by Spanish-speaking hair stylists that either don't know the Spanish word or find it easier to use the English. It comes from the English word "spray" pronounced according to phonological rules of Spanish and spelled accordingly, plus the Spanish equivalents for "of hair." It means "hairspray" (Sp. *aerosol de pelo*). In the language of computers and the internet, Anglicisms are commonplace (e.g., *el mouse* for the device one uses to *cliquear*, or click on a computer icon.) English is a very important language in a number of socially defined domains. For example, specific sports come from the U.S. Consequently, one hears many borrowed English words in international baseball (*béisbol* in Spanish) and basketball games. English from Great Britain has had a great impact on international football (*fútbol*), called soccer in the U.S.

Myers-Scotton (2002: 239–240; 243) discusses the novelty of new, dominant language forms and an unconscious association with speakers of the dominant, prestige language. In the case of additions, borrowed forms for cultural items, e.g., for foods newly introduced to the recipient community, have an immediate use (hence, the immediate usage of the Texan Spanish *fajita* in California). The words are instantly available to fill lexical gaps for terms that the borrowing language doesn't have yet.[19] (What would you call a tortilla if you didn't know the Mexican Spanish word? Or, what English word or expression would you use for the Japanese word *sushi*?) Typically, Americans know that *spaghetti*, which literally means "thin strings or twine," comes from Italian – it's an Italian food. If a word is chosen often enough by members of the recipient-language community, then it becomes an obvious candidate for borrowing.

Sometimes, a borrowed word will take on a specialized meaning. The English form *party* (often spelled "parti") has been borrowed into Chicano Spanish in the Los Angeles area (likely elsewhere, as well), initially, perhaps, as a substitution for the Spanish entry *fiesta*, but its usage has evolved into something slightly different. A *fiesta* may include typical Mexican types of music (e.g., Mariachis), dance, food, and perhaps dress, while a *party* often features music (deejays and special sound equipment) much more closely associated with U.S. Chicano-Latino popular culture. Despite the fact that the two words are taught as Spanish-English translation equivalents, they now refer to two different kinds of events.

As a consequence, borrowing can have a profound effect on the language spoken by the borrowing community, depending on the amount and kind of borrowing. When large amounts of foreign material are appropriated, embedded, and integrated into a recipient system, there will be a cumulative effect. Thus, the accumulation of individual behaviors can leave a permanent mark on a language. (This is what happened to English as massive amounts of French words were borrowed into an otherwise Germanic language.) All bilingual language phenomena exist as the anticipated consequences of contact, but borrowing is, in essence, the principal mechanism for *externally motivated, contact-induced language change*.[20]

5.   Code-switching

Code-switching (or CS) is another bilingual phenomenon that is somewhat similar to borrowing. It involves alternating between the two (or more) languages in contact, and it can manifest itself in different ways. For example, one of the results of diglossia and

---

19. It is also possible in situations of advancing shift that speakers of a heritage language may forget native terms and borrow (or switch to) dominant-language forms to shore up the gaps (Field 1994: 93).

20. The two, processes of internal and external change, obviously, can interact; external processes of change may also operate synergistically with internal processes of change to motivate sweeping changes.

the compartmentalization of languages is the more-or-less planned alternation of varieties based on the situation of speech. When one of the significant elements of a speech event changes, so does the language variety, for example, when a new speaker joins the conversation or there is a simple change of location from home to school. Importantly, the factors that determine which language or language variety is used are primarily social. This means that the situations in which people find themselves typically determine which language a bilingual uses.

For monolinguals of a language, there are different forms for different occasions, e.g., going to the dentist, dealing with a mechanic when the car breaks down, or cheering at the kids' soccer game. Registers of speech vary according to the situation of speech. Among proficient bilinguals, the choice of language, e.g., Spanish or English, is very similar to selecting from among individual registers (and equally unconscious). Spanish is typically the language of choice in informal settings (i.e., informal registers of Spanish), particularly among peers and other members of the bilingual community – an exception would be college students in formal, academic settings. For U.S.-born Chicano-Latinos, conversational code-switching is often the norm, indicating a high degree of personal involvement and, therefore, the language variety of choice among "insiders," perhaps taking the place informal registers of either Spanish or English. Speech events are dynamic and always changing because people, places, and topics are in a constant state of flux. As a consequence, language usage in a bilingual community can also be in a similar state of flux; speakers will move seamlessly from one language variety to another. In a multilingual situation, when we come in personal contact with a variety of people who may speak one or the other of our languages (or both), we need to adjust. Each time, the situation will generally determine the language variety (e.g., Spanish, English, or both), *and* the register of each language, formal-informal, informational-personal involvement, and so on.

5.1   Types of CS

When different languages are assigned to specific events, then a change in a single participant can change the language of choice, e.g., a complete change from Spanish to English when someone who speaks only English joins the conversation. A change of topic can have a similar effect, for example, if the conversation changes from gossip about friends (ex-friends) to an academic topic like linguistics. Special topics may have special terms and expressions, and the speakers may know these terms in only one language or the other. This is typical for bilinguals when one variety is used at home and another for work or school, typical of diglossic situations. Because the actual switching from one language to another occurs between completed utterances (a conversation in language A, and then a completely different conversation in language B), it is called *intersentential* CS.[21]

For instance, a bilingual Spanish-English store clerk may answer a question in English with one customer, and then turn to another and respond in Spanish. Or, a salesperson may be speaking English on the job with a manager or co-worker when another person approaches who is recognized (sometimes based on personal appearance or mannerisms) as a Spanish speaker. This change in the situation of speech may prompt a switch from English to Spanish, but the speaker, in effect, finishes – perhaps only temporarily – the English sentence before beginning the next sentence in Spanish. Similarly, a person may speak one language informally in a car on the way to some sort of formal social event, and then use a completely different language at the event.

Language choice can be rather practical, too. For example, relative proficiencies may play a role among peers. If all participants know English well and Spanish not so well, then the conversation may be pulled to English, the language all know the best. The reverse is equally possible. When all are highly proficient in Spanish, the conversation may be pulled into Spanish. Perhaps, the group will gravitate to the least common denominator, the language that the marjority of them are proficient in, when proficiencies vary from participant to participant. The symbolic nature of each language may also take hold. Spanish is often the language of *solidarity* or ethnic pride among many Chicano-Latinos, and English symbolizes the dominant culture – sometimes positive, sometimes not. There can also be momentary switches from one to the other to exploit the symbolism, and for individuals to identify with one culture or the other. This may happen when Chicano-Latinos want to differentiate themselves from monolinguals of either Spanish or English. Code-switching – the ability to switch from one to the other – can be symbolic and have its own social value (cf. Zentella 1997: 80–83, 99–101).

Intersentential CS has interested sociolinguists as a social behavior because it shows how languages (or registers of languages) can be assigned to particular social situations. However, another type of code-switching has received a much greater amount of attention, and not only by sociolinguists: *intrasentential* CS.[22] This occurs when speakers switch mid-sentence. This type is often called *conversational* code-switching since it looks and sounds like two languages being spoken at the same time. It is sometimes called *code-mixing* or *language mixing*, two terms that may also refer

---

21. *Inter-* (Latin prefix meaning between or among) and *sentential* (sentences): intersentential code-switching basically means that the switch from one language to another occurs as one utterance or sentence is completed and a new one begins (in the other language).

22. *Intra-* (Latin prefix meaning within, inside) *sentential* (sentence): the switch from one language to the other happens within the utterance, not in between sentences or a clearly marked boundaries.

to the ways native bilingual children mix their languages during Bilingual First Language Acquisition (BFLA).[23] For the present purposes, the terms conversational and intrasentential differ only in perspective; one refers to the grammatical structure of the switching, and the other to its usage.

Certain groups of people seem particularly adept at this remarkable linguistic phenomenon, skillfully weaving their way from one language to another, in a natural, flowing conversational manner. Examples might be adolescent peer groups, siblings, close friends or co-workers who usually interact in very informal ways, and so on. Participants, setting, and topic seem to have little or no bearing on the choice of language. There is a continuous stream of bilingual speech. Conversational, intrasentential code-switching can, in essence, become a separate "code" or register of speech. It also offers evidence that fluent CS is an acquired, skilled behavior. Within the Spanish-English bilingual community, it is often noted that monolingual speakers of either language do not understand the conversational switching, and certain kinds of additive bilinguals may not understand or be able to engage in it, either. (Being bilingual in Spanish and English does not necessarily mean that one will comprehend fluent intrasentential CS.) Then again, there can be social prohibitions against this "undesirable" behavior, at least with certain people, e.g., with parents, grandparents, or social superiors.[24]

Intrasentential CS does not depend on any kind of change in the speech situation. In fact, it is notable that the situation does *not* change. Speakers will speak either or both to the same people, regardless of topic or physical setting. Similar to informal registers of speech, this type of switching is typically done in informal situations, for example

---

23. Terms may be used differently by specialists in language contact, particularly those who make fine distinctions among phenomena. Not everyone will use the term code, e.g., to refer to a variety of speech. The term Mixed Language has been controversial for many years. It has been asserted that all languages are mixed in some ways (e.g., English); hence, they are the products of language mixing (in one sense). Some linguists speak of blended, hybrid, intertwined, or split languages which appear to be two languages fused together as one, for example, Michif, which is a curious mixture of French and Cree. Others do not recognize the existence of mixed languages at all, and attribute large amounts of heretofore "foreign" materials in a language to normal processes of borrowing, for instance, the high number of French words that have accrued in English. The spontaneous, unplanned usage of two languages in intrasentential code-switching does not necessarily lead to a mixed language, though it may be a factor.

24. One subject who participated in data gathering for this book remarked how surprised she was when hearing her own voice on tape. She marveled at how fast she spoke and how hard it was to understand. When she was code-switching with her best friend (who code-switched, as well), she had no problem understanding the conversation. Outside of the confines of the speech event, she had to "…try hard to understand…" what was said. She also noted that her own switches featured proportionately more English than Spanish, but her friend's switches were more Spanish than English – apparently not affecting intelligibility for either participant during the event itself.

with siblings, close friends, and co-workers, particularly during personal conversations and on the phone (e.g., personal calls on cellphones). The switching has an entirely different effect from using a single language variety in normal conversation. It demonstrates allegiance to the *bilingual* community and close personal/social attachment among participants (they can relate to each other). Social identity is connected to the ability to weave the two together.

Evidently, CS within sentence boundaries is acquired in addition to the two respective languages through contact with other speakers, just like a full range of registers are learned by monolinguals. It is most likely modeled by equally bilingual older siblings, parents, and other family and community members. Conversational CS is by no means a phenomenon restricted to Spanish-English bilinguals. In many cases, it gets a somewhat pejorative name. In Southern California, e.g., one hears *Konglish* (Korean-English intrasentential, conversational CS), *Japlish* (Japanese-English), *Taglish* (Tagalog-English), among others, and the seemingly ever-present *Spanglish*. The French-English CS of Montreal, Canada, was named *Franglais* long ago. The negative views seem to come from "purists" who want to see the respective languages maintained in their original states, i.e., according to some kind of standard variety. Purists look down on language mixing behaviors as some kind of corruption of the ingredient languages. The perception is that habitual code-switchers cannot speak either very well.[25] They seem to be losing their heritage language and failing to acquire English. Neither of these assumptions are warranted, however, when looking at CS as a skilled behavior.

5.2   Social motivations for CS

Regarding the motivations for code-switching, many authors recognize the ability of all types of CS to mark or indicate social identity (e.g., Gumperz 1982: 62–64; cf. Heller 1982). We demonstrate with speech the importance of the relationships with other members of the bilingual community and within our individual social networks, just as the choice of register for monolinguals indicates different aspects of their individual identity within monolingual communities. This will influence how a speaker interacts with the other conversational partners (*addressees*). Speakers signal their intentions, and listeners glean important information by the ways people speak, not just the content of their messages. And, this goes far beyond the kind of mood the speaker might be in.

When observing an on-going exchange, there will always be variation because not every speaker assesses the situation in the exact same way. There may be participants

---

25. Bilingualism does not *cause* CS; many bilinguals find it difficult, or simply choose not to engage in rapid, on-line CS.

who look down on CS behavior under any circumstances, and those for whom it is the normal (*unmarked*) choice for relatively informal situations. Some may engage in conversational CS while others may not to the same degree. Like the choice of an appropriate register, different kinds of CS are the result of speaker choices, usually to make the unmarked choice according to the expectations (*rights and obligations*) of the other participants under the particular circumstances of the speech event. For example, speakers may choose Spanish with Spanish speakers and English with English speakers to reflect the obligation to speak a language the addressee understands and the right for the hearer to be addressed in a language he or she will comprehend. Another expected choice may be intrasentential CS, specifically in groups where that is the normal, accepted behavior under the circumstances. Individual speakers may assess how much they feel they belong to the group, and act accordingly.

Speakers count the costs and weigh in a mental balance the costs and benefits of CS. If a group of bilinguals is speaking informally and at least one person is already mixing languages, a new participant has very little to lose by code-switching. The person who starts off the code-mixing minimizes the risk by knowing all or most of the other participants (and the choices they generally make), or he/she may test the waters with an exploratory CS (and judge the reactions of the other speakers). All personal interactions involve some kind of negotiation with respect to the appropriate language for both the individual speakers and for the situation (and scene) (Myers-Scotton 1993a: 115). There is also the possibility that an individual speaker wishes to reinterpret what is expected in a particular situation and take the *marked* choice, for example, and doing what is *not* expected under the circumstances, for instance, pulling the language of the conversation to English or to Spanish, perhaps for affect, to provoke some sort of reaction, or to demonstrate proficiency in one or the other. Conversational CS can indicate a strong bond with other bilingual speakers who have grown up in situations where it is commonplace and the accepted, expected, and, therefore, unmarked choice.

There may be a little mystery about how interaction types become more or less conventionalized and established by the community. The usual or unmarked choices are acquired through experience, by observing what people do in particular situations. And, as children watch the behaviors, they internalize the social values of those behaviors (by assessing how they are perceived by other members of the community), and perhaps emulate the ways their role models and heroes act in their unique community. It is rather important to emphasize that community norms are specific to the community. They may be very different in Los Angeles when compared to those of bilingual *nuyoricans* in New York City, *cubanos* in Miami, or *tejanos* in El Paso or those living in other borderland areas of Texas, Arizona, and California.

Although it is not associated with skilled conversational CS, apparently some bilinguals may choose a momentary switch of one particular word or phrase in order to fill some kind of gap in the speaker's vocabulary, e.g., a word that is not known in one language. In this case, just as with borrowing, the frequency of an English word may help motivate the choice of English, so a word or expression may be plucked on-line from English and used for clarity in a conversation otherwise in Spanish. The goal may be for social affect, to identify with the dominant linguistic group (demonstrating knowledge of English). In situations of advancing shift, where not all participants are highly proficient in Spanish, a bilingual whose linguistically strongest or dominant language is English may switch briefly to Spanish to identify with the non-dominant group, by "throwing" into the conversation a Spanish word or two like the discourse markers *pues* ("well"), *mira* ("look"), or *¡Orale!* (which can have a range of meanings like "right on!" or "go on, get out of here," etc.). This can sometimes be relatively deliberate and conscious. This type of CS has been called *emblematic* because the words themselves become emblems, symbolic of solidarity and group membership.

5.3   Theoretical models for CS

Only recently have researchers offered feasible models and explanations for what must be going on in the heads of bilingual speakers when they are code-switching. For example, Carol Myers-Scotton has authored two volumes for Oxford University Press on the subject (Myers-Scotton 1993a and 1993b). Her concept of a matrix (or base) language, the Matrix Language-Frame (MLF) model and the corresponding Matrix Language Hypothesis (MLH) have been particularly significant in recent discussions of the systematic nature of CS.[26] In essence, the MLF model proposes that one of the two languages involved in CS frames the utterance, the Matrix Language (ML), and into that basic frame, organized chunks of the other language, or Embedded Language (EL), are inserted. These inserted stretches are called "EL islands," and they are characteristically phrases or clauses of some kind (structural units). The MLH suggests that the ML plays the greater role in CS by providing the grammatical matrix that influences the overall structure of the CS utterance. Spanish-English CS often falls into clear patterns like this, with a Spanish matrix containing embedded phrases in English. The opposite also happens, when fluent bilinguals are speaking (Chicano) English and occasionally throw in a word or phrase in Spanish. In either case, there is a base to frame the entire utterance.[27]

It certainly seems that the concept of some sort of matrix in CS is a logical necessity, especially when one assumes that the mixing of two language systems into one

---

26. See Myers-Scotton (2002: 16–25) and Myers-Scotton (2006: 267–271) for a detailed discussion of the 4-M model, an important refinement and expansion of the MLF model of CS.

27. See also Muysken (2000) for alternative views of code-switching.

speech stream is comprehensible to the hearer. Every child and adult, when they are among other, equally bilingual people, assume that when they speak, they will be understood (the assumption of comprehensibility). When looking at transcriptions of many CS events, it appears to be systematic, despite its apparent complexity. After all, conversational code-switching must be *parsed* (analyzed as coherent speech) by the listener, even if it is only in a passive, receptive sense. But, the performance of CS involves rapid, on-line selection of forms from two entirely autonomous language systems. It seems as if only a very skilled bilingual can do such a thing. This brings into question old stereotypes of code-switchers as lacking the competence in either or both languages to carry on a coherent monolingual conversation.

One alternative to insertion into a matrix language (or alternating bases) is that code-switching is random, or somewhat random, a view that seems to have vanished from the discussion. Some other possibilities may be that the alternation between languages occurs at short, nearly imperceptible intervals, with little or no evidence of a single, underlying matrix, or that the two languages being mixed coalesce together to form a single composite or blended matrix. But, the question of intelligibility is still important to consider, and it clearly suggests that CS is a highly skilled performance. If not, then something very interesting is happening as children acquire their two languages. Whether or not one can *easily* identify the patterns of code-switching is not really relevant. Systematicity does not necessarily suggest simplicity; all languages are relatively complex. There are very complex language systems under investigation today that appear to defy description (or at least challenge strongly).

The early literature on the history of bilingual phenomena used to characterize CS as unplanned interference, e.g., that there is only room for one language inside a person's head, and when there are two (or more), one randomly interferes with the other. The imagery was like two objects banging against each other. So, the obvious complexity was viewed as randomness, similar to shaking a pair of dice and rolling them on the floor. No one knows what's going to happen, including the speaker. Current views no longer see CS in this way, preferring to seek linguistic answers to the apparent complexity. Moreover, the social motivations for conversational CS show that there is a *purpose* (intentions and goals), and the result is still comprehensible, effective communication. Note, too, that there is a great deal of current research in psychology, psycholinguistics, and neurolinguistics that shows how languages seem to be systematically stored in the brain. There will be systematic correspondences between language systems that may facilitate such things as the ability to translate from one to the other, alternate between the two (or three), and mix language systems together – systematically.

5.4   Borrowing and CS compared

The linguistic processes involved in on-line CS and long-term borrowing may overlap to an extent. In intrasentential CS, the clear alternation between/among languages seems to fade almost entirely, until, apparently, there is a simultaneous usage of both. But, once again, a continuum is evident regarding processes and the products of those processes. This is where the obvious similarity between borrowing and CS is first encountered, at the level of individual words and phrases. The difference lies primarily in how bilinguals are using the languages. In borrowing, only one language is in use, although it is drawing upon the resources of the other. In different types of CS, both languages are clearly in play.

While conversational CS can be *insertional* (demonstrating a relatively clear dichotomy between matrix and embedded languages), the amount of embedded-language information may vary from a phrase or clause all the way down to a word or morpheme. Intersentential CS is more clearly *alternational* (one language, then the other). Muysken (2000), in his typology of code-mixing, distinguishes three processes of mixing, insertional, alternational, and another he calls *congruent lexicalization*, in which words from different varieties share a single grammatical system, perhaps as a result of convergence or in the case of dialects of a single language (3). He observes that all three of these apparently distinct processes can occur in intrasentential CS. The process (language mixing) depends on the languages (and language-specific restraints on mixing) and circumstances of the individual bilingual contact situations.[28] The clearest, most obvious case of alternational CS is intersentential CS. Intrasentential CS, on the other hand, closely resembles borrowing, with much smaller chunks of the embedded language tucked into the base language. CS that is intrasentential provides occasional words that are temporarily inserted into the conversation while one language is primarily in use.

Poplack & Meechan (1995) prefer to call the word-level phenomenon *nonceborrowing*, or one-time borrowing. The most frequent nonce-borrowings are nouns, as one might suspect. They argue that it is borrowing, at least *insipient* (beginning) borrowing, and that sociolinguistic methodology is necessary to measure the degree of integration into the recipient language. For example, it needs to be determined how widespread the word has become in the community (via diffusion), or how many people consider this previously borrowed word part of their language. In this view, borrowing starts out as a one-time event, but then gradually diffuses out into the

---

28. Muysken uses the term language-mixing to describe types of processes, and claims that codeswitching implies only alternational types of mixing, to the apparent exclusion of insertional types. Myers-Scotton, in contrast, uses the term codeswitching (sans hyphen) as an inclusive term for processes and instances of language mixing.

community. They also propose that word counts will demonstrate how widespread a borrowed form is in the community, and that it is the only way to know for sure when exactly a word has been borrowed.

The likely scenario for insertion, from a psychological viewpoint, is a three-step process: First, there is simultaneous activation of both languages (they are mentally "on"). During the usage of one language, a particular word is accessed from the other language. The language in use automatically becomes the matrix into which linguistic material from the second language can be inserted. Second, the "foreign" non-matrix item or word is selected (chosen for use). Third, the form is embedded (inserted) into the bilingual speech stream, into the matrix or base language. For alternation, there is a point at which one language is "on," and then switches to the "off" position as the other language is activated.

One can remain somewhat neutral (or unconvinced) in the debate whether or not insertional CS constitutes borrowing or code-switching. However, it seems apparent that code-switching, by definition, maintains the autonomy of language systems, while borrowing (understood correctly) can produce changes in the recipient system. If the nonce-borrowing (one-time or insipient borrowing) word form enters the vocabulary of speakers of the recipient language, then and only then can it be called a "full-fledged" borrowed word. Without the social processes of adoption (acceptance), diffusion (spread), conventionalization, and so on, it doesn't seem to matter if one considers the form a result of code-switching or borrowing. There is undoubtedly some sort of transitional period during which the social and linguistic processes of diffusion and so on operate to completion (or are halted at a point prior to completion).

Where the exact boundaries might be between borrowing and code-switching is still somewhat of a point of contention among specialists, although it is probably safe to say that there is some sort of continuum between the two, with blurry lines that appear to move according to the viewpoint of the researcher. As a consequence, the two separate processes are often lumped together or confused. In the Spanish-English bilingual community, the resultant mixture of Spanish and English known as *Spanglish* is the product of the two distinct processes working separately and together (cf. Field 1994). The local, Southern California variety of Spanish is so interlarded with English that it is almost incomprehensible to native speakers of national standards including Standard Mexican Spanish, and intrasentential code-switching (with a clear Spanish matrix) *sounds* like some kind of Anglicized Spanish. The term Spanglish, therefore, appears to refer to two separate phenomena that, to the non-native's ear may *sound* almost the same. Another way to look at it is that so-called Spanglish doesn't appear to be categorized easily as a product of one process or the other because it shows clear signs of both, and clearly communicates ethnic identity (Rothman & Bell 2005; cf. Zentella 1997).

6. Language modes

The work of researchers such as François Grosjean points to the existence of different language *modes*, or psychological states, that are brought on by the kinds of social situations that speakers encounter (based on participants, setting, and so on). They are mental states that occur in the minds of bi- or multilingual speakers as they interact with their environment and with other potentially multilingual speakers. Therefore, a proficient bilingual speaker will have a *monolingual mode* for each language, in which only one language is "switched on" or mentally activated when engaging in speech with a speaker (or speakers) of only one of his/her languages. For instance, a Spanish-English bilingual will be in a monolingual English mode for people she perceives as English-speaking (and non-Spanish speaking), or when English is the expected language of interaction. A Spanish monolingual mode is activated when interacting with people in the community who appear to favor Spanish. Many proficient bilinguals (those who have grown up bilingual) will also have a *bilingual mode*, in which both languages are activated, for people who are known to be active bilinguals (e.g., Grosjean 2006: 40–43).

The bilingual status of an individual is usually (soon) evident, particularly according to the norms of social interaction that are unconsciously held by members of the community. This perception may be based on physical appearance (e.g., racial or ethnic traits), culturally based mannerisms (e.g., the way the person dresses, walks, or nods the head), or merely based on the observation of how the person interacts with companions. These are the social mannerisms that children learn in their home environments through experience, just by living day to day. Obviously, physical appearance can become stereotyped. However, within tight-knit communities such as those found in predominantly Chicano-Latino neighborhoods, the style of dress carries a lot of social information, and it can be quite overt, even intentional. Every "look" can indicate some kind of group identity. For men, it might be a shaved head, tee-shirt (of a particular color), oversized trousers, knee-length socks, and so on; khaki pants and particular brand of long-sleeved flannel shirt; a business suit and patent-leather shoes; or blue jeans, boots, and cowboy hat (of various materials such as plastic or felt, sizes, and shapes). Tattoos ("tats"), or the absence thereof, can speak volumes, as well.

Regarding the settings, in some particularly conservative, and relatively homogeneous *colonias*, a particular national-regional form of Latin American Spanish may be the norm (and, in L.A., the selection of regional varieties of Spanish can be quite extensive). Nevertheless, some sort of Spanish will be the correct, unmarked choice. Social interactions in a local *marketa*, at a multi-ethnic school campus, at a "bilingual" church (where both English and Spanish are used during a service), at a park (often unconsciously segregated by national origin), or at the county courthouse, can call forth monolingual and/or bilingual modes. During particular events, for instance, birthday celebrations, religious traditions (e.g., *quinceañeras*, baptisms, first communions, funerals), and so on, the emotional settings can vary from traditional Mexican (Salvadoran, Guatemalan…) to strictly contemporary Chicano-Latino. The proficient bilingual may need to be quite flexible.

In the bilingual encounter, because either language might be used at any particular moment, each participant needs to be prepared for just about anything, one language or the other, or both at the same time. The bilingual mode is a necessity, particularly in communities that allow and encourage various language mixing behaviors (borrowing and different sorts of CS). Such behaviors may become the norm. In many Chicano-Latino situations, conversational CS is an indicator of in-group status, and it is clearly the unmarked choice. Bilingual interaction can certainly be the norm, and all sorts of bilingual phenomena will manifest themselves, particularly in schools where children of various backgrounds are brought together, learn to socialize, and, consequently, learn to interpret important information in each social situation based on outward appearance and social behaviors. For instance, in multi-ethnic schools, most Chicano-Latinos will choose English with their Asian American and African American counterparts, but it most likely will be informal with lots of common references to pop culture. These three diverse groups, as different as they can be, share a social bond – minority ethnic and linguistic status.

It is important to emphasize that this kind of thing happens all over the world – it is clearly not just a situation found in Los Angeles. Nationally, the dynamics can vary greatly from Newark to Miami, and from El Paso to San Diego. Recent demographic trends find so-called Hispanics moving in increasing numbers to more rural areas – what could be called "Brown flight." As a result, bilingual phenomena are most certainly to follow. It should go without saying (by now) that each situation needs to be evaluated one-by-one, based on many factors, for example, the (a) immigration history of each specific group (within larger groups); (b) history in the nation of origin (and colonial history of each Latin American nation with Spain and other European countries with resultant attitudes towards dominant and minority social groups); (c) racial traits (e.g., physical stature, type of hair, skin tone, and so on that may count heavily in country of origin and in the U.S.), (d) socioeconomic status (which may include educational and professional status); (e) deep cultural traits (e.g., attitudes toward education and the professions, political involvement, etc.); and, importantly, (f) individual variation that may be based on age, sex, and multitude of hidden factors that come from personal experience.

Finally, rapid spontaneous, *online* CS between two languages (referring to unconcious processes that occur while the conversation is ongoing), whether the languages are Spanish and English or not, is *not* a social indicator of low socioeconomic status, lack of education, or low intellectual ability, despite the fact that in many areas characterized by (a) relative poverty, (b) a lack of educational opportunities, and (c) consequent high drop-out rates, various language mixing behaviors are typically found. There is no cause-and-effect relationship between bilingualism and poverty. (There may be a correlation of lack of opportunities and achievement, however.) All language contact phenomena are the *normal* consequences of bilingual situations, particularly where a social asymmetry is found to exist among members of society. The factors at play are very complex and dynamic making it difficult to predict with 100% accuracy how a particular individual will behave from moment to moment. But, as a child learns from experience, so can others; teachers and school administrators can learn to *anticipate* the relative likelihood that children will engage in bilingual behaviors and the particular social variables and language modes that may call forth those behaviors.

Key terms

adaptation, additions, addressee, alternational, Anglicism, asymmetry, bilingual modes, bilingual phenomena, borrowing, calque, code-mixing, code-switching (CS), cognitive abilities, compartmentalization, contact linguistics, contact phenomena, contact-induced language change, continuum, conventionalized, convergence, conversational CS, copying, cultural items, culturally dominant group, culturally recessive, diffusion, domain (of language use), donor language, embedded language (EL), emblematic, endangered language, etymology, externally-motivated change, foreign language, frequent/frequency, genres, global economy, goals, heritage language, individual (social) identity, information, insertional, interlocutor, intersentential CS, intrasentential CS, involvement, language attrition, language change, language choice, language contact, language death, language loss, language maintenance, language minority (LM), language mixing, lexical, lexicon, loan translation, loanblend, loanshift, loanword, marked/unmarked, matrix language, mental faculty, minority language, monolingual mode, monostylism, native speaker intuition, non-dominant, nonce borrowing, norms of interaction, norms of interpretation, obsolescence, parse, pasting, phonological adaptation, propagation, purist, receding language, recipient language, regional dialect, register, relevance, rights and obligations, rule governed, scene, semantic loan, setting, shift, situation of speech, social dialect, social dominance, sociolinguists, solidarity, Spanglish, speech event, spread, stable bilingualism, structural, subordinate, substitutions, superlanguage, superordinate, systematic, topic, variation.

Summary

There is hardly a community in the world that does not show the effects of cultural and social contact among people. One of the major results of colonial expansion of different empires has been the establishment of large national languages and the emergence of so-called superlanguages. As empires expand, people and languages come into contact. It is axiomatic that people who come into close areal and social contact typically form social, economic, and perhaps cultural ties, and subsequently learn each other's languages. One of the first consequences of contact, then, is some degree of individual bi- or multilingualism. Language contact phenomena, e.g., various types of language mixing, are the normal, expected consequences. Public and private behaviors may spread from individuals to entire communities. One person may alternate the use of languages in different ways or translate words and expressions from one into the other with no apparent loss or gain in either language. Others may do the same, but it is still an individual behavior. Other phenomena involve the behavior of groups, e.g., an aggregate of linguistic behaviors that ultimately affects the language of the entire community. If enough speakers adopt English words into their variety of Spanish, for example, their Spanish will change, perhaps to the extent that speakers of other varieties of Spanish no longer understand them. Therefore, change is a natural process that happens to all living languages; it can come from internal, as well as external causes. Spanish, itself, has changed over the centuries, diverging considerably from its parent, Latin.

A language can vary according to the place or region in which it is spoken. For example, speakers of American English in two different parts of the country may have their own special words for certain things. Their pronunciation, grammatical structure, or usage may vary, as well. Varieties linked to specific parts of a country are usually called regional dialects. There are also varieties of a language associated with groups of people called social dialects, e.g., AAVE and Chicano English. Every language that we know of consists of dialects. Our speech also changes according to the speech situation, the "who, what, where, and why" of speech. Three principle factors determine speech: (a) setting; (b) purpose, and (c) participants. For example, we generally talk differently and about different things with parents or school teachers than we do with our best friends. Our speech can be determined by the topic of conversation (part of the setting), where we are, who we are talking with, and the purpose of our conversation. Change one of those elements, and the forms of speech, or registers of speech will also change.

A register of speech is something like an individual style that a person uses according to the specific characteristics of the speech situation. Because there is a continuum of situations of speech, there will be a continuum of registers, e.g., from presenting a formal paper at a conference to having a casual conversation with (or texting) your closest friend on your cellphone. Every register is, therefore, characterized by sets of linguistic features. That is, a register is determined by the sum or totality of lexical, phonological, and grammatical features with their characteristic patterns usage. Particular linguistic features occur in relative numbers, and particular words, for example, go with particular situations of usage.

One way sociolinguists rank registers is by degrees of formality and informality. An informal register may include words and structures that don't appear in formal academic writing, e.g., contractions, sentence-ending prepositions, and slang. Pronunciation may be relatively fast and patterned after nonstandard varieties (e.g., AAVE). The grammar may also appear nonstandard and full of "ain'ts" and so-called double negatives. Formal academic English, in contrast, is characterized by the near total absence of those informal features (fewer contractions, sentence-ending prepositions, and colloquialisms), all the things that English professors warn students not to do on exams and term papers. It sounds more like Network English, and the grammar will be as close to SAE as possible. Another way to look at registers is along the lines of information versus personal involvement. Professors give lectures that contain lots of information, explanations, and instructions. However, when we talk to close friends, we may not be giving any new information at all. Therefore, one goal of education should be to encourage students to have full access to a variety of registers in each language they know, so that they can engage in all sorts of language activities, from casual speech to academic writing.

Within nearly every known language contact situation, there is some sort of asymmetry in the social relationships among groups that determines the social status of language varieties. One variety will be larger, culturally dominant, or more prestigious. Hence, a minority language may undergo a number of social and linguistic changes according to its status. The very existence of a bilingual community sets up the opposition of language shift and language maintenance. Shift is a gradual process that includes the acceptance of the dominant language and a tendency to abandon a heritage language. Maintenance of a minority language, in contrast, means simply that members of the community choose to speak their ancestral tongue, their heritage language, and transmit that language to their descendants, from parents to their children. Language minorities deal with the results of shift on a daily basis, and contact phenomena such as diglossia, borrowing, and various kinds of code-switching are typical occurrences.

According to most definitions, borrowing is the use of a word, form, or structure from one language that comes from a different language or dialect. The term may be misleading; the borrower isn't really taking anything from the donor and won't pay anything back. Haugen (1950) made distinctions among different kinds of borrowings: (1) loanwords, loanblends, and loanshifts, which includes loan translations (or calques). It is generally a one-way phenomenon, with the non-dominant or recessive language borrowing more words from the socially dominant language than the other way around, from recessive to dominant. Borrowing may eventually reach into the community as the borrowed elements diffuse into the community. Forms fan out from individuals in one social network to those of other, interlocking social networks. For a term to be acknowledged as fully borrowed, it must be conventionalized; that is, it is used in the same ways by a significant number of people in the community. Consequently, borrowing can leave a permanent mark on the language spoken by the borrowing community, depending on the amount and kind of borrowing. Thus, the accumulation of individual behaviors may have a long-term effect on a language.

Code-switching (or CS) is another bilingual phenomenon similar to borrowing. It involves alternating between the two (or more) languages, and it can manifest itself in different ways. This is typical for bilinguals when one variety is used at home and another for work or school, typical of diglossic situations. Because the actual switching from one language to another occurs between completed utterances (a conversation in language X, and then a completely different conversation in language Y), it is called intersentential CS. However, another type of code-switching has received a greater amount of attention, and not only by sociolinguists: intrasentential CS. This occurs when speakers switch mid-sentence. This type is often called conversational code-switching since it looks and sounds like two languages being spoken at the same time. Intrasentential CS does not depend on any kind of change in the speech situation. In fact, it is notable that the situation does not change. Regarding the motivations for code-switching, many authors recognize the ability of all types of CS to mark or indicate social identity. We demonstrate with speech the importance of the relationships with other members of the bilingual community and within individual social networks, just as the choice of register for monolinguals indicates different aspects of individual identity within monolingual communities.

Only recently have researchers offered feasible models and explanations for what must be going on in the heads of bilingual speakers when they are code-switching. Carol Myers-Scotton has authored two entire volumes for Oxford University Press on the subject featuring her concept of a matrix (or base) language, the Matrix Language Hypothesis (MLH). The MLH proposes that there is always one language that frames the utterance, and into that basic frame, or matrix, organized chunks of the other language, or Embedded Language (EL) are inserted. It certainly seems that the concept of some sort of matrix in CS is a logical necessity, especially when one assumes that the mixing of two language systems into one speech stream is comprehensible to the hearer. Every child and adult, when they are among other, equally bilingual people, assume that when they speak, they will be understood (the assumption of comprehensibility).

The linguistic processes involved in spontaneous, unplanned CS and long-term borrowing may overlap to an extent. In intrasentential CS, the clear alternation between/among languages seems to fade almost entirely, until, apparently, there is a simultaneous usage of both. This is where the obvious similarity between borrowing and CS is first encountered, at the level of individual words and phrases. The difference lies primarily in how bilinguals are using the languages. In borrowing, only one language is in use, although it is drawing upon the resources of the other. In different types of CS, both languages are clearly in play. Muysken (2000) distinguishes three processes of code-mixing, insertional, alternational, and another he calls congruent lexicalization in which words from different varieties share a single grammatical system, perhaps as a result of convergence or in the case of dialects of a single language. He observes that all three of these apparently distinct processes can occur in intrasentential CS. Others prefer to call the word-level phenomenon nonce-borrowing, or one-time borrowing. However, it seems apparent that code-switching, by definition, maintains the autonomy of language systems, while borrowing (understood correctly) can produce changes in the recipient system.

The work François Grosjean points to different psychological states, or language modes, that are brought on by the kinds of social situations that speakers encounter. They are mental states that occur in the minds of bi- or multilingual speakers as they interact with their environment and with other potentially multilingual speakers. So, a proficient bilingual speaker will have a monolingual mode for each language, in which only one language is "switched on" or mentally activated when engaging in speech with a speaker (or speakers) of only one of his/her languages. Many proficient bilinguals also have a bilingual mode, in which both languages are activated, for bilingual speakers. Nevertheless, rapid online CS between two languages, whether the languages are Spanish and English or not, is not a social indicator of low socioeconomic status, lack of education, or low intellectual ability. There is no cause-and-effect relationship between bilingualism and poverty.

Activities – topics for discussion

1. Have you witnessed language contact phenomena? If you are not a member of a bilingual-community, how would you describe code-switching? If you are a code-switcher yourself, explain what is going on in your head?

2. What is *your* heritage language? Discuss the pros and cons of having a heritage language other than (Standard) English.

3. Have you noticed the customs of a particular ethnic group, how members of this group talk, touch each other, or otherwise behave as a group? Make a list of specific behaviors, and discuss how you interpret these behaviors.

4. Make a list of all the words that you can think of that English has borrowed from other languages, and name the language they come from. Pick, for example, common words like *rice*, *guarantee*, and *wiener*.

5. Have you noticed how you talk differently with close friends and with different kinds of professionals (your dentist, physician, or professor)? List the ways that your speech and other factors like body language may change according to person, place, and topic.

Practice essay questions

1. Language attrition is the gradual loss or disappearance of a minority language within a community as members of the community shift to the use of a culturally dominant language. Explain the steps that are involved. What other bilingual phenomena are to be expected in such a situation?

2. Explain the many different types of linguistic borrowing, from lexical borrowing to structural borrowing.

3. Discuss registers of speech. In your response, list the social factors that influence speech (genres), degrees of formality, and the differences between informational and involved registers.

4. Describe the differences between intersentential and intrasentential code-switching. In what ways does language choice figure into the mix (pun intended)?

5. Explain the differences between marked and unmarked choices in bilingual communities where code-switching is likely to occur.

Chapter 4

Chicano English (ChE)

1. Sharing features: Vernaculars, social dialects and standards
2. Likely origins of ChE
3. Description of ChE: Vocabulary and pronunciation
4. Description of ChE: Word formation and word order
5. Standard Chicano English

In every living language, processes of change are as inevitable as rain. These dynamic processes manifest themselves as linguistic outcomes, but the forces that motivate change are typically social, the result of societal change and the pressures that accompany change. Dialects also emerge as the consequence of some kind of isolation. This isolation can be geographical, as in the case of regional varieties separated from others by natural boundaries – mountain ranges, rivers, and so on. Isolation, however, can also be social, as a result of the asymmetrical social conditions that exist in societies beleaguered by tensions among majority and minority groups and segregation practices. Language varieties can surely change over time from the inside via internal processes of change, but change can also come from the outside as a result of contact with other language varieties. The two directions of change are not mutually exclusive; they can work in concert. The language of many Chicano-Latinos in Southern California, Chicano English (ChE) is most likely the consequence of both internal and external processes of change.

ChE is considered to be a nonstandard, minority dialect. It is nonstandard because some of its characteristics differ from those that are clearly associated with Standard American English (SAE), the language of school, government, the media, and so on. It is associated with Chicano-Latinos, an ethnic minority, so it is considered a minority dialect. While it is clear that almost all of its forms (words) and structures (grammar) are essentially inherited from English, there is something about it that sets it apart from other kinds of English. Some unique characteristics stand out; these linguistic characteristics, or *features*, serve to indicate a unique social or ethnic identity, and a sense of belonging to a special group, and, perhaps, the Spanish-English bilingual community in some sense. It has already been pointed out that members of that community will vary in their levels of proficiency in the two languages, from relatively limited to relatively high levels of proficiency in either or both languages. It is possible to find monolingual speakers of Spanish living in the same household with monolingual speakers of English and bilingual speakers of both Spanish and English. Native speakers of ChE cannot be teased away from the bilingual community, unless they have acquired the dialect with no previous ethnic or linguistic connection to some form of Spanish. Even then, the influence of Spanish is likely to be felt inside the speech community as a whole via communication networks of one kind or another.

Varieties of American English can differ according to such social factors as locale (region or subregion), socio-economic strata (SES), and ethnicity – which is not always an easy concept to define, particularly in the U.S.[1] These factors can coincide; e.g., those who live in the same locale may share ethnicity and socio-economic stratum, as well, although one would expect some variability. In Southern California, many specific communities are isolated from each other by physical barriers or boundaries, along major thoroughfares (e.g., Whittier Blvd.) bounded by freeways instead of the rivers and mountain ranges that distinguish major regional dialects in the U.S. A combination of social and physical boundaries can create social islands of a sort – relatively isolated communities that have their own identities. So, one may speak of community in terms of a relatively small geographical area bounded by certain streets or public landmarks. But, these boundaries are not impermeable. Individuals move in and out according to the relatively transitory lifestyle of many Californians, in general. As recent demographic trends show, entire communities can change rather quickly. Boundaries can also move.

The concept of *speech community* is often debated, partly because it shifts the focus away from linguistic features onto social and cultural traits (Hymes 1974: 47; Wardhaugh 2006: 116ff).[2] Nevertheless, while we can certainly focus our studies in one direction or the other, the two are inextricably entwined. All language varieties, whether standard or nonstandard, are defined both by their linguistic features and the social groupings most easily identified with them.[3] Garcia (1984: 86) notes, too,

---

1.   Gender (sex roles or identity) is another factor listed in many sociolinguistic studies of language usage.

2.   See, also, Spindler and Spindler (1987) for the types of complex issues often associated with culture and ethnographic studies.

3.   In the early literature on dialects, the term *substandard* was used to indicate a hierarchical relationship among language varieties. The standard was considered higher (used by those in the upper classes) than other forms of language spoken by the lower classes. Needless to say, because all language varieties function normally within the communities that use them, one cannot construct such a hierarchy. The correct term in today's intellectual climate is nonstandard, which merely suggests that a variety that differs from a standard is merely different and not inferior.

that "…varieties may be distinguished by a higher frequency in the production of a nonstandard variant as compared to its frequency in the greater language community," meaning that particular features may manifest themselves with greater or lesser frequency according to individuals and groups of speakers. The greater the number of nonstandard features that manifest themselves in a specific speech community, the more nonstandard their language variety will be – that is, the variety associated with members of that community. For instance, the more one hears such nonstandard expressions as "ain't" and so-called "double negatives" ("I don't got nothing"), the more nonstandard the variety. Of course, the occurrence of one nonstandard variant can trigger the stereotype, so the individual may be unfairly judged by a societal perception of his/her community.

One of the most fascinating aspects of society is its ability to socialize us into identifiable groups. We all express how we identify ourselves. We reflect the social groups we feel most comfortable with, the socioeconomic class we identify with, and the racial or ethnic groups society seems to determine for us. Teachers have "teacher talk;" politicians have political talk; musicians have their talk; and so do dock workers, landscaping crews, and those who work in the food industry, from the up-scale restaurant in Beverly Hills to the local Pollo Loco in North Hills, California. Familiarity with a specific job or activity means we learn its special vocabulary, its *jargon*. Our cultures affect the ways we think and act, and society observes those behaviors and places values on them – values that are transmitted throughout society. Many linguists and anthropologists still debate the influence of culture during the acquisition of language, not *if* it shapes our thinking and behaviors, but *how* and *how much*.

One of the things that most anthropological linguists and sociolinguists agree on is that we will manifest our upbringing in the ways we behave. Because so much of language acquisition goes on beneath our conscious awareness, we don't always know exactly what it is that marks our speech, though most people will have an opinion or two based on the ways *other people* talk. We clearly size each other up by the words we choose to use, by particular pronunciation patterns, and by the many cultural mannerisms that we use *when* we talk – the use of the hands, facial expressions, body movement, and the rapidity and loudness of our speech. ChE has its own sets of linguistic features, and it has a community of speakers who identify themselves through it, by their cultural mannerisms and speech.

The purpose of this chapter, therefore, is to discuss Chicano English and how it came to be, and to focus on the types of speech associated with Chicano-Latinos in Southern California. The focus is on Southern California because its history is unique; Chicanos from L.A. are not *tejanos* from El Paso, or *cubanos* from Miami, or *nuyoricans* from New York. While there may be certain similarities and shared interests among so-called Hispanics in major urban centers such as New York, Chicago, and Los Angeles (e.g., in areas of minority language rights), each area has its own unique socio-political history, ingredient populations and residence (housing) patterns; its own individual cultural and linguistic environment; and its own influential figures, heroes, and villains. In L.A., home of major links to the entertainment industry and media visibility, having what one might call a "high profile" is quite common. Among those currently identified as Chicanos, and, therefore, those who are potential models of Chicano English, there are sports heroes (e.g., boxer Oscar De La Hoya, a k a, the "Golden Boy"); film stars (Edward James Olmos and Cheech Marin); comedians (George Lopez, Paul Rodriguez, and many more); politicians (e.g., current mayor Antonio Villaraigosa and Gloria Molina); music groups (Los Lobos, War, and El Chicano); and radio and television personalities galore.

1.   Sharing features: Vernaculars, social dialects and standards

All varieties of English share most of their linguistic features with *each other*. That is, there is a core to all varieties of English that identify them as English, particularly in grammar and vocabulary. Most linguistic differences will be relatively minor. For example, there may be differences in pronunciation and a few different words (words for regional or ethnic foods and other cultural nuances), but social varieties will be mutually intelligible with their corresponding regional standards for the most part (despite biases). The basic terms for family relationships, body parts, common activities, etc., are basically the same in London, New York, or Los Angeles. When looking at the differences among national standards (e.g., Standard American or Standard British), these differences will seem especially minor. But, this is by design. The similarities have been enforced by educators to preserve continuity (through the various points in the history of English) and to promote access to a huge shared literature. The fear is that too many changes will jeopardize its unity and intelligibility. As a result, a person who reads American English will be able to read British, Australian, and South African forms of English.

A vernacular is, in essence, the language learned as a native language in the home (from the people we love and depend on). It is typically based on the specific dialect of the locale in which the community is situated, with its own individual demographic (socioeconomic and ethnic) makeup and community standards of behavior. Therefore, vernaculars may diverge considerably from each other and from the standards. They can be quite diverse when thinking of the size of the U.S., U.K., and all the other nations where English is the primary language. The outback of Australia is a different place from streets of East Los Angeles, different people, different cultures, different foods, and different social histories. While a vernacular enjoys a very privileged place in the mind of the child, it can be subject to a lot of criticism from people on the "outside," from society in general, based on social perceptions.

Wald (1984) distinguishes the term *standard* from *vernacular*, noting that a national standard of English is not ostensibly modeled after the speech of a particular group of people or locale. It is supposed to represent the ideal form of linguistic communication that all members of a nation or society are to use in public discourse.[4]

> Since, from a linguistic point of view, the Standard is no less a dialect than other varieties of English, I use the term "vernacular" to refer to the dialect of any locally based speech community. In contrast with the Standard, which in principle does not have local connotations, vernaculars are first-learned varieties within a community, and tend to differ most in phonology and lexicon, and to a lesser degree in syntax, from each other – which gives coherence to the linguistic concept of English, whether American or worldwide. Some vernaculars are closer to the Standard and to each other than others.   (Wald 1984: 17)

A standard variety like SAE is seldom included in discussions of dialects (a dialect of what?), but it is one nonetheless. It has features that we can describe, just like every other dialect of English. The degree of "standardness" is irrelevant. And, vernaculars are not necessarily based solely on nonstandard, minority dialects. For instance, the variety that the majority of Southern Californians use at home, at work, and at school in normal, casual conversation is a vernacular form of regional (California) English that contains many nonstandard features, e.g., nonstandard uses of "like," "all," and "some." Most younger speakers have seen their English teachers cringe at the usage of some of these forms, especially "like." It can be a real challenge to speak without it, like when we're all upset, and so not into having to think about, like, what we're like saying, like when some teacher tells us to stop saying "like."[5] We may expand our linguistic capacities as we grow up, through interaction with others outside our individual communities, at work and in school, but the first language that we are exposed to will surely leave its mark.

---

4. The term *ideal* implies best. For example, the *ideal job* is the one a person dreams about: the boss and all co-workers are kind, pleasant, and patient; it pays a lot of money and requires little effort; it provides long, paid vacations and a pleasant environment. While it isn't likely that anyone would turn down such a job, the ideal is still something relative and subjective. So, calling SAE the *ideal* English is to think of it as the best, clearest, and most articulate form of English that one can possess. Even though it has specific and identifiable features, it still depends on somebody's judgment. SAE is constantly changing, and its features change in the process. It is still determined by those who are in charge of education, English teachers and authors of textbooks and dictionaries.

5. This sentence is an example of several nonstandard forms that are very frequent in So. Cal. English, in particular, the vernacular of most people from the "Valley" (San Fernando Valley). Sociolinguists call some usages of "like" and "all" *quotative*, for example: "He was like, 'Get a hold of yourself, man.'" "Some," a quantifier indicating an unknown quantity (not number) is used in place of the indefinite article "a/n," for example: "Some teacher walked up to me in the hallway."

The place where the tension among dialects is perhaps felt most is in the classroom, where children bring their vernaculars into contact with the standard. Educators may notice features in a child's speech that differ from those in a standard variety. They may have to remind themselves first of all that these differences are not the result of a conscious decision on the child's part. So, for teachers, who typically understand the destructive nature of stereotyping, there is a caveat. They must be conscious of the so-called *deficit model*, to guard against unfairly prejudging a child. The deficit model links nonstandard varieties to some sort of social or *cultural deprivation*. The assumption is that speakers of the standard have already received the benefits of American society and culture in shaping their minds and abilities, and, therefore, possess the necessary tools for unlimited advancement. Conversely, those who don't speak the standard have been deprived of these benefits, and the potential for success has been withheld from them in some way by their minority culture.

Most educators today prefer the *difference model*, an educational model that emphasizes that the differences among regional and social varieties are simply the normal consequences of language change (the evolution of language). Particular language characteristics do not necessarily imply a lack of educational, social, or cultural opportunity. In addition, individuals can certainly be *bidialectal*. Bidialectalism is the normal state of things among AAVE speakers (where switching from dialect to dialect was part of early code-switching studies).

In the not too distant past, varieties that differed from the standard were considered *substandard*, as if there were a food chain of dialects with the best and fittest at the top and the worst and unfit at the bottom. (The cultural dominance of one variety over another does not mean that it is inherently superior.) Society treats disfavored dialects as lower or less acceptable, which is all part of the process of *social stratification*. Stratification refers to the tendency of society to divide into levels, or strata, and to evaluate those levels according to social variables like socioeconomic class (e.g., middle versus working class). These variables (factors) include occupation (relative prestige of a particular job or profession), income, and education (e.g., dropout versus high school, college, or post-graduate degree). These factors are weighed subconsciously, and associated with particular linguistic features (Labov 1972:43–69). Differences can be as subtle as the pronunciation of the single phoneme [r] in different phonological environments, one of the features investigated in Labov's ground-breaking study of the stratification of English in New York City (Labov 2006). When varieties are associated with particular groups or classes, they can become socially marked, or *stigmatized*. This can be positive. E.g., desirable groups have a positive stigma, and undesirable groups, a negative one.

One of the premises of linguistics is that every language variety has identifiable features. So, we can describe SAE, and we can also describe Chicano English, not necessarily in terms of what one has (the standard) as opposed to what the other one does not have (the nonstandard). In that we all acquire our native languages from the caregivers in our immediate environments, we learn the characteristic ways those people talk. All the sounds, words, and structures that we are exposed to at home, at work, and in the media form a pool of linguistic features from which we draw whenever we speak or write. To give an example, words like *ain't* probably exist in all languages. Wherever English is spoken, ain't may occur in casual, vernacular speech. For some reason, that little negative element has been judged (without a trial) as nonstandard, bad, deficient, substandard, or otherwise wrong. Nevertheless, it appears in songs, novels, and the speech of almost every English speaker in the world at one time or another. But, by simply saying that one little word, a child may be pigeonholed for her educational career.

1.1   Social dialects – the story of Black English

Relatively recently, sociolinguists (who study the social aspects of language) have brought social dialects (or *sociolects*) to the attention of academics and language specialists. Based on the analogy that particular varieties (regional dialects) can be associated with people from different parts of a country, sociolinguists have established that some dialects can be associated with specific social groupings of people, as well. The first to be studied in the U. S. was Black English, or *Ebonics*; it has been known by other names, such as Black English/BE, Black English Vernacular/BEV, Black Vernacular English/BVE, and African American Vernacular English/AAVE.

Until very recently, it was widely thought that Ebonics/AAVE was simply *bad* English, or "broken" English, because it "deviated" from the accepted norms of those in superior social positions, mostly those of White, Anglo-Saxon business people, educators, and other institutional leaders. BE was even thought to be the result of some kind of social deprivation, or worse, that it was an indication of the *inability* of African Americans to speak *proper English*.[6] The "evidence" was usually how enslaved people of African origin appeared to learn European languages so poorly, e.g., the creole varieties of French and English spoken in the West Indies, with little regard for the impact of forcible removal from their homeland to be transported like cattle to a foreign land, along with the social conditions of enforced servitude, intense social

---

6.   It is very important, here, to recognize that the concept of a "proper" English is a misnomer – a name that is part myth and part indoctrination. First, it is saying that there is only one kind of proper English, Standard American English. (This is discussed more fully in Chapter 7, in the context of literacy.) Second, it implies that the vernacular form of English spoken by many African Americans is not proper, defective, or just plain ignorant. This leads to many forms of hypercorrection and affected speech so that vernacular speakers elevate their English to a higher, more proper level. While this may be the stuff for comedy, it is no laughing matter for children who are exposed to constant criticism against their cultural background, which is as legitimate as any other human being.

isolation, and the long-term effects of segregation in places like the American South. Biased views such as these fit right into racist theories and attitudes, particularly in the South where the practice of slavery drove the regional economy based on expansive plantations and a large, cheap, labor force. Note, too, the ever-present association of socio-economic strata and speech.

Nevertheless, the impartial investigation of so-called Black English, particularly in the ground breaking work of J. L. Dillard (1972), has emphatically demonstrated that it is indeed *systematic* in its own right and as effective in communication as any other variety of English. Speakers follow rules of pronunciation, grammar (syntax and morphology), and vocabulary.[7] The well-known court trial in 1977, "the Black English trial" of Ann Arbor, Michigan, established a *legal* definition of Black English with a list of linguistic features that described its systematic nature (see Labov 1982), not to mention the much publicized Oakland Ebonics debate (1998–9) that once again brought it to national attention.

One obstacle for the acceptance of AAVE has been that people typically associate the *value of a language variety* with the *value that society places on the people* who speak it (Wolfram & Fasold 1974: 23f). African Americans have endured a long history of injustice and blind prejudice, from the days of slavery to the present. The variety of English associated with African Americans has suffered as a consequence. Nevertheless, every dialect of American English has had its place in U.S. society. African-American culture, as expressed through language and art, has had a tremendous impact on pop culture and art internationally, e.g., in the emergence of popular forms of music such as rhythm and blues (R & B), rock 'n roll, rap and hip-hop, and Gospel music (from Spirituals to Contemporary Christian) all over the world.

1.2 From BE to ChE

Whenever the question comes up, "What is Black English?" the answer is far from simple. There is no single, monolithic version that all African Americans speak (all the time). Instead, there are identifiable features that occur in various strengths, numbers, and combinations. Every variety of a language will have some variation from speaker to speaker for a variety of reasons, all of them social (e.g., according to socioeconomic status, locale, age, and gender). We all alter our speech according to the people we talk with. We all adjust according to our impressions of the listener, so there is variation in the speech of even one speaker. Even if we were to assume that everyone we come into daily contact with is the same, with equal proficiency in our native language, equal

---

7. There is a rich literature on the subject, e.g., Rickford & Rickford (2000), Baugh (1983), Smitherman (1978), and so on.

experience (knowledge of the world), equal education, and, therefore, social status, we may vary speech according to the way we feel at that moment.

In the literature on AAVE, alternating registers and dialects (from AAVE to SAE and back) has been called *style shifting*, or code-switching (by analogy with CS in bilingual situations). Dialect switching appears to be subject to the same factors as CS and shifting among registers, the who, what, and where of speech. The focus on style in Walt Wolfram's often-cited study of AAVE in Detroit (Wolfram 1969) adds a number of dimensions to the study of social dialects. It showed that speakers of every social stratum used certain forms (vernacular variants, e.g., *bof* for "both") less often when *reading* a text.[8] In contrast, spontaneous speech, conditioned by participants, topic, and setting, produced variable results. Age also played a role: older African Americans showed a greater number (and strength) of features from Southern American English in the pronunciation of certain vowels and r-lessness (dropping the sound of /r/ at the ends of syllables).[9] Speakers who were relatively restricted socially to their inner-city neighborhoods and *had positive attitudes towards them* were more likely to use features of AAVE with other members of the community and less likely with people outside their neighborhoods. African American speech can be highly variable (Rickford & Rickford 2000: 108). One should expect the same kinds of variation and similar factors when looking at ChE.

The study of ChE owes a great debt to prominent figures of the Civil Rights Movement, especially those who conducted investigations into AAVE that inspired the brief spurt of research on ChE in the late 1960s and early 1970s. Following the renewed interest in Black English, researchers began to notice similarities among the varieties of English spoken by so-called Hispanics around the U.S. Reactions to the speech of Chicano-Latinos nationwide were similar to those of BE, that it was also bad or broken English.[10] Some early studies characterized it as "English with a Spanish accent"

---

8. This is important for a couple of reasons. One, speakers of AAVE may pronounce words according to standard norms when reading; the variation found in spoken language, however, reflects the inherently unconscious aspects of speech. Two, ESL and language arts teachers often require Chicano-Latinos to read aloud in class. Specialists complain that it is possible to read a text (especially when practiced and memorized) without the brain actually processing language and understanding the text. I can read a text even in a language I don't know, understanding nothing, but pronounce words relatively well. (This happens with Bar/Bat Mitzvahs reading biblical Hebrew and altar boys reading Latin as part of the Roman Catholic mass.) The conclusion is that being able to read an English text out loud does not mean that the child comprehends what she's reading.

9. Gender is another factor (R. Lakoff 1975; Wardhaugh 2006: 309–322).

10. Dillard (1972) expressed the ambiguous term, "broken English" (145). He mentioned that it could refer to either a "foreigner's accented English" or to a pidgin. But, when we refer to "accented" English, we usually mean an individual's speech. A pidgin is a type of language that has both rules (though they can be variable) and a community – not just an individual English language learner.

(Santa Ana & Bayley 2004: 407), and the ability to speak Spanish as a native language was even seen as an impediment to learning English (Wald 1984: 15). However, many speakers are *monolinguals* of ChE. If it were merely bad English with a Spanish accent, the question naturally follows: "How can you have a Spanish accent if you don't speak Spanish?" Native-language acquisition is always successful, so children do acquire the language of their community. As in the case of AAVE and African Americans, ChE is the native language of many Chicano-Latinos in Southern California; therefore, many are monolingual, native speakers (Bayley & Santa Ana 2004).

Nevertheless, there is still a question of what exactly constitutes ChE, who speaks it, and where it is spoken. Many misconceptions persist despite current research. For instance, many early descriptions of "borderlands" language (the varieties of English and Spanish spoken in adjacent areas on either side of the U.S.-Mexico border) borrowed terms from language contact studies such as "pidgin-like" or "creole-like" languages. The reason was that some researchers earnestly sought parallels with AAVE, which may have had its origins in plantation creoles (e.g., according to a Creolist Hypothesis).[11]

AAVE and ChE have their similarities, but there are significant differences, as well. Evidently, Black and American Indian (and Chinese) pidgin Englishes reached the American Southwest (Brandt 1982: 35–37), so pidgins were in evidence. However, pidgin varieties typically emerge among several groups that have no language in common, for a very narrow set of functions, mainly for business or trade. For instance, in African nations where many indigenous languages are spoken in particular areas, pidgin forms of English have emerged to fulfill these particular purposes. However, they are, by definition, no one's native languages. Pidgins appear to be mixtures (contact languages), with a relatively small vocabulary taken mostly from one language, the *lexical donor* (or *superstrate*), combined with the grammar of the *recipient language* (or *substrate*) reflecting greatly simplified syntactic patterns of the underlying native languages of the pidgin creators.[12] For example, a patchwork of varieties known as Nigerian Pidgin English (which can vary from village to village), is based on English words, but the grammar and pronunciation is from the surrounding African languages.

---

11. The Creolist Hypothesis states that plantation laborers of African origin may have spoken pidgin varieties of English which they brought to colonial America with them. These pidgins later developed into creoles when they became the native language of children born on the plantations. Many laborers learned their English from other laborers, so they maintained the pronunciation patterns and other grammatical aspects from their native tongues (via transfer). Some have theorized that on particular plantations, the social conditions were right for a creole to develop. Therefore, a creole gradually evolved into the dialect of English spoken by many African Americans. It has lost almost all of its creole characteristics, but many features have survived from an African past (Baugh 1983: 12).

12. See Thomason (1997: 1–7); and Holm (1988: 4–9) for definitions of pidgins and creoles.

Creole languages generally emerge in two ways, as (a) a community adopts a pidgin variety as its own language (and the language takes on a life of its own), or as (b) a community adopts an aggregate of learners' varieties (or interlanguages – ILs) as a model for acquisition instead of a pidgin, as a result of drastic and rapid shift to the language of colonizers (Field 2004: 127, 133–134). In either case, the social circumstances are generally catastrophic. Creoles become native languages, especially as children acquire them from birth, and expand in various ways to fill *all* the functions of a native language – not just the narrow range of a pidgin. This occurred in English-based creoles when African-origin people were brought to the British-run colonies as slaves and forced to learn and use English as their only language.[13]

Over the years, the literature on Chicano English has certainly grown, but not to the extent as that on AAVE. One possible reason for this is that there was insufficient evidence to support the proposed analogies. Evidently, the social situation in borderland areas between Mexico and the U.S. has never approached the same levels of servitude and oppression. It is true that learners' varieties of English were commonplace as means by which the non-dominant social group communicated with the socially dominant English speakers; the asymmetry is there with English clearly the dominant language. As expected, borrowing is much more frequent into Spanish varieties from English than the reverse. But, there is no evidence to suggest that ChE developed from a true pidgin or creole language, though some sort of language mixing (e.g., borrowing) has contributed to externally-motivated language change.

2.   Likely origins of ChE

The predecessor of any Chicano-Latino form of English in the area now known as the Southwest U.S. most likely emerged as a consequence of community-wide bilingualism. Speakers of English came into close areal and social contact with speakers of Spanish as they entered an area where Spanish was the predominant language. Individuals learned each other's languages and bilingualism had its start. As more and more English speakers entered the region in the first half of the 19th century, the two linguistic giants were probably on fairly equal footing. Spanish speakers started to learn English, probably

---

13. Field (2004) argues that community-wide learners' varieties can lead to ethnic versions of standard languages, e.g., various varieties found in Europe that have arisen among immigrant workers. They may resemble creoles morphologically (e.g., with simplified verbal morphology) but they are not legitimate pidgins for obvious social reasons. They are part of the development of a bilingual community that may or may not be headed towards shift. While a bilingual mixture and code-switching may also emerge, the children of the first generation of immigrants essentially become native speakers of the language of the host country.

to promote trade between Mexico and the U.S., and English speakers learned Spanish because they desired access to natural resources (e.g., animal pelts and silver). Spaniards were the colonists already in contact with indigenous cultures and languages, from Texas to California, with Santa Fé, New Mexico, the political and cultural center. Towards the outbreak of the Mexican-American War, the number of Anglos went up dramatically as they strove to out-populate the Mexicans and dominate the region. As the war commenced, U.S. forces invaded southward, occupying several major cities, even to the capital Mexico City. The ill-prepared Mexican Army was no match for the well-trained U.S. forces; the fruits of victory for the Americans consisted of more than one-third the territory of Mexico. The Mexican government had reason to fear losing sovereignty over the entire nation, its land and people (Nash et al 1990: 452–3).

Given this likely history, contact became more intense as English became the primary language for government, education, and the economy. While much has been written of the endless legal wrangling that resulted from conflicting interpretations of the Treaty of Guadalupe Hidalgo (which ended armed hostilities), the social and political consequences created a vast area of cultural and linguistic contact in which Spanish was clearly the non-dominant and recessive language.[14] So, it is probably best to look at ChE as emerging in a community that was becoming bilingual, and not as a variety like a pidgin or creole that rapidly and completely replaced a native language. English was foisted upon them, to be sure, but it did not develop among people who struggled to learn a language under extreme circumstances of forced labor. Mexican and indigenous families were able to maintain normal social networks though they were disrupted in various ways (perhaps temporarily) by the creation of a new national border.

Thus, the first and most obvious source for a *Hispanic* variety of English in California was contact between English and Spanish in the American Southwest. Because of the long history of contact, it is a mistake to think of it as something new or exclusive to urban areas as a result of recent immigration.[15] English was learned as a second language by many at least as far back as the mid-nineteenth century, among speakers of indigenous languages and multilinguals in Spanish and/or indigenous languages, so we might anticipate learners' varieties and "accented" English. One will undoubtedly find historic communities with a wide range of proficiencies in the various languages and an equally wide range of attitudes towards Spanish and English and their speakers, depending on attitudes towards cultural assimilation (once Hispanicized, then Americanized). Consequently, we can assume that Spanish-influenced varieties of English have existed

---

14. For an overview, see Griswold del Castillo (1990).

15. Evidence for the influence of English on the Spanish of the Southwest goes back to the very early 20th century (see, e.g., Espinosa 1915), which suggests that the existence of contact phenomena goes as far back as the late 19th century, if not earlier.

for some time, from the U.S.-Mexican borderlands northward to the rich agricultural areas of the San Joaquin Valley of central California, where the labor force has traditionally relied on immigrant workers from Mexico (e.g., the grape pickers that became symbolic of the farm workers union and famed activist César Chávez).

Fast-forward to 21st-century Southern California. The majority of the Chicano-Latino community consists of a combination of peoples, from the original inhabitants of Spanish (and then Mexican) California – the original *Californios*, along with the thousands of in-migrants from other areas of the Southwest and Mexico. Long-term immigration since just prior to statehood (1850) has also contributed to the character of this unique Chicano-Latino community. Residents of typical *barrios* or neighborhoods associated with the building of the railroad and permanent linkage with Mexico in the early 20th century, plus those in rural farming areas of the contiguous counties of San Diego, Orange, San Bernardino, Riverside, and Los Angeles have a long-standing, multi-generational status. Internally, members of various neighborhoods maintain contact with family and friends in other parts of the Southwest (and Latin America), and certainly with people in adjacent counties.

2.1   The influence of Spanish on ChE

It is not always easy to identify ChE, and to distinguish precisely between the dialect and English with a Spanish accent. It is most likely a continuum, similar to the differences among ChE and other varieties, e.g., the California regional dialect. Another possibility is that it has its own unique Chicano-Latino pronunciation patterns not necessarily linked to knowledge of Spanish or ethnicity. One doesn't have to belong to a certain race or ethnic group to live in a particular neighborhood and learn the language of its residents. Living in a relatively homogeneous, multi-generational neighborhood is how particular ethnic speech patterns can be transmitted from generation to generation in English without direct knowledge of a heritage language, for instance, the Yiddish-influenced English of New York City (and Los Angeles), German-influenced speech of the Pennsylvania Dutch in parts of Iowa and Pennsylvania, and French-influenced speech in Quebec, Canada.

In urban centers, the situations can be more concentrated, with more intense contact the rule. For example, in Los Angeles, a combination of factors has shaped the demographic nature of the community for over a century. Constant in-migration (a) directly from Mexico (and out-migration back to Mexico) and (b) indirectly via population movement from areas of Arizona, New Mexico, and Texas (with a historic link with El Paso) has created a kind of circulation effect similar to the one noted in the Las Cruces triangle (the neighboring cities of Las Cruces, NM, El Paso, TX, and Juárez, Chihuahua, Mexico) and in San Diego-Tijuana. The constant influx of monolingual Spanish speakers into Southern California helps to replenish the supply of native speakers as models for native Spanish pronunciation and vocabulary. Meanwhile, a majority of U. S.-born Chicano-Latinos speak English natively and Spanish in varying degrees, from full to zero proficiency.

The ways in which the languages are used in each contact situation can vary – each is unique. Garcia (1984) notes that vernacular English (at the time of writing) was the language of the home in East Los Angeles, an unincorporated area in L.A. county whose population is a vast majority Chicano-Latino (Mexican-American). Any person who may appear Chicano-Latino was addressed in English first because to do otherwise (speaking Spanish first) may be embarrassing, even insulting: "In East Los Angeles, people who look Mexican should be addressed in English first, and then in Spanish if necessary and the speaker is able to do so. Being addressed in Spanish by a bilingual who is a fluent English speaker is likely to offend the native-born, as the implication is that they are recent immigrants [newcomers] and therefore lower in social and economic status than the speaker" (91). Grandparents and members of older generations were also often addressed in English (whether they are proficient in the language or not). In other bilingual communities where the maintenance of Spanish is emphasized, in, say, Miami or El Paso, this is not done. In those cities, one must address one's elders formally in Spanish. Times may be changing. Newcomers, who have been arriving in the L.A. area in increasing numbers in recent decades, are characteristically Spanish monolinguals or recent learners of English and generally lack proficiency in English. They have traditionally taken the lower-status jobs and have occupied the lowest rung on the socioeconomic ladder.

2.2 Substrate and adstrate

The influence of Spanish can come from different directions, from either the NL (via transfer) or from other community sources. In historical studies of language spread, the underlying language is called the substrate language. Consequently, influence comes from underneath, from the unconscious knowledge of the original heritage language of the community which rises up, in a sense, into the language being learned. Transfer occurs during normal processes of SLA, and it is unavoidable, automatic, and natural.[16] It happens to every person who tries to learn a "foreign" language as an older adolescent or adult. It is typical of people who apply characteristics of their

---

16. Some historical linguists cite substrate sources in the development of different Romance languages throughout southern Europe, e.g., Basque in Spain and Germanic languages (the Franks) of France. It is also obvious that Irish and Scots Gaelic have influenced the native Englishes of Ireland and Scotland, respectively, and that various Hindi and Dravidian languages have influenced the development of Indian English.

native language (NL or L1) to the sequential acquisition of a second or subsequent language (SL). This also presumes that learners speak an interlanguage (IL) variety of English. They are at a stage of gaining knowledge of English from zero (no knowledge) to whatever level of mastery they might eventually reach.

The other way Spanish can influence speech is laterally, or indirectly from *adstrate* sources (surrounding language varieties). Individual neighborhoods (*colonias*) may consist chiefly of people from an individual state in Mexico, e.g., from the states of Michoacan or Jalisco. When English is spoken, it is likely an interlanguage (IL) variety. Community-wide ILs can be very successful for communication purposes, and they may very well be the principal input for acquisition for children (and adults). We all acquire the speech patterns of the people around us, and, if we are surrounded by people with characteristic pronunciation patterns, we are likely to acquire those patterns, too. A child may, therefore, be exposed to a patchwork of Spanish-influenced varieties of English from birth. Because of its unconscious and almost ubiquitous nature, this type of "accent" may go relatively unnoticed.

Multiple varieties of Spanish (from different countries of origin and socioeconomic strata) may be spoken by certain family members, among grandparents and members of the parent's generation. They may not be directed towards the child, who is most likely addressed mainly in English. While some parents may feel that their children should, therefore, understand at least some Spanish, acquiring it by "osmosis," that may not be the case. In the presence of CS and borrowing from Spanish (one-time CS), many Spanish words can still seep into the child's emerging English depending on the frequency of those words. Prime candidates are frequently used household words (e.g., *baño* – "bath-bathroom"), foods (*pan, leche, agua,* for "bread," "milk," and "water," respectively), forms of address (such as *tio, tia, abuelita* – "uncle," "aunt," "grandmother"), customs (*quinceañeras*, ceremonial fifteenth birthday for females), religious events (*bodas, bautismos* – "weddings," "baptisms"), greetings (*¡Hola!, ¿Cómo 'sta?* – "hello," "how are you?"), and so on. As forms and structures become conventionalized in the community (and regularized by child speakers), they become part of her emerging language, her ChE. It is difficult to say a person *speaks* Spanish when she is merely familiar with certain words. It is also very difficult to call it code-switching when a child intersperses Spanish words in her English, yet has minimal to zero proficiency in the Spanish.

Importantly, the bilingual Spanish-English community also consists of those who have acquired both English and Spanish natively in the U.S. It possible that they have acquired nonstandard Chicano Spanish in addition to a nonstandard form of English, unlike those who may have acquired a national standard abroad in Mexico, for example, and learned Standard English sequentially as adolescents or adults in school. Those who have learned their languages simultaneously in the Chicano-Latino community are also very likely to mix languages in various ways via borrowing and code-switching, especially in conversational CS in which both languages, local Spanish and ChE, are mentally "on."

We all acquire our own speech patterns irrespective of what the media may portray as "desirable" or correct (so-called Network or Media English), and our regional and social characteristics may outweigh what our teachers try to drum into our heads. As we grow and venture outside the home, our peers have a greater influence on the ways we speak than our parents and teachers. Hence, Spanish, through the accented speech of key people in the social environment, can influence the acquisition of English. This is characteristic of many known varieties of English, from Hiberno-English (Irish), to Indian English (that spoken on the sub-continent of India), and others like Montreal English with its characteristic Canadian French lilt. In fact, the influence of Spanish can be so pervasive that non-Latinos may acquire the Chicano accent merely through the interaction with ChE speakers, or by attending the same schools, living in the same neighborhoods, and from mutual acquaintances in their personal communication networks.

2.3   Contact with AAVE

Apparently, contact among speakers of ChE and AAVE has yet to be studied in depth. Impressionistically, of course, there are a number of ways contact can be viewed. Both Chicanas/os and African Americans typically self-identify as ethnic and linguistic minorities (Hispanics as a general classification surpassing African Americans as the numerically largest minority in the U.S. in 2003), so there is the "non-white" element. Both are so-called visible minorities unlike, say, the distinctions among Anglo-Saxon, Slavic, and Italian people. The term *Anglo* itself tends to be used by both Chicano/Latinos and African Americans to refer to all Whites and not just those who may have Germanic or British (i.e., Anglo-Saxon) origins.

Demographically, several large urban areas in Southern California have undergone significant ethnic changeover in recent times. For example, areas of Central and South Los Angeles have gone from generally White in the 1940s to Black, and then on to Latino with the considerable in-migration of Mexicans and other Meso-Americans from the late 1960s. And, because changeover is gradual, contact may be intense for a time, for example, in Compton, Carson, and Central and South Los Angeles (e.g., Watts), where large in-migrations of Central Americans have contributed a lot of diversity to the social and linguistic environment among peer groups. This kind of ethnic changeover has happened in other places, as well, for instance, in New York neighborhoods originally populated by Irish as Italians migrated to the U.S. Since the late 1960s, increasing numbers of Asians have also settled in Southern California, specifically in areas around central and eastern Los Angeles (e.g., Monterrey Park) and northern Orange County (south of Los Angeles).

There is a consequent political backlash as neighborhoods become composed primarily of a single ethnic group. Areas that show dramatic population shifts are often slow to respond to the need for political organization to elect representative officials from that new numerically significant group. Unfortunate examples of potential conflict, perhaps, are so-called "tables" or "mesas" (prison cliques for each major ethnic group) and the rather serious effects of gang membership – signs of ethnic disenfranchisement and social struggle. There is also the growing influence of non-white status as an expression against the nature of Anglo-American culture and its dominance in the economy and in the educational system (e.g., in standardized testing, tracking, and design of a national curriculum based on Anglo-American values and language). Many relatively young people acquire African American speech traits (idioms, slang, and even grammatical constructions) simply by listening to and participating in hip-hop culture, so the effects of pop culture cannot be underestimated.

3. Description of ChE: Vocabulary and pronunciation

One of the subplots of this book, and of this particular chapter, is "dialect awareness," or the ability of teachers and students to recognize that everybody speaks a dialect; for example, we all speak a vernacular that we've learned at home, and that vernacular can be close to the type of language used in school – ostensibly SAE, though impressions of what that actually is can be as biased as anything else. The aim is to inform educators and students that the job of language learning is common to every single human being on the planet. We don't want to create obstacles for ourselves, especially when the stakes seem so high.

Regarding attitudes, studies have shown that teachers can be prejudiced by the physical appearance of particular ethnic minority members – dark hair, brown skin, dress (Penfield & Ornstein-Galicia 1985: 71–73). Add to this the effects of nonstandard pronunciation patterns, and many children start out in a deep hole when entering the classroom. However, grammatical patterns can do even more towards triggering biased reactions, in both spoken and written language. Many sociolinguists who stress dialect awareness have always tried to be tactful in exposing where the ignorance of educators to social conditions can be harmful, where teachers contribute to the impression that education itself is hostile to certain (visible) minorities. Consequently, this subsection focuses on several grammatical features that pop up frequently in student speech and writing, in an attempt to explain where those features may come from – vernacular speech. Any prejudice that leads to stereotyping is unfortunate for both child and teacher – ignorance creates barriers, and teachers can be unconscious actors.

The goal is not to "tolerate" every so-called mistake. It is to understand the nature of language and that every child is capable of mastering a standard dialect. There is no reason to think that they can't. If we can learn multiple languages, we can learn multiple dialects. Discouraging, disparaging, and expressing frustration at a child can only have negative consequences. For example, in the practice of norming (discussed in Chapter 8), teachers are trained to look for particular grammatical features in student writing during class work and especially during testing, where children are expected to demonstrate their skills in the standard language. Nearly every one of those features that violate some standard "rule" can be traced to a source or combination of sources. A child may compose a sentence that fits every single rule in her own speech community, but fail the test. It is the job of the teacher not to destroy what the child knows about her language, but to raise her consciousness to the possibilities and enable her to use that knowledge to recognize differences (between home language and school language), and, therefore, acquire the skills that she needs in order to succeed.

Part of understanding the nature of language is to understand the speech environment. That in Southern California is quite diverse, with local varieties in *competition* with each other, and with the kinds of speech we hear in the media (from TV personalities) and other institutional settings (educators and government officials). Competition is what Mufwene (2001) refers to in his "population genetics model" of language ecology. Various features of English (e.g., sounds and other pronunciation traits, words, and structures) exist in the social and linguistic environment of speakers that constitute a pool – something like a gene pool – of linguistic features that speakers can draw upon. Features are selected, so they compete against each other. Chicano English needs to be situated in its cultural context to see how it has evolved. The features that are selected may be frequent (words used in many contexts); they may be particularly attractive (features that characterize the speech of notable community figures); or they may have multiple sources, from local Spanish and from local varieties of English. Therefore, discussion focuses on the possible origins of particular sets of features, if they may originate from a particular local variety or from multiple sources. Native speakers are seldom consciously aware of the formal features of their languages; native speakers of ChE may not be able to pinpoint which features of ChE can be associated with Spanish and which ones to English. So, some description of Spanish (and English) is included.

3.1   The lexicon

As a dialect of English, the lexicon of ChE (and all dialects of English) is essentially that of all other varieties of English, standard or not, with the proviso that it is generally a spoken variety and, consequently, typically informal, full of popular slang and other colloquial expressions, and characterized by a lot of personal involvement.[17] The grammar, too, is essentially that of spoken English, with a number of distinguishing characteristics. Note that some dialectal differences may be quite subtle, but they still can serve as markers of social or regional identity (cf. Zentella 2002). In that context, the following account of ChE is similar to most descriptions of the *grammar* of any language. It will include word, phrase, and sentence-level characteristics, including pronunciation (phonetics and phonology), morphology (word formation), syntax (word order and other grammatical characteristics), and semantics (how meanings are expressed).[18]

The typical lexicon that most people use on a daily basis is estimated to be around 2,000 words (give or take), based on how frequent those words appear in speech and writing.[19] Teaching texts that target vocabulary learning for ELLs often focus on the first (most frequent) 2000–3000 words that are critical for comprehension of a wide variety of texts (cf. Nation 1990: 21–24). When a speaker goes beyond the basic or fundamental vocabulary necessary for daily spoken interaction, she can draw from her knowledge of the standard or look in a dictionary.[20]

The principal linguistic issues of lexical access and dialect speakers are (a) identifying the source of some words, whether dialectal or not, and (b) the linguistic process used to get it (borrowing or switching systems). For instance, when a speaker of a nonstandard dialect selects a word from the standard, the result may be an instance of code-switching, dialect switching, or borrowing. It may also be just a reflection of the fact that dialects of a language share a basic lexicon. In practice, it may not make a lot

---

17. Slang is not emphasized here, and the reason is that almost as soon as it is recorded, it becomes outdated. It is the nature of slang that it is informal, constantly and rapidly evolving, and associated with the speech of particular "in groups," the cool kids in school and popular hip-hop artists, and not with the speech of teachers, newscasters, politicians, and the police. Nonstandard features are much more likely to pop up, as well.

18. The following descriptions contain common linguistic terms. An effort is made to make terms as transparent and easy to understand as possible, but some technical terms are unavoidable.

19. Concepts of core lexicon are used to determine the relatedness of languages. Typical words and word families include kinship terms (mother, father, husband, wife, etc.), body parts (finger, hand, head, etc.), color terms (red, blue, yellow), natural objects and substances (sky, water, mountain), common activities (stand, walk, sleep), and so on. These core words are notoriously resistant to change through borrowing. Consequently, varieties of English are expected to maintain core vocabulary; intentional substitutions will be noticeable, and great potential markers of identity. A person referring to a boyfriend or husband as *my viejo* is signifying social meaning and identity.

20. Some estimates of the English lexicon run as high as two million words (which has taken centuries to accrue). Spoken languages, in contrast, will have much smaller lexicons, but all languages, literate or not, have the means to create or add new words for new concepts. They can derive (create from existing materials) words internally, as English does, with prefixes and suffixes, or simply borrow a word from another language to represent a new item – English *sushi*, *tortilla*, *delicatessen*, etc.).

of difference, especially in light of the fact that this is a gray area where the state of our knowledge is still developing.

As in AAVE, ChE is not a separate language from SAE in the linguistic sense. Consequently, we should expect ChE to be *mutually intelligible* with other English dialects, especially regional varieties that are in relatively close contact. This means that speakers of, say, various forms of California or Western U.S. English will have little trouble understanding the ChE speaker, though their reactions may be influenced by social perceptions and ethnic stereotypes (cf. Garcia 1984:87; Wald 1984). Speakers within a relatively homogeneous speech community accommodate others based on shared perceptions of age, sex, and shared interests as members of a specific subgroup at school or work, or in neighboring communities. For example, members of various campus clubs or cliques may have their own individual ways of speaking, but they make the effort to be understood by other members of the group.

One source of Latino speech mannerisms is a growing Chicano-Latino literature of sorts (novels, television shows, music, and other performing arts) within a greater Latino discourse that includes a lot of conversational code-switching, the kind that clearly marks social identity or *in-group status*. Consequently, more and more individual Spanish words are modeled in daily conversation via intrasentential CS. There are also numerous terms for (mostly) Mexican cultural items, for instance, words for different kinds of food and so on for which there are no English equivalents (e.g., *mole*, *adobado, tortilla, taco, burrito, salsa…*).[21] The list of Mexican Spanish words for food items is extensive. Many speakers of SAE who do not identify as Chicano-Latino will recognize all or most of these terms.

It is important to note that most borrowings in ChE are from *Mexican* Spanish. They may not exist in other varieties of Spanish, or they may refer to something entirely different. For example, the word *tortilla* is translated as "omelet" in most of the world's Spanishes, and *burrito* is literally "small donkey." Most if not all varieties of English in contact with Mexican Spanish have borrowed many such words, plus a host of words from the Mexican indigenous language Náhuatl (e.g., *coyote, chocolate, cocoa,* and *tomato*). Other borrowed words in common usage represent relationships, e.g., kinship (terms of endearment) such as *mijo/mija* (from Spanish "my son" and "my daughter") and *viejo/vieja* (literally, "old man," "old lady" for one's spouse). Others may refer to social status such as *vato* (perhaps equivalent to English slang "dude").

---

21. Many of these terms have no translation equivalents simply because they do not exist in Anglo-Saxon culture. Roughly, both *mole* and *adobado* are sauces or marinades made with ingredients indigenous to Mexico, from chocolate and smoked chiles, respectively, with additional spices. A *tortilla* is a round flatbread of various grains eaten alone or used in the preparation of other Mexican food dishes. A *taco* is a "snack" made typically with meat, cheese, lettuce and tomato wrapped in a corn tortilla; a *burrito* is similar to a taco, only wrapped in a tortilla of white flour. *Salsa* technically means "sauce," but it is generally spicey hot and nearly ubiquitous in Mexican fare.

3.2   Pronunciation

The pronunciation of individual *phonemes* (language sounds), the *phonetics* of ChE, is generally the same as in other varieties of English with several exceptions that can stand out. Consonants are pronounced mostly the same as in SAE, with variation, e.g., a *dental* /t/ (with the tongue touching the teeth), as in Spanish, instead of the standard English *alveolar* /t/ (with the tongue touching the tooth gum ridge above the upper teeth). Regarding aspirated stops (the voiceless /p/, /t/, /k/), there is considerable variation. For example, the Spanish word *papas* (potatoes) is pronounced with no aspiration (a sudden burst of air) on the first "p." In English, "papas" (synonym for "dads" – as in the popular singing group from the sixties, "The Mamas and Papas") is pronounced with a strong puff of air on the first "p." The absence of aspiration is fairly typical, but more so in learner's varieties of ChE, which occur as new in-migrants assimilate into the bilingual community. Spanish (which has no aspirated stops) influence may vary in the speech of a ChE speaker, but we can't rule out bilingual speakers who may be dominant in one language or the other, and monolinguals who may be influenced by Spanish in the environment. It is likely that a lack of aspirated stops is associated with those dominant in Spanish or those who most heavily identify with local (L.A.) Spanish. Then again, the presence of aspirated stops may be a function of several social factors, including education in the English language and the pressure to acquire an "American" accent.

Regarding vowels, many ESL teachers have noted that speakers for whom English is a second language may try to force English into the five vowel system of Spanish ([a], [e], [i], [o], [u]) with relative success (e.g., the English word *cat* pronounced as /kat/, sounds like *cot*). For English dominant speakers, the vowels generally reflect the same patterns as other local varieties. The vowel system of California English has undergone the well-known merger of [a] and [ɔ] creating homophones (sound-alike words) *cot-caught, Don-Dawn, popper-pauper*, and so on, but it has not undergone the more socially marked "pin-pen" merger that may emerge in varieties in contact with various forms of Southern American speech. So, ChE needs to be compared with West Coast varieties, not with the speech characteristic of Boston, Newark, or Chicago. It shows no unique loss or simplification of the English vowel system. Another phoneme of note is the first vowel of the words *elementary* and *elevator*, which has lowered from [ɛ] to [æ], and in some cases to [a]. It is noticeable enough to have become a *shibboleth* of sorts regarding typical Chicano speech (Garcia 1984: 87; Wald 1984: 34).[22]

There is one way that vowels seem to be affected by Spanish, and that is in the occurrence of diphthongs (two-vowel combinations) featuring off-glides (when a glide

---

22. A shibboleth is a test-word used to distinguish an "accent," for example, to tell if a person is a local, ChE speaker, or not. It comes from Hebrew and the biblical story of Jephthah to detect fleeing Ephraimites (who could not pronounce the *sh*-sound) from local Gileadites (*Judges* Chapter 12, verses 4–6).

like [y] or [w] follows a full vowel) and on-glides (when the glide comes before the vowel). Language teachers like to point out that Spanish has "pure" vowels. They are monophthongs (they have one distinct vowel sound). There are relatively few double vowel combinations (e.g., in "ay" [ai] or [ia] as in *India* [India]). In Spanish, whenever two vowel letters occur in combination, each vowel is pronounced in succession – and there are no digraphs such as *oo*, *ie*, or *ei* of English. If we take the names of the vowel *letters* in English, which are pronounced as diphthongs (two-vowel combinations), we notice the lack of a single vowel sound: A (ɛy), E (iy), I (ay), O (ou), U (yu). In the latter two, there is an additional tightening of the lips for the rounded vowel [u] that can be quite noticeable to the Spanish speaker.[23] Some speakers of Chicano English substitute the pure /o/ and /u/ sounds of Spanish (e.g., in the words *boat* and *boot*) which may also relate to the tendency of ChE to be syllable timed (in contrast to the stress-timed quality of SAE), discussed below (cf. Fought 2003:64).

There is also less frequent *vowel reduction* in multisyllabic words in which vowel sounds are typically reduced to *schwa* (/ə/) in standard varieties of English (e.g., *photograph* pronounced [fóDəgræf] in the words *together* ([tugɛˈðər), *today* [tudéi], and *refuse* [rifyúz] (Fought 2003:64, 70; Garcia 1984:88). In addition, Garcia (1984) points out that the *-ing* morpheme marking progressive aspect on verbs is often pronounced with the tensed /i/ rather than the lax /ɪ/ and followed by the alveolar /n/ instead of /ŋ/, e.g., *glowing* pronounced as [glówin] – sounds like *gloween*. This, notes Fought, is typical of California English, but the final vowel is not necessarily as tense as in ChE. Apparently, there may also be a parallel occurrence of a more tensed (high-front) and lengthened or drawn out off-glide in such words as *life* [lai:f] and *take* [tei:k]. Fought notes that the Spanish /a/ is pronounced slightly more front than its English counterpart (2003:66). This Spanish vowel also appears to be characteristic of ChE.

Another unique characteristic of ChE discussed by Penfield & Ornstein-Galicia (1985) (henceforward, P & O), is the shift of major stress on noun (and verb) compounds – e.g., in compounds such as *downtówn* and *troublemákers* and verbal expressions *páy attention* and *shów up* (47).[24] There are numerous other examples where stress assignment on other lexical items differs from SAE with no correlation with

---

23. This sound may be an approximant, a type of sound that represents tightening of the lips to a point approximately at the full vowel [u]. This can vary from region to region in the U.S., and is particularly noticeable in British English and noticeably absent in the American Midwest (e.g., North Dakota).

24. The compound *downtówn* was noticeable in the theme song for the film *Born in East L.A.* sung by (and starring) the comedians Cheech Marin: "I don't belong here in downtown T.J." (lyrics sung to the melody of the rock anthem *Born in the U.S.A.* by Bruce Springsteen). The film was a comedy about an L.A. Chicano who was mistakenly deported from the U.S. and trapped in Mexico with no passport or resident "green card."

Spanish stress patterns or transfer (e.g., *operáte*). P & O also mention an interesting alternation of phonemes that has defied explanation, i.e., the alternation of /č/ and /š/ producing unexpected words like "sheck" for check while producing the more expected (via transfer) "cho" for show (also, Wald 1984: 23–24). Evidently, what needs to be explained is the unpredictable occurrence of [š]. Past explanations have ranged from confusion of the two phonemes to a merger (or *unmerger*) of the two, to the existence of /š/ in dialects of Spanish in Southern Mexico (via contact with indigenous languages). Regardless, this alternation has been reported among Chicanos in areas of Southern California. This "alternation," however, should not be linked to the simple substitution of /č/ for /š/, which is to be expected among SL learners of English, part of an anticipated "Spanish accent." Again, it is to be remembered that many Chicano speakers of English are monolinguals that may have no appreciable competence in Spanish – they may know words, but not the grammar.

ChE has its own particular cadence and rhythm, its characteristic intonation patterns – its *phonology*. P & O note that there is a rising intonation pattern characteristic more of question intonation (48, 49), what P & O call a *rising glide* (not to be confused with glide sounds/phonemes). The pitch level of a word appears to get gradually higher where in standard varieties the pitch would drop in more of a step-like manner. In the following example, this rising glide is on the main verb:

(1)   He was *cho-king* on it.

In this example, there is a rising glide that occurs on the nucleus (the [o]) of the first syllable of "choking" where the speaker of Standard English would exhibit a downward step (a more abrupt drop in pitch). They add: "Rising glides are not only used within the contour to highlight, but they are maintained in even more unusual environments. Even if the rising glide occurs on the last stressed syllable at the end of a sentence, the pitch remains up rather than falling as it would typically in a declarative StE statement…" (49), as in Example (2), below:

(2)   I want to be *awake*.

In (2), there is a rising glide at the end of the sentence, where SAE would have falling intonation in a neutral reading of the sentence – i.e., with no emphasis added to highlight information. Impressionistically, however, the gradually rising intonation pattern may not be as drastic as that of more standard varieties used in question formation.

The overall effect of ending a sentence with rising intonation (instead of falling) is to make a statement sound like a question, as if the speaker is not quite sure of herself. She may be hedging or remaining noncommittal by making a statement sound like a question. However, the rising glide does *not* indicate a question. Parenthetically, many teachers like to hear answers to questions that sound assertive and confident, that express conviction. The student's yea is a yea, and her nay is a nay, so to speak.

The ChE sentence sends a mixed signal, and the difference in intonation patterns can produce misunderstandings, especially about the intent of the ChE speaker. "…[T]here are some important implications for inter-ethnic communication which follow from the brief generalizations discussed above. Because prosody is such an ingrained and unconscious type of linguistic behavior, there is a high possibility that communication between Anglo and Chicano ethnic groups who are both 'supposedly' using the same language might break down because the same referents are not being used" (P & O 1985: 51).

Metcalf (1974) suggests, to speakers of other dialects of English, that this rising intonation pattern might sound impressionistically "wishy-washy…as if [the speaker] is asking a question when he should be making a statement, expressing doubt when he should be certain" (55). Fought (2003), in a detailed analysis of Chicano English intonation, expresses similar insights, reporting how earlier studies gave analyses of this type of intonation pattern. "Such intonations, used in English or Spanish, are sometimes heard in conversation or in the media as deliberate caricatures of Mexican speech patterns" (Fought 2003: 73). All sorts of assumptions about the intelligence level, educational background, desire to learn or pay attention, and so on can infer themselves into situations like these. P & O make quite the case that even teachers (who should know better) let visual (and aural) cues of ethnicity and language attitudes bias their reactions to students, especially those of color (71). This is only one reason why Dialect Awareness programs are needed for all teachers, administrators, educators, and students, to avoid passing prejudices and biased attitudes on to the next generation of educators and students.

With respect to the pace and alternation of stressed and unstressed syllables, and degrees of word- and sentence-level stress (the cadence of Chicano speech), Ladefoged (1975) discusses two fundamental types of syllable systems, *stressed timed* and *syllable timed*. In syllable-timed languages, syllables tend to have the same duration, as in Spanish. In stressed-timed languages, stressed syllables tend to occur at regular intervals of time, as in English. They tend not to be the same length, alternating between stressed and unstressed in a rhythmic pattern. For instance, in Spanish, a word like *poco* [pó-ko] "little," the vowels are identical in quality, both pronounced for the same length of time (duration), and relatively short.[25] They are pure in the sense described above. An English pronunciation of the same word would be something like [pʰów-koʷ], with the first consonant aspirated, and the o-sound a diphthong with the /o/ followed by an oo-sound (the tongue comes up) and somewhat tightened

---

25. Any native speaker of Spanish can demonstrate this; balanced bilinguals will be able to show the differences in pronunciation.

roundness.[26] In addition, the first syllable receives primary stress. In Standard English, syllables receive levels of stress; primary stress means that the vowel will not only be louder, it will be slightly longer and a bit higher in pitch. If the word is pronounced in a neutral way (with no special emphasis or question intonation), the last syllable receives falling intonation. The stressed-timed nature of English produces the particular character of limericks ("There was a young lady named Harris…"), the lyric patterns of pop music (e.g., hip-hop), and poetic devices like *iambic pentameter*.

Fought (2003) suggests that ChE is midway between the syllable-timed nature of Spanish (particularly suited for many styles of Latin-American music from *flamenco* to *salsa* to *cumbias*) and stressed-time nature of English, adding to the noticeably unique intonation patterns of ChE (70). Santa Ana (1991) notes a correlation between the lack of vowel reduction (with the occurrence of "pure" vowels in place of English diphthongs) and the impression that ChE is syllable-timed. However, Ladefoged (1975: 222) emphasizes that distinctions between syllable-timed and stress-timed languages are not meant to be rigid, all-or-nothing patterns. They are meant to refer to *tendencies* and the relative distribution of such characteristics. Performance in spoken language can be affected by different factors, e.g., as a result of individual variation or the desire to emphasize certain words. Then again, we can't rule out social factors; perhaps there is also a correlation between group identity (with the Spanish-English bilingual community) and the relative occurrence of specific features (e.g., short, pure vowels in place of Anglo-sounding diphthongs and off glides).

4.   Description of ChE: Word formation and word order

As a contact language, Chicano English is a bilingual mixture of sorts. The similarities in the grammatical structure of the two languages allow for borrowing on all levels of grammar. And, while the speech community includes both interlanguage and native monolingual varieties, the similarities can facilitate the bilingual speaker's ability to draw on the resources of both languages. For example, Spanish and English have relatively similar morphological systems overall, particularly in *derivational* morphology; words are formed in similar ways. The *core* vocabulary of English is Germanic, so it is safe to say that an ELL, after mastering the first 1–2000 words, will find it increasingly easy to acquire English vocabulary, particularly academic vocabulary. For ELLs, the derivational systems are so close that it is often remarked that all one has to do is learn to pronounce the words in English.

---

26. This oo-sound is called an *approximant* in that the lips come very close together without actually touching.

Speakers of French, Italian, and Spanish have a built in advantage when it comes to learning English vocabulary, in particular, that part of the lexicon known as *Latinate* (typically used in academic registers). Old English borrowed thousands of words from Latin via French (during the period of Middle English) and from Greek (in particular scientific terms), just as other European languages have done. So, English and Spanish have hundreds of translation pairs, called *cognates*, for instance (English first, then Spanish): *amiable-amable*; *inhabitant-habitante*; *electricity-electricidad*. Words in academic disciplines in both languages often originate from Greek (via Latin), so cognates are more of the rule than the exception, for example: *biology-biología*; *botany-botánica*; *linguistics-lingüística*. And, there are direct correspondences in specific derivational morphemes, e.g., *-ty* in English = *-dad* in Spanish (liberty-libertad), *-logy* = *-logía* (biology-biología), and *-ics* = *-ica* (physics-física). These suffixes were imported into English from Latin through French.

4.1   Word formation – inflectional morphology

Inflectional morphology, however, quantitatively differs in the two languages. For one, Spanish has gender on its nouns: every noun (and noun phrase) must be assigned to either masculine or feminine gender, with a very few exceptions, remnants of an old Latin neuter gender, e.g., *lo mejor* (the best). Spanish has no word for English *it*; so, a common ESL mistake is to refer to nouns as either *he* or *she* (e.g., "She is a nice house"). Spanish also has a morphologically complex verbal system and is considered morphologically *rich* as a consequence of the large number of inflections. The inflectional morphology of SAE is very simple in comparison. English is considered morphologically *poor* for its lack of inflections. The tense-aspect system of Spanish dwarfs that of English. Anyone who has taken a semester or two of Spanish knows that so-called verb conjugations can be a problem. The influence this has on speakers of ChE is not clear, but for all the Spanish speakers who learn English, it suggests that the concept of Tense is a familiar one, unlike Vietnamese or Mandarin speakers (their languages with no tense endings) for whom Tense is an entirely new and foreign concept.

Another Spanish trait that one would expect to pop up in the ILs of Spanish speakers is dropping of the subject of a sentence when it is a pronoun (e.g., *I*, *you*, and *she*). English requires that a pronominal subject is expressed – if the subject of the sentence is a pronoun, it must be there. Take note of the following translation pairs:

(3)   I want   English
       (Yo) quiero   Spanish

(4)   She said   English
      (Ella) dijo   Spanish

In the Spanish examples, the pronoun is left out, except possibly for emphasis or when the pronoun reference might be ambiguous. In English, there is no such freedom. Consequently, if an ELL leaves out a pronoun subject, it may be an instance of transfer, the unconscious application of a rule of Spanish when speaking English, and not knowing the English system yet. However, ChE is English, and no such omissions are possible, except on spoken, informal occasions when *all* speakers of English delete subjects (and sometimes verbs):

(5)   Hungry?

Proficient speakers can mentally recover the missing subject and verb and understand that this sentence is a reduced form of "Are you hungry?"

While Spanish has a different verb ending for every person (1st, 2nd, 3rd) and number (singular and plural), English has only one ending in the present tense (the infamous third-person, singular -*s*), and one regular past-tense ending (-*ed*), which is the same for all persons, singular and plural. However, the occurrence of regular and irregular verb forms makes the English tense-marking system a little more problematic. The English system is clearly a leftover from its Germanic heritage. As a consequence of contact with other nonstandard varieties of English, ChE speakers may use nonstandard verb forms. One that stands out is the use of nonstandard *brang* or *brung* instead of the standard forms *brought-brought* for the past tense or past participle forms of *bring*. Another is *seen*, the past participle of *see* used as a past-tense form (e.g., "I never seen that before"). For many Chicanos, the influence of the community is strong, particularly on informal, spoken registers. Standard forms for irregular verbs are usually learned in the classroom, where formal, academic registers of academic English are learned, not "on the street," so to speak, where the rules are clearly different.

Nonstandard forms are not exclusive to ChE by any stretch of the imagination. In that the history of the Mexican presence in Los Angeles includes those brought in to work on railroads and to offer seasonal work on farms throughout the state, it is likely that there has been influence from the speech of other migrants (e.g., those from Oklahoma during the Great Depression era in the 1930s in the Imperial Valley), from other nonstandard varieties found in Texas among lower-socioeconomic strata Anglos, and from daily contact with speakers of AAVE. So, it is not necessary to trace a single nonstandard form like *brang* to a specific dialect (e.g., AAVE); the occurrence of such forms in many dialects only increases its frequency and the likelihood that it will be adopted into ChE. The persistence of nonstandard forms may be the result of a lack of formal instruction in the national standard. Some may be the result of language acquisition, where nonstandard forms may be created through linguistic processes of analogy. Children typically learn by analogy, so forms like *bringed, buyed, singed* often precede *brought, bought,* and *sang,* respectively in the acquisition process.[27]

4.2 Word order – syntax

The other major grammatical area of language description is *syntax,* which includes such things as word order (which words typically precede or follow other words, e.g., adjectives and nouns), and the grammatical relationships among words (e.g., how some words must *agree* with other words based on strictly grammatical characteristics). Spanish and English are both considered Subject-Verb-Object (SVO) languages, but that may hide subtle differences. Spanish has been called *pro-drop* in the literature, which simply means that a speaker may omit (or drop) subject pronouns when the context allows. As a consequence, the verb often comes first in a sentence, which does not occur in English (except in commands). Most obvious to native English speakers who learn some Spanish is the order of Noun and Adjective. Adjectives in Spanish typically follow the noun they go with, but not always (which may facilitate the learning of the adjective-noun order of English). Spanish, however, includes gender- and plural-marking on adjectives (and classes of Determiners), illustrated in (6) and (7), below:

(6) la   casa   blanca
     the-FEM   house-FEM   white-FEM.
     "the white house"

(7) las   casas   blancas
     the-FEM/PLUR   houses-FEM/PLUR   white-FEM/PLUR
     "the white houses"

This points out what many linguists refer to as the interface of morphology and syntax. Inflectional morphology interacts with syntax. The form that a word is required to take conforms to the position in which it appears in a sentence (e.g., when the 3rd-person *-s* is required because the subject is 3rd-person, singular). Chicano-English speakers do not make English adjectives and determiners plural as required in Spanish, which further demonstrates that ChE is, in fact, English. There may be instances, however, in the use of pronouns when an English learner is translating on-line from Spanish to English and refers to a non-human noun as "she" or "he," when a more proficient

---

27. Analogy is often at the root of many "mistakes" like this. Even *bring-brang-brung* is constructed on the analogy of *sing-sang-sung*. *Swing-*swang-swung* is another. The forms *get-got-gotten* has even produced by analogy *buy-bought-boughten* in some of my student papers. One mustn't forget that many SAE speakers need to learn the differences between *lie* and *lay* and the irregular forms of *lie* (*lay-lain*) – and regular *lay-laid-laid.*

English speaker would use the correct pronoun *it*. (Spanish has no equivalent form for the neuter *it* because all nouns must be either masculine or feminine.) This, however, only demonstrates that some apparent ChE speakers may still be learning him (*el inglés*, masculine).

Other grammatical characteristics of ChE can be traced to the interaction of various levels or components of grammar, a characteristic found in AAVE, as well. What Penfield (1984) calls "consonant cluster deletion," is similar to the phonological process known as *apocope*, by which a final sound or sounds of a word are dropped.[28] Rickford & Rickford (2000), refer to this phenomenon in AAVE as "consonant cluster simplification," for example, in words like *just* pronounced as *jus'* (*bold*, *find*, and *fist* pronounced *bol'*, *fin'* and *fis'*, respectively) and past-tense markers (spelled sometimes *-ed*) pronounced as [t] as in the word *missed*, pronounced without the final t-sound ("He miss' the bus"). In both AAVE and ChE, the deletion is less likely when the word is followed by a vowel. Thus, there may be variation in frequency in the deletion of the final consonant, as in the following examples:

(8) She los' her keys. ([t] deleted before a consonant sound)

(9) She lost a penny. ([t] not deleted before a vowel)

However, in AAVE, final consonant deletion is much less frequent when the t-sound is morphemic and carries grammatical information (past tense) (Labov 1972:216–226). In contrast, Penfield adds that deletion also occurs when the alveolar sound is voiced ([d]), making this process even more noticeable in ChE, as in the following:

(10) "She toll me this…"   (Penfield 1984:79)

P & O (1985) mention the "[r]eduction of consonant clusters in word-final position," as a phonological process. They include the words *ward* (*war'*), *start* (*star'*), *hard* (*har'*), in all cases an alveolar (/t/ or /d/) is dropped. They also point out that tense-marking on a verb can be affected, for example, when a form like *involved* is pronounced without the last phoneme, leaving past-tense unmarked. So, nonstandard pronunciation and grammar can work together to influence the output, but it is always in systematic ways.

Garcia (1984), evidently the first in the literature to make this observation, contributes to this discussion by noting "glottalization of word-final alveolar stops" when preceded by a vowel. For example, in the words *needed* and *wanted*, the final consonants are replaced by a glottal stop.[29] (Verbs ending in an alveolar require the addition of a

---

28. Penfield (1984) cites only the deletion of /t/ and /d/, the alveolar stops.

29. Cf. Fought (2003:69–70) regarding all voiceless stops in word-final position.

vowel plus "d.") In Southern California English, word-final stops are typically unreleased (the articulators come together as if the sound will be produced, but the airflow is not restored by the sudden release of the articulators). In ChE in this particular environment, however, the word-final alveolar is replaced by a glottal stop (the consonant sound of the word *uh-oh*), which, when released, gives an audible sound (Garcia 1984: 88–89). In some past-tense forms that create consonant clusters (no vowel before the alveolar), e.g., *talked*, *cooked*, *jumped*, and *cleaned*, the final consonant may get dropped entirely, leaving an apparently uninflected form.

One problem associated with final consonant deletion is in spelling, for instance, when *lost* is spelled "loss," when letters are left off frequent expressions *used to* and *supposed to*, and when past-tense and past participle -ed forms are omitted, for example, in the following:

(11)   "You will be surprise."   (P & O 1985: 59)

Regarding literacy development, the most obvious issue is that children are often coached to "write the way they talk," and they attempt to map their spoken vernacular (colloquial and informal) onto a written medium. All school-age children need to learn a variety of registers of English, from informal through formal. They also need to acquire literacy, the ability to read and write SAE according to native-speaker norms, along with the mechanics of English (spelling, capitalization, punctuation).[30] In this respect, written Spanish and English do differ. For example, in Spanish, days of the week and months of the year are not capitalized (e.g., Monday-*el lunes*; January-*enero*). English spelling rules can be very complicated.[31] But, as with all speakers of nonstandard varieties of English, they also have to learn a new and gradiently different variety of English. Spelling mistakes under these conditions are understandable, but they can often be traced to a dialectal source or to the influence of the native language. But, this

---

30. Spanish punctuation includes the upside-down question marks and exclamation points, e.g., *¿Cómo está?* and *¡Mira!* ("How are you?" and "Look!," respectively).

31. For instance, the existence of double-letter combinations in English can seem terribly inconsistent to the Spanish-speaking ELL. Spanish is very consistent: letters are not doubled. The single "l" is pronounced one way (/l/), and "ll" is pronounced another (as the glide /y/ in many dialects). So, a word like "satellite" is spelled in Spanish *satélite*. English spelling rules need to be learned, e.g., the ones that double consonants to preserve vowel sounds but don't when the word ends in the infamous "silent 'e.'" Contrast *rap-rapping* with *rape-raping*, *bid-bidding* with *bide-biding*, *hop-hopping* with *hope-hoping*, *come-coming* with *comb-combing*. There are times when Spanish speakers overcompensate and put double letters where English would not put them, e.g. "*proffesor" (Spanish *profesor*, and English "professor"). Unfortunately for the Spanish speaker, some English spellings are idiosyncratic and must be learned one by one.

type of problem with literacy is in no way an indicator of intelligence or the ability to acquire/learn language.

Nonstandard dialects in contact with ChE clearly affect the speech of Chicanos in various areas of Southern California. In particular, some syntactic constructions appear to originate from AAVE. Fought (2003) discusses the following in her data:

a.   Invariant *be*
b.   Existential *it*
c.   Perfective *had*
d.   Negative concord and the use of *ain't*

Invariant (or habitual) *be* has been one of the most widely studied characteristics of AAVE, partly to illustrate that AAVE has resources that the standard may not have and partly to illustrate how one feature can be so marked (noticeable). The origins of this particular feature, however, are debated. On one side of the argument is the Africanist position which states that this feature survives in African American varieties of English from African languages, which may (or may not) have had this feature. The other position is that of the Anglicist, which insists that this feature originated from British varieties to which African-origin folks may have been exposed (Rickford & Rickford 2000: 113–4, 154). Its likely source in ChE is via contact with speakers of AAVE. The following examples were uttered by speakers of ChE:

(12)   The news *be* showing it too much.   (Jamie, 17) (Fought 2003: 96)

The uninflected *be* expresses *habitual* aspect, indicating something taking place over time, referring to an action that is customary or constantly recurring, a habit.

Perhaps less common is the use of *it* as an "empty subject pronoun," or expletive (a dummy place-holder to fill the subject position and make a sentence well-formed). The word is semantically empty because it has no specific meaning of its own, and it does not refer to anything in the preceding discourse (it does not get its meaning from an *antecedent* as do other pronouns, e.g., *I*, *you*, and *they*). In the literature on AAVE, this pronoun usage is called the existential *it*. "It" occurs where the word "there" would occur in the SAE expressions "there is" and "there are."[32] The term *existential* is used because such a sentence asserts the existence of a particular thing or entity. English has expletives, so-called dummy subjects *it* and *there*, but only "there" is considered existential in SAE. "It" is used in expressions such as "It is raining," and "It has been nice." In AAVE, *it* is used in both types of constructions. Contrast the following: (a) There's a

---

32. The use of contractions is associated with informal, spoken language. It is also noted that the contraction *there's* is used to represent either "there is" or "there are," required when the complement is plural: "There are *many poor people* in the U.S."

bee on your shirt," (b) "It's a bee on your shirt," (c) There are a lot of girls," and (d) It's a lot of girls" (Rickford & Rickford 2000: 111, 152).

(13) It's four of us, there's two of them.   (Avery, 16) (Fought 2003: 96)

Another nonstandard usage of pronouns related to the different uses of it is the frequent occurrence of *resumptive* pronouns, an unnecessary pronoun when its antecedent is present, which can occur in a number of constructions (Fought 2003: 97):

(14) My mother, she helped us a lot.

The use of *had* plus a past-tense verb has been noted in the speech of younger AAVE speakers (Rickford & Rickford 2000: 122). Fought (2003) refers to this type of construction as the *perfective had* because it looks similar to SAE pluperfect (or past perfect) used in reverse-order narratives.[33] Its use in AAVE is to highlight the main point of the story/narrative. For example:

(15) This is a story that happened to me Monday, not too long ago. I was on my way to school, and I *had* slipped and fell [compare "I slipped and fell"], and I ran back in the house to change my clothes.   (Rickford & Rickford 2000: 122)

Fought records the following example from a ChE speaker:

(16) The cops had went to my house.   (Jorge, 18) (Fought 2003: 96)

Probably one of the most noticeable constructions associated with ChE is the so-called double negative, which has also played a major role in sociolinguistics in the description of other nonstandard varieties of English and the debate between the prescriptivist (typically the grammarian who believes that standard varieties have "rules" that make them inherently superior) and the descriptivist (the linguist who describes actual rule-governed usage) debate (Fought 2003: 140).[34] One reason it stands out as much as it does most likely is because it is assumed to result from the influence of Spanish, and that is not necessarily so:

---

33. Reverse-order narratives contain two events that have happened in the past; one event happened before the other. Instead of stating Event A occurred, and then Event B occurred, the order is reversed, with the first-occurring event reported second. For example, "The police pulled up where a robbery had taken place." The event represented by the past-perfect, "had taken place," occurred *before* the event in simple past ("The police pulled up..."). Hence, this type of narrative is called reverse-order. However, this is not the intended meaning of *had + past tense*.

34. Fought describes what she calls the "Mick Jagger Comprehension Corollary." "...[w]hen Mick Jagger sings 'I can't get no satisfaction' it does not cause a sudden confusion in 'standard'-speaking listeners whereby they have to wonder if maybe since there are two negatives Mick is saying that he *can* get satisfaction after all" (Fought 2003: 140).

(17) No tengo   nada.
      not have-1P, SING. PRES. nothing
      "I don't have nothing"

Simply put, when a verb is marked negative (*no tengo*), the object must *agree* in that feature, negative, as well. A good example would be "I don't have no money," a type of sentence that occurs in many different nonstandard varieties of English, namely, those *not* possibly affected by Spanish. This makes the origin of this construction in ChE ambiguous. It can be associated with all sorts of varieties of English, from older British forms to AAVE. Negative concord as a *process* can certainly be reinforced by substrate (and adstrate) influence from Spanish (which requires it). Whether or not this particular feature comes from prior knowledge of Spanish, the influence of Spanish speakers in the general linguistic environment, or as a result of contact with AAVE or other nonstandard varieties is a moot point. It is more likely that all of the input conspires to create and reinforce this feature in ChE.

In addition, as far as anyone knows, the word *ain't* occurs everywhere English is used as a language and vernaculars exist, suggesting that both negative concord and the use of *ain't* likely originate from varieties of English, not Spanish, e.g., in the following:[35]

(18) Things ain't gonna never change in L.A. no more.

(Avery, 16) (Fought 2003: 142)

There are a number of syntactic features that can have more than one source. One worth noting is what Fought (2002) calls *subject-auxiliary inversion in embedded questions* (97).[36] Field (2004) lists a number of syntactic operations that are ranked according to *processability*, that is according to a precise linguistic approach to calculating complexity and degrees of learnability.[37] At the top of the list (the most complex) is *cancel inversion*. Every acquirer of English needs to learn subject-auxiliary inversion in the formation of direct questions (e.g., "Where are you going?"), in which the subject *you* occurs after the auxiliary *are*, instead of in normal word order of a declarative sentence, "You are going somewhere."[38] However, in indirect discourse – so-called embedded (or indirect) questions – this operation must be cancelled or blocked.

---

35. See, for example, Trudgill (1999: 104–5).

36. See, also, Penfield & Ornstein-Galicia (1985: 52–53), for discussion.

37. The rankings were adapted from Pienemann (1998 and 2000).

38. The discussion of subject-auxiliary inversion emerged from early depictions of Chomskyan, Transformational Grammar, which stated that underlying every question is a statement that goes through a series of transformations. Other views see such operations as alternative word-order pat-

An ELL must learn first (a), the rules for question formation, and then (b) the situations in which they *don't* apply. The occurrence of this type of construction appears to be the application of subject-auxiliary inversion when it should be blocked. For example, in a sentence like "Where do you live," all the rules or procedures of question formation apply, but in an indirect question, not all the rules apply, e.g., "I know <u>where you live</u>," not "*I know where do you live." However, in ChE, these apparent violations of the blocking principle have been conventionalized, and they are now part of the syntax of ChE. Blocking requires greater knowledge of the morphological and syntactic characteristics of *standard* English. AAVE exhibits similar characteristics, as do *all* English based creoles. Learnability (processability), then, seems to be at the root of this particular construction. Fought calls this it, "subject-auxiliary inversion in embedded questions," for example:

(19) I don't know what color are we, but it doesn't matter.

(Marina, 17) (Fought 2003:97)

Wald reports the following example (repeated in Fought 2003).

(20) ...then they asked them where did they live.   (A.R., 12) (Wald 1984:25)

Once again, various learner's varieties (ILs) are part of the Chicano-Latino bilingual community, and one must expect the features of community-based ILs to be part of the community's linguistic pool. This could, however, also be a result of the influence of Spanish, which places the subject of embedded clauses after the verb (in effect, reflecting the word order of direct questions). For example, a translation of (19), above, the equivalent Spanish pronoun *nosotros* "we" is optional, but if it occurred, it would follow the verb, as in (27), below:[39]

(21) *yo no sé   de qué   color somos (nosotros), pero da   igual*
       I   NEG know of what color are   (we),   but gives-3PS equal
       "I don't know what color we are, but it's all the same"

Fought (2003:94) also mentions variation in the patterns of subject-verb agreement, specifically, the absence of the third-person singular *-s* on verbs (and variation of *was/were* in the past).[40] This, too, can have multiple sources: (a) the influence of

---

terns, and that children acquire the various patterns as their language develops. Irrespective of one's theoretical stance, the terminology has stuck in the literature on language acquisition.

39. See, also, Wald (1984:25–26) for discussion of other, similar Spanish constructions where subjects of embedded clauses follow their predicates.

40. Subject-verb agreement in SAE is a very important issue for educators. Harking back to discussions of the deficit model, this has been one feature that has been used as a diagnostic for knowledge

community-wide ILs; (b) the speaker/writer being an ELL whose proficiency has not reached the point of mastery; and (c) the influence of AAVE. One cannot underestimate the power of pop culture, which is a very clear medium for nonstandard forms, and, inasmuch as lower socio-economic strata Asian-Americans may also speak learner's varieties and/or forms of nonstandard English, such features may be expanding, into the so-called Anglo community as well. In this case, it is also very likely that *all three sources* contribute to the variation, with the SAE of school being the primary, and perhaps only source for SAE features (i.e., the 3P-S -*s*).

The point that many scholars of AAVE make is that the absence of the third-person singular suffix is *not a lack of agreement*. The rules of subject/verb agreement in AAVE are just different from those in SAE. Trudgill (1999) gives descriptions of British dialects with the same tendencies: "In the East Anglian area, for example, including in Modern Dialects, present-tense verbs are entirely regular and have no -*s*, ending at all" (101). Trudgill goes on to explain that in many western and northern dialects, regularization is in the other direction, with all person-number combinations taking the -*s*: "I wants it," "We likes it," and "They sees them" (Trudgill 1999: 102). So, so-called *subject-verb agreement* can vary from dialect to dialect. This also complicates the job of the linguist in figuring out where a particular pattern may have come from, part of the debate in AAVE between the Africanist and Anglicist positions.

Fought (2003) suggests, also, that other changes are at work in ChE that may have come from substrate influences. For example, regarding the use of modals, Fought cites the use of *would* as an apparent substitute for subjunctive mood, and the use of *could* in the place of *can* to denote general ability. Regarding the former, English-speaking students of Spanish may have run into the subjunctive in learning Spanish (or French). It is a grammatical way (with special conjugations) to express hypothetical statements ("If I were you") that are contrary to fact, or *counterfactual*. Instead of using subjunctive (which is disappearing), English uses modals to express this same type of distinction. Fought gives the following example (99):

(22)   If Thurman Thomas wouldn't've dropped those fumbles, then the Bills woulda
       won.   (Avery, 16)

---

of standard English. As the discussion above of the morphologically poor English verbal system, there is only one inflection on present tense verbs, the 3rd-person present -*s*. It is obligatory – or required by the grammar of SAE English when the subject of the sentence is 3rd-person singular (he, she, it, or a singular noun), or when the subject is uncountable (or a noncount noun), e.g., *water*. Sentences such as "John loves Mary" and "Water runs downhill" are often used by grammar teachers to illustrate this pattern. Yes, this is an important pattern in Standard Englishes worldwide, but this in no way demonstrates that nonstandard dialects have no rules, that they are "illogical" as a consequence, or that they are evidence of cultural deprivation. Dialects with features and rules that diverge from the standard are merely different. They are *nonstandard*, not *substandard*.

(23)   *Si Thurman Thomas no hubiera perdido la pelota, los Bills hubieran ganado*
       If Thurman Thomas NEG would-have lost the ball, the Bills would-have won

As Fought's gloss (or translation) illustrates, it is not always possible to translate item-by-item from Spanish to English. Formal English does have a subjunctive form for the first *hubiera* ("If Thurman Thomas *had* not lost..."), even though historically English has lost most if its subjunctive forms over the centuries (only a few remnants remain). In the event that a speaker is mentally translating from Spanish to English, the lack of a strong subjunctive alternative in English will trigger the search for translation equivalence, which can amount to a paraphrase more than a strict translation – but this is clearly a problem only for translators, not necessarily for fluent bilinguals or ChE monolinguals.[41] To make the case that ChE modals are evolving (with substrate influence) in the Chicano community at large, a possibility suggested by Fought, one would need additional evidence from a cross-section of monolingual ChE speakers to show how they've been conventionalized across the community.

A similar situation exists with the unique usage of prepositions with clear influence from Spanish, e.g., when the Spanish preposition *en* can be translated as either *in* or *on* in English:

(24)   We're really supposed to get out of here on June.

(Christian, 18) (Fought 2003: 100)

Again, the issue may be the translation equivalence of Spanish *en* and English *in/on*. In the speech of ELLs, this is to be expected. However, in order to demonstrate conclusively that these particular occurrences are examples of permanent language change and that function words (e.g., modals and prepositions) are evolving as a result of contact, evidence needs to come from a cross section of native monolingual speakers of ChE.

5.   Standard Chicano English

As studies of registers and dialects have confirmed, speakers of AAVE, ChE, or any variety of English can show considerable individual variation; not every person speaks the same way all the time. It may depend on situational factors (the *who, what, where,* and *when*) and personal factors such as the speaker's individual attitudes of solidar-

---

41. The subjunctive in English is vanishing, but people who read the classics may encounter it through formal, written registers. In informal, spoken registers, it is almost entirely gone. E.g., today's speaker may say, "If I <u>was</u> you" instead of "If I <u>were</u> you" in everyday speech, and select that form in formal, written registers not knowing the appropriate form.

ity within the speech community (insider, observer, or outsider). For the individual speaker, there is a continuum of available forms consisting of both standard and non-standard forms and structures. Some features will surface in greater numbers and degrees as speakers switch from one register (or style) to another. The varieties available to the ChE speaker may range from nonstandard to standard, and from (a) *SAE*, with a greater number and frequency of standard forms (and correspondingly lower number and frequency of nonstandard forms) to (b) the *vernacular*, with a greater number and frequency of nonstandard forms (and lower number and frequency of standard forms).

It has never been controversial whether people from the Northeast U.S., or the South, or the West are *capable* of using SAE in formal, written contexts. One can speak SAE with a Brooklyn accent (though some New Yorkers may disagree based on their biases), a Boston accent (there are several), a San Francisco accent, or a New Orleans accent. Regional variation manifests itself typically in the same contexts as ethnic variation: in informal, spoken contexts. But, because of prejudices (based on racist, deficit models), there has been debate about the abilities of speakers of nonstandard, social dialects to learn the standard. Depending on exposure to various registers, every speaker of English will adjust her speech in response to the situation of speech. Proficiency in standard, written, academic registers is no different.

Rickford & Rickford discuss *Standard Black English*, "a variety in which the speaker uses standard grammar but still sounds black, primarily because of black rhetorical strategies and selected black pronunciations, among them intonation and emphasis" (2000: 222). While the African American community supports AAVE in informal, spoken contexts, there is a "distinct preference" for Standard Black English in formal, written contexts, at work and in the classroom. In the same way, we can propose *Standard Chicano English* (or Standard Hispanic English) in a broader, national context. After all, one can speak Standard English with a Russian, French, or Dutch "accent." There is no reason to think that a Chicano from East L.A. *cannot* speak SAE, unless we think according to racist and prejudiced beliefs (and the deficit model) that a Chicano does not have the capacity to learn the standard.

There is, nonetheless, debate over the role of SAE in the community. The debate has two sides. One side of the debate is the importance of knowing the Standard language. There is no question that mastery of Standard, written English has its benefits, though it is not always clear what those benefits actually are. Apparently, some teachers see themselves as "conduits" of SAE, with a commitment bordering on zeal. *Prescriptivists* (a k a *purists*) see themselves as responsible members of society whose job it is to teach SAE and to reinforce its importance as (a) the de facto official language of the nation, (b) the vehicle through which greater socioeconomic opportunities are reached, (c) and the language medium by which access to the political process is gained. In other words, when you learn Standard English, you learn the language of the U.S. As you master SAE, you increase your ability to get a job and a higher paying job, at that. And, in order to gain political representation and expression in local, state, and national arenas, being able to use SAE is a must. Teachers are responsible for the socialization of their students. Nevertheless, no one is assured that ethnic prejudices will go away as one's ethnic accent goes away. As recent profiling studies have shown, prejudices can certainly manifest themselves as reactions to speech patterns and a host of culturally influenced behaviors, including physical appearance. So, we can only hope – because we don't know – that the mastery of SAE will lessen or minimize those prejudices. It may only be wishful thinking that the prejudices themselves will go away.

On the other side of the debate is recognizing each student's individual identity, and how they view themselves as members of a community. One question worth asking is whether stressing SAE and Anglo-Saxon rhetorical strategies is prejudicial and demeans other forms of English by implication (standard = good; nonstandard = not good). This is a Catch-22: if the mechanics of formal, written English are not taught, children won't learn them. But, to put down a child's language is to put down that child's heritage, thereby creating a dichotomy between the language and culture of the home and the language and culture of school. It is not a strict dichotomy; it is a continuum among equals. And, as linguists like to point out, a child's peers are more likely to influence his/her speech and behaviors than parents and teachers. Another question that educators may want to ask is, "Do we want to force a child to make a decision between family, friends, and peers on the one hand, and strangers, teachers, and self-perceived social superiors, on the other?" It seems evident enough that both students and teachers need to become more aware of dialectal differences, to understand the ways society conditions attitudes, and to become more accepting of language variation in the classroom and on the playgrounds. Teachers may want to consider giving permission to speakers of nonstandard varieties to use those varieties in the classroom and to explore them so that they can become conscious of the differences between standard and nonstandard forms.

The awareness of dialects in the classroom is a way to make different varieties complementary. Because of similarities, children can access SAE via their own dialect. When children understand that everyone changes the ways they talk according to their individual backgrounds, places of birth, and the situation of speech, they may join the larger community.

Key terms

adstrate, African American Vernacular English (AAVE), Africanist, agreement, alveolar [t], analogy, Anglicist, Anglo, apocope, aspirated stops, asymmetrical, bidialectal, Black English Trial, Black English Vernacular (BVE), cognate, colonias, competition, consonant cluster, creole, Creolist Hypothesis, deficit model, dental [t], derivational morphology, dialect awareness, difference model, diphthong, double negative, duration, Ebonics, English Language Learner (ELL), ethnicity, existential *it*, gender, grammar, habitual, Hiberno-English, homophones, ideal, in-group status, Indian English, inflectional morphology, interlanguage (IL) varieties, invariant *be*, isolation, lexical access, lexical donor, lexicon, linguistic features, monophthongs, morphemic, mutually intelligible, national standard, negative concord, nonstandard (minority) dialect, number, nuyoricans, Oakland Ebonics debate, off-glide, Pennsylvania Dutch, perfective *had*, phonemes, phonetics, pidgin-like, pidgin, population genetics model, prescriptivist, processability, profiling, proper English, pure vowels (monophthongs), r-lessness, recipient, regional dialect, resumptive pronouns, rising glide, shibboleth, social deprivation, social stratification, socio-economic strata (SES), sociolect, sociolinguistics, speech community, Standard Black English, stigmatized, stress timed, substandard, substrate, syllable timed, syntax, systematic, tejano, tense-aspect, vernacular, visible minority, vowel reduction.

Summary

ChE is a nonstandard, minority dialect. It is nonstandard because some of its characteristics differ from those of SAE, the language of school, government, and the media. It is associated with Chicano-Latinos, an ethnic minority, so it is a minority dialect. Some unique characteristics stand out and serve to indicate a unique social or ethnic identity, and a sense of belonging to a special group. All language varieties, whether standard or nonstandard, are defined both by their linguistic features and the social groupings most easily identified with them. Society puts us into identifiable groups, and we all express how we identify ourselves in our speech. We reflect the social groups we feel most comfortable with, the socioeconomic class we identify with, and the racial or ethnic groups society seems to determine for us. Because so much of language acquisition goes on beneath our conscious awareness, we don't always know exactly what it is that marks our speech, though most people will have an opinion or two based on the ways *other* people talk.

All varieties of English share most of their linguistic features with each other. That is, there is a core to all varieties of English, particularly in grammar and vocabulary. Most differences are relatively minor. E.g., there may be differences in pronunciation and a few different words, but most vernaculars will be mutually intelligible with corresponding regional standards. A vernacular is the language learned as a native language in the home, from the people we love and depend on.

It is typically based on the specific dialect of the locale in which the community is situated, with its own individual socioeconomic and ethnic makeup and standards of behavior. In contrast to a vernacular, a national standard of English is not modeled after the speech of a particular group or locale. It is supposed to represent the ideal form of communication that all members of the nation are to use in public discourse. A standard variety like SAE is seldom included in discussions of dialects (dialect of what?); it is one, nonetheless. It has features that we can describe, just like every other dialect of English. Some vernaculars are closer to the Standard and to each other than others, with degree of "standardness."

One of the places that the tension among dialects is felt most is in the classroom, where children bring their vernaculars into contact with the standard. For teachers, who typically understand the destructive nature of stereotyping, there is a warning. To guard against unfairly prejudging a child, they need to be conscious of the so-called deficit model. The deficit model links nonstandard varieties to some sort of social or cultural deprivation. The assumption is that speakers of the standard have received the benefits of American society and culture in shaping their minds and abilities, and possess the necessary tools for advancement. Conversely, those who don't speak the standard have been deprived of these benefits, and the potential for success has been withheld from them in some way by their minority culture. Most educators today prefer the difference model, an educational model that emphasizes that the differences among regional and social varieties are the result of change. The differences do not necessarily imply a lack of educational, social, or cultural opportunity.

Until recently, it was thought that AAVE was bad or "broken" English because it deviated from the norms of those in superior social positions, mostly White, Anglo-Saxon business people, political figures, and educators. It was thought to be the result of social deprivation, or worse, that it was an indication of the inability of African Americans to speak proper English. Nevertheless, the impartial investigation of so-called Black English has demonstrated that it is indeed systematic in its own right and as effective in communication as any other variety of English. Speakers follow rules of pronunciation, grammar (syntax and morphology), and vocabulary. The study of ChE owes a great debt to prominent figures of the Civil Rights Movement, especially those who conducted investigations that inspired the brief spurt of research on ChE in the late 1960s and early 1970s. Researchers began to notice similarities among the varieties of English spoken by so-called Hispanics in the U.S. Reactions to the speech of Chicano-Latinos nationwide were similar to those of BE, that it was also bad or broken English. Some early studies characterized it as "English with a Spanish accent," and the ability to speak Spanish as a native language was seen as an impediment to learning English. However, many speakers are monolinguals of ChE. If it were merely bad English with a Spanish accent, the question is "How can you have a Spanish accent if you don't speak Spanish?"

The forerunner of any Chicano-Latino form of English in the Southwest U.S. most likely came as a consequence of community-wide bilingualism. Speakers of English came into close social contact with speakers of Spanish as they entered an area where Spanish was the predominant language. As more and more English speakers entered the region in the first half of the 19th century, the two linguistic giants were probably on fairly equal footing. Towards the outbreak of the Mexican-American War, the number of Anglos went up drastically as they tried to out-populate the Mexicans and dominate the region. As the Mexican-American War began, U.S. forces invaded southward. The fruits of victory for the Americans was more than one-third the territory of Mexico. Contact became more intense as English became the primary language of government, education, and the economy. Thus, the first and most obvious source for a "Hispanic" variety of English was contact between English and Spanish in the American Southwest. It would be a mistake to think of it as something new or exclusive to urban areas as a result of recent immigration. Fast-forward to 21st-century Southern California. The majority of the Chicano-Latino community consists of a combination of peoples, original Californios and in-migrants from other parts of the Southwest (e.g., Texas, New Mexico, and Arizona) and Mexico.

The influence of Spanish on a variety of English can come from different directions, from either the NL (via transfer) or from other community sources. Spanish can influence speech laterally, or indirectly from surrounding language varieties. An IL form of English could very well be the principal input for acquisition, and Spanish is only peripheral to the child. Multiple varieties of Spanish may be spoken by certain family members, among grandparents and the parent's generation, and may not be directed towards the child, who is being addressed mainly in English. Evidently, contact among speakers of ChE and AAVE have yet to be studied in depth, but there are a number of ways contact between the two can be viewed. Demographically, several large urban areas in Southern California have undergone significant ethnic changeover in recent times. E.g., Central and South Los Angeles have gone from generally White in the 1940s to Black, and then on to Latino with increased in-migration of Latino Americans from the late 1960s. Because changeover is gradual, contact between groups can be intense for a time.

As a dialect of English, the lexicon of ChE (and all dialects of English) is essentially that of all other varieties of English, with the proviso that it is generally a spoken variety and, consequently, typically informal, full of popular slang and other colloquial expressions, and characterized by a lot of personal involvement. The grammar, too, is essentially that of spoken English, with a number of distinguishing characteristics. Consequently, we should expect ChE to be mutually intelligible with other dialects, especially regional varieties that are in close areal contact. This means that speakers of, say, various forms of California or Western U.S. English will have little trouble understanding the ChE speaker, though their reactions may be influenced by social perceptions and ethnic stereotypes.

The pronunciation of individual phonemes, the phonetics of ChE, is generally the same as in other varieties of English. Consonants are pronounced mostly same as in SAE, with variation. Regarding vowels, many ESL teachers note that ELLs may try to force English into the five vowel system of Spanish with relative success (e.g., the English word cat pronounced as /kat/, sounds like cot). One way that vowels seem to be affected by Spanish is in the occurrence of diphthongs. Spanish has "pure" vowels, or monophthongs. In Spanish, whenever two vowel letters occur in combination, each vowel is pronounced in succession. There is also less frequent vowel reduction. ChE has its own particular cadence and rhythm, its characteristic intonation patterns. There is a rising intonation pattern called a "rising glide" that is characteristic more of question intonation. The pitch level of a word appears to get gradually higher where in standard varieties the pitch would drop in more of a step-like manner. The effect of ending a sentence with rising intonation is to make a statement sound like a question, as if the speaker is not quite sure of herself. However, the rising glide does not indicate a question. The ChE sentence sends a mixed signal, and the difference in intonation patterns can produce misunderstandings, especially about the intent of the ChE speaker. To speakers of other dialects of English, this rising intonation pattern might sound confused, lacking confidence, and doubtful, as if the student is unsure of her answer and is asking for support from the teacher.

As a contact language, Chicano English is a bilingual mixture of sorts. The similarities can facilitate the bilingual's ability to draw on the resources of both languages. E.g., Spanish and English have similar morphological systems, particularly in derivational morphology. Inflectional morphology, however, differs in the two languages. Spanish is considered morphologically rich because it has a complex verbal system. English is considered morphologically poor because its inflectional morphology is simple in comparison. Another Spanish trait that one would expect to pop up in the ILs of Spanish speakers is dropping of the subject of a sentence when it is a pronoun (e.g., *I*, *you*, and *she*). In English, if the subject of the sentence is a pronoun, it must be there. ChE is English, and no such omissions are possible, except on spoken, informal occasions when all speakers of English delete subjects. However, the occurrence of regular and irregular verb forms makes the English tense-marking system a little more difficult. Because of contact with other nonstandard varieties of English, ChE speakers may use nonstandard verb forms, e.g., nonstandard *brang* or *brung* instead of the standard forms *brought-brought* for the past or past participle forms of *bring*.

It has never been controversial whether people from the Northeast U.S., or the South, or the West are capable of using SAE in formal, written contexts. One can speak SAE with a Brooklyn accent, a Boston accent, a San Francisco accent, or a New Orleans accent. But, because of prejudices (based on racist, deficit models), there has been debate about the abilities of speakers of nonstandard, social dialects to learn the standard. Rickford & Rickford discuss Standard Black English, a variety in which standard grammar is used but the speaker still sounds black because of black rhetorical strategies and selected black pronunciations. In the same way, we can propose Standard Chicano English (or Standard Hispanic English) in a broader, national context. After all, one can speak Standard English with a Russian, French, or Dutch "accent."

Activities – topics for discussion

1. List the pronunciation patterns in English that you think sound the best (e.g., British vs. Southern), and the patterns you think sound the worst. Consider your personal reactions to the speakers with different accents. E.g., do they sound friendly, trustworthy, or educated? How does your own speech and that of your best friends fit into your "dialect landscape?"

2. Do you know anyone who is still learning English? Can you characterize his/her speech? Why do you think they sound the way they do?

3. Discuss the various dialects that you are familiar with. And, describe differences that you can detect between the ways that you talk with your best friends and with your teachers/ professors. What are some of the features that define these varieties of English? Give concrete examples.

4. Have you ever studied a foreign language? What are the types of problems you experienced? Did you ever speak with a native speaker of that language? How did it go?

5. Language profiling has been in the news recently. Examples are job opportunities: a person calls who has a particular accent, and the job is no longer available. The same person calls again and speaks Media English, and the job mysteriously reopens. Do you think this is fair? Why?

Practice essay questions

1. Describe hypotheses of the origins of African American Vernacular English (AAVE). What do you think is the best way to look at it (perhaps a synthesis of the two extremes).

2. Explain the process of social stratification. In your explanation, include how particular speechways become stigmatized.

3. Contrast some of the pronunciation characteristics of ChE with those of SAE. In your response, mention the "rising glide," stress, and differences in the ways vowels are pronounced.

4. What is Standard Black English? By analogy, describe Standard Chicano English.

5. What are some of the problems you might anticipate for the speaker of ChE when dealing with the mechanics of English?

Chapter 5

American attitudes to bilingualism

> 1. Ambivalent attitudes towards bilingualism
> 2. Three factors that have shaped attitudes
> 3. From the founders to the present:
>   Stages in the development of American attitudes
> 4. Reactions to the use of Spanish in the American
>   Southwest

Perceptions in the U.S. of bilinguals and their language abilities (their *bilinguality*) have ranged from one extreme to the other, running the gamut from the positive – that it enhances intellectual abilities overall, to the negative – that it is the cause of poor academic performance. Consequently, the history of bilingualism in the U.S. is inextricably entwined with the never-ending debate on bilingual education (cf., Gándara, Losen, August, Uriarte, Gómez & Hopkins 2010: 30–31). It should come as no surprise that controversies surrounding bilingual education repeatedly surface in the political arena, where budgets are hammered out and educational policy is decided. As a result, the national debate on the potential benefits of bilingualism and the high cost of bilingual education rages on. It is remarkable, however, how history tends to repeat itself.

It has become axiomatic in language studies that perceptions of a *language variety* are linked to (a) a society's value of the *people* who speak those varieties, and to (b) stereotypes based on their social behaviors (customs, appearance, and beliefs), especially when those behaviors clash with accepted norms (Wolfram & Fasold 1974: 23). Consequently, attitudes towards bi- and multilingualism most likely mirror societal attitudes towards the speakers of specific languages. For example, attitudes towards, say, French, Spanish, or Vietnamese reflect perceptions of the French, Latin-Americans, and Southeast Asians more than anything having to do with the nature of language. Evidently, some languages and their speakers are looked on more favorably by society than others. There can be historical and social reasons behind this and how stereotypes develop, positive or negative.

Unfortunately, the opinions of researchers in the science of language and its application to education (always on the lookout for new ways to deal with new issues) have not always agreed with those of teachers and administrators (practioners) who test various theories in the laboratory of life. Researchers to date may indeed be faulted for not coming up with accessible, quantifiable data, or "proof" for their theories on the benefits of bilingualism and individual bilinguality. However, there is little question that the public has been prone to biased responses and prejudice. Misconceptions based on folktales of the nature of language have led to very unfortunate results (cf. Moore & Pachon 1985: 154).

The other side of the coin in the debate on bilingualism (and bilingual education) is not bilingualism per se, but the place of English in American culture and history. It is linked to the founding fathers and to national identity, ignoring the true multilingual and multicultural origins of millions of Americans. A language is a language; there is nothing inherent to English that increases or lowers intelligence, and the same can be said of Spanish, German, Japanese, and Arabic, as well. How a language and culture may influence how we express ourselves is a debate with a long history, but any discussion of the affect of language on thought cannot be stretched to alleged links between language and intelligence, particularly regarding bi- or multilingualism.[1] Regardless of the outcome of such debates, there has never been a question about the central position of English in the U.S. All immigrants, particularly Spanish speakers from Latin America, know this and understand the need to learn its structures and uses, all prejudices to the contrary notwithstanding.

To address the issues surrounding Anglo American attitudes towards bilingualism and to provide some of the back story of the current situation in the Spanish-English bilingual community, this chapter provides a brief history of bilingualism in the U.S.[2] Many social and cultural factors have gone into shaping those attitudes. Most likely as a result of its rather unique (and relatively short) history, the U.S. has gone through different periods in which bilingualism has been viewed from a place of acceptance or neutrality, to one of repression and active discouragement. Bilingualism itself needs to be seen in its particular national context. To the average American, bilingualism is often framed as English plus another language, not just having the ability to communicate in

---

1. See Chapter 7 and discussions of the Sapir-Whorf Hypothesis, the Literacy Myth, and BICS and CALP.

2. Issues surrounding the deaf and hard of hearing go beyond the scope of this book. They deserve a chapter of their own, in particular, the struggle for the hearing community to understand the nature of American Sign Language (ASL) and other visual, signed languages. Signers have much to offer, especially concerning the nature of language and the language faculty (how language is represented in the brain). The history of ASL also includes ignorance, bigotry, and repression; the interference of the hearing community on the nature of ASL (trying to make it more like English with tense markers and so on); becoming bi- or multilingual by learning an oral (spoken) language; and becoming literate in English and all its social and cultural ramifications.

more than one language. This implies that German-French bilingualism in Switzerland may be fine and dandy, but it is irrelevant to the American psyche.

1.   Ambivalent attitudes towards bilingualism

It seems as if Anglo Americans across the nation have always had ambivalent attitudes towards the ability to speak a "foreign" language. A monolingual (or unilingual) perspective seems to be the rule. For example, in the educational systems of the U.S., U.K. and other nations where English occupies a privileged position, English is apparently the only language that counts with respect to literacy – or that's the impression one gets.[3] However, there is a good deal of ambivalence. On the one hand, it is a good thing and an indicator of superior education for a university graduate to have professional-level competence in more than one language (the more, the merrier). On the other hand, teachers and parents often believe that children in primary grades are at a disadvantage in school if their knowledge of a heritage language overshadows that of English. In this view, a high-level of English proficiency is seen as critical in such important academic areas as critical thinking and literacy, and favoring any language other than English may inhibit learning. Consequently, bilingual children may flounder in their studies without a sufficient amount of standard English.

For example, while many Americans certainly have negative feelings towards the usage of any language other than English in public, they still view the knowledge of particular languages positively in postsecondary education. For instance, it is desirable for a university undergraduate to have competence (including the ability to read "foreign" literature, journals, and periodicals) in more than one language. A student in the humanities will do well if she has access to French or Italian, for example, and the great literature of the *Renaissance*. If she is skilled in German, historically the language of philosophy and theology, entirely new ways to view classic, foundational literature are opened to her. The Russian language is a window into the thoughts of Eastern Europe and a doorway to an immense literature prior to and following the Russian Revolution of 1917 – key to understanding the Russian mind, the chief adversary of the West during the Cold War. One should expect to find a similar attitude towards European Spanish and literature, particularly in the context of a former colonial power that has influenced much of the Western Hemisphere. In addition, those who have opposed strong forms of bilingual education generally support foreign language programs for English speakers, especially those that might be viewed as important in an increasingly global economy. Some types of bilingualism (e.g., English-Japanese) are seen to be good for the economy (Baker 2006: 195).

---

3.   See Chapter 7 for discussion of literacy.

If a high school or university student is proficient in a number of languages, it is even considered a mark of intelligence. If the language is an Asian language such as Chinese, Japanese, or Korean, this is even more remarkable. There are European-Americans who learn such languages for business reasons, increasing their marketability considerably for high-paying, international jobs. It is often noted that Americans marvel at how adept the average European citizen and prominent foreign politicians are in English, while diplomats representing the U.S. are painfully inept in their linguistic abilities. Perhaps the American resistance to bilingualism needs to be put in a historical context. It isn't simply the international popularity or appeal of the English language ("everyone" wants to learn it), or the fact that the ubiquitous nature of English in the U.S. makes multilingual skills of such little value that they can be neglected throughout childhood education with no educational, economic, or political drawbacks. Other nations recognize the power of English in technology and business, and they emphasize the learning of English as an auxiliary language accordingly. However, a major drawback of a unilingual focus to the U.S. is that other nations understand American values and policies while the U.S. gains few insights into the world of its competitors – and potential foes.

In contrast to a favorable multilingual perspective for adults, many educators and parents have felt that speaking a "foreign language" will have *detrimental* effects on the complete mastery of English for children in primary grades. This is not a new idea. In some earlier research, bi- and multilingualism were thought to be to blame for "difficulties" from intellectual confusion and divided national loyalties to left-handedness (Edwards 2006: 15–18). Such a negative attitude flies in the face of common sense: the best way to become bilingual is from an early age, preferably from birth, particularly if we consider native-speaker proficiency and biliterate skills. Balanced bilingualism and biliteracy take time.

Some families in Southern California, nonetheless, have gone so far as to choose not to speak a heritage language in the home for fear that it will interfere with successful acquisition of English by children. There is little documented proof that this is in fact the case (Hakuta 1986: 14ff). There *is* evidence, though, that young bilinguals successfully keep their languages apart when acquiring them simultaneously (De Houwer 2005: 30). On the contrary, the child may experience *negative* consequences for *not* acquiring a language and the culture it represents that are integral parts of her background. She may lose, or never establish, relationships based on the primary language and culture of parents and grandparents. When the school system denigrates, discourages, or prohibits the usage of heritage languages in the school, that is one matter; but, when the child's own family acts to devalue a language and culture, that is another. This can only harm the child's self-image, her sense of belonging in American society, and the value that she places on her own cultural and linguistic background.

1.1   Early fears of certain "brands" of bilingualism

Historically, in spite of the fact that the U. S. has been populated by people of many nations and tongues from its beginnings, there has always been a certain ambivalence towards particular brands of bilingualism. Use of particular "foreign languages" in the U.S. has been repressed, even forbidden, especially at sensitive times. But, as British America developed, people from various parts of Western Europe were part of the mix from the beginning. In the so-called Old World, many nations had coexisted relatively peacefully for centuries, for example, the nations of Scandinavia in Northwest Europe. But, Norwegians are not Swedish, and Danes are neither, even though they may understand each other's languages with relative ease.[4] They've also had significant conflicts and territorial battles for political dominance. Like all other Europeans, they brought their rivalries with them to the New World. In the Midwest U.S., Americans of Scandinavian descent remember well the attitudes that their ancestors had towards each other in the "old country," the kind of jealousies and stereotypes that manifest themselves in ethnic jokes. The same goes for people of Germanic, Celtic, and Slavic background.

In particular, there was concern about the expanding German settlements in parts of Pennsylvania, enough to provoke fear that German was swallowing up English, and that it might prevail in terms of numbers. Regarding the so-called Pennsylvania Dutch (who are actually German), Benjamin Franklin noted even before the Revolutionary War that Germans were becoming so numerous in Pennsylvania that they were becoming a colony of aliens threatening to Germanize the English instead of the English colonists "Anglifying" the Germans (Crawford 1992b: 177). They seemed unwilling to assimilate into the English language and the culture that it represented. Nevertheless, German has never seriously challenged English as the national language, nor has any other so-called foreign language, all myths to the contrary. Each language minority group completed a *shift* to English over time. The pattern then was the same for Germans, Norwegians, and Russians as it is today for Chicano-Latinos: the first generation generally holds onto the heritage language, and by the third generation, a shift to English has taken place (Fishman 1991: 190–193).[5] Franklin's observations may have been the first time that a negative attitude towards language competition surfaced in an institutional setting. However, it has certainly not been the last.

---

4. Some languages are *mutually intelligible*. E.g., speakers of Swedish can understand Norwegian and perhaps with a little more difficulty, Danish as well. Norwegians, close neighbors of both Denmark and Sweden, typically can understand both Danish and Swedish. There are cases, however, when speakers of the same language do not understand each other's speech; they may speak dialects that are *mutually unintelligible*.

5. This follows the *three generation rule* discussed previously, in which individuals and entire groups gradually shift from a heritage language to a socially dominant one, in steps, one generation at a time.

Because many of the Europeans came as families to settle permanently in the colonies, children were cared for in traditional ways in the absence of established government control. Bilingual education – instruction in two languages – was a reasonable alternative to a rigid English-only stance in the American colonies (Crawford 1995: 23). In principle, it ensured that the language (or *medium*) of instruction was one that the child would actually understand. The goal was a balanced primary *education* in two languages, (a) the ancestral (albeit minority) language, the one used in the home and in the child's community, and (b) the socially dominant language of the nation, which was without question English. The transition from a minority language to the majority language would, therefore, be a natural one, not forced at the expense of a heritage language and culture or based on antagonism among ethnic groups. This was one of the cornerstones of assimilation, becoming like other Americans.

The situation was similar to what occurs nowadays in smaller Western European nations such as the Netherlands, where a number of distinct languages are taught and used as media of instruction. The first language is usually the vernacular of the locale in which the child is raised (village or region), and then comes a national language.[6] Children acquire knowledge of the world and knowledge of academic subjects so that they do not fall behind in their academic development while they learn a new language variety. Powerful languages with international prestige and academic clout come a little later, e.g., English with its associations with computer technology, international politics, and vast literature. The results have been impressive multilingualism without the repression of languages and cultures, the kind of thing Americans typically marvel at on their first trip to Europe.

1.2   Historical links to nationality and race

One important issue in the U.S. is simply race, in particular, European concepts of race. Throughout the nation's history, these theories have not just dealt with the major racial classifications (e.g., Caucasian, Negroid, and Mongoloid). They've been more specific. For instance, because the majority of Americans at the time were still mostly of Western European descent, discussions in the 20th Century typically involved a three-way distinction of Western European races: *the Alpines*, short and sturdy people concentrated in Central Europe (e.g., Hungarians); *the Mediterraneans*, dark people predominant in Southern Europe (e.g., Italians); and *the Nordic*, tall with light skin and hair, a minority

---

6.   The obvious exception would be an extremely small minority language in terms of numbers of speakers. The history of language choice in some European nations (e.g., Spain) have involved the repression of languages like Basque (Euskara) that became emblematic of separatist movements. The issue of minority languages has evolved in Western Europe, especially in the emergence of a united European economy and a political system.

worldwide except perhaps in Scandinavia (Gossett 1963: 354–355; Crawford 1992a: 59). This last group was also linked with people of Northeast Germany and England, and, presumably, their descendants in the United States. Such discussions did not yet include the vast numbers of Caucasians of Slavic origin (e.g., Russians and Poles) and many other groups considered "White" nonetheless. So, even among so-called White folks, there has been a hierarchy according to racial status, with Anglo-Saxons near or at the top. Around the beginning of the 20th century, discussions of *Americanization* made explicit the need for conformity to Anglo-Saxon cultural norms, assuming that superior culture accompanied superior racial stock, with other European "races" targets of sharp political and social pressures to abandon their languages and cultures.[7]

Some recent authors mention *visible minority* status (those who don't look European) and unequal treatment. This assumes that Anglo American attitudes have always been positive towards other European settlers, usually most favorable to those from the Northwest of Europe who shared physical traits and a similar European culture with Anglo-Saxon England.[8] But, this has not always been the case. Physical appearance may have helped the assimilation process in the long run, but there has always been social pressure to abandon Old World languages in favor of English. This pressure has been particularly strong towards relatively larger language minority groups such as speakers of various German varieties that have appeared threatening at times in terms of numbers, and especially around the time of the great world wars.

In today's cultural milieu, where visible minorities play increasingly politicized roles, there has been talk of "Hispanophobia," an irrational fear of Hispanics (and Spanish) based on racist stereotypes (Crawford 1992a: 138; Zentella 2005: 1). One common accusation is that Latinos are *unwilling* to assimilate, an accusation that has been used before against other immigrant groups. In this view, it's no wonder Hispanics have voted against making Standard American English the national language required for all governmental transactions, e.g., in the process of citizenship. Some Latinos, indeed,

---

7. The population of the British American colonies was predominantly of Anglo-Saxon or Northwestern European racial stock. The appearance of relative homogeneity was reinforced by the fact that 95% of the immigrants from 1820–1860 were from the Northwestern Europe (Wiley 2007: 62).

8. The term *visible minority* was coined in Canada to refer to citizens who were neither aboriginal/First Nation people or visibly white in color. As a term, it is under fire, partly for linking skin color with ethnicity; e.g., the term Caucasian applies to people of a wide range of physical characteristics and skin tones. In addition, minority (less than 50%) contrasts with majority (more than 50%), and in an increasing number of urban situations, traditional majorities are being outnumbered by so-called minorities, rendering both terms (majority and minority) meaningless. A candidate that receives the largest number of votes among three or more has a *plurality* of votes, not a majority. (See S. J. Gould's *The Mismeasure of Man* for a tour de force of 19th century theories of race.)

may have mixed feelings about assimilating into mainstream American culture and taking on conservative American values that seem stacked against them.

The political rhetoric typically includes allegations that Hispanics are consciously trying to out-populate Anglo Americans through massive, unrestrained immigration and high birth rates (sometimes blamed on religion and attitudes to birth control). "They" don't adhere to Anglo American views of zero population growth or the size of the ideal family (Crawford 1992a: 152). They are accused of trying to outnumber "Americans" and somehow dislodge Standard English speakers from their rightful place of dominance, as if there were a massive plot to take over the country. On one side, there are those who view themselves as the "real" Americans, gate-keepers of the American dream and proponents of Americanization. On the other, there are many who feel that language is merely a ruse or an excuse to preserve the dominance of one group over another, while concealing the real reasons for struggle, an underlying racism and an unwillingness to embrace change or truly share political power (cf. Crawford 1992a: 148ff).

The renowned sociologist, Joshua Fishman, discusses a peculiar sense of insecurity that Anglo Americans have about the leadership role of English and their fear that they may have to share power. Fishman suggests that speakers of English should rest assured of the place of English in the nation and in world affairs. He wonders why a state like California would pass legislation in 1986 declaring English its official language. After all, neither the U.S. nor the U.K. has ever declared an official language. He simply asks what has happened and why:

> In what has been called the 'century of English,' at a time when English is the world's most prestigious, most effective, and most sought-after vehicle of communication the world over; when political careers in non-English-mother-tongue countries are made or ruined partially on the basis of whether candidates for national office there can handle English effectively...; when English is still spreading and gaining uses and users in the entire non-English-mother-tongue word; why should a concern for its functional protection arouse so much interest in the wealthiest, most prestigious, and most powerful English-mother-tongue country of the world, a country in which fully 85 percent of the population is of English mother tongue and anywhere between the 94 and 96 percent of the population is English-speaking? [speaks English well]   (Fishman 1988: 165–166)

Fishman also notes that, if inter-ethnic and linguistic division are actual (not just perceived) threats to the character of America, then, following some kind of nativistic witch-hunt in search of the culprits is not the answer. Weeding out those who do not speak English well will not solve the social and economic problems of the nation. English-only advocates "are leading us away from real solutions to the causes of this threat and orienting us to the pursuit of mere symptoms and byproducts," thereby distorting the real problems and precluding real solutions.

2.   Three factors that have shaped attitudes

Historically, there have been three basic factors that have shaped American attitudes to bilingualism, each one complex in its own right with links to the economy and the evolving character of American society: (1) *Immigration*, (2) *Education*, and (3) *Language*.

The topic of immigration begins with historical trends during different periods in the development of the United States, especially the impact of immigration on such matters as (a) the availability of jobs and housing/residential patterns, hence, the economy. Controversies over (b) laws governing residency and citizenship are not far behind. The reactions of people to immigration issues may also influence or exacerbate (c) majority biases of the innate abilities of immigrant groups linked to ethnicity and race. When the complex topic of education arises, we are typically drawn to the complex interplay of (a) the socialization of children (acculturation of values), (b) educational practices such as tracking (streaming), and (c) the roles of schools in language education and the economy (e.g., the ability to gain employment and higher salaries), hence, the socio-economic effects of education. Education, therefore, includes more than merely thinking of what's best for the children.

Intimately intertwined with both immigration and education is a set of common beliefs about the nature of language, e.g., assumed links between (a) language and culture, (b) language and nationality in the search for a sense of nationality and a need for uniformity and cultural homogeneity (e.g., links to concepts of "Americanization"), and (c) reactionary views of "foreign" languages – that they are somehow competing with American English for acceptance. Perhaps the most obvious link among these basic concepts is the economy. When things are going well, little thought is paid to issues of immigrants' rights and the education of their children. However, when times are tough, one issue can definitely lead to another, like a string of dominos, and the entire national focus can shift to a host of interrelated problems. The blame is easily placed on the most visible perceived "threat."

In addition, these three basic factors can interact in dynamic ways. For instance, when a large portion of the population feels threatened by a sudden influx of "foreigners," we can expect a push for immigration reform. There may be increased competition for jobs, leading to fears by the ethnic majority that immigrants will work for less money and a sense of dread at the possibility of losing jobs, wages, and benefits. These fears can manifest themselves on the home front, as well, with rapidly changing demographics (ethnic turnover of particular neighborhoods) and increased competition (rising prices) for housing, particularly, in densely populated urban centers and their immediate suburbs. Some consequences of this chain reaction will be that concerns about educating the children of those foreigners will be negligible, amid worries of an overburdened school system. Importantly, there will be fears that immigrants and their children are threats to cultural homogeneity and an American "way of life."[9]

Nationwide, compulsory education, a relatively recent phenomenon, leads one to believe that the educational system will grow as needed, particularly in a democratic society.[10] If one of the responsibilities of education is language instruction, then it only seems reasonable that it should grow accordingly. As Gee (1992: 119) points out, experienced educators know a lot about language instruction and how to teach SAE to speakers of other languages. In U.S. society today, with the tremendous growth of native and second language-acquisition research and language pedagogy into an immense literature, one may get the feeling that language teachers must have been totally inept for millennia and ignorant of successful teaching methods. But, there is no reason to think that educators in other countries or in past centuries have had significant difficulties in teaching languages. Latin was spread by the Roman Empire, Chinese by the various Chinese dynasties, and Russian by the Russian Empire. It has always been an advantage to know the imperial language or language of a dominant social elite. Groups of people have left their homelands for various reasons and adopted new nations, as well. The movement of smaller groups of people and the survival of language minorities within empires have always included learning new languages and becoming bilingual. International, multilingual centers of trade and commerce have existed throughout the world since the dawn of civilization.

Therefore, there is no rational reason for the U.S. educational system to be in constant turmoil over language policies or teaching methods. Discussions of resources and funding are typically political. Some approaches to teaching are deemed too expensive for political reasons, e.g., specific bilingual methods regardless of their proven effectiveness. The prime example is the continuing haggling over bilingual education versus teaching English as a Second Language (ESL). Politically, no one wants to fund anything that they simply don't want. If public perceptions are that a certain immigrant or minority group is lazy or does not want to participate in Americanization and the American Dream, the idea that a humble newcomer can achieve wealth and security through hard work and determination, then that offending group should expect to be isolated and unwelcome. This has happened to indigenous peoples (American Indians), the Irish, Italians, and Eastern Europeans at different points in U.S. history.

---

9. The presence of multigenerational or multifamily homes is one example of going against Anglo Saxon norms. Although it may be a cliché, to the European American, "a man's home is his castle." There is a powerful communal influence of the extended family in most Latino cultures, something that seems contradictory to the individualism that is representative of U.S. society.

10. The state of Massachusetts was the first to pass a law making education in the primary grades compulsory in 1852. It wasn't until 1918 that all states had passed laws requiring that all children should receive an education.

Various "English-Only" initiatives are clear reactions and signs that public attitudes can be manipulated and exploited for political purposes. Immigrants don't (always) go away, but they may struggle to assimilate, making a potentially serious and long-lasting social problem worse, not better.

Educational policies are typically caught between the two, immigration patterns and beliefs about language. As a consequence, there are two over-arching themes that continue to challenge educators: (a) the *medium of instruction* – the language used to teach academic subjects; and (b) *language education* – being taught how to speak and write a standard language. These are two separate issues. English is obviously the language of power in the U.S., so a majority opinion wants children to be taught in Standard American English as the medium of instruction, as difficult as that might be to define. But, there are millions of children who don't acquire standard varieties of English at home and in their respective communities. Some acquire a different language or a different, nonstandard variety of English. This means that these children must be taught Standard English in school (which involves language education), taking valuable time away from the study of academic subjects while they learn the language of instruction. This puts many children at a disadvantage from day one. Their first exposure to school in America can be traumatic if they simply can't comprehend what their teachers are saying to them. They encounter strange, unfamiliar circumstances, unfamiliar faces, and all in an unfamiliar language. If they also encounter animosity based on ethnic or immigrant status (during tough economic times), their initial experiences can only be negative.

3.   From the founders to the present: Stages in the development of American attitudes

One of the most persistent American myths is that *our* forefathers picked up English on their own "back in the day" the hard way, by the sink-or-swim method, that is, the ones who didn't already speak English. They just naturally picked it up as they went along with no special classes for newcomers, no coddling by government agencies, and with very little sympathy from other immigrant groups. They came from their old countries in Europe to what seemed like a land of unlimited opportunity and made successes out of themselves, all with no help, no massive welfare programs, and no federal assistance. The stories of such figures as the Scottish-born Andrew Carnegie, who rose from near poverty to untold wealth through sheer determination, have long been held up as examples of the American Dream and what could happen in a land of equal opportunity through lots of hard work. The implication is that the early non-English speaking immigrants learned to swim; nobody sank or drowned (linguistically) because there was just something about those folks that led to good results and prosperity.

While there undoubtedly were dramatic success stories, many of them certainly failed. It was very likely that these early immigrants had to succeed with little or no education, as well. Finding work, assimilating into a new culture, and attaining a high degree of proficiency in a second language as an adult is no easy task, and many people would have failed without the community-based support systems that were in place.[11] The second generation, their children, were much more likely to reach mastery of English, while members of the third or fourth generation were the first in their families to finish high school or grow up as part of the middle classes. This was particularly true of the massive waves of immigrants who came to the U.S. towards the end of the 19th and beginning of the 20th centuries (Crawford 1995: 20). Unlike today, however, one could get by without a high school diploma. In today's economy, even the lowest wage jobs require a minimum of a high school education. While the U.S. still has its success stories (see Bill Gates), education plays a much more prominent role, and it still takes, on average, two or three generations for most immigrant families to reach economic and social stability. The reality is that some people do sink unless they receive some sort of help.

3.1 Colonial days into the 1800s

During the early days of Colonial America, an attitude of general tolerance and acceptance existed towards multilingualism. Apparently, it was the least of their worries. The colonies had been havens for people from a number of nations who had fled various forms of injustice in their homelands. (Large population movements around the globe today have similar causes, and the U.S. still represents a haven of sorts for many displaced people.)

In the arena of education nationally, neutrality ruled the day regarding language loyalties, although that would change in time. There was no official, national language policy for over a century from the inception of an independent U.S. In colonial times, wherever minority language groups were influential, instruction was in the ancestral language, the language acquired in the home (the vernacular), and bilingual education was left free to operate. It was up to local agencies to deal with local matters. Wherever a minority group's influence was relatively weak, monolingual education was the default. By the middle of the 19th century, bilingual programs were active in cities such as Baltimore, Cincinnati, Cleveland, Indianapolis, Milwaukee and St. Louis (Crawford 1995: 23). In 1847, Louisiana adopted legislation that allowed for education in French, English, or both along lines of an 1839 Ohio statute authorizing instruction in German – upon the request of parents.

---

11. One example was the church-based parochial school that offered an education in the minority language and a systematic, rational transition to American culture and language.

During this period of neutrality, several factors worked in favor of some immigrant groups. (1) Larger ethnic enclaves gave the impression of relative homogeneity, not intense diversity. (2) In the Midwest, schools that catered to some of these groups were situated in sparsely populated rural areas, not in high-density urban sprawls. (3) Politically, immigrant votes carried more clout in certain areas, so the lack of any firm policy was an advantage to speakers of minority languages. This helped motivate over a dozen states to pass laws that authorized instruction in languages other than English. (4) Local concerns for the well-being and educational needs of the children determined the nature of the programs, not national policy. (5) Children who came to the U.S. from many countries had the support of a community infrastructure that included churches and systematic ways to ease the transition into an American culture and educational system. With or without the support of specific legislation, local school boards, particularly in the Midwestern states, supported classes in languages as varied as Norwegian, Swedish, Dutch, German, Polish, and Czech. Education in the respective home languages/vernaculars had been the rule, and it continued to be so into the 20th century.

For most of the 19th century, the most widespread minority language in the Eastern states was by far German, and it remained so until the census of 1970 when Spanish took its place (Wiley 2007: 62–63). There was little question, however, of loyalty to the U.S. in German-speaking areas. In fact, during the Civil War, German was used to command troops in some Union regiments from Pennsylvania, New York, Wisconsin, Illinois, and Missouri (Crawford 1992a: 45). As the war loomed on the horizon, German-Americans aligned themselves with the Northern States (the Union), having in common an opposition to slavery. The plantation economy of the South, borne on the backs of African-origin slaves, took place under the control of the Southern Aristocracy, founded by English landowners and international slave traders who supplied the labor force. The plantations were large agricultural enterprises for producing cash crops, e.g., tobacco, cotton, and rice, for consumption in Europe. In the Middle states, Germans focused on family-owned and operated farms that provided for the needs of the community. Perhaps out of mutual respect and the similarities between Anglo and Germanic culture, the Germans enjoyed a privileged status, and assimilation was left to run its generational course.

Nationally, nineteenth-century thinking linked language, culture, and thought, which was particularly evident in the forced *Anglicization* processes of American Indians (Crawford 1992a: 43–44). It was thought that by eradicating their "barbaric tongues," that America's indigenous populations could be brought under some kind of social control. They had resisted the doctrine of Manifest Destiny that fueled Western expansion, and it was thought that through Anglicization, making them learn to use English as their *only* language, that their thought patterns could be brought into line with Anglo Saxon thinking. Most linguists shudder at this portrayal of language and culture, though they may agree that language is culturally transmitted (from parents and community to children).[12] Language and culture *influence* the ways we think, but they do not determine thought. Forced Anglicization involved brutal methods (e.g., taking children from their homes), did nothing to eliminate cultural resistance, and produced mostly negative results (Reymer 1992: 41–47).[13] Obviously, high-handed tactics like these were not necessary for the Germans and people of similar European stock.

Assimilation into American language and culture during the first one hundred years of nationhood was the goal for European settlers, to be sure, but their children were not left to sink or swim on their own, at least those who were considered part of the expanding social and cultural fabric of American society. (*By law*, many of the indigenous peoples and African-origin slave population did not enjoy the same civil liberties as European Americans, an issue that reached well into the 20th century.) While Americanization had community support, there was also selective respect for national and family traditions, customs, and religious observance. Since the 1900s, however, educational policy has been determined by a mixture of national laws and programs (granting or withholding funding), individual state laws, and political initiatives instigated by groups or individuals, e.g., various initiatives in California.

3.2   The end of the 19th Century and beginning of the 20th

The term *language minority* is of fairly recent coinage; in the early days of the U.S., large ethnic groups represented *nationalities* and languages, e.g., Norwegian, German, and Czech (cf. Wiley 2007: 62). Implicit in these earlier distinctions was a European view of race, plus a sense of history and loyalty towards (perhaps, reminiscence of) an original homeland, the Old Country, and culture. In today's political climate, religious bigotry is mostly associated with small-scale fringe groups or zealots, and denominational affiliation is perhaps less important nationally. However, in the late 19th and early 20th centuries, old national rivalries based in the Protestant Reformation and its aftermath (along with suspicion and resentment towards the Roman Catholic church) rose up

---

12. See Chapter 7 for discussion of linguistic relativity and the Sapir-Whorf hypothesis.

13. In the late 19th Century, the American government became more forceful in its language policy. There were widespread portrayals of Indians as poverty-stricken, destitute of civilization, and in dire need of federal intervention. Rather than confining them on reservations, Americanization efforts were focused on rapid assimilation into the mainstream of America. With the establishment of boarding schools patterned after military schools, Native American children were forcibly taken from their homes, from the familiar surroundings of family and friends, and sent to institutions far from their homes. They lived under strict disciplinary conditions, were prohibited from speaking their native languages (having their mouths washed with soap for violations), and forced to assimilate into Anglo-Saxon culture (e.g., dress, culture, and other mannerism).

vigorously from time to time (e.g., in the Know Nothing movement of the 1850s). Irish Catholics often received the brunt of such animosities.

Towards the end of the 19th century, the cultural landscape began to change, and profoundly so. Some of the major factors that appeared to hasten change were the sheer numbers and diversity of a new wave of immigration. It predictably created a backlash and a drive to recapture a feeling of national unity and relative homogeneity. Immigrants flocked to industrial centers in search of work and a glimpse of the American Dream. Ideally, the one thing that all could have in common was language, namely American English, along with a core of Anglo Saxon cultural values that were increasingly linked to what it meant to be "American." This core included the value of hard work, individualism, personal morality and ethics, and a responsibility to maintain law and order; but it entailed adopting the Anglo Saxon language, as well. Closely associated with loyalty to the United States was proficiency in English.

One pro-assimilation, Americanization organization that had an impact was the short-lived American Protective Association (APA). Active mostly in the Midwest and Northeast, it was linked to a *nativist* (native-born American) movement and a growing sense of national pride. Implicit in trends of this sort was native ability in SAE, single-minded allegiance to the ideals of American democracy, and acceptance of "American" values. To hasten the process linguistically, requirements for English-only instruction began in 1889 in Wisconsin and Illinois in all schools, public and private (Crawford 1995: 24). Many felt that it was the *duty* of the state to teach in English, and the *right* of every child to receive instruction in the language of this country. Some changes may have come naturally from competition among earlier immigrant groups as each shifted to English. For example, German was receding in schools partly because of the assimilation of German-speaking parents into American society. In a few cities, German was relegated to the upper grades. Nevertheless, in 1900, more than 600,000 children still received instruction in that language in both public and parochial schools (Crawford 1995: 25).

Change was in the air as new immigrant groups came in waves to escape political and economic turmoil in Europe. From 1899 to 1920, more than eight million people entered the U.S., mostly from Southern and Eastern Europe. The number of Italians, Slavs (e.g., Poles, who along with Italians, are typically Roman Catholic), and Jews swelled, particularly in metropolitan areas like New York City. Groups like these eventually outnumbered the Germans, Irish, and Scandinavians, Northern Europeans who physically and culturally resembled their Anglo Saxon counterparts to a great extent. The newer immigrants were culturally more diverse than the established communities, often settling in specific areas ("ghettoes") out of economic necessity and to make contact with support networks. The end of the 19th century also marked the beginning of large Jewish settlements in New York City and Chicago.

Although some religious bigotry against Jews and Catholics undoubtedly raised its ugly head, cultural diversity and the impact of sheer numbers of immigrants probably had a more powerful influence. Native-born Americans of various immigrant stock reacted to the "odd" habits and customs of an increasingly diverse immigrant population in already burgeoning urban areas. And, once again, ethnicity (nationality and race) was linked to language with ramifications in education as the number of languages increased to include Italian, Polish, Russian, Yiddish, Serbo-Croatian, and others. This may have given fuel to the idea that *not every language* could be taught – there are so many. In an atmosphere of progressive national values, political forces saw it as the *public's* responsibility to handle the newcomers. Hence, the pressure to assimilate and Americanize grew proportionately in intensity.

Americanization, though it wasn't a new term, was now the byword. For over a hundred years, assimilation had been voluntary, but it was also inevitable. As a democracy, the U.S. had envisioned itself as the ideal nation that incorporated different nationalities in a crucible of sorts, refining the ingredients into an improved nation, a stronger, synthesized version of European society.[14] As a uniquely American culture emerged in the early years of nationhood, a shared sense of history and identity indeed did develop, coinciding with rapid westward expansion and a seemingly endless array of opportunities for its citizens to own land and experience great individual prosperity. The American Dream was at its zenith. But, along with increasing national pride, there was a reaction to continued immigration.

The Immigration Restriction League, an influential group started by Senator Henry Cabot Lodge of Massachusetts, reacted in alarm to the growing number of immigrants. They pushed for literacy requirements for immigration and naturalization (Crawford 1992a: 53–55). While the "fitness" of certain groups to assimilate into American society was widely debated, Congress passed the Nationality Act in 1906, a naturalization law that included an English speaking requirement. Meanwhile, labor unions proliferated, particularly among various ethnic groups in an attempt to ensure fair wages and working conditions for their members. English instruction became widespread, offered by such organizations as the YMCA. Industrial leaders like Henry Ford required all foreign-born employees to attend evening English classes (Crawford 1992a: 56). A frantic push for Americanization was on, but it wasn't enough just to learn English. Immigrant workers were encouraged to abandon their heritage languages, values, and ways of life. This was believed to be the only way to ensure that all immigrants could function as new "Americans" in the work force, without foreign, un-American ideas creeping into

---

14. A crucible is a type of pot or highly heat-resistant container used for smelting (or melting) and purifying metals. When heated up, impurities rise to the surface where they can be extracted or removed. This analogy was used throughout the 19th century to describe the social forces occurring in America. The term "melting pot" came into popular use in 1908 after a play *The Melting Pot* by Israel Zangwill about a Russian-Jewish family and its struggles to assimilate into American culture.

society. Americanization efforts were ostensibly for the welfare of workers; efficiency and a cheap source of labor were also desirable.

On the home front, housing had become a serious concern in a land teeming with people "fresh off the boat," so to speak. An influential political reform movement known as *Progressivism* sought progress for new immigrants and equal opportunity in the housing market in view of unprecedented population growth, industrialization, and urban expansion (Nash et al 1990:710ff). To help provide this equality, progressives pushed for Americanization through education, language teaching, and social programs aimed at exposing and eliminating the exploitation of workers (children, women, and ethnic minorities). They were spurred on by the famed muckrakers of the early 20th century. The National Americanization Committee, an organization formed in 1915 with progressive ideals, contributed to an *English-first* style movement in all areas of American life, where English proficiency (and unilingualism) was the goal for new immigrants for their benefit, so they would be treated fairly in the housing and job markets. While progress in correcting social woes was the immediate and long-term goal, progressivism still operated nonetheless along racial and ethnic lines; e.g., "...progressivism did not usually mean progress for blacks" (Nash et al 1990:713). This may have appeared racist, according to today's standards, but it was quite open-minded and liberal in its social context.

3.3   The first half of the 20th Century: The Great Wars

Then came the intrigue surrounding war in Europe and entry of the U.S. into the First World War. Though the war involved nations on a global scale, it was waged mostly in Europe from 1914 to 1918, between the Entente powers, Great Britain, France, Russia, and allied nations, and the Central Powers, Germany, Austria-Hungary, and later the Ottoman Empire, with their associated nations. The U.S., still a fledgling power, had been neutral due to its isolationist policy and did not enter the war until April 1917 amid growing pressure from Britain and under the threat of continued sea attacks from German submarines. German-speaking people were suspected of all sorts of conspiracies. Using German in public or on the telephone was outlawed. In the institutions of everyday life, German was severely restricted and considered a menace to Americanism. Its usage was interpreted as a subversive ploy of the German government to undermine national unity. States passed laws against speaking German in classrooms, in public meetings, on trains, and even in church. This happened to a preferred minority whose language was spoken at the time by eight million Americans (Crawford 1992a:57).[15]

---

15. Consider, too, the plight of Japanese-Americans in WWII, confined to internment camps and suffering the same kinds of restrictions, particularly in California.

Almost simultaneous with this was the Russian Revolution and the resultant "Red Scare," the beginning of a fearful and antagonistic response to communism and the global spread of socialism. Americanization was seen as the antidote to many problems and an insurance policy against violent revolution. The Russian Revolution began in March 1917, when Tsar Nicholas II abdicated his throne as discontent with the war grew. As a result, the Russian army became less and less effective in its efforts against Germany. The Revolution ended with the establishment of the Bolshevik (Communist) government under the leadership of Vladimir Lenin, who promised to pull Russia out of the war. An armistice with Germany ensued in December of that year with details of disengagement left up in the air. In March 1918, Russia finally agreed to the German terms, handing over huge territories to the Central Powers, including Finland, Estonia, Latvia, and Lithuania, parts of Poland and Ukraine (much of which returned to Russian influence prior to WWII). Needless to say, the turmoil created by these bloody conflicts and their aftermath fueled massive emigration from Eastern Europe. (These were the days of fierce hand-to-hand combat, not smart bombs that people watched on T.V. in complete safety.) As anti-Semitism flourished all over Europe, East and West, millions of Jews began emigrating to safer places, and into that crucible known as the United States.

After WWI, the War to End All Wars, *all* foreign languages were forbidden in primary grades. The Americanization frenzy only began to die down somewhat in the 1920s, but some changes appeared to be permanent. Bilingual education was clearly on the decline, although isolated bilingual programs in the Midwest continued into the 1930s. In addition, immigration by non-English speakers lessened for a time. The Great Depression of the 1930s and severe Midwestern droughts were tremendous economic disasters that led to considerable migration *within* the U.S., e.g., as bankrupt farmers in the so-called Dust Bowl moved into the far western states.[16] As a consequence, the U.S. became less attractive as a land of unlimited potential. Economic recovery was slow, leaving a permanent mark on an entire generation of Americans.

But, once again, world events would shape the nature of emigration from a chaotic European continent. In the late 1930s, Europe was also caught up in economic woes, which contributed to the spread of Nazism in Germany, rearmament, and German expansionism. However, as massive immigration into the U.S. commenced anew, so did anti-foreign sentiments. Interest in all foreign language study declined sharply. The pace and fervor of Americanization efforts picked up to transform any remaining

---

16. The Dust Bowl was a term applied to the Great Plains region of central parts of the U.S., from the Dakotas all the way to Oklahoma and Texas. A result of improper farming methods, great clouds of dust blew into the air. It was also associated with the Great Depression which began with the Stock Market Crash of 1929, continuing the economic misery of Midwesterners practically up to the Second World War.

elements of multilingualism and multiculturalism into a primarily unilingual unity. It succeeded within one generation among Americans of similar racial stock. The tragic experience of the Depression (and its aftermath) was the impetus for national unity. Nevertheless, there was still considerable progress to be made regarding the civil rights of minority groups, particularly American Blacks, still the victims of overt segregationist policies in much of the South. As chronicled in the 1995 film, *The Tuskegee Airmen*, even the American military remained segregated until 1948.

By 1939, at the outbreak of the Second World War, Europe was again enveloped in war. While description of the war goes well beyond the purposes of this book, it started a long process that reshaped the face of Europe with hard-fought battles involving the Allied Powers (Britain, France, the Soviet Union, and, from 1942, the U.S.) against the Axis Powers (Nazi Germany, Italy, and Japan). Of course, the Holocaust involving the extermination of some six million Jews had an enormous impact on population movement (and the creation of the State of Israel). Essentially, the U.K. could no longer maintain its colonial system and the former British Empire came to a halt, e.g., with the independence of India and Pakistan. The war and its aftermath also carved a sharp distinction between Western Europe, symbolically democratic in nature following the War, and Eastern Europe, characterized by the totalitarian regimes of the Soviet Union and its satellite Eastern European nations. This also produced massive population movements within Europe, spilling over into immigration to the U.S.[17] This war had a great impact on the U.S. politically and socially, including a growing fear of communism and the rise of McCarthyism.[18]

Nevertheless, postwar America began to enjoy tremendous economic expansion and the so-called Baby Boom, the happy rise in the number of native births enjoyed by American service personnel and their spouses. Industries devoted to wartime materials such as aircraft, military vehicles, and weapons had put people to work. As factories were converted to consumer products, they brought much individual wealth. Technology grew by leaps and bounds, including a blossoming communications industry and the seeds of computer technology. Personal travel grew exponentially, including the

---

17. Significant numbers of decorated Latino war heroes focused attention on the situation in the Southwest. As devastating as WWII was, some ethnic minorities in the U.S. eventually benefited by society's renewed attention to discrimination and the increased development of national unity.

18. From the late 1940s to the late 1950s, the nation was preoccupied with the threat of the Soviet Union's ability to spy on Americans. Senator McCarthy held investigations and hearings that led to the infamous Hollywood blacklist that, by innuendo alone, affected nearly all levels of American society. Anyone who could remotely be tied to any kind of "subversive" organization was targeted; hundreds went to prison, including many in the entertainment industry (e.g., actors, writers, musicians, and attorneys), in universities and schools (professors, researchers, teachers), and those from various other professions (maritime workers, seamen, and longshoremen).

development of a national interstate highway system (freeways) and expansion of air- and seaports.[19] The automobile alone helped to transform American society. Financial stability returned, setting the stage for another round of immigration. However, many lessons were learned, especially about the excesses and violence of totalitarian regimes and the suppression of peoples and cultures.

3.4   From the second half of the 20th into the 21st Century

Following World War II, the nation went through another significant change in attitudes. Obviously, massive population movements in Europe affected the face of Europe, but the movement of displaced peoples also spilled over into the U.S. Especially in view of the Holocaust and the massacre of millions of Jews in Nazi Europe, immigrants came *en masse* to America for refuge. The famed Baby Boom began, as American military personnel joyfully returned home from oversees (from the Pacific and European theaters of war), along with a rapidly expanding economy. The result was a period of unprecedented prosperity. Along with the amazing growth of personal wealth came an attitude of benevolence towards ethnic and linguistic minorities, which culminated in the famed Civil Rights Movement. This outward shift in attitude also led to more openness towards language minorities. Following on the heals of the Civil Rights Act of 1964 (and the optimism of the Kennedy administration) was the Bilingual Education Act in 1967. However, ambivalent attitudes began to surface again as battles over funding for bilingual programs began to rage.

Again, there was the interplay of immigration, education, and language, all couched in political (partisan) terms. The single most significant event affecting immigration was the passage of the Immigration and Nationality Act of 1965 that abolished the *quota system* of immigration based on national origins. The Immigration Act of 1924 had set limits, or quotas, on annual immigration to 2% of the number of immigrants from a given country already living in the U.S. according to the 1890 census figures (turning the "clock" back more than thirty years). The Act was intended to limit the immigration of troublesome Eastern and Southern Europeans (e.g., from Russia, Poland, and Italy) who had been coming in large numbers in the 1890s. In practice, it also excluded immigration from Asian nations and severely limited immigration from Latin America and Africa, as well.[20] Abolishing this quota system in the spirit of the Civil Rights Movement

---

19. Electricity changed the ways people lived in the 1920s with widespread availability of electric lights, washing machines, vacuum cleaners, and telephones. The *Roaring Twenties* also saw the beginnings of the entertainment industry and the advent of *movies*.

20. Apparently, the thousands of Africans brought to the colonies as slaves were not counted as immigrants.

and in the interest of fairness allowed for relatively free entry into the U.S. from Latin America and Asia. This change effectively altered the ethnic makeup of immigration by stopping the preference for White Europeans that had been built into the immigration system. Northern Europeans had constituted the primary ethnic group in the U.S. and the overwhelming majority of in-migrants for over a century since independence.

Controversies concerning bilingualism in the U.S. since the middle of the 20th century have not focused only on speakers of Spanish, to be sure. Certain Asian languages (e.g., Vietnamese, Hmong, and Lao) have also received national attention. Political issues have run the gamut from the appearance of overt favoritism (e.g., federal funding for different refugee projects) to proposals to restrict immigration from Mexico. As one might expect, concerns have had a lot to do with rapidly changing demographics, so, by an enormous margin, Latino issues have risen to the top of the agendas of politically motivated campaigns for English-only legislation. Nevertheless, ambivalent attitudes towards bilingualism continue to fluctuate. Since the end of World War II, attitudes towards bilingualism of any kind have surfaced mostly in continually changing waves of legislation, first openly favoring various bilingual programs, only to evolve into laws that focus only on English proficiency and the development of national standards in education.

4.   Reactions to the use of Spanish in the American Southwest

The history of the clash of two international linguistic giants, Spanish and English, have roots that go back to territorial competition between England and Spain. Historical events have played important roles, landmark occurrences such as (a) the military intrusion of the U.S. into Mexico during the Mexican-American war; (b) the annexation of Mexican territory that became the present-day Southwest, land first owned, settled, and colonized by Spain, with its long- and short-term effects; (c) the victory of the U.S. in the Spanish-American War in 1898 that had ramifications on so-called Hispanics in the U.S., e.g., in the annexation of Puerto Rico and the Philippines (and the liberation of Cuba); and (d) growing American political and military dominance and an air of superiority internationally as the nation emerged as a world leader in the early 20th century, particularly in Latin America.

Historical forces affecting other language minority groups have also come into play, for example, trends in immigration, socioeconomic pressures, stresses on the educational system, and visions of a homogeneous American language and culture. For instance, all of these factored into the settlement of Puerto Ricans in urban centers of the Northeast in the 1930s and 40s. Ethnic majority reactions have typically linked the Spanish language and Puerto Rican culture with stereotypes of Puerto Ricans as chronically poor, unemployable, and perpetrators of violent crime (Moore & Pachon

1985: 34). Attitudes to the Spanish language have paralleled those towards other languages, but to harsher extremes, except perhaps for the near hysterical reactions to German during the World Wars.

But, nowhere have negative attitudes to languages other than English flourished more than in the American Southwest. Spanish has been spoken there for centuries; if we call it a "foreign" language in the Southwest, then we would have to call English a foreign language in the Northeast. Both were brought by immigrants to the shores of the Americas. Nevertheless, Spanish has been repressed and pushed to the fringes of society in many areas by the spread of English. An Anglo American perspective seems to have difficulty acknowledging that parts of the U.S. have been bilingual at least since the middle of the 19th century, when land belonging to Spanish speakers was forcibly taken over by the U.S. government. As a consequence of biased American attitudes towards their language, culture, and ethnicity, Latino children have experienced humiliation and embarrassment, incurring penalties from detention (being kept after school) to physical (corporal) punishment just for speaking their native language on the playground or in the classroom. During the civil rights movements of the 1960s, Latino groups stood against repressive language policies; many of the restrictions against the use of Spanish on the playgrounds and so forth were lifted or modified. But, continuing immigration from Latin-American countries continues to affect communities, raising the same litany of social, political, and other institutional concerns and objections.

Against the backdrop of constant controversy and evolving legislation, the situation in the Southwest has put the character of the U.S. to the test. To many in other parts of the country (and in other nations), some of the reactions to Mexicans and Americans of Mexican origin (Chicanos) ostensibly based on views of bilingualism and bilingual education in the Southwest may be difficult to fathom. They are no more than instances of discrimination that have no rational basis. However, in order to understand current attitudes and biases, one must consider the prevailing worldview of the time and place that undoubtedly had much to do with the events that have transpired, much as they did before the Civil Rights Movement that aimed to eliminate discriminatory practices based on race and nationality (Steele 2008: 7–9). One of the only conclusions that one can draw from the negative attitudes of Anglo Americans towards the Spanish language and its "Hispanic" speakers is that it is indeed rooted in ethnicity, with both racial and cultural elements tied to stereotypes of Spanish-speaking people, their social behaviors, value systems, religious practices, housing patterns, and family life.

Within the diverse Pan-Latino/Hispanic society (i.e., that part that reflects post-colonial identity), there is an inherited sense of ethnicity where levels of society are linked to race, a sense shared by most dominant, prestige groups throughout Latin America. The conquering Spaniards' views of race in Mexico, for instance, were based on color, with Whites typically at the top and people of darker skin hues occupying the lower socioeconomic strata of society.[21] African-origin slaves along with racial mixes of Black and indigenous stock typically have resided at or near the bottom (cf. Vigil 1980: 67–9). There has been a lot of inter-ethnic marriage and the emergence of *mestizos,* an entire class of mixed European and indigenous racial stock (Meyer *et al* 1999: 195ff). Likewise, Anglo Americans have viewed Mexicans and other Latin Americans of mixed race – conflated with various indigenous peoples into the so-called Brown race – according to American ethnic stereotypes (Suárez-Orozco & Páez 2002: 20–29), particularly in recent decades as the number of Latino immigrants has risen dramatically (Cornelius 2002: 165–189). Consequently, the territory that the U.S. annexed from Mexico was already configured according to class designations (cf. Moore & Pachon 1985: 93–95). Much of Texas, for example, consisted of rural farms and cattle ranches, worked by mestizos; the social structure of some larger settlements and cities was clearly influenced by European Spanish attitudes traceable to the 17th century and the arrival of the first Spaniards.

The advent of Anglo-American language and culture in the Southwest brought along an additional layer of stereotypes and biases. As is often the case, perceptions feed the stereotypes. Much of the labor force was composed of unskilled, uneducated, and illiterate Mexicans seeking a minimum subsistence living, traits that also characterized later migratory workers seeking to fill a labor need (Steele 2008: 9–17). Importantly, most of the "Hispanics" that Anglos were initially exposed to were principally from just one specific class. One of the curious effects of ethnic stereotyping is that some people – the focus or objects of the stereotype – internalize, perhaps, with some modification, the belief systems foisted on them by society and act out their own stereotypical patterns of behavior (cf. Ogbu 1987: 255–75). These beliefs, in turn, perpetuate themselves, in effect, reinforcing the stereotypes they may wish to eliminate, and creating what some anthropologists refer to as "castelike" minorities. While some language and ethnic minorities seek to assimilate into American culture as fast as they can through career and educational paths, e.g., certain Asian-American groups, creating their own sets of stereotypes, others appear to resist complete assimilation (from the Anglo American perspective), consistently lagging behind mainstream students in the "basics," skill areas of mathematics and the language arts. Any behavior that fits a stereotype will be interpreted by society (e.g., members of the Anglo American community) as confirming its validity.

---

21. Recall that European Spaniards are White, or Caucasian, based on broad racial characteristics. In Anglo American views, they are of Mediterranean stock, along with Italians, Portuguese, French, and so on. Currently, when Spaniards come to the U.S., however, they are typically classified as Spanish-origin or Hispanic, becoming members of a minority ethnic group. As a political construct, the term Hispanic blurs racial distinctions that are most obvious to Europeans, lumping together, for example, Cubans, Dominicans, Puerto Ricans, Mexicans, Colombians, and now Spaniards whose individual societies and cultures are racially and ethnically diverse, as well.

An example of misinterpreting patterns is the mistaken belief that bilingualism somehow *causes* low academic achievement. Academic performance may be associated (or correlated) with certain types of bilingualism, but the reasons are most likely historical and socioeconomic. Not *all* bilinguals fail in school, so there is no one-to-one, cause and effect relationship. The factors that go into the academic performance of bilinguals are many. They include (a) socioeconomic status and its effects on educational opportunity and academic preparedness; (b) proficiency levels in the language of the classroom and all the factors that may influence language acquisition (allowing participation in all academic subjects); (c) cultural and personal factors, e.g., family background, motivations to assimilate into Anglo American society, active involvement of parents in the education process, and attitudes towards English and its speakers; and (d) immigrant status, e.g. citizenship or other legal documentation regarding residence. There are additional issues with respect to non-standard dialects of English and their effects in the classroom, very controversial issues of intelligence and its measurement (and the destructive consequences of spreading biased views of innate abilities indiscriminately across entire ethnic groups), and biased testing methodologies and procedures that favor mainstream and majority groups. If a child does poorly on a test, or if first impressions seem to fit a particular stereotype, there is no simple, one-size-fits-all explanation. Blaming a child's poor performance on ethnicity is short-sighted, to say the least. And, it limits the opportunities of the teacher to offer academic instruction.

4.1   A revolving door: Immigration, repatriation, illegal aliens, and braceros

Although the area now known as the American Southwest was claimed and controlled by Spain, not all of its inhabitants were Spanish speakers. There were many indigenous people and languages, along with European Spanish settlers and others. "American Mexicans" (those affected by U.S. annexation) and native Americans have shared many of the same experiences of discrimination as conquered and displaced peoples. But, there were some differences, especially for those "Latins" of European stock who appeared to be more prepared to adapt (Vigil 1980: 129). The situation was complex, and classification as Indian or Mexican may have been relatively arbitrary depending on the languages spoken and degree of acculturation into Spanish or Mexican society. So, a Spanish-speaking (Pueblo) Indian may have been counted either way. Nevertheless, this great expanse of land was relatively sparsely populated. At the time of U.S. annexation of the four border states, one estimate has around 5,000 Mexicans in Texas, 60,000 in New Mexico, fewer than 1,000 in Arizona, and possibly 7,500 along the length of California, mainly in tightly clustered settlements. Many settlements were within 150 miles of the modern-day U.S.-Mexican border (Moore and Pachon 1985: 18). Numbers had a powerful effect on the preservation of Mexican culture and language in each of these states.

There was not much immigration into the U.S. from Mexico in the late 19th and early 20th centuries, and little formal legislation governing policy along the border. Except perhaps where border towns developed, much of the land near the border was harsh and barren, and the modes of transportation were limited. The INS (Immigration and Naturalization Service) Border Patrol wasn't set up until 1924, and entry into the U.S. without a visa was not punishable until the beginning of the Great Depression in 1929. However, a national need for cheap labor arose during WWI, particularly for work in mines, on farms, and on the greatly expanding railroad system. In the growth years of the "roaring" 1920s, the quota system was relaxed for immigrants from the Western Hemisphere (obviously affecting Mexico the most, due to its proximity). Political pressure had been applied by ranchers and other employers in the border states to allow entry into the U.S. for unskilled laborers conveniently located nearby across the border. There was also a rise in Pan-American sentiment, perhaps in an attempt to create economic and military alliances following a global war.

Revolution in Mexico (1910–1920) also led to a massive exodus from traditional homelands. In the years between 1910 and 1930, over 900,000 people crossed the border into the U.S. And, it wasn't just *peones*, those belonging to the lower echelons of Mexican society (and the most likely to engage in low-skilled, low-paying manual labor). Families belonging to the relatively small middle class were joining their ranks. The revolution seemed endless, with sporadic skirmishes among rebel groups continuing into the 1920s. Economic chaos and the constant threat of conscription (being forcibly pressed into military service) drove many young men to flee (Romo 1983: 40–43). As it is with other refugee groups, many came to the U.S. with no intent to stay. There was the hope of returning to a more stable and prosperous homeland as soon as the fighting stopped, with agrarian reforms (redistribution of farm land) and improved economic opportunity promised by revolutionary politicians and rebel leaders.[22]

By the middle of the 1920s, immigration from Mexico had risen to such an extent that some governmental officials wanted to close the revolving door through the enforcement of existing laws. Restrictions throughout Mexico were made by U.S. consular offices that determined the eligibility of its citizens for U.S. visas. The restrictions seemed arbitrary, with some applicants judged to be illiterate or unemployable (Moore & Pachon 1985: 136). The key was the selective application of existing laws; laws were hard to change, but adjusting the enforcement of immigration laws was a relatively simple task. The almost random sweeps to curb the flow of legal and illegal entry into the U.S. kept potential immigrants and those seeking seasonal or temporary work in a constant state of apprehension. But, the Great Depression effectively halted the need for Mexican laborers, motivating a drive to reverse the flow of Mexican immigration,

---

22. This was the time of Francisco "Pancho" Villa (born José Doroteo Arango Arámbula) and Emiliano Zapata, famed leaders who led their own personal armies.

and to send no-longer-wanted (surplus) laborers back home under the guise of voluntary *repatriation* (Steele 2008: 10). As early as 1921, there was so much concern for
the health of exploited laborers in Los Angeles that community organizations such as
Blue Cross (*Cruz Azul*), with the direct aid of the Mexican government, shipped 1,500
disenchanted, destitute, and unemployed *Mexicano* workers back to Mexico by sea
(Romo 1983: 153).

The U.S. economy seemed to determine how the revolving door would swing.
During the Depression and the devastating droughts of the Dust Bowl, deportations
increasingly consisted of *wetbacks*, or illegal aliens.[23] The appearance of being Mexican
was sufficient for INS agents to stop and question "suspects." This also led to a great
discussion of the increased harassment of Chicanos (U.S. citizens) who were often
confused with Mexican nationals based on physical appearance and perhaps pronunciation (a "Mexican" accent) with complete disregard for their civil rights. Welfare was
withheld to encourage repatriation, even for U.S. citizens of Mexican descent. "Mexican bureaus" were set up to promote and assist relocation (Moore & Pachon 1985: 136).
Profiteers received as much as $14.70 a head, sending trainloads of people into the
interior of Mexico. Between 1929 and 1934, approximately 400,000 people were sent
back to Mexico without any kind of formal deportation proceedings. These "repatria-
tions" had a tremendous impact on individuals and families in both countries.

The beginning of WWII reversed the trend and made cheap Mexican labor desirable once again. One consequence was the establishment of the *bracero* (contract
labor) program. Begun in 1942 (upon entry of the U.S. into WWII), the program
involving railroad workers lasted up to the end of the War, but other forms – e.g., agricultural workers, continued on. The Spanish word *bracero* refers to one who works
with the hands (from *brazo*, "arm"). A bracero was a person contracted specifically to
engage in low-skilled, low-wage, manual labor. Consequently, unskilled laborers were
recruited in Mexico to come to the U.S. on a temporary, contract basis. As expected,
many were exposed to racist practices and harsh treatment. Much as ideas of racial inferiority provided a rationale for the enslavement of African-Americans in the South,
racists beliefs towards Mexicans justified their mistreatment. The bracero program,
clouded by continuing allegations of exploitation, was stopped in 1964. However, a
ready pool of illegal immigrants were waiting in the wings. Ironically, the end of the
quota system in immigration contributed significantly to this changing situation and
the availability of cheap labor.

---

23. *Wetback* is a derogatory term that was originally used to refer to illegal Mexican immigrants who
had entered the U.S. by swimming the Rio Grande. The Spanish equivalent, *mojados*, simply means
wet (ones). However, both are offensive and meant to capture the desperation in such attempts to
come to the U.S. and to elevate the status on U.S.-born Chicanos and others who obtain documentation legally.

Immediately after the war, the number of people caught crossing the border illegally jumped exponentially. The Border Patrol picked up and deported 183,000 in 1947, and that number grew to 543,000 in 1952 (counting repeat offenders). At that time, it was not against the law to hire undocumented workers, so many farms were worked by teams consisting of both, legal (braceros) and illegal workers. This obviously complicated enforcement, especially in view of the availability of forged documentation. This contradictory practice (hiring or deporting the same people depending on legal status) reached its zenith when illegals were deported to specific spots where they could sign up for the bracero program and re-enter the U.S. with the required papers, a process called "drying out the wetbacks" (Moore & Pachon 1985: 140).

Nevertheless, the booming post-war economy once again created a need for a cheap labor pool. In 1951, Congress passed a law (Public Law 78) that superseded earlier agreements. It extended the bracero program and amended the agricultural act of 1949. Between 1951 and 1960, 356,000 Mexicans entered the U.S. (Moore & Pachon 1985: 137). So, fittingly and in complete contradiction, as a reaction to the swelling population of Mexicans in the U.S., the INS began "Operation Wetback" in June 1954. California was first to be targeted, followed by Texas, then onto the Midwest and Northwest. In 1954, over a million Mexicans were apprehended and *expelled* from the U.S. Within five years, nearly *four million people* were caught and deported. Only 63,515 of those went through formal deportation hearings. In addition, the "returned" Mexicans were not merely sent to the border; they were transported to places in Mexico near their original homes (e.g., in Sonora, Jalisco, and Michoacán). The social cost to Chicano-Latinos in the U.S. was deep-felt alienation. Hundreds of thousands of U.S. citizens were harassed with little attention to their civil rights. It was increasingly important to carry papers if you looked "Mexican." Meanwhile, in direct contrast to this anti-Mexican sentiment, 445,000 braceros were *brought into* the country in 1956, while 72,000 illegals were apprehended (Moore & Pachon 1985: 141). The issue was legal status, which could be bent and manipulated through enforcement to suit the need for a cheap source of labor.

It is safe to say that some threat of deportation still exists among undocumented aliens. Operation Wetback was not the last round of selective enforcement. One more failed attempt was made by the Reagan administration in 1982 to target illegals who received more than the minimum wage, ostensibly, those who had taken away good jobs from American citizens. Although many issues remain unsettled to this day, public attention in the 1980s began to shift to immigration laws. For example, in 1986, the Immigration Reform and Control Act (IRCA) gave political amnesty to over three million previously undocumented aliens. As an act of Congress, it made it illegal to hire undocumented workers *knowingly*. But, it appeared to be a compromise of sorts in that it granted citizenship and immunity from prosecution to those who had lived continuously in the U.S. since January 1982. Legislation is one thing; changing a culture of prejudice is another.

4.2   Schools and segregation

Segregation in schools has a long history in the U.S., but it is often difficult for Anglo Americans to separate it from the Black and White context of the American South. However, the Southwest, particularly in the border states of Texas and California, has experienced its own brand of segregation. In these states, Chicano-Latino children were typically assigned to "Mexican" schools that reflected their low status. "Segregation was seen as a solution to educating Mexican Americans, not as a problem to overcome" (Steele 2008: 13). A second-rate education was deemed good enough; in fact, the establishment of Mexican schools was seen as the crowning achievement of many administrators in Texas. Discriminatory practices in Texas, for example, involved shorter days and academic years, and fewer years of education overall for Mexican American children. According to one account, during WWII, 42 percent of school-age Mexican children got no education at all (Steele 2008: 12). Schooling was often seen as irrelevant to the Mexican American experience and not necessary for survival. By lowering academic expectations, schools were doing them a service. However, the legacy of exclusionary practices is the reinforcement of low self-esteem and the fostering of a separate social identity, a sense of belonging to an inferior socioeconomic caste.

These so-called Mexican schools were under-funded (fewer resources like textbooks, reference works, desks, and other educational materials), housed in inferior facilities (run-down buildings), and staffed by teachers with lower qualifications (including fewer degrees earned and the lack of other certification). Fewer teachers were assigned to these schools, as well, meaning larger class size when compared with mainstream, principally Anglo schools. In California, many educators simply ignored the concerns of the Mexican community or assumed that Mexicans did not place much of a priority on education. Plus, as one sociologist suggested, increased education only made them "unhappy" with their lot in life (Romo 1983: 138–9), making them overqualified for the types of jobs they would eventually hold.

The Los Angeles School District maintained separate facilities based on the theory that Mexican American children have special needs (Romo 1983: 136–142). Educators thought that they were not interested in traditional academic pursuits, easily tired by sustained mental effort, and handicapped by their lack of academic preparation (due to lack of parental support and educational history). They were typically shy and reticent (quiet when compared with their more aggressive Anglo peers), which inhibited "normal" participation in class. Separate schools were thought to correct this imbalance. In a mixed school (with both Anglos and Mexicans), English learners were at an obvious disadvantage. By having separate facilities, the Mexicans avoided awful comparisons with the "superior" Americans who performed much better in school on average. While Americanization was the goal (as it was in the rest of the U.S.), it seems that segregation would work against that goal. In California, segregation was accomplished by drawing boundaries around barrios and establishing neighborhood schools. This ensured that Chicano-Latinos would attend specific schools. Even though there may not have been uniform legislation throughout the state, the effect was de facto segregation. White neighborhoods had their schools, Black or Asian neighborhoods had theirs, and ethnically mixed neighborhoods presented challenges.[24]

The practice of *tracking*, or streaming, also contributed to the continual separation of socioeconomic classes. Such an approach fit well with prevailing prejudices; e.g., vocational training, introduced in 1910, has been the hallmark of minority education in Los Angeles. Students are assigned into tracks, or groupings according to their perceived similarities. Some children are destined for higher education (so-called college or academic tracks); some destined to be auto mechanics, domestic workers, or homemakers (vocational tracks); and some fall somewhere in the middle, perhaps finding some kind of white-collar jobs (general tracks). However, this type of system was based in biology, not on socioeconomic criteria. The philosopher and psychologist John Dewey had a tremendous influence on education in the U.S., especially among Progressives. He saw education's role as the shaping of citizens into interlocking segments according to their natural capacities; a strong America needed its workers and soldiers just like it needed its leaders. As strong proponents of the scientific method, Dewey and other progressive educators saw tracking as a scientific approach, based on Darwinian principles, to the problems of American education. Its goal was to prepare children for the "real world" out there and to help them adjust their expectations to reality (Oakes 1985: 23). It would provide equal opportunity for individual progress within prescribed limits.

There were additional "Jim Crow" laws that barred service for minorities in restaurants and such things as burial plots. Latino veterans, returning from the battlefields of WWII, led a drive to dismantle all laws that were based on discrimination and race. Their efforts eventually led to the repeal of the last segregationist statute in Californian's education code, signed into law by Governor Earl Warren in 1946 (Romo 1983: 168).

4.3 The suppression of Spanish

Perhaps the most humiliating aspect of discrimination was the prohibition against the use of Spanish in the schools – in the classroom, and on the school grounds. There have been two primary arguments, one that appealed to a sense of national morality, and

---

24. This was also the era when housing practices were also determined by ethnicity and race. Unspoken agreements existed that the purchase of property (homes and businesses) in specified neighborhoods would only be allowed for members of certain groups.

the other related to teaching. The moral argument states that English is the language of this country, and it needs to be used at all times. (A related idea is that it is impolite to use a language that the majority of people don't understand.) The pedagogical argument is based on the popular (yet misguided) belief that bilingualism itself is mentally confusing. Languages randomly interfere with each other causing confusion and the inability to express oneself clearly in one language. So, rules against Spanish usage appeal to both national unity and the myth of a homogeneous America, plus the idea that this is all for the child's mental and psychological good. It is in the child's interest (and in the interest of the entire nation) that she not speak Spanish or any other "foreign" language, especially in school. It follows that Spanish speakers have ample opportunity to use their heritage language at home with members of their family and community, and that they should use the school as a place to practice their English skills (Crawford 1992a: 79). By establishing penalties (in the form of fines and so on), teachers reinforced their views that learning English was the priority of the schools, and they had the support of the community.

In 1919, the Texas legislature made it an offense punishable by law to teach in any language other than English – foreign-language teaching was still allowed in the upper grades. Children were routinely punished for speaking Spanish. Such penalties as "Spanish detention" continued into the late 1960s. One principal, explaining the rationale behind this practice, was quoted in the Civil Rights Commission's 1972 report:

> Our school is predominantly Latin American – 97 percent. We try to discourage the use of Spanish on the playground, in the halls, and in the classroom. We feel that the reason so many of our pupils are reading two to three years below grade level is because their vocabulary is so limited. We are in complete accord that it is excellent to be bilingual or multilingual, but we must…stress the fact that practice makes perfect – that English is a very difficult language to master. Our pupils speak Spanish at home, at dances, on the playground, at athletic events…We feel the least they can do is try to speak English at school.
> (Cited in Crawford 1995: 33)

The punishment for children who spoke Spanish on the school grounds (and offending school authorities) ranged from corporal punishment (paddling, a k a swats) to being held after school. They were fined (e.g., a nickel for each infraction or as much as one penny a word). During recess or after school, they were required to stand on a special mark (e.g., a black box) for long periods of time or walk along a painted line ("walking the line"). And, they were given repetitive writing assignments, e.g., "I must not speak Spanish in school," presumably to occupy their time while in detention (Ramírez & Castañeda 1974: 22).

Moreover, the U.S. Commission on Civil Rights, which was responsible for monitoring violations of the Civil Rights Act, found that rules outlawing Spanish were applied more frequently to schools in low socioeconomic areas. It also found a correlation between the *number* of Chicano-Latino students and the existence "no Spanish" rules – the higher the ratio of Latino students in the student population, the more likely rules were enforced (Peñalosa 1980: 162). Whether there is any benefit at all to bilingualism or not, the suppression of the language rights of children is unconscionable. Is it any wonder that many Chicano-Latinos feel alienated from Anglo American society?

Key terms

Allied Powers, Alpines, Americanization, Anglicization, Anglo American, Axis Powers, Baby Boom, Central Powers, Civil War, Colonial America, cultural homogeneity, dominance (hegemony), Entente Powers, European races, ghetto, Great Wars, Great Depression, Hispanophobia, interethnic, language minority, Manifest Destiny, McCarthyism, Mediterraneans, Midwest, muckrakers, nationality, nativist, naturalization, Nordic, plantation economy, progressivism, residency and citizenship, Southern Aristocracy, totalitarian, unilingual, visible minority, Civil Rights.

Summary

The opinions of Americans towards bi- and multilingualism have swung from one extreme to the other. Perceptions of bilinguals and their language abilities have ranged from the positive (that it enhances intellectual abilities overall) to the negative (that it is the cause of poor academic performance). Attitudes towards those who are bilingual have been shaped by societal attitudes towards the *speakers* of specific languages. Evidently, some languages are looked on more favorably by society than others; the knowledge of some European languages is highly valued. However, feelings towards Spanish and its speakers in the U.S. have consistently been negative, to the point of hostility.

In general, it seems that Anglo Americans have always had ambivalent attitudes towards the ability to speak a "foreign" language. For a university graduate, on the one hand, it is an indicator of superior education to be truly competent in more than one language. On the other, bilingualism in children appears to be a "problem." Many educators and parents have felt that speaking a "foreign language" has *detrimental* effects on the mastery of English for school-age children. Nationally, the fear of languages other than English has had a long history. In colonial times, there was concern over expanding German settlements in Pennsylvania, enough to provoke fear that German might prevail in terms of numbers of speakers and swallow up English. For most of the 19th century, German was the most widespread minority language in the U.S., and it remained so until the census of 1970 when Spanish took its place. Nevertheless, German never seriously challenged English as the national language, all myths to the contrary.

In retrospect, some facets of national history have been idealized. One persistent myth is that *our* forefathers (those who didn't speak English already) picked up the language on their own the hard way. They just naturally learned it on their way to greatness. The truth is that many had the help of a variety of community organizations, and many failed anyway. But, they were welcomed with open arms. These first Americans also tended to accept multilingualism; it was the least of their worries. Many had come from Northwestern Europe to remote, rural areas where ethnic enclaves gave the impression of cultural homogeneity. To be sure, assimilation into American language and culture was a goal, but the children of European settlers were not left to sink or swim on their own. As today, second and third generation immigrants were typically the first in their families to finish school and master English. *Americanization* had community support, but there was also respect for national and family traditions, customs, and religious observance. In the U.S. today, immigrants find a very different environment.

By the end of the 19th century, attitudes began to shift due to the sheer numbers and diversity of new immigrants. From 1899 to 1920, more than eight million people entered the U.S., mostly from Southern and Eastern Europe. They flocked to urban centers to pursue the American Dream. One reaction was a push for a feeling of unity and ethnic homogeneity. Thus, a national drive for forced Americanization emerged through education, focused on the learning of *American* English. The first half of the 20th Century was a time of great hardship worldwide, with WWI and WWII, and the Great Depression in between. Attitudes towards bilingualism deteriorated further in the U.S. to one of suspicion and fear. But, following the Holocaust and huge population shifts in Europe, many Americans again felt sympathy for displaced peoples, welcoming them again as the Post-War economy rapidly expanded. This reached its zenith in the Civil Rights Movement of the 1960s. However, as the warm glow of the sixties faded, attitudes again changed. From sympathy for struggling minorities and establishment of bilingual programs, positive attitudes waned, and support for bilingual education gradually stopped.

The Southwest: Nowhere have negative attitudes to languages other than English flourished more than in the American Southwest, where Spanish has been spoken for centuries. Spanish is not a foreign language anymore than English is a foreign language in the Northeast. The only conclusion that one can draw from a biased attitude towards Spanish and its "Hispanic" speakers is that it is rooted in prejudice, based on stereotypes of Spanish-speaking people, their social behaviors, value systems, religious practices, housing patterns, and family life.

A revolving door: As the U.S. economy expanded in the 20th Century, the need grew for immigrants from Mexico as a cheap source of labor. The Mexican Revolution (1910–1920) forced thousands to flee. By the middle of the 1920s, immigration from Mexico had risen to such an extent that the government wanted to close the revolving door through the selective application of existing laws. The almost random sweeps to curb the flow of legal and illegal entry into the U.S. kept those seeking a safe haven in a state of fear. Nevertheless, the U.S. economy determined how that revolving door would swing. When laborers were needed, the door opened; when they weren't, the door would slam shut. During the Depression and the devastating droughts of the Dust Bowl, deportations increased. The *appearance* of being Mexican was enough for INS agents to stop and question "suspects."

The beginning of WWII reversed the trend and made cheap Mexican labor desirable once again. One consequence was the *bracero* (contract labor) program. After WWII, laborers who were no longer wanted were sent back under the guise of "voluntary" repatriation. The number of people caught crossing the border illegally jumped exponentially. But, the booming post-war economy once again created a need for cheap labor. Laws changed again and again, some encouraging immigration, while others (e.g., "Operation Wetback") reversed the trend. E.g., in 1954, over a million Mexicans were apprehended and *expelled* from the U.S. Within five years, nearly *four million people* were caught and deported. Only 63,515 of those went through formal deportation hearings. Segregation in schools also has a long history in the U.S., but it is often difficult for Americans to separate the idea of segregation from the Black and White context of the American South. However, the Southwest, particularly in the border states of Texas and California, has experienced its own brand of segregation. In these states, Chicano-Latino children were typically assigned to "Mexican" schools that reflected their low status. Perhaps the most humiliating aspect of discrimination was the prohibition against the use of Spanish in the schools – in the classroom, and on the school grounds.

Activities – topics for discussion

1. Discuss your own attitudes towards bi- and multilingualism and those of your parents. Are attitudes changing? What do you think are the reasons?

2. What are the popular attitudes towards the Spanish language and its speakers in your part of the country (that you are aware of)? In what ways do you see attitudes manifested towards so-called Hispanics?

3. Many languages were spoken in North America before Europeans came to establish colonies. Make a list of all the languages that you know of that were "here first."

4. Many Americans come from a mixed ancestry, with a little bit of this and a dash of that in their heritage. Do you have family stories what your ancestors encountered in "coming to America" and learning English?

5. What are some of the differences between today's immigrants and those of 100 years ago? List the causes for these differences, including laws and the development of transportation and communication. Speculate on what the future may hold.

Practice essay questions

1. Describe the Civil Rights Movement in the U.S. Discuss the connections between the Civil Rights Movement and changing immigration laws.

2. Describe the bracero program. Include in your response how contradictory immigration laws reflected the need for a cheap labor source in the U.S.

3. Describe the idealized tale that "our" forefathers learned English the hard way and just naturally assimilated into American culture. What are some of the different conditions that recent immigrants face as they pursue the American dream?

4. What are the three factors that have shaped American attitudes towards bilingualism and bilingual education? Explain each one and how they may be linked to the economy.

5. Describe some of the factors that went into the constantly changing U.S. immigration policies in the 20th Century. What is the most pressing factor in the 21st century.

Chapter 6

Bilingualism and education

1. The second half of the 20th Century:
   Waves of legislation
2. What's in a name?
3. Poor academic performance: The achievement gap
4. Different types of bilingual programs
5. Some preliminary conclusions

In the previous chapter, two separate areas of education were discussed: language instruction and academic *achievement*. Some issues seem to boil down to the desired purposes and outcomes of the educational process. Historically, from the beginning of the 20th century, Americanization efforts and cultural assimilation as an ideology have been focal points of education, especially in times of social and economic stress (cf. Wiley 2007: 53–54). The role of the English language has been a critical part of the debate over what it means to be a "real" American. Indeed, attitudes towards bilingualism have fluctuated considerably, but the specific area in which attitudes manifest themselves the most clearly (and ambiguously) is education. Specifically, a lack of English skills implied in some views of bilingualism has been viewed very negatively, for example, as disloyal to the U.S. and its ideals, even as un-American. Yet, there is constant controversy over the definition of American ideals and confusion over the costs-benefits of bilingualism. Is the real American a person who speaks only one language?[1]

---

1. There is an old joke. Question: "What do you call a person who speaks three languages? Answer: "Trilingual." Q: "What do you call a person who speaks two languages?" A: "Bilingual." Q: "And what do you call a person who speaks only one language?" A: "An American." It is difficult in chiefly monolingual societies for many people to understand the concepts of bilingualism and bilinguality. Obviously, this occurs in nations where the so-called superlanguages are nearly ubiquitous, e.g., in the U.S. and the U.K. But English speakers are not the only ones; similar attitudes exist in Spanish-speaking nations, and in parts of China and Russia, where imperial languages have pushed out nearly all of their competitors.

When considering a nation ostensibly built on democratic principles, one may wonder where cultural pluralism ranks and how a cultural synthesis (*a la* the melting pot) is supposed to work. But, the key issues of education remain distinct: educators have the responsibilities to *educate* and prepare children for their roles in American society. Society is, however, changing. We live in an evolving, multilingual and multicultural world, and in a global economy. The role of education is more than merely teaching basic skills and socializing children into a particular brand of Americanism. The responsibility to educate needs to extend into broadly based programs for all children. To be sure, language instruction is a part of it. Spolsky (1988) notes that the mismatch of home and school language and the need to teach a "standard" language are common on a global scale: "The fact that most children in the world do not come to school already controlling the language or variety that the school itself values and teaches means that most education has a large component of language teaching in it" (103).

For at least the last century, however, the role of language in education has been routinely confused with the purpose of schools to educate. It may be difficult to say for sure how much the perceived problems in education are artifacts of public perception and biases that get dramatized in the media, e.g., vivid portrayals of urban centers teeming with poor immigrants and threats of being overrun by hordes of illegal aliens on our borders. But, if there are real flaws in the educational process, solutions can be found. Even to the casual observer, there must be something behind the increasingly strident tone in discussions of failure rates on state and national tests. Unfortunately, these failure rates are typically attributed to ethnic and language minority students who fall within very narrow demographic profiles – the children of recent in-migrants and members of particular ethnic minorities. We all know the potentially harmful effects of stereotypes, but we still have to ask ourselves how much national biases influence our perceptions of the issues.

Perhaps nothing can illustrate the ambivalent and often conflicted attitudes of Americans to bi- and multilingualism than the history of bilingual education in the latter half of the Twentieth Century. The previous chapter chronicles many of the twists and turns up through the Civil Rights Movement. This chapter continues that discussion, focusing on the waves of legislation that occurred in the second half of the 20th century and continue into the present century. It also takes a critical look at various approaches to bilingual education, from "sink or swim" approaches, e.g., *submersion* (monolingual) programs, to strong versions such as *dual immersion* and *heritage language instruction*. Weak versions of bilingual education typically emphasize a rapid transition to English and ignore any form of language maintenance. They are bilingual in name only. Strong versions emphasize the bilingual and *bicultural* aspects of education and seek to develop the skills and knowledge children already possess in their native languages. Such programs are truer to the ideals of bilingual education. A key concern is student *achievement*, the academic progress in skill and content areas that seem to underlie today's concerns of the U.S. educational system as a whole and its inability to move bilingual students along in the system. All major approaches aim to incorporate increasing numbers of immigrants into American society. Different approaches achieve different outcomes.

1. The second half of the 20th Century: Waves of legislation

From the beginning of the 20th century to the end of World War II, the U.S. went from an isolated nation willing to live in its corner of the world to an international military and economic juggernaut. In roughly half a century, Americans forged a national identity in the face of incredible adversity. As a consequence of increasing diversity brought on from the outside and growing prosperity on the inside, its internal politics also began to shift. Prevailing sentiment evolved (perhaps superficially) into something more open and inclusive towards people of color. This change culminated in the Civil Rights Movement of the 1960s and the idealism associated with the new *Camelot* and the presidency of John F. Kennedy. Sweeping changes were enacted in laws concerning civil rights, education, and immigration, setting a ball in motion whose effects have been felt for decades.

Year	Legislation	Notes
1906	**Nationality Act**	Added English requirement to the requirements of immigration and naturalization
1923	**Meyer v Nebraska**	Ended arbitrary restrictions on teaching foreign languages
1950	**Amendment to Naturalization Act**	Added literacy requirement for citizenship
1954	**Brown v Board of Education**	Segregation in schools ruled unconstitutional
1958	**National Defense Act**	New legislation that promoted foreign language teaching

Figure 6.1 Language legislation prior to the 1960s

The federal government prior to 1965 had enacted only a few laws that affected bilingual education and the usage of languages other than English. After the Nationality Act of 1906, which added an English language requirement to those of immigration and naturalization, the U.S. Supreme Court took a stance against arbitrary restrictions in the teaching of foreign languages in its landmark 1923 ruling in *Meyer v Nebraska*. A state law had prohibited foreign language instruction to elementary school pupils, and a case was filed against a teacher for reading a Bible story in German to a 10-year old child. The Court ruled the law unconstitutional, and "that proficiency in a foreign language was 'not injurious to the health, morals, or understanding of the normal child'" (Baker 2006: 191). However, a 1950 amendment to the Naturalization Act added a literacy requirement for citizenship, expanding its English requirement to reading and writing, putting more pressure on immigrants to conform to an Anglo-Saxon mold.

Two other critical pieces of national legislation appeared in postwar America reflecting a profound change in race relations. The first, a Supreme Court ruling in *Brown v Board of Education of Topeka, Kansas* (1954) made racial segregation in schools unconstitutional, attacking the "separate but equal" doctrine that had allowed such racist practices to persist (Baker 2006: 201; cf. Crawford 1992a: 73). (Almost simultaneously, there were other similar state rulings in California and Texas.) While this ruling specifically dealt with issues of Black and White, it had ramifications that reached into Latino communities. The other was the National Defense Act in 1958. As fears grew of the developing scientific technology of the Soviet Union and the launching of *Sputnik*, the world's first space satellite, a national debate began to develop about the relative quality of the U.S. educational system. To improve the system and make it more competitive on a global scale, Congress passed legislation that *promoted* foreign-language learning in elementary schools, high schools, and universities (Baker 2006: 191). While this meant encouraging bilingualism from an English plus perspective (English as primary language along with another, auxiliary language), greater attention was paid to language minority groups in the U.S. and the possible benefits of other kinds of bilingualism (e.g., heritage languages plus English).

1.1 The Civil Rights Movement and the Immigration and Nationality Act of 1965

Until the Civil Rights Movement, discussions of racial or ethnic minorities had been confined to issues of Black and White. Indeed, the movement was originally focused on the struggles of African Americans to achieve the rights that they had been granted a century earlier by the Emancipation Proclamation of 1862. But, despite legislation, discrimination and segregation had endured for over a hundred years. The Civil Rights Act of 1964 outlawed segregation on the basis of race and nationality in schools, the workplace, and public places. Its ramifications have reached into nearly every layer of American Society. In that same spirit, in the interest of diversity and long-held American beliefs of freedom and equality, Congress opened the floodgates to increased immigration from Latin America and other so-called Third World nations with the passage of the Immigration and Nationality Act of 1965. This act effectively stopped the complex quota system of immigration that had restricted immigration from certain countries. While the Act's supporters may have anticipated sweeping changes, it has become more of a Pandora's Box to those who now want to restrict immigration.

Year	Legislation	Notes
1964	**Civil Rights Act**	Ended discrimination based on race and nationality
1965	**Immigration and Nationality Act**	Ended immigration quota system based on nationality
1965	**Elementary and Secondary Education Act**	(ESEA) Granted funds to children who had been denied equal opportunities in education
1967	**Bilingual Education Act**	Title VII of the ESEA, established funding for bilingual programs—poorly defined; term LEP (limited English proficiency) first appears
1970	**Beginning of Lau v Nichols**	S.F. Court case regarding equal opportunity of language minorities in schools; appealed to Title VI of Civil Rights Act
1974	**Court Decision in Lau v Nichols**	Ruled against S.F. Unified School District in favor of parents
1974	**Equal Educational Opportunity Act**	(EEOA) Turned Lau decision into law
1974	**Reauthorization of ESEA**	Native-language instruction became a condition for grants
1975	**Lau Remedies**	Established guidelines for schools re LEP students
1978	**Bilingual Education Act reauthorized**	Limited grants for native-language instruction, paving way for transitional programs

Figure 6.2 Language legislation in the 1960s and 1970s

That same year, on the educational front, landmark legislation known as the *Elementary and Secondary Education Act* (ESEA) set the stage for the rebirth of bilingual education as one extension of the Civil Rights Act (Wiley 2007:64). It provided federal funds to meet the needs of disadvantaged children who had been denied equal opportunities in education as a result of overt segregation. It affected *all* language minority children. By virtue of numbers, Spanish-speaking children stood to benefit the most, including Puerto Ricans in the Northeast, Mexican-Americans throughout the Midwest and Southwest, and Cubans in Florida – Hispanics nationwide.

In 1967, not long after, Ralph Yarborough, a senator from Texas, introduced an amendment to this legislative landmark known as the *Bilingual Education Act*. The goal was to help native speakers of Spanish who were failing in schools. Enacted as *Title VII* of the ESEA, it established funding for bilingual programs for children who did not speak English and were from lower socioeconomic strata.[2] However, definitions were vague on what actually constituted bilingual education. Local jurisdictions were left to interpret the provisions of the Bilingual Education Act on their own. While it was a huge step forward in giving help to growing numbers of immigrant children, the differences between bilingual education and merely teaching English as a Second Language were blurred considerably. Studies of the effectiveness of various bilingual programs did not always specify the precise nature of the programs, so it was difficult even for the experts to determine exactly what caused programs to succeed or fail. Language maintenance (the preservation of heritage languages) was not addressed, leaving room for various and conflicting interpretations down the road.

An important court case testing some of these issues was *Lau v Nichols* which began in 1970 (Baker 2006: 192). It involved a group of Chinese children (with limited English skills) in San Francisco whose parents claimed that their children were being denied the help they needed to succeed in school. The case appealed to Title VI of the Civil Rights Act, which had banned discrimination on the basis of national origin. The U.S. Supreme court accepted the case after other courts had rejected it. It ruled in 1974 that the San Francisco Unified School District had violated the children's civil rights by not offering educational services in Chinese. It was not enough to provide the same textbooks and instructional materials used for proficient English speakers to students who did not understand English. The Lau decision, often cited as an authority for all language-discrimination cases, acknowledged the close ties between language and national origin, and that discrimination based on language was in effect discrimination based on national origin. It tested the limits of the Bilingual Education Act by challenging the practice of merely providing English (ESL) instruction to children who did not speak English. Programs were established to provide help for students as they gradually progressed from bilingual-education classrooms to so-called mainstream classes.

The same year as the Lau decision (1974), the *Equal Educational Opportunity Act* (EEOA) turned the *Lau v Nichols* decision into law. The EEOA required every school district to take appropriate action to overcome language barriers that interfered with the equal participation of its students in instructional programs. The ESEA was also up for renewal; this gave lawmakers an opportunity to revisit the specifics. As a consequence, the reauthorization of Title VII of the ESEA produced an amendment to the Bilingual Education Act. It added for the first time a requirement for native-language instruction as *a condition* for bilingual education grants. However, bilingual education was specifically defined as *transitional*. In other words, it would be temporary, and a means of placing students into English-only classes. Clearly, this was to quell fears that students might receive instruction in their native languages without end.

---

2. A *title*, in legal parlance, is a major section of written legislation, typically book length.

In 1975, the very next year, a document known as the Lau Remedies was published by the former Department of Health, Education, and Welfare (HEW) setting guidelines for schools on their responsibilities to English Language Learners.[3] It required bilingual education (broadly defined) in districts where students' civil rights had been violated. However, public debate was becoming progressively more vocal and political. In 1978, another reauthorization of the Bilingual Education Act (Title VII of the ESEA) further limited grants for native language instruction, this time specifying that such programs could only provide the help necessary for a child to achieve proficiency in English, once again addressing fears that bilingual education programs would somehow be open-ended and, thus, never-ending. The tide had changed again, and there was growing pressure to limit reliance on heritage languages and to focus on what was perceived as *the goal of bilingual education*, namely, full proficiency in English. In an almost complete reversal of the spirit and intent of Civil Rights legislation, heritage-language maintenance programs were no longer eligible for federal funding.

1.2 The Eighties and beyond

As the warm glow of the 1960s and the Civil Rights Movement faded in the 1970s, attitudes had once again turned. From a feeling of empathy for struggling immigrants and the establishment of promising bilingual programs (e.g., Florida's innovative programs with Cuban exiles), the attitudes of many Anglo Americans gradually turned against bilingualism amid nationwide pressure to adopt English at the expense of heritage languages. In the 1980s, American attitudes towards bilingualism and bilingual education continued to spiral downward. And, again, the reasons were evidently reactions to increased immigration, economic stresses on education and the economy, and the desire to maintain a uniform culture. *English-only movements* were popping up and picking up steam. Their growing influence had the effect of changing the concerns of the public and the government from an equal opportunity in education to issues of cultural assimilation, from how to meet students' educational needs to finding the fastest way to make them proficient in English. Bilingual education was portrayed as divisive and encouraging loyalty to minority cultures. So, the terms of the debate over bilingualism and bilingual education changed, answered by charges of racism (Crawford 1995: 68–78).

---

3. Most of the so-called Lau remedies and other guidelines became tools of the federal Office of Civil Rights (OCR), which played a role in the enactment of the Equal Educational Opportunity Act (EEOA). However, this office has always been in the middle of the debate concerning the intent and long-range effects of various proposed laws, e.g., (a) whether federal agencies should require strong forms of bilingual education and language-maintenance programs, and (b) whether or not such programs fostered allegiance to ethnic minority cultures instead of allegiance to majority, Anglo American culture and language. Needless to say, these issues remain highly controversial.

Year	Legislation	Notes
1981	**Castañeda v Pickard**	Established guidelines to evaluate bilingual programs
1983	**US English Movement begins**	Debates become more prominent regarding the place of English in education and society
1984	**Bilingual Education Act reauthorized**	Funding for maintenance programs once again allowed; most money to go to TBE and special English-only programs
1988	**Bilingual Education Act reauthorized**	Mandated 25% of funding go to English-only SAIP (Special Alternative Instructional Programs)
1994	**Bilingual Education Act reauthorized**	Eliminated 25% quota, and funded dual-language programs
1998	**Proposition 227 in California**	Infamous "Unz initiative," effectively eliminated bilingual programs in California
2001	**No Child Left Behind**	Replaced Bilingual Education Act; makes schools (and teachers) responsible for student performance
2009	**Race to the Top**	$4.35 billion incentive program of competitive grants to encourage school reform; part of the American Recovery and Reinvestment Act of 2009.4

Figure 6.3 Language legislation from the 1980s to the present

Much of the criticism of the English-Only movement, founded in 1983 by California Senator S. I. Hayakawa and various Official English movements (e.g., *US English* and *English First* organizations), has been cast in the light of Civil Rights legislation. For example, Baker and Jones (1998:291) cite six typical criticisms of the English-Only Movement: (1) it ignores U.S. civil rights traditions; (2) fails to support the full integration of language minority children; (3) neglects the needs of U.S. business to communicate with foreign markets (demanding that they use English); (4) limits government's ability to serve all citizens; (5) disenfranchises minority citizens (by not making full participation possible); (6) and encourages divisiveness and animosity towards people whose native language is not English.

Nevertheless, the political debates became more and more divided along partisan lines. For instance, in 1980, a document known as the Lau Regulations was an attempt by the Carter administration (Democrat) to formalize the Lau Remedies. Opponents saw it as an overt appeal for the Hispanic vote. These regulations would have required bilingual education for limited English proficiency (LEP) students but *only when feasible*. The proposal was withdrawn the next year by the incoming Reagan administration (Republican), which looked like it was opposed to bilingual education. This left the responsibilities of schools unclear. One court case, *Castañeda v Pickard* (1981), resulted in an Appeals Court decision that created specific criteria to help the government decide if a school was meeting responsibilities of the ESEA. It stated that programs for LEP students needed to be based on (1) sound educational theory, (2) implemented with adequate resources, and (3) evaluated and proven effective. As vague as these three criteria are, they have proved to be valuable in assessing programs, particularly, those that were only half-hearted attempts to comply with the EEOE.

A cabinet-level Department of Education (which superseded HEW) was created by the outgoing Carter Administration in 1979 to oversee federal funding programs and enforce laws regarding privacy and civil rights. (It does not control curriculum and has no role in the accreditation process.) Secretary of Education William J. Bennett, who arrived on the scene in 1985, wound up being a spokesman for anti-bilingual education interests. He almost singlehandedly dismantled nearly twenty years of legislation. In his first major speech, Bennett alleged that there was no proof that bilingual education had helped anyone, after seventeen years and nearly two billion dollars of federal expenditures. He was hailed as a leader who could stand against the powerful bilingual education lobby and as a proponent of innovative educational programs (although they were the same old, English-only programs that post-Civil Rights legislation had sought to rectify). In so doing, he alienated significant portions of the Hispanic community. However, he directed many of his statements against federal policy, not specific programs, while pandering to a growing anti-immigration sentiment in political circles that were against native-language instruction (Crawford 1995:85).

The death knell for Bilingual Education programs in California, however, began in 1998 with the passage of Proposition 227 in California, the infamous *Unz Initiative*. It was presented as a political measure that would strengthen English-language instruction and improve the success of bilingual students – under the slogan "English for the children" (Wiley 2007:70). Ron Unz, a San Francisco Bay Area political figure, was motivated by his own assimilationist views; he had been a vocal critic of bilingual education and multiculturalism. His campaign targeted what he perceived as the ineffectiveness of bilingual education – the slow academic progress made by English-language learners in the state. It proposed that English-only programs replace those with heritage language instruction. Similar measures were passed in Arizona (2000) and Massachusetts (2002), though another brought by Unz in Colorado was defeated (Baker 2006:195–6; Wiley 2007:70). It is still debated whether or not the voters who passed 227 understood that it would effectively outlaw bilingual education of any kind. Its appeal had been for English Language Learners to reach English proficiency as fast as possible. Nevertheless, Proposition 227 had a profound impact on California's educational policies and produced long-lasting consequences (see Wentworth, Pellegrin, Thompson & Hakuta 2010).

Into the 21st century: legislation runs full circle. Under the George W. Bush administration, US legislation was enacted in 2001 that completely repealed the Bilingual Education Act of 1968. At this point, the term "bilingual" disappeared from federal education legislation regarding English Language Learners (ELLs) to reflect the emphasis on cultural assimilation and the subtractive nature of future programs and federal education laws (Wiley 2007: 69). Known as the No Child Left Behind Act (NCLB – often pronounced "nickelbee"), it was the first federal legislation that effectively did away with the rights of state and local agencies to interpret compliance with laws and regulations derived from Civil Rights legislation. It made school districts and states accountable to the federal government for the performance of LEP students. Districts are required to (a) identify languages other than English used by the student population; (b) develop academic assessment in both skill and content areas; (c) assess proficiency in English annually for all LEP students; (d) include grade 3 through 8 LEP students in the assessment of reading and mathematics; and (e) assess reading skills in English for all students who had been in US schools for three years.

Some of these requirements were relaxed somewhat in 2004, but in essence, English Language Learners were to be tested yearly in both English and mathematics. Individual teachers and administrators are held responsible for their progress, risking punitive actions (e.g., firing, lower pay, and loss of funding) for consistently low test scores. There is no mention in this act of bilingualism or the development (or maintenance) of native-language skills, or the preservation of heritage languages. Any research that questions the effectiveness of English-only approaches appears to be irrelevant. Most critics point out that compulsory, standardized testing, or "high-stakes assessment," will transform the established curriculum, leading to a "teach to the test" mentality in those specific areas that are continually tested, rather than a focus on educating children in a broad manner in the arts, sciences, and humanities. The ramifications have also led to the massive reorganization of school districts, the emergence of *charter schools*, and the upswing of private and parochial schools.

2. What's in a name?

All bilingual programs are ostensibly designed to educate and take care of the needs of bilingual children and the communities to which they belong. But, as the waves of legislation demonstrate, there does not seem to be any kind of consensus concerning what works and what does not work. To get at the roots of the controversy, educators compile mounds of data that supposedly indicate the positive (or negative) affects of particular approaches and pedagogical methods. However, the data is not always easy to decipher. Terminology is key. While a rose by any other name may smell just as sweet, putting a name or label on a child may have a lasting, perhaps harmful effect. By ascribing a name or label to a cluster of individuals like *immigrants* or *aliens*, we differentiate between those who fit into accepted norms (*normal* being members of the dominant or mainstream society) from those who deviate from it.

With respect to immigrants and their assumed poor language abilities, a new class of people has been created for exclusionary purposes, one that is often labeled deficient, remedial, at risk, nonstandard, or merely limited in their linguistic abilities (Wiley 2005: 121–122; cf. Baker 2006: 206). It may appear that this class of people is so broken that it can't be fixed, but it is not static and unchanging. The more extreme reactions suggest that members of this class are societal liabilities that are nothing more than a drain on the economy. Those who are against relaxed immigration laws and the education of immigrant children can certainly stir up public opinion. However, one's response to those issues is a sure indicator that prejudices are lying at the door. If one believes that there is intrinsic value to every human life, then the response may be to deal with a changing reality, not to demonize a certain group and call for their eradication.

First of all, by assuming that there is a norm of some kind, anything that deviates from that norm becomes abnormal, defective, or deficient. The same holds for Standard English. For decades, AAVE (Ebonics) was considered *substandard* because it deviated from standard norms determined by educators, dictionary writers, and English teachers. Nevertheless, by creating the categories of standard or normal, behaviors that differ are automatically assumed to be *below* standard, therefore, substandard. Whether they appear valid or not, such terms and labels imply a social *hierarchy*: some language varieties (or people) are better or higher than others.

The issue of terminology is more than just political correctness; it's a matter of accuracy. For instance, the term *ELL* (an acronym for English Language Learner) has replaced the more stigmatized *LEP* (Limited English Proficiency) and its caustic nickname *leper* that has been carelessly tossed about in "lunchroom conversation" (Wiley 2005: 123–125). The term *limited English* focuses only on what a child does *not* know, not on what she does know. And, because of the political importance of Standard English, incipient bilinguals get no credit for knowing their own native language(s). Whether a change of name has truly altered perceptions and biases is, however, debatable. The label itself, though not overtly linked to race, can act similarly to stigmatized classifications based on race (Wiley 2005: 120–121).

Perhaps the biggest obstacle in determining the causes for poor performance in schools lies in the categories themselves. The data from which educators need to work are put into different boxes: one is racial/ethnic, another dependent on socioeconomic status (*SES*), and a third based on language abilities. All three categories refer to different ways of labeling people. Combine these with immigrant status, and there are many possible overlaps, obscuring important information that could shed some light on causes. Immigrant status seems to be the least likely cause from a rational standpoint. All of the original European colonists were immigrants, but that didn't mean they were doomed to failure as a consequence. And, even if a child can be placed in all of these categories (a non-native English speaking Hispanic immigrant from a lower SES background), it does not follow that this child will do poorly or fail.

There are a number of reasons why these particular categories can cause confusion. First, SES is clearly not a racial category, stereotypes notwithstanding. There are poor Anglos just as their are poor Latinos, poor African Americans, and poor Asian Americans. Not all poor people are Latinos, and not all Latinos are poverty-stricken. Sweeping generalizations are simply not accurate; in fact, they are logical fallacies. SES may influence a child's readiness for the school environment, but educators need to look at specific communities where SES plays a key role, whether that community is populated by immigrants or not. There may be deep, underlying cultural issues that come into play. In addition, not all Chicano-Latinos in the U.S. are bilingual in Spanish and English. Millions of Latinos are monolingual, native-speakers of English, while only a small minority speaks only Spanish. A bilingual community consists of all types. While perceptions of race and ethnicity have influenced language policy and attitudes towards bilingual education in the Southwest, data about bilinguals is independent of race. While the two categories may overlap somewhat, they are distinct.

Ethnic classification, is controversial, to say the least; and again, we see the mixing of categories. Traditionally, race, nationality, and culture are included, but the same criteria do not always apply equally to each group. E.g., Anglo Americans, in today's scheme of ethnicity, may include any person born of European racial stock (so-called Whites), ignoring the old three-way classification of the early 1900s. African Americans are generally classed according to race and U.S. nationality. (Blacks from African nations are not ethnic African Americans.) Asian Americans are primarily classified by racial characteristics. So-called Hispanics can be of any race, from many different nations, and from diverse cultural and historical backgrounds. As a consequence, all data that use Hispanic, Latino, or other similar designation may refer to people of many different nationalities, language backgrounds, physical appearance, cultural beliefs, and SES. As discussed in Chapter 1, so-called Hispanics are not one, homogeneous, and "happy" family. There are many rivalries between groups. Consequently, not all data based on such a fluid definition of ethnicity will have a direct bearing on bilingual education.

Another set of issues arises when we focus on schools. There are questions about the *quality of various approaches* to bilingual education and *the ability of schools* to carry out specially-designed programs that always seem to have an emphasis on language learning. We can find excellent programs (based on sound educational principles) that are half-heartedly applied that fail miserably because teachers lack specific training or motivation. In contrast, we can also find older, perhaps outdated approaches that are carried out by experienced, caring teachers with positive results. Consequently, we not only need to look at various types of testing and the interpretation of data, we have to look at the feasibility of different program models across the curriculum and across age groups – what works for preschool children may not work for adolescents and adults. There has been a lot of work done regarding what makes programs effective, but an abstract "theoretical" approach may not weigh as much in the equation as the social make-up of the teachers and others (reflecting the background of the student population) who interface with children on a daily basis (Lucas, Henze & Donato 1990). In this respect, the role of popular culture may be significant: teachers need to be sensitive to cultural nuances affecting large numbers of ethnic minority children. Educators need to ask themselves how they can use the interests of the students as bridges into the world of academics.

One of the ramifications of the No Child Left Behind Act has been that schools and entire districts are hamstrung by the conflicting demands of the federal government and the needs of their students. Pressure from the government has led to the restructuring of entire school districts and programs and the growing influence of charter schools (with special mandates) where *parents* have greater control over curricula and school spending. (These schools may specialize in the arts or sciences, offering alternatives to public schools and their emphasis on standardized tests.) Charter schools in the U.S., both primary and secondary, receive state and federal funding in addition to donations or grants, but they generally don't have the strictures placed on public schools. They are accountable for student performance specified in each school's charter agreement – a performance contract. Admission is often by lottery because of long waiting lists. In general, they do not charge tuition, have no selective admission requirements, and have no religious affiliation. Some have been established by universities or other non-profit organizations in response to the restrictive atmosphere of state-run schools. This may leave the average public school with even greater pressure to comply with NCLB to prove their worth.

In any case, particularly in the state of California, discussions of bilingual education since passage of the Unz Initiative have been curtailed to include only programs specifically designed for ELLs to get them from low English skills to full proficiency as quickly as possible. These may be English-only programs that continue the cycle of subtractive bilingualism jeopardizing students' long-term academic success. So, one of the issues for school districts is how they can allow current knowledge (informed approaches) to influence the models they are required to adopt. They must establish realistic goals, and the expectations of teachers and students must be free of biased perceptions. Their problem is not one of immigration; it is one of serving students. And, although the school is the main arena for cultural and linguistic assimilation, the research into effective programs suggests that the best approaches are sensitive to the *students'* needs (and those of their communities), flexible (able to adjust to the individual student's environment), and open-minded (free of racist beliefs of cultural and linguistic inferiority). But, when a program's chief aim is language instruction, the impartation of academic knowledge (and knowledge of the world that forms the backbone of academic language) suffers accordingly. Major pedagogical approaches whose entire focus is to assimilate increasing numbers of immigrants into American society fail to recognize that language minority students need to learn and acquire real-world knowledge that cannot only impact their circumstances and increase their ability to gain material success, but also increase the likelihood that they may lead fulfilling lives.

3.   Poor academic performance: The achievement gap

As the numbers of immigrants have gone up, so have reports of their academic failings, reminiscent of old arguments that bilinguals are at an academic disadvantage and reports of so-called semilinguals. Continual dire press reports keep immigration in the national spotlight prompting reactions that can be genuinely xenophobic. Typical allegations include low reading scores (when compared with national norms), lower grades (when compared with mainstream students), and characteristic high drop-out rates (when compared to those of different ethnic groups). We need to take care not to blame immigrants for all that ails schools in the U.S.

Categories are often mixed in public sectors, just as they are for educators. There seems to be a general tendency to put all immigrants, language minorities, and English learners into one general category despite the fact that they are three separate populations. However, because public opinion plays such a large political role in legislation, immigrant status (in place of ethnicity) has a disproportionately large influence on public perceptions of what is wrong with the system. Thousands of immigrants arrive each year from the U.K., Canada, Australia, and the Caribbean, from dozens of officially English-speaking nations, who are neither language minorities nor English learners. Speakers of Chicano English (ChE) and African American Vernacular English (AAVE) are members of language minorities, but they are neither immigrants nor ELLs. Tens of thousands of U.S. citizens are born each year who acquire a language other than English in the home, e.g., speakers of indigenous languages. They're not immigrants, though they may eventually get classified as members of a language minority and enter the ranks of ELLs. We certainly don't have to look exclusively at people coming from outside the U.S. to see the need for equitable educational practices and intelligent language-teaching programs.

3.1   Fixing the blame

When looking for the causes of poor academic achievement, we have several options. We can blame the children – the victims. But, this might be like blaming a shooting victim for standing in the wrong place at the wrong time (see Wiley 2005: 98). We can also look to causes outside the child in her social environment or to the school system itself. How much does socioeconomic status influence students' success? When there has been such obvious inequity in the educational system as segregated classrooms, inferior facilities, inexperienced and poorly trained teachers, and clearly limited educational opportunities for language minority students, we can blame individual schools. In addition, the costs of subtractive types of education seem obvious when entire heritage languages and cultures are devalued and established skills are ignored and swept aside. The subtractive nature of particular educational programs undoubtedly has a role in alienating students and the communities they come from.

In spite of a chorus of voices from linguists and language acquisition specialists to the contrary, beliefs persist that somehow bilingualism causes some kind of mental confusion and delayed development, and that it is the root cause for the achievement gap between immigrant children and their mainstream counterparts. In the U.S., this is typically discussed in the context of a gap in the academic performance between ELLs and proficient English speakers (Rumberger and Tran 2010: 86–87). But, if we start looking at bilingualism as a cause, we are immediately faced with different kinds of bilingualism. Bilingualism is multifaceted, complex, and dynamic, not monolithic, simple, and static. There are segments of the bilingual population in the U.S. composed of highly-skilled, balanced bilinguals who achieve high academic standards.

However, there may also be bilingual communities where particular aspects of both language varieties appear to be underdeveloped, not necessarily to the extent of semilingualism where a child seems unable to communicate fully in either of her languages, but enough to affect competence in the language variety required in school settings. In this respect, social and economic factors can influence exposure to specific kinds of English. Academic performance depends on exposure to academic registers in each language, forms of the language that are gained through literacy training and conscious study, and not necessarily through natural processes of language acquisition. Children learn the varieties that they are exposed to. So, when a child does not receive enough exposure to specific academic registers of English, educators need to look for causes in their environment, in the schools and their influence on children, and in the communities that shape attitudes. If we wish to put blame for low test scores on underdeveloped language varieties, we need to look into the social conditions that give rise to them and how communities contribute to the lack of language development.

Chicano children in some areas of Los Angeles receive little or no formal training in Spanish, so some local varieties (vernacular Spanish) consist almost exclusively of informal, spoken registers used in the home and in other non-academic contexts. Formal training in Spanish may be restricted to Spanish foreign language classes, which can be problematic for teachers as well as students when natives and non-native speakers are in the same classroom. Their problems will differ according to levels of proficiency. Some districts in California and other states make available Spanish for Native Speakers (SNS) courses that give additional support in a standard form of (Mexican) Spanish for those who are heritage-language speakers and for those who speak nonstandard forms of Chicano Spanish. Bordering on irony, there are also Advanced Placement (AP) Spanish classes supported by the College Board throughout the U.S., in both AP Spanish language and AP Spanish Literature.[4] However, the vernacular is not always considered "real" Spanish: there are frequent Anglicisms (English words and structures) that are considered "substandard." It is stigmatized like nonstandard varieties of English.

Schools are exploring ways to make the content of language arts courses more relevant to language minority children. This is done to draw these children into the learning process. By making quality resources available to the community (children's books and other reading materials), educators hope to encourage the entire community to stress literacy, to gain academic knowledge, and to promote a culture that endorses the acquisition of knowledge and respect for the educational process.[5]

Indeed, some Latinos do live in high-density, low income areas where material poverty is particularly severe, and access to educational resources is limited. The work of James Diego Vigil (e.g., 1988, 2007; Moore & Vigil 1993: 27–49) has shown strong connections between life in low-income housing projects (barrios) and criminal activity associated with gang membership. But, it is a combination of low SES and a sense of disenfranchisement brought through decades of social struggle that lie at the heart of this alternative to mainstream culture. Just as exposure to academic registers of English or Spanish can encourage participation in academics, the lack of exposure can act as a barrier. Nonstandard varieties develop in response to social pressures. Factors such as individual and group identity can shape a language variety, for example, in nonstandard forms of Chicano Spanish and Chicano English. Consequently, children are often caught between (a) their social identity (which is often reinforced by stereotypes and biases shown by teachers and administrators) and the ways that identity manifests

---

4.   Advanced Placement (AP) programs offer rigorous, specifically designed courses that make university credit available to high-school students. AP courses are provided and supported by the College Board, a non-profit organization established in New York in 1955. Tests are administered nationally and internationally once a year by the Educational Testing Service, headquartered in Princeton, N.J.

5.   To imagine the impact of children's books, consider the wealth of literature that has been translated from other languages into English, for example, the tales of the Brothers Grimm in German (*Rapunzel, Hansel and Gretel, Cinderella, Little Red Riding Hood, Sleeping Beauty, Snow White*, and *Rumpelstiltskin*). Add to that the works of the Dane Hans Christian Andersen (*The Emperor's New Clothes, The Little Mermaid*, and *The Ugly Duckling*), and one can see the depth of imagery embedded in English and European literature. Where would literature studies be without English translations of Miguel de Cervantes Saavedra (*Don Quixote*) and images of the hero fighting windmills, and the translations of Russian literary giants Dostoevsky (*The Brothers Karamazov*) and Tolstoy (*War and Peace*). Once a reader is familiar with the characters and plots, learning to read in German, Spanish, or Russian is greatly aided. All one has to do is learn the structure of the language; much information is already known.

itself in language, and (b) the desire to gain an education in highly literate registers of a language variety to which they've had little exposure.

The argument for blaming socioeconomic level has apparent advantages. For example, it rightly shifts blame away from the child (as victim) and onto society to explain lack of opportunity and achievement. Home life needs to be considered, as well, e.g., the possibility of neglect or abuse, material circumstances, and living conditions. This may include psychological and social factors of discrimination, racial prejudices, depression, and immobilizing feelings of inferiority (Baker 2006: 207). But, *SES does not explain everything.* Some children do well in spite of their social and material circumstances. Lack of academic achievement cannot be pinned on one and only one cause. While there may be a correlation between (a) the lack of literacy in any language and low academic achievement and (b) low SES, there is no direct cause-and-effect relationship. Low SES may account for lack of opportunity, but the reverse may also be true, that low academic performance and lack of literacy play negative roles in poverty by lowering prospects for employment (Wiley 2007: 102ff.). One needs to analyze the possible effects of SES, e.g., the influence of parents' attitudes to education and literacy (according to their educational background and experience), and the reaction of family members to stress and the hardships of merely surviving in their adopted homeland.

3.2   Strong versus weak bilingual programs

Some attempts to fix the blame for poor academic performance on bilingual education are subtle and misleading. One strategy to promote bilingual approaches has been to emphasize a mismatch between school and home environments. This may be true, but it can also be misleading. Emphasis on a mismatch can suggest that the English language learner should want to abandon her heritage language and culture to increase her chances of gaining complete mastery of English, and that her unique background is a detriment to success in the majority language and culture. A transparent attempt to create and maintain a uniform, mainstream society, it discourages pluralism and diversity. One can't help but suspect that the motivation for such an argument is rooted in biases with perhaps a tinge of racism. The argument for a uniform culture often starts with assertions like "those people have come here, to the U.S., and it is up to them to learn our American language and ways. We Americans don't have to adjust to them; they have to adjust to us." Such a view is obviously condescending and patronizing. But, if heeded, it invariably leads to weak forms of bilingual education, to English-only instruction and subtractive education that can have negative consequences in the bilingual community and in society.

Strong forms of bilingual education show promise in addressing actual causes for low academic performance by being inclusive (drawing students and their families together with educators) and non-discriminatory, thereby minimizing feelings of alienation. For sequential learners, they enable language minority students to grasp academic concepts in their native language while still learning their second. Learning a new form or label for a concept is a relatively easy process when a child already knows the concept. Vocabulary learning is only one small part of language acquisition; speakers of European languages like Spanish have a tremendous advantage in view of the large number of common lexical items and cognates available, particularly in academic registers. For native and nonnative speakers alike, explicit learning and conscious attention are required for literate, academic registers of speech, and that type of learning is easily extended to include the awareness of cognates.

In the social context of both ChE and AAVE, or *bidialectal* settings, children do in fact know the basic syntax and morphology of English, albeit a non-standard form of it. As spoken varieties, both cover informal, non-academic registers, core vocabulary, and basic grammar. All dialects of English share the majority of their characteristics with minor grammatical differences and variation in pronunciation and vocabulary. By building on what the child already knows, the transition to academic registers is partially complete. The native language or dialect functions as a bridge to the acquisition of Standard English. In true bilingual settings, when a child already knows the meaning of the word, the task of learning its English equivalent is half completed.

In general, weak bilingual programs produce weak results, and strong programs produce strong results. For example, students enrolled in strong programs have scored at or above average in reading achievement (Baker 2006: 204). Nevertheless, many people still blame *bilingual education* (as a blanket term) for the poor results they read about in their daily newspapers, not realizing that there are (a) many types of programs that lead to very different results and that there are (b) many more possible causes for poor academic performance than a flawed program. With content instruction in the native/heritage language, the English that ELLs hear is made more comprehensible (easier) because they are prepared and poised to learn new vocabulary items. Simply put, strong forms of bilingual education produce *better English proficiency* because they promote acquisition. This may be counterintuitive by going against traditional ideas of language learning, but preliminary research backs up the claim. A byproduct of a strong program may be a degree of language maintenance. However, one cannot confuse language instruction with a general education and simply substitute more English training in place of knowledge that can actually help them master English and become better educated.

So-called *mainstreaming* programs try to speed up the process of language acquisition by cutting out the middle man, so to speak, the language that the child already knows. But, they do not speed up anything. Some programs, in fact, may wind up doing more harm than good. They effectively ignore the skills the child already has in her home language and her ability to comprehend academic materials. They undermine her sense of self-respect and confidence in her own abilities by implying that they are somehow inferior (e.g., by saying knowledge gained in Spanish doesn't count). Instead of building on the existing foundation, which is what educators do for speakers of the majority language (giving them an inherent advantage), they ignore that skill set by substituting another one that the child has not yet attained. Then, when *academic* scores don't go up, the child gets more of the same medicine, more remedial English-only instruction. It is reminiscent of outmoded methods of artificial respiration used to resuscitate drowning victims. Make the victim lie prone and pull her arms back to force the water out of their lungs – out with the bad air, in with the good air. Another water metaphor applied to teaching methods known as "sink or swim," unfortunately, fails to consider the possibility that a child may sink without help.

4. Different types of bilingual programs

The term *bilingual education* means many things to many people, so any definition can be ambiguous and potentially confusing. It can mean almost anything from (a) the education of a child in two (or more) languages with the goal of a full-blown bilingual and biliterate student to (b) a systematic program designed to eliminate a child's native language. Therefore, different bilingual programs will reflect conflicting goals and contrary anticipated outcomes. In order to bring these differing aims and outcomes to light, the following section takes a look at several basic types of program. They are not static, unchanging entities. There are many variations (upon variations). How individual programs play out also relates to numerous factors along with the characteristics of individual student populations and of the teachers, administrators, and support staff available. (Tables 6.1–6.3 are adapted from Baker 2006: 215–216.)

4.1 English-only programs

The two kinds of programs pictured in Table 6.1, below, aim to assimilate language minority children into the majority culture and language by using only the politically predominant language as the medium of instruction. They tend to be subtractive in that the children's native language is ignored or neglected; the preferred outcome is monolingualism in the culturally dominant language. With respect to language learning, we would expect no appreciable development of bilingual skills, with the students' home languages falling by the wayside due to neglect, or that the languages would develop in some kind of lopsided way, causing a sharp distinction between home and school varieties. Home languages fall into the category of heritage languages that contract as a result of attrition. As far as academic achievement, we would still expect it to be of lesser concern than the attainment of English proficiency. Assimilation and Americanization are priorities, apparently in the interest of the children and society.

Table 6.1 Monolingual education for bilinguals

Type of program	Children, language	Goal/outcome
Mainstreaming/submersion (structured immersion)	Language minority in majority language	Subtractive; with monolingualism
Mainstreaming/submersion (Sheltered English, Content-based ESL)	Language minority in majority language (with pull-out classes)	Subtractive; with monolingualism

Mainstreaming is the practice of placing language minority students into majority language classrooms, whether from the beginning of instruction or gradually through some sort of transition arrangement. Mainstream classes are regular classes in school that are populated mostly by NSs of the majority-language and that do not offer assistance for language minority students. (The term is also used for disabled students or those with special needs, placing them in mainstream classes or similar work environment, perhaps with some accommodation.) Mainstreaming in the U.S. may involve an ESL component, a special provision by which children are assured of some specific ESL training (presumably by teachers who are trained in specialized ESL teaching methods).

Submersion, a. k. a. "sink or swim," is a term applied to an approach characterized by placing children into a classroom with curriculum and instruction only in the culturally dominant language. It has the connotation of tossing a child into a river or lake, or into the deep end of a swimming pool where she can't touch the bottom and expecting her to learn to swim without the help of a raft, flotation devices, lifeguard (and lifeline), or swimming coach (Baker 2006: 216). *Structured immersion* is one example. Only language minority children are involved, and their native languages are rarely used as the language of instruction. They are replaced by a simplified form of English while allowing for some use of the L1 in the very beginning. However, there is no L1 support (even when all students speak the *same* native language), no books, lessons, or sustained effort from the teacher that make content available to the students outside the medium of English. The desired outcome is cultural *assimilation*, and the approach is *subtractive*, meaning that acquisition-learning of the dominant language is at the expense of the culturally recessive, minority language.

Sheltered English programs are offered as alternatives to English as a Second Language classes. *Sheltered* English means that children are protected in some way from the full force of submersion by the way the instructor constructs the curriculum. The language of the classroom is simplified so that the lessons themselves form comprehensible input (along the lines of hypotheses of Stephen Krashen). According to the Input Hypothesis (Krashen 1985), comprehensible input consists of the forms of language that are needed for acquisition and not merely basic comprehension. They must be one small step beyond what they have already acquired. If it is too far past the acquirer's ability, it will not be understood. If the acquirer has already learned it, there's no challenge – acquisition is moot. It must be just slightly beyond their current level for true language acquisition to kick in (and not just conscious learning). Although the hypothesis has harsh critics, it certainly appealed to the intuitions of classroom teachers, and it provided considerable grist for discussion during the 1980s and 1990s.

Sheltered classes often emphasize gesturing and visual aids to assist the learning of concepts. There is frequent repetition and summaries of the main points. Vocabulary is basic, and the syntax is simple, with no long, complex sentences. The teacher's speech is slow and careful, and she often checks the students for feedback regarding their understanding. However, the classes are typically closed and students have little interaction with native speakers (NSs). Interaction is mostly with teachers and other ELLs. Apparently, there is little room for the students to ask questions and to think critically (along lines of abstract reasoning). Instruction is basically teacher centered (with full frontal teaching via lectures). Students are, therefore, passive observers. Some researchers believe that the students learn too little English to move to higher, critical thinking tasks that would have been available in their native languages (Valdés 1988). There is usually a high ratio of students to teachers with teachers teaching to the lowest common denominator (not to lose less-proficient students in the process). So, lessons are simplistic rather than challenging, while there is also a lot of attention on form rather than to content, consistent with approaches that seek specific progress in grammatical accuracy and not in the acquisition of knowledge.

One type of sheltered English instruction is called SDAIE (Specially Designed Academic Instruction in English). It is also known as Sheltered Content Instruction. It is "sheltered" in the sense that minority-language students are taught according to a specially-designed curriculum in content areas such as language arts, math, science, and social studies. Teachers also use a simplified-form of English and specific methods involving cooperative learning techniques (students interact with other students), visual aids (e.g., realia), demonstrations, hands-on experiences, and frequent checks by teachers of student comprehension (Baker 2006: 220). The English-language texts are progressively more demanding, gradually introducing more advanced vocabulary items. Nevertheless, all instruction is in English, and the goals can appear to be socialization and *subtractive bilingualism*.

Sheltered instruction frequently involves *pull-out* classes in which students are segregated from their mainstream counterparts. The advantages to segregated classrooms is that English Learners (ELLs) are with other students who may have similar strengths and problems. However, by being set apart, they are less likely to interact with their peers who are native speakers of English. And, the curriculum they are presented with may be simplified and less challenging with respect to academics. Some see this as "dumbing down" their course work, in a sense, and holding them to lower standards. To critics of such programs, it is another example of giving ELLs language instruction in the place of a quality education, masking deep-seated biases against language minority students (Baker 2006: 217–221).

When sheltered English or ESL methods are involved in classroom teaching, insufficiently trained teachers may have little flexibility in the ways they communicate with their students, particularly during the first few months of schooling when some children simply don't understand what the teachers are saying. This only emphasizes the value of specialized training and experience. If ELLs are inserted into mainstream classes with both Native Speakers (NSs) and Non-native Speakers (NNSs), then some children may get lost in the shuffle. The teacher may have difficulty in separating students according to needs. In addition to learning the language (sometimes from scratch), students have the added stress of trying to pick out important concepts from scattered bits of information, concepts that they may be held accountable for and tested on. It is not difficult to conclude that some children may stay significantly behind their native-speaking counterparts. The worst-case scenario is that children may be denied promotion to the next grade. If held back multiple times, some children are no longer in age-appropriate grades, undoubtedly one reason for high drop-out rates – clearly the case with some Chicano-Latinos. Children get discouraged by a lack of measurable progress and systematic retention. They can't help but internalize a sense of failure. If the child needs a source of self esteem, she will have to look elsewhere.

While pull-out classes are preferable to no help at all, they may still carry a stigma, identifying those with language "problems," who need remediation. On the positive side, their interactions with teachers and classmates may be less inhibited without the intimidating presence of native speakers, and their individual needs will inevitably become more apparent to the teachers. And, despite the fact that they can also develop some sort of self-identity ("we're in this together"), the accompanying stigmatization and lack of interaction with native speakers as role models work against both cultural assimilation and language acquisition.

4.2   Weak forms of bilingual education

Weak forms of bilingual education can be thought of as compromises of sorts. They allow for some instruction in the child's native language to alleviate concerns of drastic submersion programs. The prevailing type of program in the U.S. is *transitional bilingual education* (TBE), the type supported by Title VII funding that received a lot of attention in 1980s. Overall, its goal is assimilation into the majority language and culture, so transitional programs are still subtractive in nature. However, because there is some attention spent to the children's L1, there may be a limited amount of language maintenance, and strict unilingualism is not necessarily an outcome. It is *transitional* in that there is a time limit put on native-language instruction – a move that seems to satisfy those who resist unlimited bilingual education (strong forms) and long-term language maintenance programs. It is an alternative (a kinder, gentler approach) to the sudden nature of sink-or-swim approaches, so it is a middle position in that respect. The so-called transition is incremental, with increasing instruction in the majority language and gradually decreasing exposure to instruction in the native language. In effect, the child is weaned from her mother tongue and gradually immersed in the language of the dominant culture. Mixing the metaphor, children are given a temporary raft until they're ready to learn to swim in the new language.

Table 6.2 Weak forms of bilingual education

Type of program	Children, language	Goal/outcome
Transitional	Language minority	Subtractive; with some bilingualism
Mainstream with foreign language teaching	Language majority, majority lang. with L2/FL lessons	Limited enrichment, some bilingualism

With a limited amount of bilingualism being an outcome, we would expect that a small minority of students may achieve relatively balanced bilingual status, sufficient enough to enjoy any possible cognitive benefits. And, the same outcome can be anticipated regarding academic achievement – some children may thrive, depending on individual factors. However, we would still have to anticipate that large numbers of students will encounter difficulties, with younger children being the least affected. A one-size-fits-all approach will most likely lead to a mixed bag of advantages and disadvantages for the school, the community, and the children.

The argument behind TBE is a familiar one in the context of Americanization efforts and assimilationist policy. The rationale suggests that all children need to learn the language of this nation in order to function in American society, so it is to their benefit to leave the old language and culture behind and progress as soon as possible to proficiency in the culturally dominant language. Through a quick transition, they may avoid, or at least minimize, falling behind their majority language schoolmates academically in content areas. However, this argument ignores the long-range effects of subtractive educational practices. Therefore, while it may appeal to the patriotic instincts of some Americans, it does not necessarily represent what is best for the children, and it may even hinder assimilation (by forcing the issue).

Generally speaking, there are two types of transitional programs: *early exit* and *late exit*. Each seems to be adaptable to the types of students they are designed to serve. For instance, in urban schools where numerous different L1s are spoken, an early-exit program may be more practical because it is not so dependent on qualified bilingual staffing. Early-exit programs usually allow a relatively short maximum period of time of L1 instruction, e.g., for 1 or 2 years only. (A three-year limit still is, in principle, consistent with the aims of early-exit programs.) In much of the Southwest, where Spanish-English bilingual students greatly outnumber those from other groups (e.g., Chinese-English or Japanese-English), a late exit program, which allows a longer amount of time for the acquisition/learning process, may be easier to provide because there is a greater supply of Spanish-English bilingual teachers, teacher's aides, and other forms of support to facilitate communication with parents and other members of the community. Late-exit programs also permit a percentage of classroom instruction (established by individual districts) to be conducted in the students' native language throughout the primary grades. Children are expected to transition fully when they move on to secondary schools (middle and high school). As a consequence, U.S.-born, native bilinguals, or *early* learners, probably benefit more from late-exit programs, and, in a sense, the transitional aspect loses some of its sting.

Early-exit programs, nonetheless, are found much more frequently, especially for older students, hence *late* learners. Even though Spanish-English bilinguals outnumber all other bilingual groups put together, the sheer number of students from different bilingual communities necessitates alternatives to long-term transitional approaches. In addition, older immigrants have usually received at least some education in their native language in their nation of origin. For example, many Mexican immigrants today come from lower socioeconomic classes in Mexico. The vast majority of immigrants from Mexico come to the U.S. before their 25th birthday. Most reports state that only a small percentage enter the U.S. with high school or higher education. Usually, children from rural areas of Mexico complete their primary grades, and continue on to secondary school (*secundaria*) at around 13–15 years of age.[6] They then come to the U.S., around the time a young male culturally begins to assume his individual responsibilities to contribute monetarily to the family.

Transitional programs, however, are often criticized for the same things as English-only approaches. There are criticisms of segregated (separate) classrooms and

---

6. A secondary education is considered sufficient preparation for those entering the trades, jobs involving manual labor that may require some specialized training (e.g., agriculture, welding, repair). Other students who go on to college preparatory courses, in essence, belong to a different educational track that leads to a university education.

watered-down instruction because so much attention is spent on English-language instruction (ESL). At least some of the teachers need to be bilingual (fluent in Spanish) for even a limited amount of native-language instruction. However, in another bit of irony, bilingual teachers often become promoters of shift. Because of their enthusiasm for learning English, they become great salespeople for assimilation ("If I can do it..."). These teachers come from inside the bilingual communities, and their attitudes towards learning English may be influential. Monolingual English speakers, particularly Anglos, are outsiders who may lack credibility. The value system is everywhere, built into the social structure of many schools. The power structure constantly sends subliminal messages to students. For instance, the principal, other administrators, coaches in athletics, and most teachers are likely to prefer English for official communication, while those most likely to use Spanish will be janitors, food service employees, and groundskeepers. So, the usage of Spanish may be stigmatized as belonging to a service class. Members of the power group (authorities) may wish to avoid Spanish, especially if it is of the local variety. (It may come in handy for one-on-one encounters when educators wish to bond socially for affect.)

Another weak form is *mainstreaming with foreign language* teaching. It often involves elementary schools composed mostly of native speakers of the majority language in which a few foreign-languages are introduced ostensibly for enrichment as an element of a "well-rounded" education. At one point, preferred languages were classical Latin and Greek. Modern languages such as Italian, French, Spanish, or German have replaced them. These languages are much more commonly taught in secondary schools (middle and high schools), but they are always added as electives – the children choose to take the courses. Because foreign-language instruction is limited to one short class period per day (perhaps as little as 30 minutes long) one would have to expect that few children will attain proficiency. (In the U.K., there is movement to have all primary schools teach various foreign languages.) But, in essentially monolingual cultures like the U.S. (and the U.K.), motivation to learn a foreign language will also be low. However, in European nations (e.g., the Netherlands and Sweden), English is taught as a foreign language with a good deal of success. For older students, there is a strong link to success in international business when one is proficient in English (although, principally the British kind).

4.3   Strong forms of bilingual education

Strong forms of bilingual education all share the desired outcome of bilingualism and biliteracy, proficiency in both languages. In principle, minority languages are given equal status with the majority language. Programs are built on an additive, enrichment model, rather than on a compensatory model (temporarily making up for the pressure

Table 6.3 Strong forms of bilingual education

Type of program	Children, language	Goal/outcome
Two way/dual language	Mixed majority-minority in both languages	Maintenance (pluralism)/ additive; with bilingualism & biliteracy
Heritage language	Language minority, in both with emphasis on L1	Maintenance/additive; with bilingualism & biliteracy
Immersion (dual immersion)	Language majority, in both with emphasis on L2	Pluralism (enrichment)/ additive; with bilingualism & biliteracy
Mainstream bilingual	Language majority; with two prestige languages	Maintenance (pluralism)/ additive; with bilingualism

to lose a heritage language and culture) that weak forms are patterned after. They are also designed to last longer than TBE, going for at least four or five years, ideally from kindergarten until the sixth grade and beyond. Nevertheless, there may be a few differences among strong programs. For example, the ratio of language majority and minority students and the amount of time spent in each language may vary. Language maintenance is a minimum goal. Stronger programs aim for high levels of bilingualism and biliteracy and superior academic performance. Because there are so many variations, program names can be confusing, leading the bystander to believe a program is potentially strong when it is still intrinsically weak.

Two-Way/dual language programs are sometimes referred to as *developmental bilingual education* (DBE). Both languages are used as media of instruction. Because there are two targets for acquisition, this has the effect of emphasizing the languages. Language minority and majority students meet together in integrated classrooms where there are typically two cultures represented as well through decorations, posters, announced meetings and cultural events, and the observance of special days. NNSs of English are in continual contact with NSs who serve as models for majority language learning and classroom behaviors (the reverse is obviously also true). Each class period in the day is reserved for only one language (the separation of languages), with accommodation to the proficiency levels of the students. Classroom work is designed to be challenging and not merely to appeal to the lowest common denominator. Students who may lag behind have bilingual teachers to assist them.

The ideal student population is half language majority and half language minority (non-English 50% and English 50%). If the percentage slips significantly either way, there might be an imbalance favoring the usage of a particular language in the classroom. Typically, in bilingual programs, the number of language minority students is high because the attraction is language maintenance and the preservation of minority culture, satisfying many minority parents. Depending on the community being served, the number of NSs of English may be low as a consequence, so monolingual English speakers may need to be actively recruited. Because participation in the program involves learning another language and culture, this may be a concern in some communities, particularly in the case of a socially stigmatized variety such as Spanish. In school districts that are heavily populated with language minority students where the 50–50 ratio cannot be achieved, instruction may start out at 10% in the majority language, and 90% in the minority language. The percentage may increase in yearly increments (roughly 10%), and instruction can reach 50% in each language by the fourth to sixth grade.

Because one of the main goals is equal status of both language varieties, care must be taken not to create the impression of a language hierarchy, but that is not necessarily an easy task. If the academic topics are arranged by language, for example, English for math, technology, and science, and Spanish for social studies and art, then students may associate English with cutting-edge technology (super computers and communication devices like i-pods and cell phones) and Spanish with topics that are not so easily associated with pop culture. Some programs will alternate languages by the day, so science may be taught in Spanish on one day and in English the next.

However, there are some issues that underscore the linguistic hegemony of English. English is the dominant language of the web, even though it is not the *only* language available. Further, Spanish borrows words from English, for a number of reasons (see Chapter 3 on borrowing). English terms tend to be short and quickly pronounced, and some seem to be nearly ubiquitous in internet usage. A few examples of English words (or phrases) adopted into Spanish are *internet, e-mail (email)*, (the verb "to e-mail") *emailear, software, mouse* (instead of the Spanish *ratón*), *clickear (cliquear* or *haz clic aqui* – to click), *ISP* (v. Spanish *proveedor de servicios Internet*), *SPAM* (*mensajes no deseados*), and *módem/modem*. There is some variation where both Spanish and English terms are used, e.g., *browser* along with *navegador*. So, the powerful influence of English in science and technology may present an additional obstacle to making each language appear of equal status.

The educational goals of Two-Way programs are a high degree of proficiency in both languages, the ability to read and write at grade level in both, and academic achievement at or above grade level in the content areas (e.g., math, science, and social studies). Additional goals are social, for example, to foster positive intercultural attitudes and behaviors through exposure and understanding, and to benefit society by producing highly skilled bilingual and biliterate citizens, e.g., in the international workforce (global economy). Idealistically, students learn to become more tolerant and less prejudicial and discriminatory of languages and cultures. Some commentators, however, have pointed out that in becoming proficient bilinguals, benefits are enjoyed more by language majority students (e.g., Anglos) who can use their bilinguality and biliteracy skills to greater economic advantage.[7] While it is a valid hope that society can be changed one person at a time, individuals still have to live in today's society which may lag a good distance behind the ideals of certain blocks of educators. It seems that some segments of U.S. society are quite happy with TBE and its token service to language minorities, and easily persuaded of the urgency of Americanization and total cultural assimilation.

According to the Center for Applied Linguistics, there are currently 336 Two-Way immersion programs in the U.S. California alone has 103, with over ninety Spanish-English programs, four Korean-English, three Cantonese-English, two Mandarin-English, and one French and Mandarin-English (www.cal.org). Despite the restrictive language policies instituted by Proposition 227 in California, dual-language education is expanding in California's public schools (Linton and Franklin 2010: 176). As a consequence, there is now a growing number of opportunities to demonstrate the effectiveness of Two-Way programs.

In *heritage language bilingual education*, the children's home language is used as the medium of instruction, for example, in specific programs used for indigenous languages such as Navajo, Ojibwa, Cherokee, Dakota, Inuit (Eskimo), native Hawai'ian, and also for Spanish in areas where it is a common home language and where it is the majority vernacular in the community. However, there are warnings against the use of the term *heritage*. It emphasizes the child's past and perhaps present minority status, rather than her future potential. In the U.K. and Australia, the term is not used in favor of *community language*. In such places, English is referred to as an *additional* language, not second language. To add a touch of ambiguity, the term "heritage language" in the U.S. is also extended to include a broad range of immigrant languages (e.g., Russian, Yiddish, and Serbian) (Wiley 2007: 75). In this case, heritage language schools have sprung up in grassroots fashion, particularly by language minority groups who are keenly aware of the cost of language attrition and loss of cultural values that total assimilation produces. These schools are mostly private, so presumably, parents and other community members are from upper socio-economic strata. The students come from language-minority homes, and the parents choose to place their children there. On average, instruction is half in the minority language and half in the majority language, although the minority language may be used exclusively in the early grades.

---

7.   Data from the National Chicano Survey (1979) which was designed to measure attitudes towards bilingualism and biliteracy in Mexican-American (Chicano) homes suggested that there is a strong correlation between family income and literacy in English, but that Spanish literacy is also important. By comparison, those who were nonliterate showed significantly lower family income. Family income among biliterates was slightly lower than that of those literate in English only. Biliterates, however, had higher rates of employment than those literate only in English (Wiley 2005: 103).

It is assumed that the children will eventually be able to transfer skills and knowledge to the majority language.

The goals of heritage language schools, in general, are to preserve the ancestral language (maintenance) and culture; therefore, bilingualism and biliteracy are byproducts. However, where endangered languages are concerned, there is a good deal of ambivalence within the communities about the future of their languages. Well-meaning educators (and linguists) who push for maintenance may be convinced that they represent the best interests of the community, but the social, political, and economic pressure to shift to English may be so strong that languages are lost despite their best efforts. This has happened with hundreds of indigenous languages in North America that have "died" as a result of disuse; it occurs worldwide as a common theme of studies of language attrition (cf. Edwards 1994: 104–118; see also Dorian 1989, 2006). If learning English means that a community has a better chance to survive economically, get an education, and advance in society, it may be a tough sell to motivate them to preserve a language that is no longer perceived as useful (cf. Crystal 2000: 76–88).

Immersion programs have received a lot of attention in the U.S. due to their obvious success in other parts of the world (Hakuta 1986: 93–4, 228; Baker 2006: 244–250; Crawford 1995: 138–142) and perhaps because of the lack of unambiguous reports of the success of Two-Way programs up through the 1980s. Immersion programs are especially known from Canadian efforts to become (or remain) a fundamentally bilingual nation, with both English and French *majority* languages. The term, itself, is intended to mean that the child is immersed in two languages and cultures, without the connotation of being thrown into the deep end of the pool and forced to swim according to the sink-or-swim approaches of monolingual education (perhaps she can still touch bottom, her L1). However, the key point is that the students are immersed in two *prestige* languages. Consequently, the term *immersion* can be misleading. If it is used to mean immersion in only one language, then it effectively becomes an English-only approach.

The experiment that gathered the first burst of interest was done in the 1960s in the affluent Montreal (Quebec) suburb of St. Lambert. English-speaking parents wanted their children to become bilingual and bicultural in French (the dominant language of Francophone Quebec). Traditional French classes as grammar-focused "foreign" language courses were insufficient, and these French-speaking parents were concerned that their children needed to be very proficient (bilingual and biliterate) in order to function well in an essentially bilingual society. In St.Lambert, the English-speaking (Anglophone) children were put into classes in which only French was spoken; they were totally immersed in a second language. All teachers were proficient bilinguals. Around grade two, English was gradually introduced. Such programs have been widespread and successful in Canada, spreading throughout Europe in nations with similar language policies.

However, the question is, would it work in the U.S.? In Culver City, California, this experiment was reproduced in the early 1970s with similar success (English-speakers immersed in Spanish in kindergarten and gradually introduced to English instruction). But, the roles of Spanish and English in U.S. society are very different; there is no palpable desire to make the U.S. a bilingual nation as in Canada. English is the prestige language, and Spanish is not.[8] Consequently, critics of bilingual education (strong and weak versions) have favored immersion for all *language minority children into English*, which essentially defeats the purpose of Canadian-style dual immersion programs. They have opposite goals and outcomes: in the immersion programs of Canada and elsewhere, majority-language children are immersed in second-language teaching for the purpose of becoming bilingual, biliterate, and bicultural. In (structured) immersion classes in the U.S., it is quite the opposite: language minority children are immersed in the majority language. This is nothing more than warmed-over English-only, monolingual education. The irony is amplified by the fact that legislation that favored TBE and SAIP programs (special alternative instructional programs) in the 1980s portrayed structured immersion as helping language minority children learn English and become bilingual. The outcome of such subtractive programs, however, is monolingualism.

As with other terms, "immersion" can also be an umbrella term for different types of programs. In general, however, on the international level, they have similar characteristics. For example, there is more than one prestige (or politically important) language represented; there are social and economic advantages associated with bilingualism and biliteracy; teachers are practicing bilinguals; and classroom communication is authentic and linked to the curriculum. Language acquisition is, therefore, a byproduct of interaction. These bilingual programs offer the same curriculum as mainstream (language majority) classrooms, with a focus on academic achievement (Baker 2006: 248). There are early (infant, kindergarten), late (secondary school), and middle (e.g., at age nine) entry models, and various programs will vary between total (100%) to partial immersion (50–50) (Baker 2006: 247). Such immersion programs can be found in Europe, for example, in Spain (Catalonia and the Basque Country), the U.K. (Wales and Ireland), and in France (Brittany); in Australia; Hong Kong; Singapore; and South Africa.

A final type of strong program involves *mainstream bilingual education*, in which the emphasis is not on language education per se. For example, in nations like Luxembourg and Singapore, there are multiple "national" languages that are not necessarily spoken by a numerical majority. In Nigeria, there is the former colonial English that

---

8.   In sociolinguistic terms, English is the "high" or H variety, and Spanish is a "low" or L variety based on the perceptions of society in general.

functions as a unifying political language, which is paired with several important community languages such as Hausa, Ibo, and Yoruba. In Singapore, English (also a former colonial language) is paired with Mandarin (for ethnic Chinese people), Malay (ethnic Malays), and Tamil (from India and Sri Lanka). In most European nations, English is taught as an additional language to promote international communication. On a global scale, international schools operate for children of diplomats and international (transnational) corporations; they may offer education to local citizens as well and usually feature English and/or French as a language of instruction.

In recent years, there has been a rise in European schools that also stress multilingualism and a united Europe (the EU) and a common European identity. These schools often configure various pairings of French, German, and English. Belgium is an officially multilingual nation, with both French and Flemish (Dutch) varieties spoken by two large and distinct Belgian groups, with a relatively small German-speaking minority. Switzerland has four "official" languages, Swiss German, French, Italian, and Romansch (a rapidly contracting Latin survival spoken by about 1,000 people); nevertheless, English is a popular additional language among the Swiss. Each of the 26 cantons (provinces) of Switzerland is individually responsible for its own language policies, so bilingual pairs exist in many combinations, e.g., French-German, Italian-French, Italian-German, with frequent trilingualism that includes proficiency in English. Luxembourg, which is another model of multilingualism, features its own language, Luxembourgish (a variety of German). Most people become bi- or multilingual in French, German, and English through schooling.

Such international models are, of course, of interest to Americans, but they are not likely to have much impact on attitudes to bilingualism and bilingual education. By far, the most prominent in the U.S. are transitional programs, with a growing interest in Two-Way programs.

4.4 A special case: Coral Way

Florida has been an exception to almost every pattern and rule. Cuban refugees flooded into the Miami-Dade area following the 1959 revolution in Cuba when Fidel Castro came to power. The unique thing about this population was that many were members of the Cuban intelligentsia fleeing the oppressive communist regime. Many were of European stock (descended from Spanish colonizers) and professionals who brought with them job skills, education, and professional expertise. Politically, the first Miami Cubans were typically more assertive of their rights than other Latino groups, noticeably more than Mexicans in the Southwest. Almost from the beginning, *cubanos*, as a special political case, perhaps, received federal assistance through the Cuban Refugee Program, which helped get Cuban teachers recertified in the educational system of Florida.[9]

In Dade County, ESL programs for the refugees were quickly set up, and a program was begun in 1961 that provided for Spanish instruction for Spanish speakers. In 1963, full-fledged bilingual programs, most likely the first in the U.S. since the early 1920s, began to pop up. The school mentioned in nearly every text on bilingual education is Coral Way Elementary School in Miami, where a program was set up that could accurately be called "bilingual." It was *dual-immersion*, providing Spanish for English speakers and English for Spanish speakers in addition to native-language instruction. In a sense, it was an experiment in making two groups equally bilingual. It was organized for first through third graders, with the English speakers receiving all morning instruction in English and, after lunch, instruction was in Spanish. The Spanish speakers received the reverse, Spanish instruction in the morning and English in the afternoons. Each group started the day in their native languages, and spent the afternoons in the other. During lunch, on the playground, during music and art, either language could be used, and teachers used both. The results were remarkable, and both groups progressed academically.

Initial reports suggested that students were becoming bilingual and bicultural. In English reading, both groups did better than monolingual counterparts in the Miami area, and the Cuban children read up to national standards in Spanish, as well. The only apparent disappointment was that the Anglo American students did not progress in Spanish skills as well as hoped. There were probably several reasons for this. One was that the Spanish speakers had quality Spanish input at home through the community (exposure is an important factor), while the English speakers apparently did not, though one can anticipate that if the entire community were to become bilingual that would change, too. Kenji Hakuta, an expert and noted author in bilingual education, has remarked that the disparity in Spanish proficiency in the two groups was to be expected because of the environment, the social milieu surrounding each child, and the lack of exposure and possibilities of interaction with Spanish speakers that the Anglo Americans encountered. Nevertheless, a precedent was set, only this time with speakers of Spanish as the example. The Coral Way "experiment" demonstrated that the problems of ESL could be overcome (Hakuta 1986: 194–198).

---

9. Professionals such as medical doctors, attorneys, psychiatrists, and teachers must be certified in their respective professions to practice in the U.S. Foreign certification is not considered valid, with the exception of some doctorates for university employment. So, many foreign professionals must start over from the beginning to be certified through examinations given in English – of course, attorneys need to understand the American legal system, which differs in many respects from the systems of any other nation, and requirements in other fields may differ significantly, as well. This is one reason why medical doctors (surgeons) from Latin American countries often can only find jobs as physician assistants in the U.S., dentists clean teeth, and attorneys find work as legal aids or translators.

The experiment was stopped as a consequence of a change in the laws, and not for a lack of documented results. The dual-immersion program was not recognized as the innovative approach to bilingual education that it truly was. Politically, there was talk of the special treatment that the Cubans were getting through federal assistance programs, and other groups felt entitled to government money, as well. There were perceptions that federal aid for Coral Way was nothing more than a poverty program, and there were many more deserving groups that could benefit from federal money. Consequently, the success of the program became almost irrelevant. The more serious social issue was that Anglo Americans do not appear to want their children to become native speakers of Spanish or bicultural in Cuban (or other Latino) culture, at least not to the extent that the new Cuban-Americans wanted their children to succeed in American society. The Cubans did not want their children to lose their own Cuban heritage and language in the process.

5.   Some preliminary conclusions

It should be apparent that the education of bilingual individuals is far from simple. The advantage of strong forms of bilingual education are principally that more attention can be placed on the acquisition of various types of knowledge, which should be the goal of education. A child can then use this knowledge to attain maximum levels of competence in English, including communicative competence, knowledge of the world (facilitating the acquisition of sophisticated vocabulary, terms, and concepts), and specific skills that lead to the mastery of literate registers of English. This can be done without the subtractive effects of English-only approaches. The child can learn to be proficient in literate, academic English, and proficient in her native language, as well, effectively becoming biliterate for great economic and social benefit for the individual and society (Wiley 1988).

Weak forms of bilingual education may help young bilingual children temporarily cope with learning English, but as it is with English-only approaches, the tendency is to aim low to a minimum functional type of proficiency (and literacy) that leads to a cycle of failure. In the current culture of No Child Left Behind (and The Race to the Top), educational policy puts an inordinate amount of emphasis on short-term, measurable progress. It does not deal with the kind of sweeping changes in educational philosophy that can accomplish real results. The irony is always there: short-term gains often have to be sacrificed in order to reach long-term results, especially when a short-sighted approach makes long-term benefits nearly impossible to achieve.

Key terms

achievement, bicultural, bidialectal, Bilingual Education Act, biliteracy, Brown v Board of Education, compensatory model, Coral Way, cultural assimilation, developmental bilingual education (DBE), dual-immersion, early- or late-exit programs, Elementary and Secondary Education Act (ESEA), ELL (English Language Learner), enrichment model, Equal Educational Opportunity Act (EEOA), FEP (Fluent English Proficiency), heritage language bilingual education, immersion, Immigration and Nationality Act of 1965, L1, labeling (categorization of people into groups), Lau v Nichols (1970–1974), Limited English Proficiency (LEP) – or *leper*, literacy training, mainstreaming, National Defense Act of 1958, native speaker (NS), No Child Left Behind, non-native speaker (NNS), normal/abnormal, Proposition 227, pull-out courses, quota system, race-ethnicity, Sheltered English (SDAIE), sink or swim, socioeconomic status (SES), Special Alternative Instructional Programs (SAIP), strong versus weak programs, structured immersion, submersion, Title VII (of the ESEA), the Bilingual Education Act (1967), transitional bilingual education (TBE), Two-Way program, Unz initiative, US English Movement (English First, English Only, English for the Children), William Bennett.

Summary

In the first half of the 20th Century, the U.S. went from being an isolated nation to being a world power. Attitudes towards social justice also changed as the nation went through the Civil Rights era and a new kind of idealism. As the rights of citizens expanded to include people of color, attitudes changed on bilingualism and bilingual education, as well. However, public opinion kept wavering. From the start of the 20th century, Americanization and cultural assimilation have been focal points of education, and proficiency in English has been a large part of the debate on national identity. Lack of English skills has even been viewed as disloyal to the U.S. and its ideals. Around the globe, most children learn a new or standard language to attend school, so language teaching is a part of education worldwide. But, for at least the last century, the role of language in education in the U.S. has been confused with the goal of schools to educate. *Language policy often reflects perceptions and fears of being "overrun" by foreigners.*

Prior to the 1960s, only a handful of laws had been passed concerning language and education. However, in the 1950s, laws prohibiting segregation in schools began to surface. The Civil Rights Act outlawed segregation based on race and nationality. In the same spirit, Congress opened the floodgates of immigration from Latin America and other so-called Third World nations with the passage of the Immigration and Nationality Act in 1965. It did away with the quota system that limited immigration from particular countries. Such legislation has had a major impact on bilingual education. The ESEA (also in 1965) set the stage for the rebirth of bilingual education. It provided funds for children who had been denied equal opportunities in education because of segregation. It affected *all* language minority children, but by virtue of numbers, Spanish-speaking children stood to benefit the most. The Bilingual Education Act (Title VII of the ESEA) was established to help Spanish-speaking children failing in schools. However, definitions were vague about what constitutes bilingual education, which led to a wide range of interpretations. One important case was *Lau v Nichols*. It involved a group of Chinese speaking children in San Francisco whose parents claimed that their children were denied the help they needed to succeed in school. The case challenged the practice of merely giving ESL instruction. It is often cited as the authority in language-discrimination cases. The same year as the Lau decision (1974), the EEOA made the provisions of *Lau v Nichols* law. The EEOA required school districts to take action to overcome language barriers that affect student participation. Laws continued to evolve in the 1970s.

Eventually pressure grew to eliminate reliance on heritage languages and to focus on the goal of education, proficiency in English. A cabinet-level Department of Education was set up in 1979 to oversee federal funding programs and to enforce laws on privacy and civil rights. In the 1980s, debates became more vocal regarding the place of English in education and society. In 1983, the US English Movement began, heralding a shift away from any kind of bilingual education. William J. Bennett was named Secretary of Education in 1985. He became a spokesman for groups against bilingual education. He almost singlehandedly dismantled nearly twenty years of legislation. In 1998, the infamous Unz initiative, Proposition 227, was passed, eliminating bilingual programs in California, touching off similar measures around the country. Legislation in 2001 completed the circle, repealing the Bilingual Education Act of 1968. The term "bilingual" disappeared from federal legislation to emphasize cultural assimilation. Known as the No Child Left Behind Act (NCLB), it did away with the rights of state and local agencies to interpret compliance with laws derived from Civil Rights legislation.

Irrespective of the opinions of language specialists, beliefs persist that bilingualism causes some kind of mental confusion or delayed development, and that it is the root cause for the achievement gap between immigrant children and their mainstream counterparts. In the U.S. this typically is discussed in the context of a gap in the academic performance of ELLs and proficient English speakers. As a consequence, some attempts to fix the blame for poor achievement on bilingual education can be very subtle and misleading. Lack of academic achievement cannot be pinned on one and only one cause. For example, while there may be a correlation between (a) low academic achievement and (b) low SES, there is no direct cause-and-effect relationship. SES can explain some of the problems for the achievement gap, but it does not explain everything. It is also evident that performance in school relates to proficiency in academic forms of language, registers of speech. Lack of exposure to literate forms of language can be influenced by community attitudes, so educators need to address social issues (attitudes and motivation) in the communities they serve. They need to increase literacy training regardless of which language is used. By overemphasizing a mismatch between home and school environments, a child may conclude that her own unique background has no value – not true. English and Anglo culture are clearly stressed, forcing the issue and inclining educators towards subtractive approaches.

Bilingual education means many things to many people. In general, weak forms of bilingual education produce weak results, and strong forms, strong results. English-only programs aim to assimilate language minority children into the majority culture and language. They are subtractive because preferred outcome is unilingualism in the culturally dominant language. Sheltered English programs are alternatives to ESL classes. Children are sheltered from the full force of submersion by the way the instructor constructs the curriculum. E.g., the language of the classroom is simplified. While pull-out classes are better than nothing, they still carry a stigma, identifying those with language "problems," who need remediation. Weak forms of bilingual education are compromises of sorts. They may allow for a limited amount of instruction in the child's native language. One typical program in the U.S. is *transitional bilingual education* (TBE), the type supported by Title VII funding that got attention in the 1980s. The goal is assimilation into the majority language and culture, so they are subtractive in nature. The argument behind TBE is a familiar one. It says that all children need to learn the language of this nation in order to function in American society, so it's to their benefit to leave the old language and culture behind and progress as soon as possible to proficiency in English. A quick transition may minimize falling behind their majority language schoolmates in content areas.

Strong forms of bilingual education have in common the desired outcome of proficiency in both languages, bilingualism and biliteracy. They build on what the child already knows, so the transition to academic of English is partially complete. The native language acts as a bridge to formal, academic registers of English. Such programs are built on an additive, enrichment model, rather than a compensatory model (that makes up for losing a language and culture). The Coral Way Elementary School in Miami, Florida, was the site of a well-known experiment (dual immersion) in bilingual education. It involved Cuban refugees after the 1959 revolution in Cuba. It was successful, but it was eventually dropped amid cries of special treatment for Cubans (other groups felt entitled to government money), not for lack of documented results.

The education of bilinguals is far from simple. In the current culture of No Child Left Behind, educational policy puts an inordinate amount of emphasis on short-term, measurable progress in specific skills, not the kind of sweeping changes in educational philosophy that can accomplish real results. The irony is always there: short-term gains often have to be sacrificed in order to achieve long-term results.

Activities – topics for discussion

1.   Make a brief outline of the differences between language instruction and education. Focus on all the things that you believe a student should learn in school.

2.   Discuss your opinions of English and its relationship with national identity in the U.S. Would you go so far as to say that lack of English skills is un-American? Besides the time and effort

that go into learning Standard English, what other factors can you think of that bring this extreme view into question (e.g., who were the original Americans?).

3. Only a few laws were passed regarding language in the U.S. before the 1950s. Discuss why that is, and what changed after World War II.

4. Laws since the 1960s have changed considerably, from apparently pro-bilingual education to laws that restrict the use of heritage/foreign languages. Explain the reasons for these changes, and include factors such as immigration, social perceptions (public opinion), and bipartisan politics in the U.S.

5. Since the late 1990s, laws regarding bilingual children in public schools have come full circle, and the push for English-only methods dominates national policy. How can these laws be improved?

Practice essay questions

1. Discuss the Civil Rights Movement of the 1960s and its effects on bilingual education.

2. Compare and contrast weak versus strong bilingual programs.

3. What are some of the benefits that Sheltered English Programs and Transitional Bilingual Education can provide for ELLs?

4. Discuss the Lau v Nichols case. How does it relate to the problems Spanish-speaking students have in school.

5. Compare how children assimilate into U.S. culture today with the ways that people assimilated in the 1800s. How different is it today with respect to the importance of education and job requirements in the 21st Century (e.g., regarding technical literacy).

Chapter 7

Literacy, biliteracy, and the cognitive effects of schooling

1. Literacy: Facts and myths
2. Definitions of literacy
3. Biliteracy
4. The impact of pre-literacy training
5. Different kinds of language (codes)
6. Contrastive rhetoric: Developments and criticisms

Without a doubt, the most significant issue in education in the U.S. today is *literacy* and the empowerment that seems to go along with it. However, just as we've seen with definitions of bilingualism and its role in American society and education, literacy is a complex and multifaceted topic. One popular definition of literacy is "the ability to read and write." This is both obvious and naïve (Gee 1996: 22). No one needs to argue that reading and writing skills are two rudimentary elements of literacy, but there is considerable debate over what it means to be truly literate in a language, and, in particular, how such an abstract concept as literacy can be quantified and measured.

Beyond the basic concepts of literacy, there is a host of related issues, in particular, the assumed links between literacy and intellectual capacity (cognition). It is certainly true that by being literate in English, we have access to an immense and timeless literature in that language. We are also granted access to the many types of information that can be gleaned from countless books, journals, periodicals, and other available printed media. Perhaps as a side bar to this discussion is that the current generation has at its fingertips instantaneous responses to questions of any kind. Web sites such as Wikipedia and other similar sources make the task of walking from book stack to book stack in the traditional library almost a thing of the past. This not only creates problems regarding the meaning of literacy, it also presents problems for teachers who want their students to build a solid foundation of knowledge that is not so easily manipulated by biased and mistake-prone internet writers.

Discussions of literacy also deal with the assumed linkage between language and thought. Even before literacy was an acknowledged topic of academic interest, there have been discussions of links between language and culture. The debate comes from two equally plausible positions, one that looks at how language influences culture, and the reverse, how culture can influence language. One important theory is the Sapir-Whorf hypothesis. In its strong form, it asserts that one's native language determines thought. It seems clear enough that people from various cultures think differently; they express themselves in wide ranging ways, even when they use the same language. It is also clear that the languages of the world are structured in very distinct ways. European languages all seem to share particular characteristics (e.g., word classes such as nouns and verbs, and grammatical features such as various tenses). The languages of the Far East, Africa, Australia, and the Americas can differ in almost unimaginable ways from this *Eurocentric* model. E.g., a language like Vietnamese has no present or past tense, and no singular and plural nouns. The indigenous languages of North America contain words that can be so long and complex that, in certain instances, it would take an entire sentence in English to translate just one word. These observable differences led to the concept of linguistic relativity, that language and thought are not universal as previously thought. It is no surprise then, that nonnative speakers of English have so much trouble learning English and in reaching the more advanced levels of literacy.

While much of this particular debate continues to be unresolved, there is a temptation for many of us to rely on intuition and to take a position that appeals to our individual experience and to, perhaps, our cultural upbringing. This chapter, therefore, investigates the multiple issues surrounding the concept of literacy. It discusses the role of pre-literacy training, i.e., how children are socialized into the practice of literacy, a process that can be influenced by culture and such practical things as SES. It looks into popular beliefs about language, for example, the idea that there is some sort of threshold that a child can reach in her two languages that allows for improved academic performance. It takes a critical look at the Sapir-Whorf Hypothesis and its ramifications, in particular how language-specific rhetorical strategies determine such things as information flow (how we order the information in discourse, especially in written genres). Finally, it examines a study of the rhetorical patterns of Spanish speakers and Spanish-English bilinguals in order to see if, indeed, Spanish leaves a discernable mark on the English of Chicano-Latinos. As one might expect, children who are *not* educated in Spanish-language literature are not likely to show the influence of Spanish literature. They do, however, show a lack of education and familiarity with any kind of literate language.

1.   Literacy: Facts and myths

One simple observation is significant from the linguist's perspective: While every human child acquires a native language, not all will learn to read or write in that or any other language. First of all, reading and writing are not natural processes in the same sense that language acquisition is. The ability to read and write is not acquired merely through observation and interaction or as a result of some sort of "biological endowment." Reading and writing involve skills that are typically learned through planned instruction, study, and practice (*schooling*). Secondly, not every human language has a written literature. There are hundreds of languages spoken today that are simply not written down and have no writing systems at all, alphabetic or otherwise.

There are numerous persistent myths about literacy and its link to education. Public perceptions of literacy are overwhelmingly positive, to the extreme. Accordingly, by becoming literate, a person is more likely to be happy and informed, find a job, and earn more money.

> Claims for the powers of literacy are, indeed, yet more specific than this: literacy leads to logical, analytical, critical, and rational thinking, general and abstract uses of language, skeptical and questioning attitudes, a distinction between myth and history, a recognition of the importance of time and space, complex and modern governments (with separation of church and state), political democracy and greater social equity, a lower crime rate, better citizens, economic development, wealth and productivity, political stability, urbanization, and a lower birth rate.
>
> (Gee 1996: 26)

Literacy is often thought to be a social panacea and a gateway to different kinds of knowledge, the ability to make logical connections, and the attainment of "higher levels" of thinking. But, does literacy equal higher thinking? The development of particular kinds of skills may provide a means, but it does not guarantee an end. One must be very careful to separate language proficiency and socio-economic, cultural, and educational factors whenever making claims about cognition and the dubious linkage to standardized tests that purport to measure intelligence or academic achievement. It is very difficult to make the claim that literacy (in English or any other European language) has the effect of civilizing the savage, as suggested by J. Goody's (1977) book, *Domestication of the Savage Mind*.

1.1   Literacy counts, but only in English

There is a question whether being literate in languages other than English counts as literacy in the U.S. National assessments (e.g., surveys of language use) are typically limited to literacy in English. In such tests, when a respondent is literate in another language, it is not relevant, and, therefore, it is not counted. The effect is that many

Spanish-English bilinguals, especially immigrants, are considered nonliterate (or illiterate) when they are, in fact, educated and literate in Spanish. Consequently, perceptions of a "literacy crisis" are made larger than they really are (Wiley 2005:80), and immigrants are often to blame for the skewed numbers. Such a narrow view of literacy also ignores the fact that native-language literacy (e.g., in Spanish) can be used as a foundation upon which literacy in English can be built.

Having a literate tradition, however, does not make a language inherently superior, and, conversely, the absence of one does not render a language variety inferior by comparison. A written language is merely a human language that happens to be written down. Nevertheless, such views persist, especially in the case of English. There are also views that a particular time in the history of a language, a golden age, represents a language in all of its glory and elegance, and most likely because of a notable literature. To *purists*, the many spoken varieties (vernaculars) and colloquial usage (replete with slang and "uneducated-sounding" words) pale in comparison to the classic literate forms (e.g., Hip-Hop versus Shakespeare, popular culture versus the classics). But, there is no reason to assume that a language at any particular stage in its development is better or worse, that it works better or is more beautiful. The English spoken in 17th century London is neither better nor worse than the English spoken in Los Angeles today, although there are those who would disagree. One can be reasonably sure that, when Early Modern (Shakespearean) English first emerged, there were those who reminisced about the "good old days" of Anglo Saxon and complained about the influence of the French (or the Danes).

A literate person can also fall into the trap of assuming that anything that is in print is, therefore, true, and that it is somehow validated (vetted) by a society (Gee 1996:27). When the print media present any message to the public, it adds credibility, partly because it is assumed – rightly or wrongly – that the message has been subject to prior scrutiny and correction. There is little question that most of us who reside in the U. S. and other developed nations live in literate cultures and typically assume that what we read in our newspapers, magazines, and journals is generally true and accurate. In the present political, technological, and philosophical environments, this view may be losing ground, as evidenced by current debates of a "liberal press" and "conservative agenda." One prominent worldview suggests that all truth is relative, that it emerges. In the absence of absolutes, truth is subjective, and individuals assemble their own individual "truths." Consequently, living in an age of instantaneous communication and social networking via the Internet (not to mention "reality" television programs), we should not find it surprising that massive social change is underway.

Those who live in literate cultures may think that the lack of literacy and a literature means that a culture or society has no reliable source of its own history. On the contrary, in oral cultures (where *oracy* is the counterpart to literacy), character, accuracy in transmission, and truthfulness are critical concerns of the entire community. The integrity of the individual story teller is a critical component of the credibility of a social, cultural, or historical narrative. Passed from individual to individual, these narratives are political statements affecting the identity of the community. Individual storytellers are akin to modern day pundits. They are entrusted with the maintenance of the history of a people (and the individual, social, and cultural identity that it defines). Consequently, they speak for and represent community leaders, and, in so doing, become accountable to those leaders. Oral accounts are monitored and greatly influenced by other responsible members of the community, to preserve accuracy and objectivity in the transmission of history. In such tight knit societies, there is typically a strong sense of community, social cohesion, ethics and responsibility, and family structure.

Many histories of modern societies often consist at least in part on earlier oral traditions; they have simply been written down. In addition, oral histories reveal facts and experiences that a biased or narrow-focused literature may have missed. For example, the telling of slave narratives of the American South has given us a lot of information about the practice of slavery and what it was like to *be* a slave that go well beyond merely stating numbers, dates, and places, statistics that are basically meaningless outside of the social context of the trafficking of human cargo. The oral narrative is an art form that shares many characteristics with written narratives. As such, they are often subject to the same types of literary criticism as written pieces as they wend their way into a modern written literature (Makgamatha 1999: 1–13). Evidently, where oral histories coincide with the written, they can be verified. But, that is not the only way that oral narratives can be judged for their accuracy. When multiple accounts apparently conflict, details can be verified by comparing them and weeding out obvious additions and omissions, standard practice in textual criticism (cf. Mous 2003: 17–50).

1.2   Standardization

Even if one accepts that literacy in English is the only kind of literacy that matters, there is still the question of what *kind* of English. Of the many regional and social dialects, what counts as literate language in the U.S.? Standard American English (SAE) is the obvious answer, but deciding what constitutes SAE is not as easy as it looks. It is a language variety with identifiable features – just ask an English teacher. Theoretically, it is also an ideal – ideal in the sense of the "best" kind of English that a person (i.e., an American) can imagine or use. It is held up by society as the variety that all civilized, educated people in the U.S. must emulate as the standard for performance and unifying language of society. In actuality, its features can seem like arbitrary linguistic demands that can sound stilted and contrary to the ways "normal" people talk.

To the child reared in a home where a nonstandard dialect is spoken, there may be significant differences in grammar and pronunciation between the language of the home (the vernacular) and the variety used at school. According to some dissenting language specialists, the concept of standard usage is based on faulty assumptions of the nature of language, "to justify judgments that have more to do with race, national origin, regional affiliation, ethnicity, and religion than with human language and communication" (Lippi-Green 2004: 292). The notion of a national language is based on an ideology, a *belief* in the existence of a single, unified, monolithic, almost mythological language called English:[1]

> In critical language studies ideology is taken as *the promotion of the needs and interests of a dominant group or class at the expense of marginalized groups, by means of disinformation and misrepresentation of those marginalized groups* [emphasis the author's]. More specifically, when looking at the larger issues of language standardizations, linguists often refer to a "standard language ideology," that is, a bias toward an abstracted, idealized, non-varying *spoken* language that is imposed and maintained by dominant institutions. Of course, everyone speaks a dialect, and a uniform language is an impossibility.
>
> (Lippi-Green 2004: 293)

The process of *standardization* entails institutionalizing language forms and making one particular variety or set of norms the official and socially preferred variety. It usually comes from *above*, implying that it is the variety that is used by particularly influential groups, upper classes or higher levels of society. Some forms and structures may also come from *below*, from surrounding dialects and vernaculars associated with the lower classes as forms are adopted into broader usage. It involves codifying all levels of grammar plus, in the case of written languages, mechanical facets of language such as spelling, punctuation, and capitalization in formal situations of usage, e.g., in the media, government, and education.

To the student of English, it is obvious that Standard American English is not modeled after the speech of any particularly city or region, according to the ways people talk in the Northeast (e.g., Massachusetts), South (Virginia), Midwest (Ohio), or West (California). One could argue, however, that it is patterned after the speech of the ethnic group *traditionally* with the greatest influence in politics (diplomacy and international relations), the economy (distribution of land and wealth), and education

---

1. A related point is that all conceptualizations of "standard" English are entirely subjective. We, as individuals, put our own idealized structures and usages into categories – this is standard and that is not – based on what we've been taught in school and how we see those who seem to represent "educated" speech behave linguistically. We are always changing the ways we speak as we are exposed to new forms and new social contexts. These changes are typically unconscious; we merely opt for the form that fits, in our mind's eye, the situation at hand. A good example of this may be the ever changing usage of slang terms, which can become old and outdate in a very short time.

(how children are socialized into American culture) with a good deal of regional and individual variation. This influential group happens to be the Anglo Saxon founders of England and the British-American colonies, the masters of a vast empire. Nevertheless, the speech habits of all social groups change over time, as they have with American and British varieties (and dialects thereof). Conservative elements in government and education may wish to slow down the processes of change to keep it under control, but they cannot bring change to a complete standstill – that's not possible.

Schools may prohibit words or structures that they consider offensive, undesirable, or less than standard (hence, substandard), and block them from seeping into the language system, e.g., words like *ain't* and so-called double negatives. But, they cannot eliminate such forms from popular usage. Typically, such words and expressions come from vernacular speakers who are associated with the lower socioeconomic levels of society, but they have a way of surfacing in a variety of settings via popular culture. No matter how well nonstandard varieties and forms may function in their linguistic and cultural environments, they are, nonetheless, frowned upon by those whose opinions apparently count. Because of the existence of different kinds of dialects, one child may grow up with consistent exposure to a relatively standard variety in the home, and, as a consequence of upbringing (the *where* and by *whom*), may coincidentally have command of the language of school. Another child from a different social background or part of the country may grow up speaking a nonstandard variety. And, as a consequence of her upbringing, she may have to learn the standard language in school. This is a particularly gnawing problem for speakers of Chicano English and AAVE, when the language that is learned in the home is held in such low esteem that it has no place in the classroom.

2. Definitions of literacy

Not long ago in parts of the U.S., being able to write one's name constituted literacy – if you could sign your name, you were considered literate, and you knew how to write. This vague concept is common in many nations today, making published literacy rates very much open to interpretation. If a particular nation or state claims that 100% of its citizens are "literate," it may simply mean that they can mark an "X" on an official form. Perceptions of literacy are also key to understanding the many controversies that exist in governmental and educational circles. It is always implied that literacy is good, and it is somehow linked to education and intelligence. Its opposite, *illiteracy*, in contrast, is somehow bad. As with other labels, entire classes of people can be created. When individuals or groups of individuals are referred to as *illiterate*, they are assumed to be uneducated and ignorant, and both of these qualities or states are considered serious limitations and disabilities in today's modern, "literate world." This is why other terms such as *nonliterate* or *preliterate* are preferred in polite discourse, to reduce the stigma of the term illiterate and its assumed link to ignorance and lack of formal education (Wiley 2005: 119). Despite its pejorative nature, the term "illiterate" is still common.[2]

Among our first concerns is definition, and perhaps to expand on the notion that literacy is merely the ability to read and write. The first, practical place to start is a *functional* definition, which identifies the kinds of skills an individual needs just to function satisfactorily within a society. This first step includes the ability to *decode* print – that is, to convert the printed word into understandable expressions and structures or their spoken equivalent. Specifically, all U.S. citizens are expected to be able to read road signs and warning labels (e.g., poison, often represented by a symbol, the skull and crossbones), street names, and job applications that they encounter on a daily basis. They need to be able to read the bills (coupons, advertisements, and offers) and school notices that they receive in the mail and perhaps gain important political information about their communities from local newspapers. They will need to be able to fill out those job applications, sign checks to pay their bills, pass tests for a driver's license, and respond to the miscellaneous notices they receive. This also implies a degree of *numeracy*, basic arithmetic skills required to balance a checkbook. These abilities form the core of *basic* literacy skills that are deemed important for basic survival. Not coincidentally, this type of literacy is often the goal of educators for many of their students, in particular immigrants and ELLs in short-term, English-only programs (and adult education ESL classes).

A functional definition can also be expanded to include the different types of skills required for an occupation or profession, for example, specific kinds of computer and/or equipment skills. (Skillful use of the internet today indeed includes a set of skills, but it is debatable if those skills pertain to any meaningful notion of literacy. Locating bits of information in a moment's notice, in fact, is often a substitute for the much more time-consuming activity of reading books and other pieces of literature to obtain a long-term knowledge base.) *English for Specific Purposes* (ESP) courses are often structured for the nonnative speaker with this explicit functional goal in mind. Many community organizations such as adult schools and community colleges cater to businesses that require specialized literacy skills (e.g., being able to read instruction manuals, safety booklets, claim forms, and schedules) to successfully run assembly plants and to deliver products and services.

A second, deeper kind of literacy (or stage in a process towards a more complete view of literacy), *cultural literacy,* includes more complex analytical skills than the

---

2.   See Wiley (2005: 67–70) for a more comprehensive review of definitions of literacy.

surface skills required merely to function reactively in a society. All culturally-based behaviors are learned behaviors. They are usually learned through such culturally-defined institutions as schools and the media. They involve the values, assumptions, and the kinds of cultural knowledge that are reflected in school curricula across the nation. This school-based knowledge embodies the information that citizens of a country are expected to know, for example, the basic A to Zs of an "American" worldview (in the context of the U.S.).

Educators have long known the necessity of a common body of knowledge (e.g., "what it means to be an American") for meaningful communication among the various sectors of society and to interpret the messages that appear in various media. All U.S. citizens are expected to be familiar with generally accepted beliefs of the roles and responsibilities that they have within a democracy. Living up to those expectations entails understanding one's legal rights and responsibilities (and their limitations), participating in the political process, and supporting other institutions such as education, health care, and social welfare. This goes beyond merely being able to function, read the mail, and contribute tax dollars to the public coffers if a greater cultural knowledge is to have any meaning at all. At first glance, this may appear to be a quantitative measure – know more stuff and you'll know how to use it, but that may underestimate the complexity of the associations that need to be made in order to arrive at subtle inferences.

Nevertheless, one would be hard pressed to find a precise listing of the things an "informed" citizen must know. Every segment of society can conceivably draw up its own list of the books an educated U.S. citizen or resident must read. Ask a scientist, philosopher, English teacher, political scientist, music or art instructor, or coach of any sport to list the 100 written works that all productive citizens should be familiar with, and you can imagine how different those lists might be. Nevertheless, this is the exact job that educators take on in deciding basic school curricula – and, of course, this is taking place at the national level as a consequence of NCLB and the organization of nation-wide, content-based tests for teachers (e.g., the California Subject Examinations for Teachers, or *CSET*, in California). To be qualified to teach, every teacher is expected to have a knowledge base vetted by a segment of the federal government.

In a text for teachers, *Teaching Culture: Strategies for Intercultural Communication*, H. Ned Seelye responds to the influential and controversial work of American educator E. D. Hirsch, Jr., who, like many, decries the sad state of cultural literacy in the U.S. and the decline of cultural knowledge, and argues for sweeping changes in the educational system:[3]

---

3.   The full title of the text cited below: *Cultural Literacy: What Every American Needs To Know*.

To this end, Hirsch's bestselling *Cultural Literacy* [1987] inventories 4,600 items that every educated American should be able to identify. These are listed in an alphabetized appendix titled "What Literate Americans Know." These items range from people and places (Hank Aaron, Achilles, Maya Angelou, Adirondack Mountains, Argentina) to sundry concepts (act of God, adagio, animism) to songs ("Amazing Grace") to science and medicine (antigen, anthropomorphism, arthritis) to adages ("All work and no play make Jack a dull boy") and so on. Some other items under the letter A are Jane Addams, Addis Ababa, AEC (Atomic Energy Commission), Aeschylus, amniotic sac, "As flies to wanton boys are we to the gods," and Atlantic Charter.   (Seelye 1994: 27)

It should go without saying that the people most likely to be *culturally literate* are those who have gone through the mainstream educational process from start to finish, who share mainstream values, and, of course, are part of its culture – at least that part that influences and defines its literate traditions. Seelye adds, "And, unfortunately the sector [of society] that can remember esoteric bits and pieces of their formal education more often than not is poorly (but admirably) representative of a nation as a whole. Historical biases conspire to deny many sectors equal access to formal education. Rural people, working-class people, women, indigenous peoples, and linguistic minorities often suffer in this regard" (27). In other words, the cultural and institutional bastions of power belonging to those groups in charge (a privileged elite – without reflecting on *how* those groups got into power) are upheld and preserved, while the voices of less privileged, marginalized groups are systematically excluded from the discussion.

One may want to ask how Hirsch arrived at his list, what his motivations were (or how one man came about such an authoritative position), and who might be excluded intentionally or unintentionally from such standards of cultural literacy. Can a person who is similarly literate in the cultures of, say, Latin America (including indigenous nations), Africa, West or East Europe, Asia (including Islamic, Hindu, Confucian, and Buddhist cultures) be counted among those having cultural literacy? There is little doubt that if the items of Hirsch's list truly define the term *cultural knowledge*, then the only kind of knowledge of value in the U.S. is that of Anglo-American culture. This is contrary to any concept of ethnic or cultural equity and diversity.

When we read today's American newspapers, we find discussions of literacy crises and the growing problems in the educational system at state and national levels. But the perceived problems do not appear related to the simple ability to read and write. As Gee (1996) points out, "[Thus], we see that young adults do not have an 'illiteracy' problem (80 percent of them can read as well as or better than the average eighth-grade student), rather they have a schooling problem. As tasks become more complex and school-like, less and less of the population can do them, with failure being most prominent among those least influenced and most poorly served by the schools." (1996: 23). The problems that many otherwise literate people appear to have may not be so easily linked to basic literacy skills as one might initially suspect. The issues are more clearly related to *access* to critical types of information and the social involvement that accompanies it (e.g., access to super computers, cutting edge technology, and understanding how the political process works). If access is the sole possession of a small number of individuals or elite groups, then large portions of the population are kept from informed participation in societal levels of the educational, political, legal, and other institutional processes. Regarding the school-like nature of problems, many secondary students develop skills for scoring high on particular kinds of exams (as evidenced in various AP programs), but this is still no guarantee that they will graduate from a university or find meaningful employment. Unfortunately, the distribution of academic wealth perpetuates the appearance of class struggle, with the children of privileged parents enjoying the advantages of material wealth, time to study, resources, and access to the top schools. Experience is still a wonderful tutor.

A third type of literacy that follows from cultural literacy is often called *critical literacy*. It is the ability to recognize the underlying social and political assumptions of particular authors. Clearly, this type of literacy skill requires mastery of cultural literacy and more. It includes the ability to "read between the lines" to the motivations of a particular author (and to spot persuasion and manipulation), being able to recognize expressions of Anglo-American cultural values, and having the ability to analyze texts critically and expound on the types of meanings expressed. This implies having sufficient knowledge of the historical, cultural, and social backdrop of the writer and what he or she has written. (This still seems to suggest a quantitative measure of the access necessary to learn such things.) Any educator who has gained valuable insights into the challenges faced by rural folks, the working-class, women, indigenous peoples, and linguistic minorities knows what a daunting task this can be. Anyone who claims to teach critical literacy skills must be familiar with the kinds of knowledge that critical reading entails, qualitatively, as well as quantitatively. It goes much farther than merely teaching a child how to read and write and to achieve functional literacy – and it bears repeating that the endpoint of many English-only programs is just that, functional literacy.

One conclusion regarding literacy on a mass scale, perhaps with the lowest common denominator as a guide and functional literacy as its goal, has been a utilitarian view that literacy should be linked to academic and employment opportunities. By attaining high levels of literacy, one might expect to reach higher levels of academic achievement (higher test scores and more years of schooling) and better jobs (consistent employment and higher salaries/wages). Society's perceptions of literacy, however, have certainly changed since the beginning of the 19th century, making expectations that were once held of society's elite apply universally to all groups – a type of inflation of literacy standards (Wiley 2005: 104–107). For example, Resnick and Resnick (1988) provide the historical backdrop of how continually rising expectations have shaped views of literacy. They estimate that current views of large-scale literacy instruction have lasted for the last two or three generations. In the past, high levels of literacy were expected only of the upper and middle classes, while minimal, more basic levels were required of the lower classes, the factory workers, mechanics, and general laborers (harking back to the days of John Dewey, progressivism, and "scientific" approaches to education and literacy). More recent approaches to literacy on a mass scale have risen to include all sorts of "new" *literacies*, e.g., computer and techno-literacy and the kinds listed above, cultural and critical literacies.

In addition, as a consequence of the Civil Rights Movement, competencies were raised a great deal nationwide due to the expansion of educational opportunities for ethnic minorities. Skills that were once considered specialized and specific to higher education became more widespread and available to an increasing number of people. As a result, the stakes have been raised and unskilled workers in today's economy need to exhibit higher levels of literacy, well beyond the minimal skills necessary a generation or so ago, when a national production-based industrial economy used to exist in places like California. Educational credentials (certificates, diplomas, degrees) have similarly shrunk in value. A few generations ago, a high school diploma was the only prerequisite for many jobs, but no longer. Having some college credits, a BA, or even a graduate degree are now the types of credentials that dot résumés for entry-level positions in the current service-oriented economy. Those whose academic achievement fall below the new norms will find barriers to employability, income, and equal status.

The implication is that the tremendous gains in the 60s and 70s of post Civil Rights-era language minorities (and those from lower SES backgrounds) have been minimized, lessening their impact. From 1950–1975, ethnic minorities found greatly expanded educational opportunities, but Anglo Americans (men and women) also entered colleges and universities in record numbers. So, *all* groups progressed in academic achievement and literacy skills, minimizing the gains made by ethnic and language minorities and inflating the minimum requirements for even the lowest paying jobs. One of the limitations of surveys of literacy and levels of education is that one group is always measured against other groups, e.g., Latinos compared with African Americans or Whites; progress within groups (e.g., Chicanos in 1950 compared with Chicanos in 1990) is seldom the focus. The perception of progress and social equality among minority groups is clouded as a result. In other words, even though tremendous progress has been made in the education of various minority groups, the bar is always being set higher. What may have constituted superior qualifications at the beginning of the 20th century (e.g., functional literacy and a high school education) does not even meet the minimum requirements for the lowest paying jobs.

3.   Biliteracy

American attitudes towards *biliteracy*, like bilingualism itself, are ambivalent at best, even when all indications are that bilingualism and biliteracy have socioeconomic and, perhaps, cognitive advantages for individuals and the community. But, when literacy in English is emphasized so much that it is the sole measure of one's abilities, we should expect some sort of reaction from speakers of minority languages. There is little pressure for English-dominant bilinguals to become highly literate in Spanish, but the many thousands of Spanish-dominant bilinguals face the dilemma of either merely maintaining the language at the spoken level or developing advanced cultural and critical literacy skills in Spanish in the face of active discouragement. They have to find the motivation necessary to put forth the effort and time it takes to become equally literate in two languages. However, because of the international position of English, becoming (bi-)literate in English is almost a necessity in academics, irrespective of one's native language. Many European students must read texts in (International) English, and often need to write papers in the language to be able to contribute to the more prestigious international journals (printed mostly in English). In fact, many universities worldwide require that theses and dissertations be written in English as members of an international scientific community where it is the *lingua franca*.

As stressed above, literacy myths have persisted, including the belief that a good citizen is a literate one. Consequently, literacy, as a force for democracy, was once thought to be a virtue, like Prudence and Justice. With the lack of it came a social price. Words like *illiterate* were demeaning. Being illiterate meant more than just lacking a specific skill; it implied a "lack of proper judgment" (Cook-Gumperz 2007b: 2), or it was a symptom of cultural deprivation and personal failure. Nevertheless, as a consequence of the uneven relations between English and minority languages, a young student may be highly literate in her native language, but be considered a failure because she has not mastered the technical facets of English literacy.

The role of schooling is seldom questioned. It has been seen as an important medium of social change, Americanization, and stability. Since the early 1900s and the advent of universal education, "it has been unquestioningly assumed that literacy is both the purpose and product of schooling…and that the possession of literacy will improve the quality of life for individuals, social groups, and even society as a whole" (Cook-Gumperz 2007c: 19). In this social context, literacy is synonymous with English literacy. Therefore, when national literacy rates are down, the entire educational system has failed, or so it seems. Nevertheless, literacy in other languages can have the same effects, despite the clear bias towards English. The development of literacy in general can provide a means to acquire knowledge and technology that has the power to transform society (for the better, we assume), provide paths to the accumulation of personal (and corporate) wealth, and access to power. But, this also applies to Spanish in nations where it is the politically dominant language. Thus, it is literacy per se that enriches the human mind, not just literacy in (Standard) English.

Early research into biliteracy focused on the children of immigrants (and indigenous minorities in the U.S.) learning the culturally dominant English as a second language (sequentially). It primarily defined biliteracy in terms of the mastery of reading and writing in two languages, and that children can leapfrog from literacy in their native language to literacy in a SL. Degrees of proficiencies and how those proficiencies may interact were topics yet to be explored. These early studies were limited, too, in that they focused primarily on second-language acquisition in school according to a rigid skills-based view of literacy. But, as we have seen, literacy is more than the acquisition of a simple set of technical skills like decoding and encoding print or just being able to read and write. It is a social construct, a prescribed collection of communicative practices necessary to succeed in a literate society. In contrast, recent work has focused on the many facets of literacy in general and literacy development in multiple language varieties, according to a more complete view of the nature of language. In that literacy studies have widened their focus to the complexities of literacy, we can only imagine how literacy in two or more languages has proved to be even more complex.

Variation is key: there are registers and styles ranging from very informal to formal, written versus spoken modes, and regional and social dialects (with registers in each). Some varieties are typically spoken, while others are written. Consequently, we are drawn to the multifaceted nature of literacy and the interdependence of language varieties. Degrees of proficiency are also significant. Bilinguals know their languages to different degrees, and typically use them for different purposes: "They may understand, speak, read, and write these languages very well, or they might be in the process of developing any of the language skills in either of the languages. The use of each language can vary from casual daily conversation to academic uses. Proficiency and use are closely interrelated because proficiency facilitates use and use facilitates proficiency" (Brisk et al 2007: 4). We should expect that when continua of proficiencies in each language are evident in a community of speakers, that there will also be continua of proficiencies in their abilities to read and write those languages.

Acquisition scenarios are similar to those of bilingualism; biliteracy can be acquired sequentially and simultaneously. That is, a child learner may acquire literacy in one language and then apply that knowledge to a second, or simultaneously acquire literacy in two languages at the same time. She may learn literacy skills through either and apply those skills to the other.[4] Therefore, biliteracy is bidirectional; it is

---

4. Biliteracy can also develop in families, homes, and communities in a powerful second language – it is not solely dependent on institutional settings.

not necessarily sequential (L1 then L2). Even though a native bilingual's languages may develop simultaneously, they nonetheless develop separately and independently (García et al 2009: 209–212).

As the literature has progressed, perspectives have broadened, in the sense that they have attempted to view the acquisition of biliteracy in a greater context. First, the term *literacy* (singular) has given way to *biliteracies* (plural) or even *pluriliteracies* to emphasize the complex, multifaceted nature of literacies in more than one language variety.[5] (The term biliteracy, singular, implies that it proceeds as a single, uniform process. *Literacies*, plural, refers to the many elements of a speaker's linguistic and cultural repertoires, and the interdependencies among them.) Martin-Jones & Jones (2000) propose the term *multilingual literacies* to underscore the complexity of individual and group linguistic and communicative repertoires, all the available language varieties and behaviors that are modeled in their own speech communities.[6] For example, bilinguals use more than two varieties on a daily basis; they have varying degrees of "expertise" in each language and literacy; and they draw on their individual repertoires in multiple ways (4–7). In this approach, literacy is not an autonomous (unified and unchanging) set of skills that can be removed from its cultural contexts. Thus, Martin-Jones & Jones do not approach biliteracies as a simple dichotomy of L1/L2; to them all literacies have equal value and are equally valid – a child's attempts at written expression should be greeted with acceptance and encouragement, not disdain or discouragement.

One apparent breakthrough has been the concept of *continua of literacies*. The work of Nancy Hornberger and her colleagues has been influential because it points to significant sociolinguistic and political factors around the emergence of biliteracy as these factors interrelate and intersect (Hornberger 2003a; Hornberger 2003b; Hornberger & Skilton-Sylvester 2003). In this model, particular sets of continua are "nested" within each other, so issues of language/literacy development interact with continua of social contexts, types of writing systems, and continua of oppositions based on minority-majority status, oral-written language, and so on (twelve individual continua of biliteracy). While the impact of this important work may be felt only indirectly, it does portray the complexities of biliteracies in a comprehensive way. It draws attention to

---

5. The European Union apparently promotes plurilingual practices; however, the social and linguistic situation is somewhat different from that of the U.S. Except for England, which is still mostly monolingual English-speaking, E.U. nations have their own national languages and a host of regional varieties that are acquired from birth. Additional languages such as English are all learned as second languages. Though international Englishes have certainly gained influence as a consequence, they are not native languages. A pluriliteracies approach, however, has a long tradition in postcolonial societies, for example, in South Asia (see Canagarajah 2009).

6. See Street (2009: 17–24) for a comprehensive discussion of terminologies and issues relevant to concepts of biliteracy and multiliteracies.

the obvious asymmetrical relationships between minority and majority languages and ethnic groups, and how literacy instruction in one language (a politically dominant variety) is typically valued more than that of minority languages and cultures. (Their aim is to illustrate that knowledge of such power relationships can be utilized for social change. In a conservative political environment such as one finds in the U.S., even with its push for school reform, it may not be entirely clear how such a research framework can be turned into pedagogical practice.)

Information about the complexities of biliteracy should guide pedagogical practices, and it does. Regarding materials, there is a range of teaching texts: (a) those that teach each language/literacy as monolingual literacy (children can enjoy the benefits of the full range of literacy training and practice), or (b) specialized texts that may appeal to adolescents and adults who are acquiring a second-language and literacy in that language. The former (a) is associated with strong bilingual programs in which biliteracy is the goal, and the latter (b) is associated with weak programs and sheltered classes that rely on *scaffolding* and simplified texts.[7] Every approach will yield its own set of outcomes – the buyer beware.

Recent literature has suggestions, too, regarding the bilingual, biliterate classroom. For example, Baker (2009) outlines the characteristics of effective pedagogy: "An effective curriculum tends to include bilingual and biliteracy development across the curriculum (including science and information technology), with smooth transitions across ages and stages. Biliteracy and multiliteracies can be developed throughout the subject curriculum" (146). So, they should be interwoven among content areas (in monolingual fashion) so that children receive the full benefits of gradual instruction. Baker points out that biliteracy reinforces the oral languages, particularly concerning vocabulary and fluency (use facilitates proficiency). Baker also provides the motivation: "Reading literature in two or more languages may be for education, recreation, instruction, and gratification. Whether minority language literature is regarded as aiding in moral or religious teaching, of value as an artistic form, or as a means of vicarious experience, literacy becomes both an emancipator and an educator" (Baker 2009: 146).[8]

---

7. Scaffolding is a term derived from the concept of a scaffold, a temporary platform used to support workers as they work on a building. It involves providing support or a model for learning by demonstrating similar structures. Therefore, it features the use of analogies, the teacher's direct intervention and encouragement, and the gradual increase of the amount of information the child receives until she can solve the problem herself without adult help.

8. Obviously, there is the potential for conflict. The "emancipator" role of literacy in the minority language gives the child permission to explore her own roots, puts value on her background language and culture, and validates her life in the present. But, for educators, it might require a greater context. It is implicit that the values espoused by the heritage language and culture will not be destructive or

4.   The impact of pre-literacy training

Certain groups seem to manifest socioeconomic advantages in tangible ways through shared cultural experiences and hands-on training that can lead to superior literacy skills even before their children learn to read and write. *Pre-literacy* training essentially corresponds to the quality time that a student is mentored or apprenticed into literacy. It involves the amount of time a child practices particular literacy activities in the home prior to attending school and engaging in those activities in formal contexts. When such behaviors are modeled and practiced frequently in the home, children are taught the values of those activities. They learn to place importance on reading and writing even before they venture onto a school campus. Mainstream students, defined as middle-class, Anglo-Americans or others holding very similar values of education and literacy, get a great deal of their individualized pre-literacy training by caregivers through story telling and the reading of bed-time books, so-called "talking books" – interactive books that "talk" the story from the printed page – and exposure to other printed material specifically directed to children. These privileged children learn to expect outcomes in the stories, identify characters and plots (according to Anglo-American literate discourse patterns), and learn to view the entire activity as fun and entertaining.[9] A child from a home that lacks this type of environment may acquire a very different set of values, to the point of indifference.

"A correlation between social class and reading seems to be indisputable…" (Adger, Wolfram & Christian 2007: 125). For example, according to the Washington Post (June 20, 2003), on the 2002 National Assessment of Educational Progress (NAEP), children from low-income homes scored significantly lower than their more affluent peers in reading in spite of the best efforts of schools to close this achievement gap. Pre-literacy training offers a possible explanation for this gap. Gee (1992) discusses a long-term study of beginning readers (Adams 1990) which estimated that mainstream children (subjects in the study) engaged in such activities for more than 3,000 hours *before* entering first grade. In contrast, a child's first grade teacher spends around 360 hours, with a group of 20 or more children – of course, in states like California, the number of students in a classroom can be much higher.

---

promote excessive antagonism towards U.S. culture and the secular values it espouses. As value sets among equals, they should be complementary, where the values of U.S. culture are woven together with heritage moral and religious values and traditions in a synthesis of sorts.

9. Not often made explicit is the intellectual elite, those who belong to upper socioeconomic strata and who are especially privileged with regard to well-funded schools and districts (or the alternative, private schools), accelerated classrooms, nannies, and tutors. This group is favored in Advanced Placement (AP) programs that make university credit available through rigorous high-school courses.

In a separate study of families from lower socioeconomic strata, Adams estimated that these poorer families spent about 225 hours per child on school-based preliteracy activities, including "25 hours of storybook experience and perhaps 200 hours of general guidance about the form and nature of print" (Gee 1992: 124). To appreciate the difference, children from the mainstream households had more than thirteen times the exposure to literacy practices that their lower socioeconomic counterparts had. The disparity may be even greater with respect to the amount of time linguistic minority students receive in areas like South and East L.A. where both parents work more than one job, and children become "latch-key kids" (those who have their own keys to the home or apartment and go directly to and from school unescorted by parents or caregivers).[10]

The work of anthropologist John Ogbu (1987) compares the educational progress of various ethnic minority groups. In general, minorities fare less well than their majority counterparts. Nevertheless, there are important differences among minority-status groups. Some are relatively successful while other specific, U.S.-born groups are prone to much higher failure rates, drop out rates, and general lack of success in all school-based, academic activities (which obviously involve literacy skills). He calls such non-immigrant groups as African-Americans, Chicano-Latino, and American Indigenous groups "castelike minorities," groups who have been "incorporated into a society more or less involuntarily and permanently through slavery, conquest, and colonization" (Ogbu 1987: 258).[11] They are castelike because they do not seem to be able to escape the "denigration and rationalization" of their minority status, and often accept "what may be called *an institutionalized discrimination perspective*" (261). They may grow to accept the expectations and stereotypes that society in general has placed on them.

While some of Ogbu's generalizations have been controversial, many of his observations and conclusions deserve some thought: individuals often live up to the expectations that society places upon them, and lack of academic achievement seems to fall in that realm. "I conclude by pointing out that ultimately the wider society is responsible for persistent disproportionate school failure of castelike minorities. Schools are implicated because they tend more or less to treat minorities so as to prepare them for subordinate positions in the prevailing stratification system" (Ogbu 1987: 274). Two other generalizations seem to affirm this conclusion: (1) mainstream students seem advantaged by the culture within which they live, and by participating in mainstream school-based literacy practices; and (2) the existence of tracking or streaming

---

10. This type of situation undoubtedly exists in many nearby communities, e.g., in densely populated Huntington Park, Bell Gardens, Pico Rivera, Montebello, and Whittier, and elsewhere, e.g., in Orange, San Bernardino and Riverside counties.

11. *Caste* is used in the sense of the Hindu system of hereditary social classes.

systems, conceived with perhaps the best of intentions, which often reinforce the low self-expectancies of individuals and particular ethnic and linguistic minorities. If the adage "wealth breeds success" is true, one may posit, equally "poverty breeds failure."

5. Different kinds of language (codes)

Questions about the connections among society, language, and education have been around for some time. Obviously, there is something about these connections that appeal to the intuitions of teachers and others in education. It seems apparent that children from poor backgrounds don't do as well in school as their wealthier counterparts, and poor kids often share certain speech characteristics (e.g., a nonstandard dialect). But, finding exactly what those connections are has been elusive, and the topic itself seems to feed biased attitudes that link ethnicity, culture, and language with poverty. They also may appeal to outdated evolutionary ideas that certain groups of people are ideal for certain positions in society, that an upper, elite class is destined to lead, and lower echelons of society are meant to follow and serve the elite.

Very similar in scope to later discussions of *BICS* and *CALP* (see below) was the work of the late Basil Bernstein, a British sociologist who focused on the connections between language and processes of socialization, particularly the effects of culture and social class on language according to an apparently strong version of the Sapir-Whorf hypothesis (linguistic relativity). In the 1960s and 1970s, he developed the terms *elaborated* and *restricted* code. According to Bernstein, a restricted code is characterized by relatively simple speech patterns. Used in informal situations, it contains lots of gesturing, colloquialisms, and context-bound deictic expressions (e.g., words like *this*, *that*, *here*, and *over there*). The term contrasts with *elaborated code* (or, earlier *formal* code), which is portrayed as context free (hence, abstract), complex speech patterns used in educated situations. It does not depend on extralinguistic contexts such as gesturing and shared beliefs (Crystal 1991: 118). Both terms are typically associated with cultural stereotypes and concepts of social class, how Bernstein thought a working-class person behaves in contrast to how a middle-class person behaves. (We should anticipate that this kind of approach would be applied to the perceived deficits of second language learners who have yet to learn "educated" registers of English.)

Bernstein described restricted code as characteristic of the speech of members of lower social classes. It contains short, simple sentences, sentence fragments, *poor* syntactic form, and much repetition; and it is less logical (cf. Wardhaugh 2006: 326–332). He also claimed that elaborated code uses *accurate* grammatical order and syntax, complex sentences, propositions to show *logical* relationships, and a wide range of adjectives and adverbs. Citing the behavior of middle-class mothers, he noted that they explained things better and more fully to their children than working-class mothers.

Needless to say, terms such as "accurate," "poor," and "logical" appeal to the biases of educators, but they are not based in objective fact. For instance, the term "accurate" is obviously subjective; it confuses the use of standard English forms with accuracy. His descriptions are at odds with the work of sociolinguists who write of the logic (systematic variation) of nonstandard varieties, e.g., in the work of William Labov (Labov 1972), though they have also been thought of by some educators as insightful descriptions of language usage in many classrooms. Despite persistent controversies, some of his distinctions have resurfaced in education, with refined meanings. While it may be possible to link socioeconomic stratum with success in school for social and economic reasons, it is not possible to link a particular language variety with inherent intellectual capacities, despite one's prejudices. Even at first glance, there are those who can switch from one "code" to the other, from standard to a nonstandard variety, depending on the situation of speech. One cannot spontaneously switch SES, nor change the ways one thinks.

Framed by more recent discussions of various registers and dialects of language, it is obvious that public perceptions of language variation differ from those of linguists and other language specialists. While linguists point to the "equality" of language varieties, there is still a lingering view that some varieties are inherently better than others, and that those who speak superior varieties are consequently privileged and cognitively (intellectually) advantaged. The distinction between elaborated and restricted codes is one more manifestation of this. The terms and concepts have been met with great skepticism by their critics, though they have also been received by some educators as insightful descriptions of the differences in language usage found in many classrooms around the globe, particularly in English-speaking countries. However, among the criticisms is that Bernstein was less than clear of what exactly constitutes a *code*. His distinctions, too, of (lower) working-class and middle-class lack definition. He also made the very controversial claim that working-class children not only have little experience with the so-called elaborated code, but they might be *harmed* by exposure to it because it communicates cultural values that go against the child's lower-class upbringing, in recent terms, perhaps, a form of cognitive dissonance.

5.1   Thresholds Theory

There are a number of claims made about links between bilingual language acquisition and thinking, particularly the debate about the role of language and a student's bilingual abilities in the classroom. Though not specifically linked to literacy, per se, some educators maintain that language can be linked to a child's cognitive abilities.[12]

---

12. This may be a little like linking proficiency in English with overall intelligence – there are billions of intelligent people on earth who do not speak English.

However, no link has been demonstrated between language and *cognition* (the mental ability of knowing) or any ability that is testable by any non-linguistic means. This is one aspect of the popular (yet controversial) "Thresholds Theory," which proposes that higher levels of abstract thinking are only available to those bilingual children who are highly proficient in both their languages, presumably a first or native language, and then a second-subsequent one (the dominant language of the community and language of education whose proficiency is of concern). This theory is obviously intuitive and appears to match certain social conditions in the classroom, but it is debatable how it pertains to simultaneous bilingualism and the complex topic of dominance.

The theory, credited to the early work of Jim Cummins (1976) and Toukamaa & Skutnab-Kangas (1977), began (again) with the observation that children who are still learning a second language often struggle in school settings. It further states that an emerging bilingual must reach a turning point, or *threshold*, at which competence in both languages is developed enough so that she can enjoy the cognitive advantages of balanced/proficient bilingualism, enough to handle the demands of a curriculum taught in that second language. Critics have argued that the theory is not specific enough about the types of language that must be mastered (e.g., academic registers that tend to be formal and written), and that any alleged deficit a bilingual child might have is most likely semantic and in the area of vocabulary. Incipient bilinguals just haven't learned the terms and concepts via background knowledge necessary for academic achievement, particularly in subtractive educational settings.

The main problem, as many language specialists see it, is precisely identifying proficiency levels and teasing out the much more general effects of schooling (or the lack thereof). There are two distinct issues that need to be considered: (1) overall proficiency in formal, written English, a linguistic issue; and (2) the types of knowledge one gets from going to school, a schooling issue, that clearly implies the need for a tradition of literacy and education, academic resources (a socioeconomic factor), and exposure to a quality academic environment and skilled teachers. The schooling issue involves the intentional, focused attention on both culturally-based knowledge and the linguistic forms necessary to express that knowledge. Indeed, many children have been educated in a native language other than English who would be able to transfer prior academic knowledge and literacy skills significantly reducing the time necessary to acquire formal registers of English. Such children are familiar with the academic concepts and aware of the differences between conversational skills and the adjustments student writers need to make in written registers.

5.2   BICS and CALP

As an outgrowth of Thresholds Theory were claims by Cummins in the early 1980s of two different kinds of language skills, BICS (basic interpersonal communication skills) and CALP (cognitive/academic language proficiency). The first is associated with informal, spoken language, and the other with formal, written, highly literate written language. This distinction has appealed to the intuitions of teachers in the U.S., who see their bilingual students struggle with an English-based school curriculum (Joergensen & Quist 2009: 155–157).

As with the discussion of codes, such theories are open to criticism, particularly by linguists and other language specialists, because they apparently (1) lack empirical evidence in the form of well-constructed research; (2) fail to consider a child's semantic and pragmatic competence while looking only at surface grammatical performance on standardized tests; (3) they are full of implicit, subjective judgments about language and supposed links to intelligence, while oversimplifying the true nature of language acquisition; and (4) they typically understate the complex relationships among a child's language development, cognitive development, social environment, and experience in the classroom (Baker 2006: 170–180; Romaine 1995: 265–273; & Hoffman 1991: 130–135).[13]

While distinctions like BICS, CALP, and restricted versus elaborated code encapsulate what educators seem to witness in the classroom, objective research has offered little support. Studies have not been able to identify two distinct kinds of "language" and clear, unambiguous links to cognition and learning. However, when considering a child's developing semantic competence, pragmatic knowledge in writing, and the interaction of the many factors that can influence school success, a different picture emerges. In addition, it is not only possible to identify different levels or kinds of literacy, it is also possible to argue that there is a continuum of literacies, that literacy itself is a gradient concept marked by special vocabulary and knowledge attainable only through direct instruction. The linguistic focus is the role of registers of speech (discussed in Chapter 3) and the gradual acquisition of a continuum of language forms.

The academic registers that children need to negotiate the demands of higher education (secondary and beyond) typically correspond to formal, written, informational genres (situations in which large amounts of information is critical). The correspondence of information and formal speech suggests that children need to develop large vocabularies, which takes time. Academic speech requires in depth knowledge

---

13. For a discussion of early attempts at linking bi- or multilingualism with intelligence, in particular, some "dated" conceptions of the detrimental effects on intelligence and social skills of multilingualism see Edwards (2006: 15–18).

of a range of topics and all the specialized and technical vocabulary items associated with fields of study, words that are not necessarily frequent outside of their individual contexts nor learned in casual speech on the playground. In contrast, informal, spoken genres correspond to more involved registers of speech linked to a high degree of personal involvement and familiarity among participants. They also involve a smaller, less sophisticated vocabulary.

Correlated with access to (a) the practice of literacy and (b) educational opportunities is access by English-language learners and bilinguals to academic, literate registers of English. Children with high literacy skills typically have access to both, educational opportunities and the practice of literacy. It seems reasonable, then, that the more exposure to literate registers of English a student has, language learner or otherwise, the more likely it is that the student will acquire the knowledge these registers convey – of course, individual factors such as motivation, attitude, and learning styles will also be significant. Exposure to formal, informational registers can be a significant issue for speakers of nonstandard varieties of English and children from low SES homes who may have neither exposure to the practice of literacy in the home nor access to the educational opportunities that encourage learning.

If a child or young learner is expected to acquire English literacy in its deepest, most academically useful sense, then all the information that a child has learned via her native language can be exploited to develop familiarity with concepts, to make important distinctions of meaning, and to see associations ("connecting the dots") that only a genuinely literate person can make. Moreover, the acquisition of knowledge is not dependent on any particular language, despite what the dominant culture might say. Stopping all education in a native language, the most important source of information for a child, effectively chokes off the kinds of literate associations a child can make while she learns a second/subsequent language, a process that can certainly take years of sustained effort. Educational practices that limit participation can only exacerbate the problem of high drop out rates among many ethnic and language-minority groups, particularly in states such as California, New York, Florida, Texas, and Hawaii, where the sheer numbers of minority students and high drop-out rates frustrate educators. Crying "problems of illiteracy" based on "low standardized test scores" obscures the real issues; it ignores causes.

With respect to how much time children need in order to develop proficiency in a variety of registers, there are consistent estimates of the time required for young bilinguals to attain conversational fluency in their second language. Cummins (1979) found that everyday conversational skills took approximately two years, and more complex language abilities might take five to seven (cf. Romaine 1995: 265–266). However, R. C. Gardner claims that near native-like proficiency requires a level of expertise that takes around ten years of "persistent practice" (Gardner 2001: 4), approximately the same amount of time that a native-speaker takes. A key element is the motivation of the learner to draw closer and closer to the dominant language and culture. Gardner also defines this integrative motivation as (a) putting forth effort, (b) desiring to achieve native-like proficiency, and (c) *enjoying* the task of learning (Gardner 2001:6; cf. Field 2004:135). This is a far cry from the one to three years allowed in transitional bilingual programs for children to catch up to their peers and participate in mainstream, English-only classrooms.

5.3   Language skills: Passive versus active knowledge

It is not difficult to estimate the importance of such things as vocabulary and the types of skills that an English learner must acquire in order to reach the more complex levels of literacy. And, as the previous section implies, cultural and critical literacy, which necessarily includes being able to read and understand published texts in a wide variety of genres, will have an impact on *writing* academic prose (composition). And, progressing past basic, functional literacy will simply take time. The amount of time will depend on both motivation and ability of the educational establishment to encourage (rather than discourage) participation. A quick look at what is involved in the two distinct processes of reading and writing may prove instructive.

Brown (1994:217) addresses the four language skills that have been discussed and dissected by teachers for decades: listening, speaking, reading, and writing. Reading entails *perception* and the *passive* (receptive) knowledge required to recognize written forms. Writing involves *performance*, the *active* (productive) knowledge required to select appropriate forms from among grammatically correct alternatives. The demands of performance reach into larger cultural, social, and linguistic contexts. Two books, Nation (1990) and Weltens & Grendel (1993), deal specifically with the kinds of knowledge required for nonnative learners from a pedagogical perspective. They point to perceptual, formal (syntactic), functional (in discourse), and specific semantic knowledge by contrasting receptive and productive aspects of language. With respect to the receptive knowledge needed to understand (retrieve) spoken forms, all a speaker has to know is what the word sounds like, and in written form, what it looks like. In contrast, the productive knowledge required to *use* the word includes how the word is pronounced and how it is written (spelled). As far as where the word may occur, receptive knowledge involves merely learning to anticipate the syntactic patterns in which the word may occur (e.g., noun, verb, or adjective). But, in performance, the speaker must *select* a word from a list of possible synonyms plus the types of words that must occur before and after from a theoretical list of alternatives that can number into the hundreds when considering long written assignments, for instance, selecting the correct article or quantifier for a noncount noun (<u>much</u> information) according to the count-mass distinction or a specific preposition required by a noun, verb, or adjective ("A is different <u>from</u> B").

There is more. Word recognition is passive requiring a simple mapping of form to meaning, but choosing an *appropriate* word includes knowing both how common the word is (e.g., *and* versus *furthermore*) and in which register(s) it can be used based on frequency and appropriateness. Because many words have multiple meanings (a simple glance at a dictionary will do), active/productive knowledge also entails both *denotation* (what the word literally means) and *connotation*, all the possible meanings that a word can have in a broad range of contexts (Nation 1990: 31). There is clearly an asymmetrical relationship between receptive knowledge of phonological (or orthographic) form and the productive knowledge to which a *performance error* can be attributed. Relatively simple observations such as these help illustrate the traditional distinction between competence and performance. Being able to recognize words within grammatical (phrasal or clausal) frames requires a minimal linkage of form to meaning. Productive knowledge requires active selection of the grammatically correct form based on syntactically generated word order patterns, e.g., picking the correct preposition, determiner, adjective, and noun patterning of the English prepositional phrase. Performance errors suggest that native and nonnative writers alike may select words to further a message based on meaning or translation equivalent. However, in academic settings, that choice must be from formal registers of SAE, forms that can be quite elusive to the ELL or speaker of a nonstandard variety.

As discussed in Chapter 2, ELLs need to go well beyond merely acquiring the ability to produce grammatically correct sentences. They also need to attain high levels of communicative competence involving at least three overlapping types of knowledge. For instance, a student must have pragmatic knowledge, knowing the norms of written language in the academic community (how to cite sources and to observe the mechanics of writing such as spelling, punctuation, and capitalization. Discourse knowledge is knowing how to structure larger units of discourse beyond the sentence to paragraphs, and how to order information according to the academic community within various disciplines. That is, they need to learn how the predominant model of education determines the ways information is to be presented in narratives and other formal, academic genres (e.g., in argumentation, persuasion, and many types of scientific and expository writing). Sociolinguistic knowledge refers to how usage varies according to social variables like status (the roles of students and teachers) and other cultural variables (e.g., how to refer to authority figures).[14] While direct, cause and

---

14. One example of this is how student writers sometimes refer to authors. An important author, say Albert Einstein, may be referred to as "Albert," which is not accepted practice in academics. It implies being on a first-name basis with a renowned scholar, not likely of secondary students in urban classrooms. Calling a figure such as Einstein by his first name would only be acceptable by social intimates (family members or colleagues) in spoken, involved registers.

effect links between reading and writing are somewhat problematic (whether good writing is inferred from extensive reading without direct instruction and explicit learning), it is still safe to say that the demands of academic writing require cultural and critical literacy.

As an example of the implicit nature of Anglo-Saxon writing practices, in many secondary schools, young people are taught to follow a form typically referred to as *the five-paragraph essay*. Paragraph 1 is the Introduction (with three points a–c). The next three body paragraphs are additional information about each point, one at a time. The last paragraph, the Conclusion, then, restates points a–c. Every essay must have a *thesis statement*, a guiding sentence of its overall purpose-topic, in essence, what the essay is about and the claims it makes (assertions of truth). Each paragraph needs to be built around a single sentence, a *topic sentence*, that structures the flow of information. A claim is made, and evidence is ushered in as proof for that claim. To writers from many other cultures, this is boring, predictable, and just a bad rhetorical strategy. It also features *deduction* (stating a general principle first, and presenting evidence later), a typically Anglo-Saxon method of reasoning *a priori* (a la Sherlock Holmes). Other cultures may favor a "discovery" technique in which the writer gradually comes to a conclusion inductively (*a posteriori*).

This perhaps simplest of essay formats is one example of a *product* of conscious learning. Those children who have grown up in other cultures may be at a disadvantage; they may have fairly high-levels of linguistic competence in English and yet not have the required discourse and pragmatic competence to write papers that conform to Anglo-Saxon norms. In fact, some students may have been taught explicitly that it is not a desirable model to follow, as in the case of Latin American (e.g., Mexican) school systems that encourage completely different rhetorical strategies that conflict with the American model (more on that later). All U.S. teachers should be aware that this basic type of (Anglo Saxon) rhetorical style is implicit in nearly all academic writing (outside of such fields as creative writing and screen writing, for example) in the American educational system. For the students' sake, however, it may be comforting to know that it is not a fact that it is *the best way to write* when taken from a global perspective. It is simply *preferred* in academic settings in the U.S., the U.K., and other nations where English is the politically dominant language, and where this format (and rubric) is emphasized in courses on essay writing. In many cases, it needs to be taught and consciously learned as such, but without denigrating the students' culture, upbringing, or past educational practices. As in additive types of programs, the five-paragraph essay is merely one writing strategy that can be learned and added to existing alternatives. It does not need to be enforced as the *only* true way to write at the expense of other culturally appropriate rhetorical strategies.

6.   Contrastive rhetoric: Developments and criticisms

Continuing this line of reasoning, that ELLs may write differently from native English speakers, and that writing (as a written form of speech) seems to reveal the culturally based ways we *think*, an entire field of inquiry has emerged. The study of *Contrastive Rhetoric* (CR) arose from the evaluations of student essays in English courses written by speakers of other languages (ESL and EFL students) (Connor, Nagelhout & Rozycki 2008). It was originally based on the relatively simple observation that nonnative writers may indeed have near-native-like control of the lexical and syntactic devices of English of proficient speakers and writers, yet fail to demonstrate the pragmatic skills necessary to compose coherent papers according to native-writer norms and patterns of usage. Instead, they typically rely on the rhetorical patterns of their native languages and cultures, in fairly predictable ways. "A large body of earlier work has established that L2 written discourse and text are invariably affected by NNSs' first language (L1) discourse norms and paradigms" (Hinkel 2002: 1). Connor (2002) points out that this insight is based on the idea that "language [usage] and writing are cultural phenomena" (494). It also fit into then accepted pedagogical practices based on behaviorism, that "…learning equaled the reinforcement of correct responses" (Connor 2008: 301). Where differences existed, we might anticipate a learning problem.

The inaugural piece, Robert Kaplan's (1966), "Cultural thought patterns in intercultural education," brought a key insight to the field of applied linguistics in the U.S.: "Writing is culturally influenced in interesting and complex ways" (Connor 1996: 495). Kaplan's pioneering work came under criticism that it did not pay enough attention to subtle differences among cultures and that it appeared to "privilege the writing of native English speakers," in essence setting it up as the standard for academic writing (Connor 2002: 494–5). Despite admitted drawbacks (e.g., that it led to stereotyping), this article has had a tremendous impact on the teaching of English to speakers of other languages (TESOL). If a literature (thus, literacy) is culturally influenced, it follows that writing will also be culturally influenced. One goal for many ESL writers in the U.S. is, therefore, *to write according to the expectations of native users* of English, structuring written discourse according to the culturally-defined patterns of literate (written) genres and corresponding registers. The goal is more than merely constructing grammatical sentences in English; it is to organize information in ways that are consistent with the norms of academic institutions, according to the dominant culture.

One of the major criticisms of contrastive rhetoric has been that it creates stereotypes because it tends to associate *group behaviors* with that of *individuals*. That is, an educator may assume that an individual is a member of a particular group and anticipate that the individual will behave like all other members of the group, which denies the fact that each and every one of us consists of our own constellation of personality traits, abilities, interests, and types of motivation. Setting up stereotypes may merely be inherent to the quantitative methodology characteristic of such studies (as an artifact) that attempt to uncover large-scale cultural patterns. It is something to be aware of. Nevertheless, contrastive rhetoric reveals interesting patterns that upon retrospection seem to fit the intuitions of teachers and other language specialists in composition. The patterns observed are also consistent with current conceptualizations of transfer (the influence of a native language) in perception and performance (Gass & Selinker 1993a, 1993b; Eubank, Selinker & Sharwood Smith 1995).[15]

Another, perhaps more significant criticism of contrastive rhetoric is a concept of *culture*. A traditional view is that culture is monolithic and based on clear national, geographical, and perhaps ethnic lines (*British*, *Japanese*, or *American culture*). Such a unitary view sees cultures as entities of some sort that act in uniform ways to condition the thought patterns of their members (Connor 2002: 503–504). This can lead to an oversimplification of concepts of society, and the multifaceted ways that culture manifests itself in human behavior. An alternative view suggests that culture is not as homogeneous as one might believe within various levels of society. For instance, in modern urban societies there is a dynamic interaction among subcultures, socioeconomic strata, ethnicity, sex/gender, views of morality and ethics, and the like. Within literate (and oral) domains, we see a subtle interplay of factors that (a) manifests itself in various genres (affecting reader/audience expectations), and therefore, (b) influences the rhetorical strategies available to an individual writer. Atkinson (1999) discusses concepts of identity, hybridity, existentialism, and power that characterize criticisms of the traditional view:

> So used, these terms indicate the shared perspective that cultures are anything but homogenous, all-encompassing entities, and represent important concepts in a larger project: the unveiling of the fissures, inequalities, disagreements, and cross-cutting influences that exist in and around all cultural scenes, in order to banish once and for all the idea that cultures are monolithic entities, or in some cases anything important at all.   (Atkinson 1999: 627)

All societies have their dissenting voices, and while we might be able to speculate that one's culture is something that is to a great degree unconsciously acquired and expressed (much as language is), it is nonetheless something that can be brought into the realm of objective study. Cultures intersect to form new, hybrid subcultures that acquire new social identities, much like the unique Chicano-Latino identity.

The contrasts that seem evident among cultures, moreover, should be looked at in the light of differences among equals. One may look at one's own culture as superior because of its familiarity. We tend to understand the rationales and justifications for our own value systems, but that does not necessarily make one system better, higher, or superior to another. Consequently, we shouldn't look at contrastive rhetoric as

---

15. See, also, Ulla Connor's review of contrastive rhetoric in TESOL Quarterly (2002).

measuring various cultural patterns in writing *against* English or Anglo-European patterns, and assume the cultural and linguistic superiority of English over all others, e.g., English over Spanish or Russian (Connor 2002:495). The intent of contrastive rhetoric is only to understand the differences, not to place languages and cultures on some sort of scale or hierarchy. Unfortunately, it has been common in the West to assume some sort of cultural and linguistic superiority, perhaps based on technological advances and economic and military dominance. At various stages in Western history, the sense of superiority resurfaces from time to time in various forms of racism, an idea that is generally acknowledged as wrong, or at least questionable, by Anglo Americans today.

Contrastive Rhetoric, today, is responding to earlier criticisms; it has come a long way. Looking at writing as an "intercultural encounter" (Connor 2008:299) CR, perhaps under a new heading as *intercultural rhetoric*, has expanded its focus from a product-oriented approach to one that includes the experience of writing cross-culturally in general, and continues to bring insights into second-language pedagogy and the teaching of writing to non-native speakers of English (Xiaoming Li 2008).

6.1   Linguistic relativity and the Sapir-Whorf hypothesis

Connor (2008) also suggests that one likely inspiration for Kaplan's work was the so-called *Sapir-Whorf (or Whorfian) hypothesis* (301). In the early twentieth century, anthropological linguist Edward Sapir and his student, Benjamin Whorf, observed links between language and culture in their study of indigenous languages and cultures of the Americas. The hypothesis that emerged is an American version of *linguistic relativity* that has had an impact on education, and perhaps on public perceptions of the concept of culture, especially relative to Anglo Saxon culture and its imprint on American society. Briefly, linguistic relativity suggests that we all view the world according to the words and structures of our native languages. We do not see an objective reality shaped by universal characteristics of thought or language. Our views of the world are shaped by the culture and language in which we live. Each language, therefore, contains and communicates a particular worldview. This is especially relevant to American attitudes towards "foreign" cultures and languages. The concept of linguistic relativity, consequently, may also play a prominent role in debates over a uniquely American culture and the roles that Anglo Saxon culture and language play in national unity.

This hypothesis fit U.S. anthropological theory in the first half of the 20th century – cultural anthropologists, including Edward Sapir (1921), held to the doctrine of cultural relativism. They believed that each cultural group had its own unique world view, based partly on a long-term connection to the physical environment, but mostly on the long-term connections of group members to each other (Connor 2008:301).

The hypothesis itself is now attributed mostly to Whorf because he carried the ideas of Sapir a bit further. Thus, in its strongest version, the Whorfian hypothesis argues that a person's first language *determines* thought, that "one's native language influences and controls thought, consequently barring fluent second language acquisition" (Connor 1996:29). A weaker version takes the view that a native language may affect thought, but to a lesser degree. It influences, rather than determines thought. This modified form has regained respectability in cognitive linguistics, psychology, and comparative studies of composition and rhetoric, resulting in renewed interest in cultural differences (Gumperz & Levinson 1996:495). There is little doubt of a connection between culture and its various expressions, but it may be over-reaching to say that language determines perception of the world (a position known as *linguistic determinism*), which has become one of the larger issues of cognitive linguistics and debates over various versions of the Sapir-Whorf hypothesis.[16]

Whorf concluded that human language is not universal in its structure, and, therefore, does not represent human thought in uniform ways. If it were universal, our languages would be much more alike than they apparently are, and we would all think in similar ways.[17] Whorf also argued that the language a person speaks (assumed to be acquired natively) *classifies and organizes experience*, according to the categories that it contains (e.g., grammatical categories such as Tense and Gender and the subtle ways a language makes implications), and that this cultural and linguistic classification scheme is objective only up to a point (Lucy 1992:26). For instance, through grammatical categories such as *animacy* linked to classes of nouns and pronouns, agreement markers (e.g., subject-verb agreement), or other structural characteristics, one language may indicate rankings of human versus non-human; another may make finer distinctions based on human, higher animal, lower animal, other animate things (e.g., plants and trees), and other things such as water, thunder, and rain. But, to one group of people (or culture) a tree may be an inanimate object, and to another, it may be a spirit-being, having the same life force within it as classes of animals and human beings (Croft 1990:111–117; Comrie 1989:185–200). Therefore, the categories expressed by a language may shape how we view the things we "see" in the world around us.

On perhaps the opposite side of the debate, particularly since the early 1960s, is the concept of linguistic universals in the form of *Generative Theory* and concepts of *Universal Grammar* (UG) (Chomsky 1976, 1986). In general, this theory argues that human language is a *biological* endowment (a property of our species), and that the language

---

16. See, e.g., Gumperz & Levinson (1996) and G. Lakoff (1987) for discussion of the links between language and thought.

17. "…Whorf's own considered positions seem to have been that language influences unconscious habitual thought, rather than limiting thought potential…" (Gumperz & Levinson 1996:22).

faculty, therefore, is universal, hence uniform (in all human beings) in some, perhaps hidden way. It also suggests that we are all born with innate grammatical categories such as Noun and Verb; grammatical functions of Subject and Object, and semantic notions of Agent and Patient (cf. Cook 1988: 110–117). Parenthetically, a different view of language universals was suggested by Sapir (1921) and renewed by Comrie (1989). It seeks to take the rich data provided by the world's languages and to construct a reasonable theory of what is in fact possible in human languages and, therefore universal to human language(s).[18]

Both general sides of the debate on relativity, however, acknowledge the universality of the language faculty, but the amazing diversity of linguistic systems gives a good deal of credibility to linguistic relativity. There is not much question, based on evidence, that rhetorical patterns represent the ways that information is ordered and expressed in a language. For example, every language has its own unique ways to classify and describe entities (people, places, and things that exist), order events, express relationships of cause-and-effect, contrast old and new information, and emphasize the relative importance of events. The basic functions of a language to form negatives, give commands, imply, request, and so on can be very specific. In academic writing, there is always a task and a purpose, and one can include concepts of elegance (skillful discourse) and effectiveness (reaching the purposes and goals of written discourse). The ways different languages allow a user to perform these tasks can vary considerably.

The Whorfian hypothesis, however, has not been without its critics. In fact it has found some of its harshest of critics on methodological grounds (e.g., Fishman 1989) and, more recently, on philosophical grounds (cf., Pinker 1994: 57), because it appears to equate thought and language. The first and, perhaps, most obvious problem is the fact of bilingualism. Fishman (1977) notes that many bilinguals go about their day-to-day lives switching from language to language with no problem. It seems that if language determined or controlled thought, then a bilingual would think one way in one language and differently in another. Some bilinguals may indeed be bicultural and able to "think" as monolinguals in each language; however, true bilinguality and biculturalism most likely belong to the relatively rare minority of ambilinguals (balanced bilinguals) who have acquired their languages simultaneously.[19]

In addition, there are multilingual societies where individuals use various languages for various purposes (the phenomenon known as diglossia), e.g., one at home, one at work, and one for religious observance, a situation that occurs in many urban areas where speakers of different languages form well-established minority communities and

---

18. See Comrie (1989: 1–5) for a discussion of the two approaches to universals of language.

19. See Chapter 2 for discussion of different types of bilingual individuals.

compartmentalize language usage. The ability to *translate* from one language to the other also points to the facility with which many fluent bilinguals can represent their thoughts in each of their languages. It's difficult to envision that a bilingual "thinks" one way in one language and an entirely different way in another, although bicultural-ism implies behaving in appropriate ways according to the norms of two autonomous cultures. After all, a bilingual person is not two monolinguals in one body (Grosjean 1995: 259). Every bilingual is a unique individual with specific linguistic abilities. In essence, a bilingual is one speaker with two languages. It can be argued, too, that cultural elements of speech can be teased away from language. More than one culture can be represented by one language, e.g., African American or Chicano-Latino culture as it is expressed via the medium of English.

Despite the potential for controversy, recent work in the area of contrastive rhetoric has opened new ways to analyze literate, academic discourse by looking at specific rhetorical strategies that can be linked with various cultures. University students from a wide range of cultural and linguistic backgrounds appear to use English in ways that differ fundamentally from usage in the Anglo-Saxon mold, as any ESL teacher will attest. As a result, linguistic relativity, as a concept, is becoming more widespread in its weaker form, that language (and the culture it represents) can influence the ways we think and communicate our thoughts (as a linguistic behavior), but it certainly does not determine thought in a rigid sense. But, it is an entirely different topic to discuss whether or not Chicano-Latinos or any other language minority in the U.S. can or cannot *think* like Americans and make significant, positive contributions to society. One must remain vigilant with respect to harmful stereotypes wherever they may originate.

6.2 Contrasting the rhetorical patterns of Spanish and English

As discussed in Chapter 5, American attitudes towards bilingualism have certainly been ambivalent; and public perceptions have predictably vacillated at particularly trying economic times in the history of the nation. So, it may be especially important to investigate the rhetorical patterns that Chicano-Latinos exhibit in academic settings, sometimes questionably linked exclusively to a biased view of Spanish-English bilinguals (that all Latinos are Spanish dominant, and therefore, limited in English as a group). However, the research has proceeded in fits and starts, and the conclusions have sometimes been met with skepticism, even cynicism. As a consequence, the positive and negative sides of contrastive rhetoric (and the tendency of its quantitative focus to foster stereotypes) and the limitations of a strong view of linguistic determinism need to be kept in mind. To that end, the following paragraphs trace the early development of research on the rhetorical strategies of Chicano-Latinos.

Among the earliest studies of contrastive rhetoric were papers on Spanish, though such studies have yet to be included in major anthologies. There was also a significant time gap following the initial work, most likely a reaction to criticisms that such studies may have prejudiced teachers by the stereotypes they implied. Nevertheless, a number of more recent studies of large groups of subjects and extensive qualitative analyses of texts have produced some interesting results. In general, they suggest that Spanish-language writers prefer a style described as *flowery*, detailed, elaborate, and ornate, with longer chunks of discourse "decorated" with long, complicated sentences and long, "educated sounding" words, language that, in an English model, appear glib and perhaps pretentious (Montaño-Harmon 1991: 419–420). Clauses are loosely linked (without strong transitional elements such as *consequently*, *as a result*, etc.), giving what has been described as a rambling effect. In a study of an essay portion of the TOEFL (Test of English as a Foreign Language), Reid (1988) found that native speakers of Spanish used pronouns and longer sentences more frequently than native English speakers, so ideas and referents expressed by Spanish L1 writers of English appeared to lack cohesion. In contrast, from the Anglo perspective, the use of short (concise) clauses and nouns linked specifically by different types of conjunctions appears to make the association of ideas clearer and direct according to an English model, rather than implicit in a Spanish model.

Montaño-Harmon (1991) compared texts on a 50-minute writing task (850 total essays) written by four groups of students: native Mexican Spanish speakers, Spanish dominant ELLs, English-dominant Chicano English speakers, and native English speakers (all secondary school students). The initial purpose of her study was to observe the discourse patterns of writers who were speakers of Chicano English. It soon became apparent, however, that ChE speakers *did not show the effect of transfer from Spanish*, and little effect of literacy training in either language. Instead, they showed writing patterns associated with the informal, spoken nature of ChE and "all the problems associated with a limited level of literacy in English." Most noticeable in these compositions was a very informal, conversational tone (style or register) that made them "unacceptable in an academic setting" (420). To point out what one should expect as a result of transfer of rhetorical strategies from Spanish, her results showed the following:

Table 7.1 Word counts (means)

Discourse feature	Mexican Spanish	Anglo-American English
text length	184.86 words	155.70 words
number of sentences	5.38	9.90
average length of sentences	41.10 words	17.10 words

Sentences tended to be long, run-ons (linked by the additive conjunction *y*, "and"), or with no conjunction and no punctuation at all to mark sentence boundaries. The writing of the Anglo-American students tended towards simple sentences (single-clause sentences) or relatively short complex sentences (cause and effect, linked by *because*).

Table 7.2 Sentence types (means)

Discourse feature	Mexican Spanish	Anglo-American English
fragments[20]	.58	.76
run-on	2.66	1.30
simple	.73	3.20
compound	.18	.56
complex	.90	3.40

Montaño-Harmon (1991) also notes that the Mexican Spanish-speaking students relied on synonyms more than their English counterparts to achieve cohesion, a strategy that is overtly taught in the Mexican school system. "Their strategy was to state an idea, place a comma, and then repeat the same idea using a synonym, the same word, or a semantically related word to create a build-up effect" (421). In contrast, Anglo-American writers frequently used enumeration (e.g., first, second, etc.) to signal temporal or spatial order, or the order of importance (in descending order), a strategy typically taught in U.S. schools (e.g., in the typical five-paragraph essay). The use of *and* in English, the additive equivalent to *y*, is most often associated with the writing of children and young adolescents, so this particular strategy in the writing of Mexican Spanish looks unsophisticated from the Anglo-American view. A large number of digressions (conscious deviations) were found in which there were abrupt changes of topic. This would make the text seem disjointed and unorganized, despite the fact that the writer would later return to the topic. The Anglo-American students used relatively simple (common, frequent) vocabulary, few synonyms, and no "flowery" language.

Montaño-Harmon's results regarding the differences between native Spanish speakers and native English speakers were repeated in a dissertation done on university-level Ecuadorian Spanish writers and university-level native English writers in the U.S. (Lux 1991). These and other studies point to the likelihood of Spanish L1 transfer into L2

---

20. Fragments, or "frags," are not considered "complete sentences." Either an overt subject (e.g., a nominal of some kind) or a tensed verb is missing, or the clause is introduced by a subordinator rendering the construction a dependent clause, and therefore not a "complete" sentence.

English by native speakers of Spanish with respect to elaborate and ornate style and other particular characteristics, for example, frequent run-ons, sentence fragments, and an organizational pattern that looks flowery, disorganized, and rambling to the native English speaker. And, if the papers are written in an inductive or quasi-inductive style (from a specific evidence to a general conclusion), it would be difficult for the Anglo-American to find "the point," the thesis, or the controlling idea of a paper. The predictability of Anglo-American rhetorical style may appear rigid, simple, and therefore, boring to the Mexican Spanish writer and contrary to the ways that rhetorical strategies are overtly taught in Mexico, but it showcases the lexical and grammatical clues that (a) link ideas and (b) help the reader see easily how ideas are connected. In the Anglo view, it is the writer's responsibility to make his/her text clear, and not the reader's to figure it out.

The most significant finding was the contrast between the rhetorical styles of the English-dominant ChE speakers and the native-English speaking Anglo Americans. Unfortunately, Montaño-Harmon's paper did not provide quantitative data on the Chicano-English speakers; it only described differences impressionistically and stated that the expected results of transfer did not occur. However, we can still see the importance of formal registers of English in education. Consequently, the pedagogical strategies to teach formal, academic English for Chicano English speakers will be entirely different from those proposed for native speakers of Spanish, but in either case, bridges can be made to literacy in SAE via the students' native varieties. For the nonstandard English speaker, the bridge comes through increased exposure to literate registers of English, vocabulary instruction, and the awareness of dialects (standard and nonstandard) in the classroom. For the Spanish L1 speaker, a connection can be made to literate forms of Spanish (and rhetorical strategies) via overt instruction in the literacy practices of native users of English.

For both groups, awareness of individual rhetorical patterns can assist teachers in raising the awareness of young writers to the often unconscious, cultural patterns of speech. Some direct and explicit instruction in either case may be needed to describe the rhetorical demands of Anglo Saxon culture, the dominant culture in the American educational system (and not likely to change in the near future). More objective, quantitative research is obviously needed, with the knowledge that negative stereotypes will only lead to more problems, not solutions. The lack of a coherent "plan," and merely lumping Chicano English speakers together with ELLs has surely contributed to the frustration of educators, including administrators and classroom teachers.

Key terms

active knowledge, animacy, appropriateness, basic literacy skills, BICS, biliteracy, biliteracies, biliterate, biological endowment, CALP, castelike minority, cognition, computer literacy, connotation, continua of literacies, contrastive rhetoric (CR), critical literacy, culture, cultural literacy, decode, denotation, discourse feature, elaborated code, empowerment, English for Specific Purposes (ESP), Eurocentric, five-paragraph essay, flowery language, frequency, functional, functions of language, Generative Theory, hybridity, identity, ideology, illiteracy/illiterate, intercultural rhetoric, language universals, linguistic determinism, linguistic relativity, literacies, literacy myth, literate tradition, multiple literacies, NAEP, nested, nonliterate, numeracy, online sources, oracy, overt teaching, panacea, passive knowledge, perception, performance error, plurilingualism, pluriliteracies, pragmatic skills, pre-literacy training, preliterate, purist, receptive knowledge, restricted code, rhetorical strategy, run-on sentence, SAE, Sapir-Whorf (Whorfian) Hypothesis, scaffolding, schooling, standardization, techno-literacy, thesis statement, thresholds, transfer, translate, Universal Grammar (UG), universalism.

Summary

There are numerous myths about the power of literacy. For example, it is thought that a literate person is more likely to be happy and informed, find a job, and earn more money. Stronger versions state that literacy leads to higher-order thinking skills, abstract use of language, a questioning attitude, recognition of complex and modern governments, greater social equity, lower crime rate, better citizens, economic development, wealth and prosperity, and a lower birth rate. Such myths are obviously subjective, and there is no empirical research to back them up.

Defining literacy, however, is not a simple task. The lowest, most basic level is functional literacy: a person with this level of literacy can basically decode printed texts, read the mail, and pay the bills (which involves numeracy skills, as well). There is also cultural literacy, which entails understanding all or most of the facts and beliefs an educated reader is *assumed* to know. But, who decides what all literate Americans should know? Critical literacy is yet another type that involves being able to recognize the underlying social and political assumptions of authors. This requires background knowledge that goes beyond functional literacy. However, the endpoint of many English-only programs is merely functional literacy, probably a minimum requirement for menial labor or to prepare students for the so-called trades such as welding and auto (refrigerator, computer) repair.

American attitudes towards biliteracy, like bilingualism, are ambivalent at best. It is important to recognize that literacy is more than the acquisition of a set of technical skills. It is a socially constructed phenomenon, a prescribed collection of communicative practices necessary to succeed in a literate society. Most recent research has focused on the complex and multifaceted nature of literacy; so one can imagine how literacy in two or more languages has proved to be even more complex. One expects continua of proficiencies in each language, and that there would also be continua of proficiencies in abilities to read and write those languages. Early studies were limited, in that many focused on literacy in a SL in school and from a skills-based view of literacy. In contrast, recent work has focused on the many facets of literacy in general and literacy development in multiple language varieties, according to a more complete view of the nature of language itself. As the literature has progressed, perspectives have broadened. They have attempted to view the acquisition of biliteracy in a greater context. One apparent breakthrough has been the concept of *continua of literacies*.

Though not specifically linked to literacy, per se, some educators maintain that language can be linked to a child's cognitive abilities. But, no link has been demonstrated between language and *cognition* (the mental ability of knowing). This is one part of the controversial "Thresholds Theory," which proposes that higher levels of abstract thinking are only available to those bilingual children who are highly proficient in both their languages. The theory began with the observation that children learning a second language often struggle in school. It states that an emerging bilingual must reach a threshold at which competence in both languages is developed enough so that she can enjoy the advantages of balanced bilingualism. But, there are two issues: (1) proficiency in English (the linguistic issue) and (2) the types of knowledge one gets from schooling (the schooling issue). So, came the concepts of BICS and CALP. The former is speech used in informal situations, and the latter is the speech required for academic usage. Linguists disagree on numerous grounds, stating, e.g., that such theories understate the complex relationships among a child's language development, cognitive growth, and social environment. The more exposure to literate registers of English a student has, the more likely it is that the student will acquire the knowledge these registers convey. Not only can we identify different levels of literacy, but we may argue that it is a gradient concept, a continuum of literacies.

To see the effect of a native language on SL writing, Contrastive Rhetoric (CR) is based on the observation that nonnative writers may fail to demonstrate the pragmatic skills necessary to compose coherent papers according to native-writer norms and patterns of usage despite having native-like control of the grammatical devices of English. They typically rely on the rhetorical patterns of their native languages and cultures. The danger of CR and similar approaches is that they may lead to stereotypes. Another is a concept of *culture*. A traditional view is that culture is monolithic and based on clear national, geographical, and perhaps ethnic lines (*British culture*). Such a unitary view sees cultures as entities that condition the thought patterns of their members. An alternative view suggests that culture is not homogeneous. In modern societies, subcultures, SES, ethnicity, sex/gender, and views of morality and ethics interact. In spite of its drawbacks, contrastive rhetoric reveals patterns in useful ways.

Among earlier empirical studies of contrastive rhetoric were papers on Spanish. A number of more recent studies have produced some interesting results. In general, they suggest that

Spanish-language writers prefer a style described as *flowery*, detailed, elaborate, and ornate, "decorated" with long, complicated sentences and long, "educated sounding" words, language that, in an English model, appear glib and perhaps pretentious. Montaño-Harmon (1991) compared texts written by four groups of students: native Mexican Spanish speakers, Spanish dominant ELLs, English-dominant Chicano English speakers, and native English speakers (all secondary school students). It soon became apparent that ChE speakers did not show the effect of transfer from Spanish, and little effect of literacy training in either language. Instead, they showed writing patterns associated with the informal, spoken nature of ChE and problems associated with a limited English literacy. Most noticeable in their compositions was a very informal, conversational tone (register) that made them unacceptable in school settings.

Activities – topics for discussion

1. What is SAE? Is it the way all people talk in your family, neighborhood, community, and school? Discuss other possible language varieties that you encounter on a daily basis.

2. Make a list of the potential economic and social benefits of developing bilingual, biliterate *groups* in the U.S. Also, make a list of the potential drawbacks. Then discuss how being literate in a heritage language can help a child become literate in English.

3. Various literacy myths have persisted in modern-day classrooms. Have you ever heard some of the arguments about the power of literacy? How did you react to them? Do you know anyone who is non-literate? How does that person feel?

4. Discuss literate culture versus oral culture. It has been said that once a language is written down, people forget how to memorize. A similar phenomenon happens when children rely on calculators in classrooms: they learn how to do simple arithmetic in their "heads."

5. Explain why Standard American English is the only language variety that counts in literacy in the U.S. Concerning the history of the U.S., consider the importance of oral accounts and multiple views of history (e.g., from the perspective of ethnic minorities and women).

Practice essay questions

1. Compare and contrast the various types of literacy needed in academic English. For example, what are some of the subtle differences between cultural literacy and critical literacy?

2. Define multiple literacies. In your response, trace the evolution of terms from old views of biliteracy (as L1, then L2) to current views of continua of literacies and pluriliteracies.

3. Identify what is intuitive about Thresholds Theory, and also what seems to be wrong with it. For instance, examine the importance of vocabulary building and the roles of knowledge and classroom experience in academic achievement.

4. Describe linguistic relativity and the Whorfian hypothesis. How do you think English influences our thought patterns?

5. Discuss Contrastive Rhetoric and how culture may influence such things as the flow of information or other rhetorical strategies in English.

Chapter 8

The current state
of the Chicano-Latino community

News articles on the failure of state schools to progress according to federal standards and the No Child Left Behind (NCLB) initiative are commonplace in places like California. School reform, particularly since the beginning of the Obama administration and his proposed *Race to the Top* program, is gathering steam in unprecedented ways, affecting nearly every area of education from the government through union membership and into the classrooms.[1] As all educators know, schools are not just buildings; they are composed of administrators, teachers, teaching assistants, students (their parents and other caregivers), and a host of others, all intent on serving school-age children. One possible inference that can be drawn from the continual reports of failure is that it is the teachers' fault, that they are underprepared. Perhaps the accusation that rankles educators the most is that the tenure system – that teachers reach a state of seniority passed which they can no longer be fired or disciplined – breeds lazy teachers

---

1. Created by the U.S. Department of Education, the Race to the Top initiative is a $4.35 billion incentive program of competitive grants designed to encourage reforms in state and local K-12 education. It is funded by the ED Recovery Act as part of the American Recovery and Reinvestment Act of 2009. While many states have tried to comply with application guidelines, the Race to the Top competition has met considerable opposition from teachers' unions and some states (e.g., Texas) opposed to federal interference in their educational policies. Critics argue that the reforms being promoted are unproven or have not been successful in the past and that selection of "winners" is subjective and biased, not based on objective evidence of superior compliance with reform criteria.

who cease caring about their students' education. Hence, teachers are under constant scrutiny and consequent risk of sanctions by school districts for low test scores.

In many states, the establishment of data bases to measure student performance on standardized tests is a key element of reform and the move towards greater teacher accountability. The blame for lack of school achievement, if it is not placed squarely on the shoulders of educators, can conceivably be placed with the parents for their lack of involvement, or on the children's respective communities, or society in general for not preparing children for the rigors of formal schooling. It is not likely a case of "none of the above," but it could be one of "all of the above." The only actors in this drama who seem to escape blame are the children, who can't be faulted for the inadequacies and lack of resources of a system that seems to be collapsing around them. Nevertheless, language minority students often find themselves in the middle of a tug of war: a major issue is still the role of language proficiency, particularly in Standard American English. It will not go away.

Despite substantial research demonstrating the effectiveness of bilingual education, it is no longer an "official" option in California – a casualty of political turmoil. The reality is that today's teachers go into an environment where bilingualism is the norm, with little or no specific preparation for the task at hand, that is, how to teach bi- and multilingual students of varying levels of competency in English to compete with monolingual users of English on a formal, academic level. We certainly don't wish to let social perceptions, stereotypes, and attitudes towards ethnic and language minorities influence our view of the job ahead of us in education and jeopardize the academic careers of the children. They appear to be pawns in a struggle for hegemony among language and cultural groups. As discussed in the previous chapter, the educational playing field is not a level one; most mainstream children are advantaged in concrete ways, in preliteracy training and in the material benefits of privilege.

If the state university system, ostensibly the principle vehicle for teacher training in a state like California, is not preparing teachers for the realities they will face, then that needs to be addressed, and as quickly and efficiently as possible. When new teachers are sent into densely populated school districts where the vast majority of students are non-native speakers of English (e.g., Spanish-English bilinguals of varying proficiencies), where (a) resources for teachers and students are scarce, (b) area residents are more likely to be from low-income families, then those teachers are destined for a career of frustration. Add to this the constantly evolving teaching methodologies and professional pressure to raise children's scores on standardized tests, and it appears that our new or experienced educators are put in a position to fail. If they are underpaid (relative to the amount of specialized education they need, their workload, and the type of stress they have on the job regarding their own safety), as well, then it should be no surprise to read reports that there is a shortage of teachers. Perhaps the place to start in educational reform is in teacher preparation. Find what teachers need to perform more effectively, knowing that they are the ones charged with carrying out the mandates of well-intentioned reform movements.

A fairly recent article (10/23/02) in the *Daily News* titled, "LAUSD seeks more ways to teach English," reported that "According to the district, 54 percent of elementary school students, 31 percent of middle school students and 24 percent of high school students are English learners." The percentages in the higher grades cannot help but increase as time passes – and that may be the best-case scenario. The article cited the *Los Angeles Unified School District's* (LAUSD) efforts to improve its effectiveness in reaching this obviously expanding group and improving literacy and writing skills. Evidently, there is an implicit connection between test scores and language proficiency (literacy and rhetorical skills). A more recent article in the *Contra Costa Times* (7/24/06), "Change in education: As Latino students near a majority in public schools, questions arise on how California will address shift," states that in three years (from 2006), "California will become the nation's second state, after New Mexico, in which a majority of public school students are Latino…." As of November 2010, Latino students accounted for 50.4 percent of the student population in California's public schools (Blume 2010).

In keeping with the recent emphasis on standards and accountability in education, a new standardized exam designed to measure basic skills in Mathematics and English Language Arts, the *California High School Exit Exam* (CAHSEE), has exposed huge gaps among ethnic groups concerning their academic success. While the numbers may present a somewhat glum picture of the future of California's public school system (depending on one's perspective), there is some indication that the statistical effect for ethnicity, evidently the clearest factor in student success on the standardized tests, gradually disappears as English language proficiency goes up. A related issue is the contrast between the children's "home" language and the formal, literate forms of Standard American English needed for academic success that affects specific ethnic minorities. When a student's native variety (language or dialect) is indeed a factor in his or her failure, there is reason to believe that ways can easily be found to lessen its impact and the consequent disparity between traditionally privileged groups and those with a history of failure. The question follows whether or not the educational system wants to eliminate the disparity.

In order to assess the situation and perhaps to make recommendations for the future, this chapter takes a brief tour through California's student population to gauge the current state of the Chicano-Latino bilingual community. The final section, "Conclusions," discusses some of the social, economic, and linguistic issues covered in this book, and a few of the ramifications of current school practices. Many of these issues affect other states in the Southwest U.S. and elsewhere around the country. Ultimately, they are a national concern as Latinos of all backgrounds constitute the largest and fastest growing ethnic minority in the nation (Gándara & Contreras 2009: 1). It is hoped that discussion will provide points to consider for other states as they anticipate their own changing demographics and the consequences, for example, in the American South, Midwest, and Northeast, where pockets of Spanish-English bilinguals from various regions of Latin America have emerged in the past few decades. These communities, in addition to the already established bilingual communities in major urban areas, have the potential to impact the political and educational landscapes of the nation (Suárez-Orozco & Páez 2002).

1. Student demographics: Language issues

It is not difficult to project that the majority of California's public school children will soon be non-native speakers of English, if they are not already. This obviously influences public education at all levels. Note, too, that, according to U.S. Census figures, California has approximately 40% of the nation's school-age English Language learners (ELLs), formerly known as English as a Second Language (ESL) students. Higher education feels the impact. The system needs to respond to this reality, particularly with respect to teacher preparation/training, hiring and retention (e.g., of bilingual Chicano-Latino faculty), and payroll practices.

Since the early 20th Century, one of the now traditional gripes against bilingual education, per se, has been that there are just too many languages spoken by all of the English Language Learners, and it isn't feasible to have bilingual classes for every student who speaks a language other than English. If we had classes in Spanish, for example, it wouldn't be fair to the others, or so goes the complaint. However, this is not sufficient reason to ignore the numbers of Spanish speakers who are a numerical majority in many districts statewide and who could clearly benefit the most. According to *California Department of Education* (CDE) statistics covering the last twenty years, by far the most widely used language in California other than English is Spanish, followed by Vietnamese. Current figures show that for every ELL student who is a Vietnamese speaker, there are nearly *forty* who are speakers of Spanish, nearly double the ratio of only ten years ago. In 1992, for instance, there were 828,036 Spanish-speaking ELLs enrolled in CA public schools, and 45,155 Vietnamese speakers, a ratio of about 18 to one. In the school year 2005–2006, thirteen years later, the numbers are 1,351,369 to 34,263, a ratio of over 39 to one (Field 2005).

Importantly, the overwhelming majority of these Spanish speakers reside in one continuous geographical area, the five neighboring counties of Los Angeles, Orange, Riverside, San Bernardino, and San Diego. Consequently, it is not uncommon for teachers in these counties (regardless of teaching experience) to face classrooms of

30 or more students who are all native-speakers of Spanish, and who exhibit a wide range of proficiencies in English, from English Language Learners (ELLs) at the very beginning of the learning process to relatively competent bilinguals, or those who have been reclassified as Fluent English Proficiency students (FEPs) – but are, nonetheless, non-native speakers. (All data cited in this chapter were obtained from www.cde.gov, the official web site of the California Department of Education.)

1.1 Numbers in terms of English proficiency

As discussed previously, the sole use of English in California public schools has been an emotionally charged political issue for many years. As a result, propositions such as the Unz initiative of 1998 (Proposition 227) have been passed that have given English, the de facto "official" language of the state and nation, legal status and, in effect, outlawing bilingual education, i.e., prohibiting the use of so-called "foreign" languages in the state's classrooms in content areas (Gándara 2002). Outside of dismantling fledgling bilingual programs of various types and instituting English-only programs in their place, it may be interesting to know what effect these movements have actually had, and whether or not the state has improved its effectiveness in its handling of non-native speakers of English. (Critics point suspiciously to relatively higher test scores that merely demonstrate the success of "teach-to-the-test" classroom methods, not necessarily to actual improvement in a range of academic disciplines, for example, in the social sciences – i.e., history and civics – or the arts.)

Table 8.1 Statewide enrollment in terms of ELLs and FEPs

CA Statewide enrollment (2005–2006)	6,312,393
ELL (English Language Learners, formerly ESL)	1,570,424
FEP (Fluent English Proficiency)	1,123,954
Total NNS (Non-Native Speakers)	2,694,378
% of total	42.7

Table 8.1 shows that 42.7% of all students enrolled in California public schools are designated non-native speakers of English, and, hence Language Minority (LM) students. Of course, this begs the question of how the figures are reached. For example, are bilingual students who test as proficient English speakers as they enter school counted as natives or non-natives? The answer is that they are most likely included among native speakers, as many Spanish-English bilingual children certainly are native speakers of English, as well (native bilinguals), and, therefore, do not require special services or placement into particular programs. They are enrolled in mainstream classes from the beginning.

1.2 Numbers based on ethnicity

One of the major problems in determining the gravity of the situation in education is the fact that the important figures are tallied in different categories, which undoubtedly reflects how issues of ethnicity and language become intertwined ethnographically, socio-economically, and especially politically. Ethnicity typically includes a heritage language, particularly among groups whose members include recent arrivals. A heritage language can play a significant role in a community despite the fact that not all members actually speak it. Relatively balanced, native bilinguals, though being designated native speakers of English, may have younger siblings and other family members who speak little or no English. Consequently, they may not use English all the time, particularly in situations of diglossia in which language varieties are compartmentalized according to situations of usage.

The home is also one likely place for a social dialect (or vernacular) to develop that can, consequently, spread throughout the community. Children will undoubtedly bring that language variety with them into the classroom. Consequently, educators need to consider the relationship of SAE and nonstandard varieties of English such as Ebonics (African American Vernacular English – AAVE), Chicano English (ChE), and *Vietnamese English* (VE), all recognized social dialects.[2] Children speaking these varieties may be counted as native speakers of English, despite the fact that they may also be considered LM students *entitled to certain rights as a result*. The existence of social varieties of American English, particularly in the case of African Americans and Chicano-Latinos, goes a long way in accounting for the disparity in the data on academic achievement according to language status (NS v. NNS) and ethnic affiliation.

Therefore, one can safely assume some correlation between language and ethnicity, though that correlation can never be absolute, even if that connection is obscured somewhat by the data types. Standard varieties of American English also infer their way into the data on mainstream student populations; after all, SAE is a dialect – it is merely the one endorsed by the media and educational institutions. If looked at through the lens of a social dialect, it can also be linked to a social group, albeit one that is privileged in educational circles. In a wide-angled view, the CDE published the following figures regarding ethnicity in the academic year (AY) 2005–2006:

---

2. For informative material regarding AAVE (Ebonics), see the work of Dillard (1972), Baugh (1983), Rickford & Rickford (2000), and Wolfram & Thomas (2002); regarding Vietnamese English, see Wolfram (1985, 1989), Wolfram & Hatfield (1986), and Wolfram, Christian & Hatfield (1986).

Table 8.2 Statewide enrollment by ethnicity AY 2005–2006

Ethnic group	number enrolled	percentage of total
Hispanic or Latino	3,003,726	47.58
White-not Hispanic	1,915,449	30.34
Asian	517,167	8.19
African American not Hispanic	495,012	7.84
Filipino	165,571	2.62
Multiple or no response	124,324	1.97
American Indian or Alaska Native	50,758	0.80
Pacific Islander	40,386	0.64

One cannot help but immediately notice that there are over one million *more* Hispanic or Latino students than White-not Hispanic (a ratio of a little more than 3 to 2). Apparently, one can be White-Hispanic (e.g., Spaniards), yet be excluded from the "White" category. The other two major groups, African American and Asian, together number a little over a million.

Note that members of the largest ethnic minority group, a plurality and near majority statewide, are densely concentrated in the same areas where there are high concentrations of Spanish speakers in the public schools. Despite the obvious drawbacks of cross-categorical comparisons, it can still be inferred that Spanish speakers (and Spanish-English bilinguals) most likely constitute a subset in the data based on ethnicity. Therefore, ethnicity is the larger and more inclusive category. Table 8.3, below, displays the enrollment of Chicano-Latino students (Hispanic or Latino) in Los Angeles, Orange, Riverside, San Bernardino, and San Diego counties during the AY 2005–2006:

Table 8.3 Enrollment of Chicano-Latino students in five key So. Cal. counties

County	enrollment	Hispanic-Latino (%)
Los Angeles	1,708,064	1,060,535 (62.1)
Orange	510,114	225,830 (44.3)
Riverside	395,183	211,366 (53.5)
San Bernardino	427,631	229,829 (53.7)
San Diego	495,228	211,641 (42.7)
	3,541,634	2,093,450 (**59.11**)

While Chicano-Latino students are heavily concentrated in these adjoining counties, this specific subgroup, nevertheless, accounts for over 56% of the *total* number of students enrolled in the state's public schools in a total of 56 counties. We certainly cannot say that this is only an urban concern (some of this area is rural farmland) or that ethnicity is an issue that impacts only Southern California. However, it does point to the relevance of student demographics for those teachers responsible to teach this sizable numerical majority in these five counties. Note, too, in the following, Table 8.4, that the statewide population trends over a thirteen year period in terms of percentage of students from the four largest ethnic groups:

Table 8.4 State public school population AY 93–94 to 05–06, based on four ethnic groups

AY	Asian	Hispanic/Lat.	African-Am.	White
05–06	8.2	47.6	7.8	30.3
04–05	8.1	46.8	8.0	31.3
03–04	8.0	46.0	8.1	32.5
02–03	8.1	45.2	8.3	33.7
01–02	8.1	44.2	8.3	34.8
00–01	8.0	43.2	8.4	35.9
99–00	8.0	42.4	8.6	36.9
98–99	8.1	41.3	8.7	37.8
97–98	8.1	40.5	8.8	38.8
96–97[3]	8.2	39.7	8.7	39.5
95–96	8.2	38.7	8.8	40.4
94–95	8.2	37.9	8.7	41.4
93–94	8.2	37.1	8.7	42.3

Note the gradual increase in the percentage of Hispanic/Latino students and the decrease in that of White students. There is a clear pattern: The percentage of the statewide population composed of (so-called) Hispanics has gone up by approximately 1% per year, while that of Whites has dropped by 1% per year. It is noteworthy that both African American and Asian American populations have remained relatively constant in contrast. It does not take a statistician to project what the next ten years may hold, despite the fact that there is little or no objective research dealing with how profound changes in demographics and varying language proficiencies may affect teacher training, hiring practices, teaching methodologies, and pedagogical practices such as tracking in skill, not to mention content areas that may assume that basic language skills have already been attained. It is not merely a matter of speaking English that is significant. It is what kind of English and to what degree or extent proficiency has been achieved in literate, academic language.

---

3. The 1996–97 school year marks the only time there was parity between Chicano-Latino and White populations.

1.3 Age and grade levels with respect to language proficiency

Table 8.5, below, displays the number of public school students who are native speakers of Spanish statewide. It illustrates another important point: the younger the student population, the greater the number of Spanish speakers (and higher the percentage of ELL students to native English speakers), a significant issue for current and prospective teachers in primary grades:

Table 8.5 Native speakers of Spanish statewide, ELLs and FEPs, 2005–2006

Grade	ELL	FEP	totals
1	147,003	26,130	176,882
2	140,600	30,096	175,800
3	136,754	35,554	176,072
4	127,492	44,996	176,345
5	107,252	66,284	171,954
6	98,141	75,680	163,797
7	87,323	82,767	161,762
8	78,346	85,867	153,722
9[4]	89,308	89,603	154,039
10	69,225	82,892	132,334
11	51,761	70,966	109,154
12	39,067	64,515	90,132
ungr.	18,360	1,133	19,493
Totals	1,351,369	774,983	2,126,352

Even if we assume that a higher drop-out rate among particular ethnic minority students affects the tallies in the upper grades (e.g., those in middle and high school identified as Hispanic and African Americans), ignoring for the time being the causes, it is evident that issues concerning the education of this group of children will grow in importance as each year passes. Along with the sheer growth in terms of numbers, the ratios of non-native speakers of English to native speakers will grow, as well. Note, too, the figure at the bottom, right of the chart, the combined total of ELLs and FEPs who are all, nonetheless, native speakers of Spanish: 2,126,352. Subtracting this total from 3,003,726, the total number of Hispanics enrolled in California's public schools, we have a remainder of 877,379. This subgroup likely consists of either (a) monolingual speakers of English (or some kind of English) or (b) relatively proficient Spanish-English bilinguals, those who were proficient enough to be lumped together

---

4. By grade 9, the numbers of Spanish-speaking ELL and FEP students are *roughly equal*. This seems to indicate a possible point at which the numbers of ELLs reclassified as FEP becomes significant.

with other native English speakers when they entered school, a potential reservoir of proficient bilinguals.

Estimating how long it takes the average ELL student to transition to mainstream classes and reach FEP status is another concern. For example, grade 1 ELLs number 147,003. In order to estimate the time it may take all of them to be transitioned into mainstream classes and reclassified as FEP and to reach an equivalent number of FEPs, we need to total the numbers of FEPs, beginning at grade 2 through grade 5. Thus, a preliminary estimate for the shortest possible length of time it might take to transition *all 147,003* students currently in first grade to FEP status (a rate of about 44 thousand a year) would be around four years. However, this optimistic projection fails to factor in the number of students currently in grades 2 through 4 who may also transition during that span of time (some go quicker, and some slower), and the number of transfer students from other districts classed as FEPs. We must assume that there is some sort of continuum in effect, and that some ELLs will transition each year until all will reach sufficient command of English to be redesignated as fluent English proficiency and enter mainstream classes in all skill and content areas. As discussed in the previous chapter, depending on district, type of program, and the availability of content instruction in Spanish, this suggests that each ELL student goes through at least four years of English-only courses despite not being fluent enough for mainstream classes. What does that mean with respect to their academic development? How long can we anticipate it to take for them to be at grade level in all subjects? These are tough questions to answer.

Robert C. Gardner, one of the leading experts on the affects of motivation on language mastery, has estimated that *ten years* is a reasonable amount of time for non-native speakers to catch up to their native counterparts in *academic* English (2001). Thus, there may be a significant amount of time between (a) being transitioned to FEP status and (b) sufficient mastery of academic English to compete with monolinguals (or native bilinguals). Moreover, there has been little objective data on how well the typical FEP student, balanced bilingual or otherwise, fares on standardized tests in content areas. Raising test scores is not necessarily going to improve language skills or increase the type and amount of knowledge the children actually need for a well-rounded education. This is especially true if the goal of the teacher is *to teach directly to the test* and not to increase general skill levels and the kinds of knowledge that can form the real basis for academic success. Given a choice, in the event that students will not be allowed to advance to the next grade level or to graduate, many teachers may find teaching to the test the only alternative, for the *students'* sake. And, in view of standardized testing and accountability demanded by NCLB and state equivalents, student failure is to be avoided.

2.   The California High School Exit Exam (CAHSEE)

The connections between reading and the ability to write college-level academic prose (the two sides of literacy) are tenuous at best. And, there is a dearth of objective, scientific data proving links between reading on the one hand and writing academic prose on the other, despite the intuitions of teachers. However, data is now available concerning skill areas – the California High School Exit Exam. Indicative of the California Department of Education's earnest attempt at conformity with federal standards, the state now administers standardized exit exams in two skill areas, Mathematics and English Language Arts (ELA). Table 8.6 presents the results by ethnicity for all grades, for all tests administered in 2006:[5]

Table 8.6 CAHSEE results based on ethnicity 2005–2006

Ethnicity	Subject	number tested	passed (%)
African American	Math	85,298	34,435 (40)
	ELA	75,376	37,934 (50)
Hispanic/Latino	Math	391,090	189,680 (49)
	ELA	383,506	190,719 (50)
Asian	Math	54,812	45,335 (83)
	ELA	62,782	43,983 (70)
White	Math	221,611	170,166 (77)
	ELA	214,999	173,215 (81)

Table 8.6 displays some truly remarkable figures. Asian and White students significantly outperformed African American and Chicano-Latino students on the standardized tests. The disparity between White and Asian students, on the one hand, and African Americans and Chicano-Latino students on the other, seems to fit well with accounts of "castelike minorities" in the work of John Ogbu (e.g., Ogbu 1987). Of particular interest are the figures relating to the performance of African American students on the English Language Arts exam, which seem to suggest that there may, indeed, be a language issue as mentioned previously. If a majority of these test-takers are speakers of AAVE/Ebonics, the skewed test scores could very well reflect a clash of dialects. There must be a reasonable explanation for this gap, an explanation that still eludes us despite the furor created by the Oakland Ebonics debate (Rickford and Rickford 2000) and its predecessor, the Black English trial of Ann Arbor, Michigan (Labov 1982). Both asserted that children were not having the "desired" academic success because they spoke a nonstandard dialect of English. The verdict of the Ann Arbor case mandated

---

5.   Data from DataQuest at cahsee.cde.ca.gov, prepared 2/23/09, last modified 9/03/08.

corrective action, and spelled out a legal definition of Black English by listing its most prominent linguistic features.

Regarding Hispanic/Latinos, a pass rate of roughly 50% also needs an explanation. In contrast with African Americans, there is a significant number of English language learners that one can assume pulls the scores down somewhat. However, there is still another kind of language issue. Chicano English, spoken among Chicano-Latino students, may very well have a significant impact, particularly regarding Language Arts. Apparently, any sort of social dialect that might be spoken among Asian Americans (e.g., Vietnamese English) does not seem to hinder overall performance in either Math or Language Arts. Being a member of an ethnic minority is not in itself a factor in low scores; it is the type of minority, again suggesting the existence of castelike minority status, the causes of which are a topic for discussion.

2.1   Testing results for NNSs

To measure the influence of language specifically, we look at scores for the same tests among ELLs and FEPs statewide in the following, Table 8.7. Once again, the numbers tell an interesting tale. In Table 8.8, the focus shifts to the five key counties (the number of FEP students who passed is in boldface type).

Here, again, we have some striking figures. FEPs passed, on average, at roughly the same rate as their White and Asian counterparts in both Math and ELA. To state the obvious, ethnicity loses its affect as English language proficiency goes up, at least among those still enrolled in public school. Consistent with bilingual studies of the *cognitive benefits* of bilingualism, FEPs, as relatively proficient bilinguals, have apparently caught up to their monolingual, Anglo peers, and, in some instances, passed them. Granted, those FEPs who stayed in school and persevered may represent the best in their category, the relatively high scores demonstrate that FEPs are indeed capable of keeping up with the mainstream under specific conditions.

2.2 Discussion of CAHSEE results

The results of the high school exam suggest that increased proficiency in Standard American English can cancel the obvious effect for ethnicity, but they also imply that certain stereotypical ethnic groups are likely to continue failing standardized tests at significant rates. The question that needs to be asked is not *who* fails, but *why* they fail. Perhaps the causes are concealed by the data. One explanation for the highly contrasting scores of ELLs and FEPs is that many ELLs in grades 9–12 are most likely relative newcomers, recent immigrants (e.g., adolescent males who have migrated to the U.S. in search of work) who see the importance of English proficiency in finding employment

Table 8.7 CAHSEE results based on program (ELL and FEP), statewide figures

	Subject	number tested	passed (%)
ELL	Math	176,752	62,613 (35)
	ELA	199,857	56,944 (28)
FEP	Math	92,741	**69,791 (75)**
	ELA	85,801	**70,607 (82)**

Table 8.8 CAHSEE results based on program (ELL and FEP), five key counties[6]

County	Subject	number tested	passed (%)
Los Angeles			
ELL	Math	57,569	19,205 (33)
	ELA	61,706	17,971 (29)
FEP	Math	40,407	29,206 (72)
	ELA	36,225	29,766 (82)
Orange			
ELL	Math	14,820	6,139 (41)
	ELA	16,995	5,749 (34)
FEP	Math	6,101	**5,437 (89)**
	ELA	5,902	**5,481 (93)**
Riverside			
ELL	Math	11,822	3,707 (31)
	ELA	13,065	3,383 (26)
FEP	Math	4,634	**3,337 (72)**
	ELA	4,179	**3,354 (80)**
San Bernardino			
ELL	Math	10,251	3,530 (34)
	ELA	11,103	3,314 (30)
FEP	Math	3,090	**2,405 (78)**
	ELA	2,967	**2,428 (82)**
San Diego			
ELL	Math	13,488	4,841 (36)
	ELA	15,780	4,235 (27)
FEP	Math	7,028	**5,353 (76)**
	ELA	6,409	**5,364 (84)**

6. There was no category by ethnicity among ELLs and FEPs, nor for specific language.

and job advancement, and who enroll in English Language Development classes. The specific subgroup of FEPs are typically long-term residents who have spent a number of years in various ELD programs and have successfully transitioned into mainstream classes at some point in their academic careers. So, it may not be surprising that FEPs do well while the general ELL population still struggles.

The pass rate among African Americans is comparable to that of ELLs (even lower in some respects). Speakers of African American Vernacular English are presumed to be native speakers of English, and rightfully so – it would be extremely controversial *not* to do so. Therefore, the native language of many African Americans is not a standard variety, and this fact is at least enough to skew scores on standardized tests. Consequently, ethnicity, either African American or Chicano-Latino, appears to be a greater predictor of success on the high school exit exam than specific language status. Nonstandard dialects of English infer their way into the data for African Americans and perhaps those Chicano-Latinos who were also designated as native speakers of English, bilingual or not. (There is presently no data that indicates bilinguality – the proficiency levels in *both* languages.)

The "why" may lie in a growing, research-based literature on the mismatch of home language versus school (or academic) language. But, similar to issues pertaining to Native Americans and indigenous languages, the results appear to highlight a clash between the language of a child's individual, social, and ethnic identity and the utility of mastering Standard American English for educational and employment (socioeconomic) reasons. Much research is surfacing on dialect awareness in the classroom, orality versus literacy, formal versus informal registers of speech, and the affect of pop culture – particularly in inner-city environments. As a result, resources are becoming increasingly available for educators (and those who become exam readers). Teachers certainly can improve their ability to see the differences between how their students communicate among themselves (spoken, informal, and highly influenced by pop culture) and how they need to express themselves in a formal, *written*, academic setting.

The educational system clearly needs to avoid the appearance of systematic exclusion, and this is surely the impression that the test scores create. When high percentages of very sizable student populations fail a standardized exam, attention needs to be placed on characteristics of the *test takers* as well as characteristics of the tests in order to find equitable ways to increase the likelihood of success and their systematic inclusion. Dialect awareness, knowledge of students' home language, and their cultural background are merely ways that today's teachers can equip themselves for the challenges ahead in a multilingual, multicultural classroom. Finally, bilingualism and its very close kin, bi-dialectalism do not have to be viewed as "problems." They force all of us to look past our immediate social environments and implicit societal norms onto the cultures and language varieties of others.

3.   The double whammy

For one plausible explanation of how minority dialects may contribute to low exam scores, we can look at the dual focus of scoring practices on exams of Standard American English (SAE).[7] As a consequence of a particular conceptualization of the nature of Standard English, language minority writers are often penalized twice (or on two levels) because they may show systematic variation in both (a) surface-level, grammatical aspects of language and (b) deeper, culturally-based divergence in rhetorical styles (e.g., organization and narrative style).[8] So, a student writer may exhibit control of the grammatical features of a standard dialect and not have command of standard rhetorical strategies, and vice versa, having control of one but not the other. Writers receive a kind of double whammy when they are penalized twice, for lacking control of the structures of the standard variety (producing so many surface mistakes that the reader is distracted from the content of the essay) *and* not having command of standard, Anglo Saxon rhetorical patterns – which may be viewed as muddled thinking according to a particular bias against non-English rhetorical strategies.

Some educators and teachers of the language arts may need to be reminded that SAE is an idealized form of English and that testing practices often reflect a particular ideology (see Chapter 7). A candid look at so-called deficit models and their educational counterparts, difference models, may reveal underlying prejudices that can certainly influence teachers' attitudes towards language and ethnic minorities. First, speaking a nonstandard dialect is not the result of any type of cultural deprivation; a language is a language and a culture is a culture. Where a standard variety differs from a nonstandard variety, they merely differ. The same goes for the cultural resources of language and ethnic minority students and their communities. A minority culture is merely different from a majority culture – whose leadership and preeminence may

---

7.   Obviously not a new expression, the term *double whammy* was used in Field 2004 to refer to specific testing practices of language minorities in the U.S. and in nations where creole languages are used by the general population. In both situations, a prestige national standard is used in institutional settings such as in the media, commerce, government, and in educational settings. Biased reactions to nonstandard, native varieties of children put them at a disadvantage in the classroom.

8.   The term *surface features* in this context refers to production errors that manifest themselves in writing. It does not imply that the knowledge of English syntax, for instance, is not "deep." However, based on studies of language acquisition, pragmatic knowledge is typically acquired much later by native-language users and requires additional awareness of the culturally based conventions of language usage. Hence, command of rhetorical strategies can be considered deeper in the sense that it requires a deeper reservoir of pragmatic and linguistic knowledge.

only seem to be threatened by minority views. SAE is that particular evolving variety of English whose roots lie deep in Anglo-American culture, one that has been considered politically dominant since the founding of the original British-American colonies. Other varieties certainly exist. This fact should inform educators' views of standardized testing, how to interpret test results, and how to react appropriately to the alleged "deficiencies" they uncover.

Readers for exams of all levels of English proficiency in writing typically score exams *holistically*; they grade an essay exam as a *whole*, based on an overall impression of the skill of the exam taker, whether she has skillfully fulfilled the writing task. It is often based on such criteria as organization, development (completeness), style (clarity of expression, presentation of evidence), and the mechanics of writing (spelling, capitalization, punctuation, etc.), not as individual characteristics, but as a whole. These readers are often directly or indirectly trained as a group to focus attention on particular characteristics of student writing, a practice called *norming*.[9] This is ostensibly designed to keep scoring as consistent and objective as possible with respect to the *features* of Standard American English. For instance, exam readers pay attention to inflections such as plural and possessive markers on nouns, and tense-aspect markers on verbs, in particular the third-person agreement *-s* (3ps), appropriate forms of the copula/auxiliary *be*, tense markers (e.g., regular and irregular past), and standard forms of the so-called past participle (i.e., in the expression of perfect aspect, e.g., the *present perfect* as in "He has went/gone to the school"). Anyone familiar with nonstandard dialects of American English will immediately notice that this is a veritable laundry list of problematic forms.

All such exams are intended to measure proficiency in the standard, so it is easy to see the situation that the readers find themselves in. All deviations from the standard must be considered *errors* if the test is to measure proficiency in SAE. These performance errors create problems when they become distracting, diverting the attention of the reader from the content of the essay and onto the form. Of course, those who expect or demand standard forms will take note of every offending, nonstandard form.[10] In general, surface errors may be noted with little or no knowledge by exam readers that nonstandard forms systematically diverge from standard forms; nonstandard varieties are systems unto themselves. Native speakers of AAVE and ChE, for example,

9. For example, the California State University system has a junior-level or "exit" exam that goes by various names. On the national level, there is the Early Assessment Program (EAP) for high school juniors sponsored by the Educational Testing Service, and the national Advanced Placement (AP) exam, administered to advanced placement students around the U.S., it's territories, and worldwide.

10. Even the terms such as *error*, *deviation*, and *offending* reflect the deficit model of learning discussed below.

may leave visible surface evidence of their nonstandard dialects, the varieties that they speak at home with family and friends, and with their peers at school between and during classes, on the school yard, and at all after-school functions. The variety that students use to define themselves in everyday social circumstances is the one that they know the best and feel most comfortable with and use the most (most likely, their native language variety). Thus, nonstandard features, typically characteristics of spoken and informal speech, may surface in student writing, especially when students have been instructed to "write like they talk" to encourage fluency. The mismatch is not one marked by an inability to learn SAE; it is marked by the greater social value placed on relationships with peers.

The second part of the double whammy can be equally unconscious. It goes beyond surface characteristics to culturally-based rhetorical practices. For example, for non-native speakers of English (and native speakers of nonstandard varieties), the development and the flow of the writing may diverge considerably from standard, written Anglo-Saxon English norms, as well, with its prescriptive emphasis on argumentation, thesis statement, topic sentences, characteristic flow of information (general to specific, old before new information, etc.), and according to traditional deductive reasoning. Volumes are being written on African American rhetorical strategies with their characteristic emphasis on *oral* language and the *sounds* of words, parallelism, repetition, etc., with influential models such as the work of Dr. Martin Luther King, Jr. and a host of other African American dignitaries, religious leaders, novelists, poets, statesmen, and entertainment and sports heroes.[11]

3.1   The effects of Spanish on the Chicano-Latino writer

With respect to native speakers of Spanish, Contrastive Rhetoric (CR) has addressed Spanish-language rhetorical patterns, according to a "Romance" model that is decidedly *not* the Anglo-Saxon model. However, there were charges that CR created stereotypes similar to those used in language profiling to discriminate against certain minorities. Some of the initial concerns may have been somewhat warranted, but they followed primarily from the quantitative design of the early research. Whenever particular characteristics are averaged together and linked to specific populations, there can be a tendency to overgeneralize and form stereotypes. The individual can get lost in the crowd. They should not be viewed as predictive tools because of the danger of stereotyping. For example, if we say that all Chicanos do pattern X, then, when we see this particular pattern, we conclude that the writer must be a Chicano. First, not

---

11. For relevant examples of African American rhetorical strategies, see Rickford & Rickford (2000) and Jackson & Richardson (2003).

all Chicanos write in identical ways, and, second, many student writers who are not Chicanos may exhibit similar patterns of grammatical mistakes and informal usage. (The patterns may be spreading; they are fairly common in the writing patterns of many children in Southern California.) Nevertheless, some observations of patterned usage can still be informative. They can be used for their informational value in retrospect, in looking back at a child's linguistic background to identify possible sources of influence.

Then, too, there have been important developments in CR in the past 40 years that have motivated researchers to adjust and broaden their approaches, including increasing the types of texts that are considered and acknowledging the social contexts of writing (Connor et al 2008: 3). One may expect proficient, native Spanish writers to show the influence of a literate Spanish model via transfer in academic writing, in particular ELD students born abroad and educated in Latin American schools.

However, even with this renewed interest in native Spanish speakers and writers, there is a lack of research on Spanish-English bilinguals, a significant group of writers that includes FEP students who have transitioned into mainstream classes, though steps are being made to correct this (see, e.g., Suárez-Orozco & Páez 2002). But, recall that the vast majority of native speakers of Spanish and their bilingual counterparts in the U.S. are transitioned into English-only courses as quickly as possible by the various programs, as is the case of all transitional programs where mainstreaming is the objective (discussed in Chapter 6). Instruction in academic registers and the literate forms of Spanish is typically neglected in favor of either a weak approach to heritage-language maintenance or an aggressive, subtractive approach that does not consider proficiency in any language other than English necessary or desirable.

While one can argue that the influence of European Spanish in the writing of Chicano-Latinos is minimal, there is indeed a growing literature that is intimately tied with the Spanish language and Chicano-Latino culture. Much of this literature is written in English and Spanish, or in "Spanglish," a combination of the two in a type of literary and sometimes conversational code-switching. Relatively early works that have become part of a modern-day Chicano-Latino canon include English-language books by such authors as José Antonio Villarreal who wrote *Pocho* (1959), one of the first Chicano novels to gain recognition, and Rudolfo Anaya, who wrote *Bless Me Ultima* (1972), which helped contribute to the establishment of a uniquely Chicano literature. *Pocho*, set in California during the Great Depression, is a story of a young man's struggle in becoming American while trying to honor his Mexican roots. *Bless Me Ultima*, set in New Mexico during WWII, details the struggles of a young man who questions the meaning of life, good and evil, and his internal conflict between folk religion and established Catholicism. Much of these early works depict the conflicts Chicano-Latinos experience while attempting to assimilate into U.S. culture, particularly in the American Southwest.

Tomás Rivera, a revered educator and former Chancellor of the University of California, Riverside, was born in post-Depression Texas and became another key figure in the early development of Chicano literature. He was also an advocate for higher education in the Chicano-Latino community. He was probably most known for his collection of short stories and poems written in Spanish, *Y no se lo trago la tierra*, published in 1967, translated under various titles (e.g. ...*And the Earth Did not Part*). The book consists of fourteen vignettes that together present a year in the life of an anonymous Chicano-Latino child, the son of migrant workers in Texas, revealing autobiographical glimpses of Rivera's humble roots as a migratory field hand. A little later but in a similar vein, prominent author and poet, Gary Soto, also came from humble beginnings. He worked in the fields of the San Joaquin Valley and factories of Fresno in Central California and has continued a tradition of writing of everyday life and experiences as a Chicano. His first collection of poems, *The Elements of San Joaquin*, won the United States Award of the International Poetry Forum in 1976, and his second, *The Tale of Sunlight* (1978) was nominated for a Pulitzer Prize.

Much recent literature is more overtly political (and feminist) in nature, focusing on a search for cultural and individual, often sexual, identity while challenging traditional value systems. This newer wave is also highly critical of the racist and discriminatory practices of Anglo Saxon culture (and language). For example, the work of Sandra Cisneros, *The House on Mango Street* (1983/4), is a collection of stories of coming of age in a Hispanic barrio in Chicago. The feminist and Chicana author Gloria Anzaldúa writes in her major work, *Borderlands/La Frontera: The New Mestiza* (1987) of the artificial and arbitrary nature of the U.S.-Mexico border as metaphor, and how Anglo Americans (gringos) see things in clear, unambiguous categories of good and evil – the border forms a barrier to keep out the evil. Ana Castillo, like Cisneros, from inner-city Chicago, wrote *So Far from God* (1993) another collection of short stories set in the village of Tome, New Mexico, that details the lives and loves of Latinas on the border. The book is written in the form of a *telenovela* (T.V. soap opera) in melodramatic fashion giving the reader clues of what will happen in the next episode.

Two more recent Chicana authors of note are Susana (Suzanne) Chávez-Silverman, a professor of Romance Languages and Literatures at Pomona College, and the more light-hearted and pop-culture oriented Michele Serros. Chávez-Silverman's *Killer Crónicas: Bilingual Memories* (2004) uses both languages in a "Spanglish" style to express her *crónicas*, memoirs or chronicles of her experiences living in various parts of the world such as Argentina, the U.S., Spain, Mexico, and South Africa. Serros published her first work, *Chicana Falsa and Other Stories of Death, Identity and Oxnard* while a student at Santa Monica City College. A collection of poems and short stories, she tells of her problem being Chicana and not knowing Spanish very well ("Mi problema"). The book has become required reading in many Chicano Studies programs.

Another of her books, *How to Be a Chicana Role Model* (2000), is a comical retrospective of her adventures and quest for identity on the road to commercial success – which extends to, among other things, a brief stint writing for the *George Lopez Show*.

Another side to Chicano-Latino literature portrays modern urban life, for example, the work of Luis J. Rodriguez, poet, novelist, critic, and journalist. Born in El Paso, his family relocated to South L.A. when he was two. He became a member of his first gang at 12 when the family later moved to the San Gabriel Valley on the eastside of L.A. Rodriguez may be best known for *Always Running: La Vida Loca, Gang Days in L.A.* which received the Carl Sandburg Literary Award. While critically acclaimed, the book has been controversial for its graphic descriptions of gang violence, which can run the risk of glorifying gang life. For that reason, serious work on gang life in Chicano-Studies programs often focus more on the work of anthropologists such as James Diego Vigil (currently of the University of California, Irvine) who take particular care not to foster stereotypes of gangs and their members, while delving into socioeconomic causes and what can be learned from the reality of gangs.[12]

3.2 The power of pop culture

The findings of the Montaño-Harmon (1991) study are tempting. Her discussion of the informal, conversational style of the writing patterns of her Chicano-Latino subjects seems to resonate with the sentiments of current educators. But, the danger is that such results can be used to prejudge the work of students according to questionable stereotypes. Informal speech is not necessarily a sign of muddled thinking, just a lack of exposure to particular literate forms. And, rhetorical strategies can be taught and learned.

Today's teachers often find the writing of Chicanos deficient (according to a deficit model of education, discussed in Chapter 6), just as teachers in the past believed that speakers of Black English failed to show the cultural knowledge of their White counterparts as a result of cultural deprivation (Lindflors 1980:366ff). This view fails to acknowledge that access to academic registers of English, or the relative lack thereof, is a likely contributing factor to the students' reliance on a conversational, rather then an academic tone, not the child's cognitive abilities. As discussed in Chapter 7, socioeconomic status (SES) can affect the amount and quality of preliteracy training and limit the kinds of educational advantages that traditionally privileged groups have. But, ethnicity by itself cannot be blamed for the lack of academic achievement. When children do not receive instruction at age- or grade-appropriate levels in content areas

---

12. See, for example, Vigil (1988 and 2007).

(a common result of English-only education), the lack of focused instruction can also add to the appearance of ignorance or the lack of sophistication in English.

The CAHSEE data imply that the presence of nonstandard varieties of English may be a factor in low test scores. But, first, we need to ask whether speaking Spanish (or any other non-English language) limits proficiency in English. If the child is a native bilingual, the answer is a clear and emphatic "no!" There is nothing inherent in learning Spanish natively that affects the acquisition of English adversely, particularly in cases of additive bilingualism. Importantly, the Montaño-Harmon study showed *no influence of Spanish* in the performance of English-speaking Chicanos, which may surprise those who have equated Chicano English with "accented English" (Montaño-Harmon 1991:419).[13] More specifically, the results showed a lack of literate registers in *both* languages. Perhaps the fact that no Spanish influence was found should be of concern to the Spanish-English bilingual community because it portends the loss of a language and culture. It provides evidence of subtractive methods of education that do not necessarily hasten the acquisition of English, though they may hasten the loss of Spanish. If high levels of Spanish proficiency were indeed exhibited by the Chicano writers, we would expect the *positive* transfer of both academic knowledge and literacy skills. This was clearly not the case.

If the model for rhetorical strategies is not a literate tradition, then this begs the question of what that model might be. There are a number of possibilities. One is that the primary model for English is the speech (informal, spoken registers) of peer groups, the voices of Pop culture, so to speak. A second is that the subtractive nature of many "weak" bilingual programs has eliminated all traces of Spanish and any cognitive or academic advantage bilinguals might have had. Yet another is that many Chicanos are the unwitting recipients of the exclusionary practices of tracking (streaming), with its long tradition of favoring language and cultural majority students and assigning minority groups to less challenging courses in occupational tracks or streams – it might be quite the challenge to acquire strong literacy skills in a woodshop class, one in auto repair, or one on remedial math. (The same applies to students in math, engineering, and computer science compared with those in history, philosophy, and language arts.) The lack of familiarity with formal, academic registers of English may simply be a byproduct of the kinds of courses that they are expected to take and pass. All three of these factors can work in concert to create the *impression* of a learning deficit. The situation is far from simple, and it extends to a multitude of

---

13. It should go without saying at this point that *every* English speaker has an "accent," whether he or she is from London, England, or London, Ontario, Canada. We all seem to assume that we, as individuals, don't have an accent when we stay close to others who speak the same as we do (from our respective communities). It is only when we move away from that community that we notice the speech patterns of others. But, *they* notice ours, too.

social issues. For instance, U.S.-born bilinguals may become bilingual in two non-standard languages, nonstandard Chicano English and an equally nonstandard form of local Spanish. Those Spanish-speakers who have grown up in Mexico may at least have knowledge of Standard Mexican Spanish, which is not guaranteed in the barrios of Southern California.

On a national level, each individual bilingual situation is dynamic in its own unique social and linguistic ways. For instance, there can be significant differences in each group's original homelands affecting their political status in the U.S. As mentioned in the introductory chapter, many Cubans fled the communist regime in Cuba, so, as a group, Cuban Americans began mainly as refugees. Puerto Ricans are citizens because Puerto Rico is a U.S. territory. They need no passports when traveling back and forth from the island to the U.S. mainland. With Mexican Americans, it is even more complex, particularly in the American Southwest, because so much of Mexico's territory was annexed after the Mexican-American War and the signing of the Treaty of Guadalupe Hidalgo (1848). Each group, heterogeneous to start with, has its own political history in relation to the U.S. It has its own socio-economic history and outlook (prospects in the job market), cultural values (e.g., those placed on formal education, literacy, the accumulation of academic knowledge, individual responsibility, and community involvement), and attitudes towards Standard English and its speakers as a reaction to decades (or centuries) of discriminatory practices by Anglo Americans. On the local level, these types of social situations can be rather fluid, changing a great deal along the age continuum from generation to generation as a result of social change.

4.   School reform: Reinvent the wheel?

Clearly, one of the biggest issues facing education in the U.S. today is that of school reform. With the current Race to the Top Program, change is encouraged. However, if some "old" programs are being replaced for the sake of change and reform, then it stands to reason that the correct choice would be programs that address the real problems of student performance and teacher training in the long run. Short-term fixes can create long-range problems by producing unexpected results or by continuing discriminatory practices that have alienated entire communities. Perhaps, there is no need to force the pendulum of education to swing radically and quickly to a new emphasis. Maybe, what we need is a renewed sense of urgency to apply the knowledge that we already have. For instance, evidence is out there of bilingual programs that work.

Two decades ago, the *Harvard Educational Review* published an exploratory study by Lucas, Henze, and Donato (1990) of six high schools known for their success with language minority (LM) students according to state and local accolades and recommendations from their peers. Five were located in California and one in Arizona, schools that provided environments in which LM students thrived and achieved academic success.[14] The study went beyond those on densely populated urban environments that are typical of the literature of the schooling of LM students. Issues of LM students are no longer the exclusive concern of inner-city schools. The authors took a methodical approach to what they considered the key features of these particularly effective schools. As an aside, there's no reason to think that their suggestions would not work in urban situations just as well.

The researchers' approach was holistic in the sense that they did not concentrate solely on language instruction or the language of instruction. They looked instead at the total learning environment and the factors that go into the process of education. As part of the discussion, they considered previous approaches that focused on *structures* (e.g., the kinds of leadership hierarchies the schools may employ or the types of programs from an administrative view) and those that dealt with specific *attributes* of the schools, qualities such as openness that participants exhibited in the process. As discussed in Chapter 7, there is no guarantee that what works for one school district will work for another. A school can take an otherwise ideal program and achieve mediocre, even poor results if the program is run halfheartedly or if teachers and staff are inexperienced and not trained sufficiently in the purposes and goals of a particular approach or method of teaching. The reverse is equally true: a mediocre program run by experienced and caring teachers can produce positive student outcomes. Further, for one school to emulate particular attributes of another may be similarly counterproductive. The kinds of features that mark success come from within the individual school as it deals with its unique configuration of personnel, student population, and the socioeconomic and ethnic makeup of its community.

The researchers investigated these schools for the patterns behind their effectiveness, looking for a total system that could generate an atmosphere conducive to student success. For example, they were looking for strong and positive leadership, high staff morale, high expectations for their students (believing in their students' capacity for learning), and instructional programs that encouraged academic performance and that specifically denied the deficit model. The generality of the issues that the researchers addressed can be questioned for vagueness, and the validity and generalizability of their qualitative results may be subject to criticism. However, when the rather extensive literature on effective schooling shows that numerous studies come to the same or similar conclusions despite their alleged deficiencies, then one might suspect that there is indeed some truth lurking beneath the cynicism.

---

14. The schools were Anaheim, Artesia, Newcomer (San Francisco), Overfelt (San Jose), and Sweetwater (National City), high schools in the state of California, and Nogales High School in Nogales, Arizona.

As discussed in previous chapters, we err when we try to fault children for their lack of success. We may look at the socio-cultural milieu in which they live, but it is also very difficult to pin blame on parents. Socioeconomic factors may command a different set of behaviors from parents of language and ethnic minority children than from parents of mainstream students. Adult caregivers from lower socioeconomic strata may spend a lot of time working low-wage jobs just to pay the bills; not many can afford the nannies and private tutors that some privileged folks have. For some middle-class people, it may be difficult to imagine how people from the proverbial "other side of the tracks" live, and how much socioeconomic status influences not just attitudes towards education but more practical issues like the nature of parental involvement, pre-literacy training, and school readiness. Individual parents may be 100% behind their children and support teachers explicitly, but have neither the skills nor the time needed to help their children with their homework on a consistent basis. This can surely impact the children's perceptions of the value of education unless the child or the school somehow picks up the slack. In times of economic difficulty, these issues are exacerbated, diverting parents' attention away from their children's education and onto survival.

In each school, English literacy was the primary goal, but it wasn't the only goal. Four out of six offered Spanish for Spanish speakers and encouraged improving skills in the native language. Three schools offered advanced Spanish courses and promoted Spanish literacy through Advanced Placement (AP) courses that gave proficient bilinguals the opportunity to earn college credit. One school required all students to have one year of Spanish, unless they tested out of the requirement, in which case they were allowed to study another language. Five provided content courses in Spanish. They also understood the diverse nature of the Latino community, that it is multinational with different histories, customs, and varieties of Spanish. All had some type of mentor program, and hired from within the community when feasible. Evidently, all ESL courses were transitional (no two-way programs), but alternatives still existed for proficient bilinguals to continue to progress in Spanish. Of course, two-way programs offer even stronger possibilities for students to advance both in English and in academics.

The qualitative data that the researchers accumulated was obtained through extensive interviews with administrators, teachers, staff, and students, contributing to the descriptions of each school, and then they highlighted the features that all the schools shared. Each school had large populations of Chicano-Latinos with minority White populations, so the principle LM group was Spanish speakers. (If one chooses to fault the research because of an inability to generalize from the results, then one still must consider the specific community from which they were obtained.) Even though the socioeconomic situations at each school differed, at the heart of each feature were many of the issues that concern both (a) Chicano-Latinos and the Pan-Latino community (e.g., prejudice, stereotyping, lack of academic success) and (b) Spanish-English bilinguals in general (language acquisition, sensitivity to Chicano-Latino culture, academic preparation, and parental involvement).

Table 8.9 Features of the six high schools (adapted from Lucas et al 1990)

1. Value is placed on the students' languages and cultures
2. High expectations of language-minority students are made concrete
3. School leaders make the education of language-minority students a priority
4. Staff development is explicitly designed to help teachers and other staff serve language-minority students more effectively
5. A variety of courses and programs for language-minority students is offered
6. A counseling program gives special attention to language-minority students
7. Parents of language-minority students are encouraged to become involved in their children's education
8. School staff members share a strong commitment to empower language-minority students through education

They not only identified eight features, but they gave concrete examples of the many ways each feature was manifested. For example, concerning the first feature, placing value on students' languages and cultures, principals, administrators, counselors, teachers, and other staff "celebrated" diversity.[15] They gave the Chicano-Latino students and community the impression that their culture was respected and that a positive value was attached to the ability to speak Spanish. This ability was recognized as an advantage, rather than a liability (or sign of cultural deprivation). This obviously promotes a positive sense of individual and group identity that stands in stark contrast to the humiliating and belittling effects of the often harsh treatment experienced by other Chicano-Latinos throughout the history of the Southwest – e.g., in the segregated school systems of California. Concrete expression was given by teachers actually learning of their students' cultures (and languages) and treating them as individuals and not as members of a stigmatized group or demographic category. They emphasized this value by hiring bilingual staff with backgrounds similar to that of the students, actively encouraging students to develop their native language skills, and offering content courses in their primary language. They paid attention to the customs, values, and holidays of their LM students: "While many schools pay lip service to these aspects of culture, for example, by celebrating Cinco de Mayo and serving tacos on that day," these schools honored students' cultures throughout the school year (Lucas, Henze, & Donato 1990: 323).

Their high expectations (feature two) were shown by challenging students in class, providing college-prep courses for the LM students, bringing in representatives from

---

15. Unfortunately, terms like *celebrate* can become buzzwords or slogans with little substance. It is pointed out here and by Lucas et al that the various school personnel demonstrated the features that they identified. As a result, the significance lies not so much in the terminology but in the effects. We can easily substitute other terms such as *respect*, *honor*, *recognize*, or *acknowledge* as long as we look at the specific actions of the school and their effects on the students.

colleges to speak to students, showcasing minority graduates as role models, and by providing counseling services in Spanish. They encouraged them to pursue post-secondary education and university degrees. Staff development (feature four) always included programs (e.g., workshops) that exposed teachers and staff to principles of language acquisition, current ELD teaching methods, and cross-cultural communication (this may be seen in contrast to the top-down mandating of specific approaches and methods that all teachers must follow uncritically). The schools did not assume that teachers who are highly skilled and expert in the instruction of mainstream students would automatically be equally successful with LM students. As a consequence, all teachers were encouraged to participate in staff development, not merely those who were directly involved in ELD classes. In all, there was a feeling that everyone was part of a single, unified community dedicated to the success of all students, language minority and majority.

There was some expected overlap in the categories and how they were expressed due to their general nature, but the features were not presented as formulae to be followed to the letter. They are posited as general principles that can inform the practice of teaching in multilingual, multicultural environments. Many volumes on the topic of bilingualism and bilingual education seem to overtly promote specific programs, e.g., two-way bilingual instruction. This study, in contrast, took a "whole-school" approach and did not hunt specifically for individual classroom practices as "secrets to success." The literature on language attrition (e.g., Dorian 1989) suggests that languages and cultures maintain their vitality internally, from within the community, and not from the outside via government funded programs – although, in many cases, nationally funded programs can give minority groups the resources to establish bilingual programs, for example, programs for indigenous/First Nation groups in the U.S. and Canada (see also Fishman 1991 on the obstacles to reversing language shift). And, because the eight features reflect characteristics of effective schools, they underline the fact that most if not all critical information is readily available for present educators and those in teacher-prep programs.

5. Conclusions

In this final section, we look back on some of the major issues brought up in this book and what today's educators can bring to the learning experience of Chicano-Latino students. From the first chapter, it has been emphasized that bilingualism is a normal condition that affects people around the globe – there is no urban society that is untouched by recent economic conditions and large population movements. In order to understand a changing world, educators, parents, and students in the U.S. may need to reconsider preconceived notions of language and culture in the light of the nation's true multilingual and multicultural history, particularly with its position in a global economy (Chapter 1).

Some things are to be expected as a consequence of multilingualism: there will be bi- and multilingual individuals, families, groups and communities. Children will acquire and use more than one language almost from birth (Chapter 2). Beyond historical considerations, we've discussed the nature of bilingualism, from a perspective that is linguistic, social, and psychological. It has been linguistic in that we have looked at the language development of individuals and the different types of bilingualism that exist in the Chicano-Latino bilingual community (e.g., additive versus subtractive, sequential and simultaneous). It has been social in examining the effects of societal attitudes towards bilingual individuals – that outsiders have of them and that they have of themselves. Because communities are composed of individuals and their families, there are as many different expected outcomes as there are situations of contact. The discussion of different types of bilingualism includes the psychological in pinpointing the processes that go into the acquisition, development, and expression of bilinguality, from language and cultural contact as a national issue to that of language and cultural contact as a continual mental state among individuals in community.

From this pluralistic cultural and linguistic matrix, language usage has predictable characteristics. For instance, some multilingual people will use there languages separately, one at a time according to the situation of speech, but they may also use them at the same time, perhaps intermingled like forms of "Spanglish" (Chapter 3). More than one language will be used throughout the community, from the classrooms, boardrooms, and into the bedrooms of America. And, because language contact is a present and on-going process, the discussion moved to bilingual phenomena such as the various kinds of code-switching, linguistic borrowing, and diglossia that characterize *all* situations of contact worldwide.

The next chapter in this cluster is Chapter 4, which provided a glimpse into the variety of English associated with Chicano-Latinos in Southern California. The standing of English has never been stronger in the U.S. and in the rest of the world, but there is still competition among languages. There is little question of the role of Spanish in California because of the numbers of people who speak it. No one doubts the leadership position of English or the role of a uniquely American culture. But, one reaction to the omnipresence of English by specific groups is the development of a variety of English that can be used to express their own cultural and individual identity. The greatest examples are African American Vernacular English (AAVE or Ebonics) and the patchwork of varieties of Hispanic English (e.g., Tex-Mex and Puerto Rican forms of English). ChE may show some linguistic similarities with these other social varieties of English, yet it remains unique, manifesting itself in different degrees according to its many situations of usage (from the spoken to the written). The point is, however, that groups who have felt marginalized by Anglo Saxon culture and language often tailor the English language to their own needs. This has happened worldwide in such varied places as India (and Pakistan), Singapore, Ireland, Scotland, and throughout the Caribbean nations known as the West Indies. There is much to say about a language and its effects on culture, but there is also much to say about a culture and its influence on a language.

Despite the creativity of English speakers and their ability to adapt the language for their own social purposes, the drive towards a unifying language variety (bordering on a national obsession) has not been without its excesses, to be sure. Since the end of the 19th Century, the U.S. has grappled with the dilemma of a national identity forged in a crucible of multilingualism and multiculturalism. In many ways, the nation still seems conflicted by its own vision of the rights of minority groups and the legacy of the Civil Rights Movement of the 1960s (Chapter 5). The nation still faces the challenge of (a) understanding the effects of centuries of linguistic and cultural contact and the dominance of Anglo Saxon culture and (b) learning to embrace its own language and ethnic minorities in the light of the diverse nature of its founding populations. The obvious context is the numerous Native American peoples who were conquered and subjugated by an expansionist American government (and the reluctance to accept total assimilation that it engendered) and all the other groups who knowingly jumped from the frying pan of immigration (as a nation of immigrants) into the proverbial Melting Pot. A very large question remains whether the U.S. will ever learn to harness its own multiculturalism and multilingualism.

One particular theme that has been interwoven either directly or indirectly into the fabric of each chapter is *education*. Chapter 6 provided an explicit overview of the history of bilingual education in the U.S. and the ever-increasing waves of legislation affecting it, some of which have been based on public perceptions more than actual academic concerns. There has been much discussion of a gap in academic achievement between LM students and their "mainstream" counterparts. Some of its possible causes have been discussed, for example, low SES and lack of opportunity. In addition, there is discussion of the nature of testing and the difficulties formal standardized tests can present (e.g., testing bilingual children as if they are monolinguals in each of their languages), and how misunderstanding test results can lead to biased practices that do not solve the problems that the tests are purported to diagnose. There are also many types of bilingual programs to consider. Each has its characteristic goals and expected outcomes. Simply bombarding children with more SAE and prohibiting the learning and usage of native languages/dialects has not proved to be effective, except in certain draconian instances in which native languages and cultures have been eliminated, and that ignore the social cost. In fact, some programs whose goals are clearly subtractive may even aggravate an already tense situation, adding to a sense of disenfranchisement that lies at the root of the achievement gap and many associated social problems.

Literacy has been a concern since the first "Why Johnny can't read" article was written. Chapter 7 deals extensively with literacy, the literacy myth (that people are happier and better citizens when they know how to read in English), and other mis-understandings of the power of literacy. First and foremost is the fact that literacy is a complex, multifaceted concept that goes well beyond simple descriptions that it is merely the ability to read and write in a language – it involves much more. Literacy has particular relevance in linguistic minority communities because so much time and energy has been invested in recent decades in raising the standards of education in the U.S. For teachers in all levels of education, rhetorical issues in composition studies are once again at the forefront, specifically the impact of culture on *thinking* and the students ability to conform to teachers' expectations. It seems clear to most researchers that the type of educational program influences the abilities that students acquire. There are successful programs, and there is responsible research. And, while many approaches to bilingual education may be well-intentioned, there may be heavy and far-reaching educational and socioeconomic costs, especially when the approach is essentially subtractive and a child's linguistic and cultural heritage is looked at as a liability, rather than a potential resource. The positive effects of bilingualism and biliteracy were also discussed, two topics that are systematically ignored in the school reforms being discussed around the country (in view of the Race to the Top initiative).

Two remaining issues worth discussion, particularly amid concerns of ill-prepared and underpaid teachers and teacher shortages, are (a) the responsibility of teachers to teach Anglo Saxon culture to our increasingly diverse student population and (b) the practical limits of cultural homogeneity. At what cost is a monolithic view of Ameri-canization, and how feasible (or desirable) is it to ignore the multicultural and mul-tilingual nature of the nation that the U.S. truly *is*? In the past, some educators have felt that those making important educational decisions in government are doing so for political reasons that fail to recognize the real needs of real children. All are faced with the day-to-day task of justifying expenditures for programs that may not yield clear and positive results in the short-term. But, short-term fixes may actually hinder the long-range success of the children. In the final analysis, much work still needs to be done to find the most productive and cost-effective ways to educate the burgeoning population of bilingual children in states like California. The Chicano-Latino com-munity in this sense is key, by virtue of its size, vitality, and potential for impacting the economic well-being of the State of California and the nation in an increasingly globalized economy.

6.   Final comments

In Chapter 5, there was a discussion of three factors that continue to shape Americans' attitudes towards bilingualism and bilingual education. These factors are immigration, education, and language. Each one is complex and multifaceted, and each can be linked to various other social issues and to the economy in some way. All seem to incite very heated responses in the many arenas where cultural and political battles are waged.

With respect to immigration, a typical concern is that it has reached a kind of critical mass, and something needs to be done about it. This has been a recurrent theme in U.S. politics for well over a century. Some things do need to be considered that are not solely based on the self-interest of one country. For example, since the 1960s, the population of the planet has more than doubled; the growth of the U.S. has lagged behind only very slightly, even with massive in-migration. The U.S. is increasingly tied to world markets for its economic survival, the recent "economic downturn" a case in point. Any discussion of immigration reform needs to be intelligent and not based solely on a national bias. The reality is that the U.S. is (and always has been) a multicultural and multilingual haven. The Civil Rights Movement of the 1960s was inevitable as the social conscience of the nation evolved from one that was patently racist and exclusionary to one that is egalitarian and inclusionary, at least in principle. The U.S. cannot return to a policy that favors only particular immigrants on the basis of race, creed, or color. The alternatives are to be increasingly restrictive by closing the borders and returning to the days of isolationism prior to the Great Wars, or to be selective in some way. If the government does become selective once again, who makes the choices? On what basis can the U.S. government choose which group is acceptable and which one is not? National security is a necessity, but there must be a better way to insure it than to resort to racial profiling. These are more than rhetorical questions. They are some of the biggest issues facing the U.S. in the 21st Century.

With respect to education, children are not the cause of the problems we find, but they are often the victims. They appear to be caught in a tug-of-war pitting two warring factions and ideologies. If educators were to consider what is best for the children, then compromise may be in order. With respect to the Spanish-English bilingual community, there can be many economic benefits of having a highly educated population. Parents, caregivers, and community leaders may also need to make certain adjustments and compromises by supporting literacy practices that could help LM children become better prepared for the sometimes artificial environment of school and the demands of formal, academic, and highly literate forms of language.

Perhaps a national discussion can intelligently address changes in the educational system that truly takes the needs of children as a primary focus, in a nonpartisan manner. It should involve listening to the experts and encouraging research, and it should also include the participation of practitioners, those whose primary concern is education, e.g., administrators, teachers, and other educators responsible for teacher training. Bi- and multilingualism do not have to be considered national problems or strains on the economy. Multilingualism can be developed into a national and regional resource. And, perhaps, the government can develop economic incentives, tax breaks, and so on, to cultivate industry in parts of the country that would negate the need for off-shore expansion by manufacturers, providing work for members of many socio-economic strata. This does not mean the continued exploitation of an ethnic underclass; it means expanding opportunities for U.S. citizens to the benefit of the nation.

In response to concepts of national unity, Americanism, and the desire for cultural homogeneity, there is more than one alternative. As current figures attest, 92% of Americans speak English and speak it well. Two-thirds of all native speakers of English live in the U.S. This demonstrates the role of the English language in the everyday lives of Americans. However, in the interest of freedom, mutual respect, and individual civil rights, linguistic and cultural pluralism is a reasonable alternative. Compromise needs to come from all corners.

Key terms

accountability, additive education, advanced placement (AP), Americanization, barrio, Black English trial, California Department of Education (CDE), California High School Exit Exam (CAHSEE), copula *be*, cultural homogeneity, cultural pluralism, double whammy, English Language Arts (ELA), English Language Development (ELD), expectations, expository writing, flowery language, holistic scoring, language arts, Los Angeles Unified School District (LAUSD), norming, Oakland Ebonics debate, parental involvement, past participle, pop culture, positive transfer, Race to the Top, reform, stigmatized group, structures v. attributes of schools, subtractive education, teacher preparation, test takers, top-down, tracking (streaming), transition, Vietnamese English (VE).

Summary

The state university system is the principle vehicle for teacher training in states like California; its job is to prepare teachers for the realities of the classroom. However, new, inexperienced teachers are often sent into densely populated school districts where the majority of students are NNS of English (e.g., Spanish-English bilinguals of varying proficiencies), where (a) resources for teachers and students are scarce, (b) area residents are more likely to be low-income families, and (c) students and their families are not likely to have a tradition of higher education. It certainly appears that teachers and children are put in a position to fail. While federal initiatives such as the Obama administration's Race to the Top encourage educational reform, there is much controversy on how minority groups can benefit.

For some background, California Department of Education (CDE) figures on student demographics (2005–2006) state: (1) According to English proficiency, 42% of all students enrolled in California public schools are NNS of English; this does not count bilinguals who were considered native in both languages. (2) According to ethnicity, so-called Hispanic or Latino students comprise 47.58 % of the total; Whites comprise 30.34%, by comparison. (3) In the five contiguous counties of Los Angeles, Orange, Riverside, San Bernardino, and San Diego, 59.11 % are Latino; this subgroup accounts for over 56% of the total in the state. (4). In addition, more than two million children in CA public schools are native speakers of Spanish; the younger the student population, the greater the number of Spanish speakers, a significant issue for current and prospective teachers in primary grades.

One of the issues is obviously time, particularly how much time ELLs are allowed before they transition into mainstream classes. Psychologist Robert C. Gardner, an authority on motivation in second language learning, has estimated that ten years is a reasonable amount of time for NNS to catch up to their NS counterparts in written, academic English. Therefore, there is a significant amount of time between (a) being transitioned to FEP status and (b) sufficient mastery of academic English to compete with monolinguals. Raising test scores is not necessarily going to improve language skills or increase the type and amount of knowledge the children actually need for a well-rounded education and to use academic English skillfully.

The California High School Exist Exam (CAHSEE) gives some indication of the state's high school population and their rate of success on standardized exit exams in English Language Arts (ELA) and Mathematics. Results based on ethnicity in 2005–2006 showed that Asian and White students significantly outperformed African American and Hispanic/Latino students on both. Ethnicity appears to be a better predictor of success on the exam than status on proficiency. Regarding NNS, FEPs passed at roughly the same rate as White and Asian populations, proving that cognitive benefits for bilingualism are possible. Test results also suggest that increased proficiency in SAE can cancel the statistical effect for ethnicity. And, it is implied that certain ethnic groups will continue to fail standardized tests.

Minority dialects can contribute to low exam scores. LM writers are often penalized twice (or on two levels) because they may show systematic variation in both (a) surface-level, grammatical aspects of language and (b) divergence in rhetorical styles (e.g., organization and narrative style). So, a student writer may exhibit control of the grammatical features of a standard dialect and not have command of standard rhetorical strategies, and vice versa, having control of one but not the other. Writers get a double whammy when they are penalized twice, for making so many surface mistakes that the reader is distracted from the content of the essay *and* not having command of standard, Anglo Saxon rhetorical patterns – which may be viewed as muddled thinking according to a bias against non-English rhetorical strategies. The question is not *who* fails standardized tests and exit exams, but *why* they fail. Nonstandard dialects of English infer their way into the data for African Americans and Chicano-Latinos because of test bias. The "why" may lie in a mismatch of home language versus academic language. Dialect awareness and knowledge of students' home language and cultural background are ways that teachers can equip themselves for the challenges ahead in multilingual, multicultural classrooms.

Despite a growing Chicano-Latino literature, the model for rhetorical strategies of Chicano-Latinos is evidently not a literate tradition in Spanish. One possibility is that the primary model for written English is the speech (informal, spoken) of peer groups, the voices of Pop culture.

A second is that the subtractive nature of many "weak" bilingual programs has eliminated all traces of Spanish and any cognitive or academic advantage bilinguals might have (that can be transferred to the task of writing). Another is that many Chicanos are the unwitting recipients of the exclusionary practices of tracking/streaming, with its long tradition of assigning minority groups (based on negative stereotypes) to less challenging courses in occupational tracks or streams, where students don't have to write nearly as much as in college prep tracks. All three can work in concert to create the impression of a learning deficit. But, to fix the problems, educators may not have to reinvent the wheel. It is possible to apply the knowledge we already have.

Activities – topics for discussion

1. Describe the roll that a state university system has in teacher preparation in your area. Do campuses provide scholarships and job placement services? Do they provide ample, quality preparation for the realities of the classroom, e.g., how to deal with a diverse student population?

2. Why do you think there is a correlation between low socio-economic status and low scores on standardized tests? Identify causes, and propose solutions.

3. What does the student demographics in California tell you about the typical classroom in the state? In view of the fact that there are so many LM students in certain counties and cities, what can be done to help those specific children?

4. Imagine a teacher saying, presumably in jest, "I think some children should be left behind." She works at a school where nearly 100% of the students are Hispanic, and most of them speak Spanish, so her comment may have come from a feeling of frustration. Be a child advocate and convince her that all of her students deserve an education. Make a list of reasons.

5. Discuss the amount of time that school districts near you give ELLs to transition to English-only classes, and what additional steps could be taken to improve their proficiency in academic English. In addition, explain how you would interest children in reading formal English.

Practice essay questions

1. Describe the double whammy in grading practices. List the features that you would expect in a "conversational" style of writing. Refer to the characteristics of informal, involved registers of English discussed in Chapter 3.

2. Certain minorities consistently score lower on the CAHSEE than mainstream students. Explain how minority dialects and languages can account for some of the disparity in scoring patterns. And, is there such a thing as "White" English?

3. Identify at least three possible reasons why Chicano-Latinos are not influenced by a literate tradition in Spanish. What influence do you see that a growing Chicano-Latino literature may provide?

4. Identify some of the characteristics of schools that have considerable success with LM students. What does this say about school reform?

5. Evidently, there is a long history that can explain why some speakers of minority dialects of English are not motivated to learn SAE. Demanding proficiency in SAE has never helped before. Explain some of the pressures *against* learning Standard English.

References

Acuña, R. F. 1995. *Anything But Mexican: Chicanos in Contemporary Los Angeles*. New York NY: Verso.

Adams, M. J. 1990. *Beginning to Read: Thinking and Learning about Print*. Cambridge MA: The MIT Press.

Adger, C., Wolfram, W. & Christian, D. 2007. *Dialects in Schools and Communities*. Mahwah NJ: Lawrence Erlbaum Associated.

Anaya, R. 1972. *Bless Me Ultima*. Berkley CA: Quinto Sol Publications.

Anzaldúa, G. 1987. *Borderlands/La Frontera: The New Mestiza*. San Francisco CA: Spinsters/Aunt Lute Books.

Atkinson, D. 1999. Culture in TESOL. *TESOL Quarterly* 33: 625–654.

Bailey, G. & Tillery, J. 2006. The Lone Star state of speech (Texas). In *American Voices: How Dialects Differ from Coast to Coast*, W. Wolfram & B. Ward (eds), 36–41. Malden MA: Blackwell.

Baker, C. 2006. *Foundations of Bilingual Education and Bilingualism*. Clevedon: Multilingual Matters.

Baker, C. 2009. Becoming bilingual through bilingual education. In *Handbook of Multilingualism and Multicultural Communication*, P. Auer & L. Wei (eds), 131–152. Berlin: Mouton de Gruyter.

Baker, C. & Jones, P. 1998. *Encyclopedia of Bilingualism and Bilingual Education*. Clevedon, Multilingual Matters.

Bakker, P. 1997. *A Language of Our Own: The Genesis of Michif, the Mixed Cree-French Language of the Canadian Métis*. Oxford: OUP.

Barent, G. P. 2006. Sign language – spoken language bilingualism: Code mixing and mode mixing by ASL-English bilinguals. In *The Handbook of Bilingualism*, T. K. Bhatia & W. C. Ritchie (eds), 312–335. Malden MA: Blackwell.

Baugh, J. 1983. *Black Street Speech: Its History, Structure, and Survival*. Austin TX: University of Texas Press.

Bayley, R. & Santa Ana, O. 2004. Chicano English grammar. In *A Handbook of Varieties of English: Morphology and Syntax*, Vol. 2, B. Kortmann, E. W. Schneider, K. Burridge, R. Mesthrie & C. Upton (eds), 167–183. Berlin: Mouton de Gruyter.

Becker, A. 2006. As Latino students near a majority in California, questions arise. *Contra Costa Times* (7/24/06).

Bhatia, T. K. & Ritchie, W. C. 2006. Introduction. In *The Handbook of Bilingualism*, T. K. Bhatia & W. C. Ritchie (eds), 1–2. Malden MA: Blackwell.

Biber, D. 1988. *Variation across Speech and Writing*. Cambridge: CUP.

Blume, H. 2010. Grade school enrollment falls statewide and in L.A. *Los Angeles Times* (10/12/10).

Brandt, E. 1982. A research agenda for native American languages. In *Bilingualism and Language Contact: Spanish, English, and Native American Languages*, F. Barkin, E. Brandt & J. Ornstein-Galicia (eds). New York NY: Teachers College, Columbia University.

Brisk, M. E. & Harrington, M. M. 2007. *Literacy and Bilingualism: A Handbook for ALL Teachers*, 2nd edn. Mahwah NJ: Lawrence Erlbaum Associates.

Brosnahan, L. 1963. Some historical cases of language imposition. In *Language in Africa*, J. Spencer (ed.). Cambridge: CUP.

Brown, H. D. 1994. *Teaching by Principles: An Interactive Approach to Language Pedagogy*. London: Longman.

Brown, R. 1973. *A First Language: The Early Stages*. Cambridge MA: Harvard University Press.

California Department of Education. <http://www.cde.ca.gov> (20 September, 2005).

Campbell, L. & Muntzel, M.C. 1989. The structural consequences of language death. In *Investigating Obsolescence: Studies in Language Contraction and Death*, N. C. Dorian (ed.), 197–210. Cambridge: CUP.

Canagarajah, S. 2009. The plurilingual tradition and the English language in South Asia. *AILA Review* 22: 5–22.

Castillo, A. 1993. *So Far from God*. New York NY: W.W. Norton.

Chambers, J. K. & Trudgill, P. 1980. *Dialectology*. Cambridge: CUP.

Chavez-Silverman, S. 2004. *Killer Crónicas: Bilingual Memories*. Madison WI: University of Wisconsin Press.

Chomsky, N. 1965. *Aspects of the Theory of Syntax*. Cambridge MA: The MIT Press.

Chomsky, N. 1976. *Reflections on Language*. London: Temple Smith.

Chomsky, N. 1986. *Knowledge of Language: Its Nature, Origin, and Use*. New York NY: Praeger.

Cisneros, S. 1983. *The House on Mango Street*. Houston TX: Arte Público Press.

Comrie, B. 1989. *Language Universals and Linguistic Typology*. Chicago IL: University of Chicago Press.

Connor, U. 1996. *Contrastive Rhetoric: Cross-cultural Aspects of Second Language Writing*. Cambridge: CUP.

Connor, U. 2002. New directions in contrastive rhetoric. *TESOL Quarterly* 36: 493–510.

Connor, U., Nagelhout, E. & Rozycki, W. (eds). 2008. *Contrastive Rhetoric: Reaching to Intercultural Rhetoric* [Pragmatics & Beyond New Series 169]. Amsterdam: John Benjamins.

Connor, U., Nagelhout, E. & Rozycki, W. 2008. Introduction. In Connor, Nagelhout & Rozycki (eds.), 1–8.

Cook-Gumperz, J. 2006a. The social construction of literacy. In *The Social Construction of Literacy*, 2nd edn, J. Cook-Gumperz (ed.), 1–18. Cambridge: CUP.

Cook-Gumperz, J. 2006b. Literacy and schooling: An unchanging equation? In *The Social Construction of Literacy*, 2nd edn, J. Cook-Gumperz (ed.), 19–49. Cambridge: CUP.

Cook, V. J. 1988. *Chomsky's Universal Grammar: An Introduction*. Oxford: Blackwell.

Cook, V. J. 1993. *Linguistics and Second Language Acquisition*. New York NY: St. Martin's Press.

Cornelius, W. 2002. Ambivalent reception: Mass public responses to the "new" Latino immigration to the United States. In *Latinos: Remaking America*, M. M. Suárex-Orozco & M. M. Páez (eds), 165–189. Berkeley CA: University of California Press.

Crawford, J. 1992a. *Hold Your Tongue: Bilingualism and the Politics of "English Only."* Reading MA: Addison-Wesley.

Crawford, J. 1992b. What's behind official English? In *Language Loyalties: A Source Book on the Official English Controversy*, J. Crawford (ed.), 171–177. Chicago IL: University of Chicago Press.

Crawford, J. 1995. *Bilingual Education: History, Politics, Theory, and Practice*. Los Angeles CA: BEA.

Croft, W. 1990. *Typology and Universals*. Cambridge: CUP.

Crystal, D. 1991. *A Dictionary of Linguistics and Phonetics*. Oxford: Blackwell.

Crystal, D. 2000. *Language Death*. Cambridge: CUP.

Cummins, J. 1976. The influence of bilingualism on cognitive growth: A synthesis of research findings and exploratory hypotheses. *Working Papers on Bilingualism* 9: 1–43.

Cummins, J. 1979. Cognitive/academic language proficiency, linguistic interdependence, the optimum age question. *Working Papers on Bilingualism* 19: 121–129.

De Houwer, A. 2005. Early bilingual acquisition: focus on morphosyntax and the Separate Development Hypothesis. In *Handbook of Bilingualism: Psycholinguistic Approaches*, J. Kroll & A. M. de Groot (eds), 30–48. Oxford: OUP.

De Houwer, A. 2009. *Bilingual First Language Acquisition*. Bristol: Multilingual Matters.

Dillard, J. L. 1972. *Black English: Its History and Usage in the United States*. New York NY: Random House.

Dorian, N. C. (ed.). 1989. *Investigating Obsolescence: Studies in Language Contraction and Death*. Cambridge: CUP.

Dorian, N. C. 2006. Minority and endangered languages. In *The Handbook of Bilingualism*, T. K. Bhatia & W. C. Ritchie (eds), 437–459. Malden MA: Blackwell.

Dressler, W. 1988. Language death. In *Linguistics: The Cambridge Survey*, Vol. IV: *Language: The Sociocultural Context*. F. J. Newmeyer (ed.), 184–192. Cambridge: CUP.

Edwards, J. 1994. *Multilingualism*. London: Penguin Books.

Edwards, J. 2006. Foundations of bilingualism. In *The Handbook of Bilingualism*, T. K. Bhatia & W. C. Ritchie (eds), 7–31. Malden MA: Blackwell.

Elías-Olivares, L. 1976. Ways of Speaking in a Chicano Community: A Sociolinguistic Approach. PhD dissertation, University of Texas at Austin.

Elliot, A. J. 1981. *Child Language*. Cambridge: CUP.

Espinosa, A. 1915. Speech mixture in New Mexico: The influence of the English language on New Mexican Spanish. In *The Pacific Ocean in History*, H. Stephens & H. Bolton (eds), 408–428, reprinted in 1975 in *El Lenguaje de los Chicanos: Regional and Social Characteristics Used by Mexican Americans*. E. Hernandez-Chavez, A. D. Cohen & A. F. Beltramo (eds). Arlington, VA: Center for Applied Linguistics.

Eubank, L., Selinker, L. & Sharwood Smith, M. 1995. *The Current State of Interlanguage*. Amsterdam: John Benjamins.

Fennel, B. 2001. *A History of English: A Sociolinguistic Approach*. Malden, MA: Blackwell.

Field, F. 1994. Caught in the middle: The case of Pocho and the mixed language continuum. *General Linguistics* 34(2): 85–105.

Field, F. 1999. Long-term effects of code-switching: Keys to structural borrowing. Paper presented April 17, 1999 at the 2nd International Symposium on Bilingualism, University of Newcastle upon Tyne, UK.

Field, F. 2002. *Linguistic Borrowing in Bilingual Settings* [Studies in Language Companion Series 62]. Amsterdam: John Benjamins.

Field, F. 2004. Second language acquisition in creole genesis: The role of processability. In *Creoles, Contact and Language Change: Linguistics and Social Implications* [Creole Language Library 27], G. Escure & A. Schwegler (eds), 127–160. Amsterdam: John Benjamins.

Field, F. 2005. School-age population in California: A changing demographic. Paper presented at conference on English Language Learners sponsored by Teachers for a New Era at the Warner Marriott Hotel in Los Angeles, CA, September 13, 2005.

Finegan, E. 1994. *Language: Its Structure and Use*, 2nd edn. Fort Worth TX: Harcourt Brace College Publishers.

Fishman, J. 1977. The sociology of language: Yesterday, today, and tomorrow. In *Current Issues in Linguistic Theory*, R. W. Cole (ed.), 51–75. Bloomington IN: University of Indiana Press.

Fishman, J. 1988. The displaced anxieties of Anglo-Americans. Reprinted in 1992 in *Language Loyalties: A Source Book on the Official English Controversy*, J. Crawford (ed.), 165–170. Chicago IL: University of Chicago Press.

Fishman, J. 1989. Whorfianism of the third kind: Ethnolinguistic diversity as a worldwide societal asset. First published in 1982 in *Language in Society* 11: 1–14, and reprinted in *Language and Ethnicity in Minority Sociolinguistic Perspective*, 564–579. Clevedon: Multilingual Matters.

Fishman, J. 1989. *Language and Ethnicity in Minority Sociolinguistic Perspective*. Clevedon: Multilingual Matters.

Fishman, J. 1991. *Reversing Language Shift*. Clevedon: Multilingual Matters.

Fishman, J. 2006. Language maintenance, language shift, and reversing language shift. In *The Handbook of Bilingualism* T. K. Bhatia & W. C. Ritchie (eds), 406–436. Malden MA: Blackwell.

Fought, C. 2003. *Chicano English in Context.* New York NY: Palgrave MacMillan.

Gal, S. 1989. Lexical innovation and loss: The use and value of restricted Hungarian. In *Investigating Obsolescence: Studies in Language Contraction and Death,* N. C. Dorian (ed.), 313–331. Cambridge: CUP.

Gándara, P. 2002. Learning English in California: Guideposts for the nation. In *Latinos: Remaking America,* M. M. Suárez-Orozco & M. M. Páez (eds), 339–358. Berkeley CA: University of California Press.

Gándara, P. & Contreras, F. 2009. *The Latino Education Crisis: The Consequences of Failed Social Policies.* Cambridge MA: Harvard University Press.

Gándara, P., Losen, D., August, D., Uriarte, M., Gómez, M. C. & Hopkins, M. 2010. Forbidden language: A brief history of U.S. language policy. In *Forbidden Language: English Learners and Restrictive Language Policies,* P. Gándara & M. Hopkins (eds), 20–33. New York NY: Teachers College Press.

Gándara, P. & Hopkins, M. 2010. *Forbidden Language: English Learners and Restrictive Language Policies.* New York NY: Teachers College Press.

Gao, H. 2002. LAUSD seeks more ways to teach English. *Daily News* (10/23/02).

Garcia, M. E. 1984. Parameters of the East Los Angeles speech community. In *Form and Function in Chicano English,* J. Ornstein-Galicia (ed.), 85–98. Malabar FL: Robert E. Krieger.

García, O., Bartlett, L. & Kleifgen, J. 2007. From biliteracy to pluriliteracies. In *Handbook of Multilingualism and Multilingual Communication,* P. Auer & L. Wei (eds), 204–227. Berlin: de Gruyter.

Gardner. R. C. 2001. Integrative motivation and second language acquisition. In *Motivation and Second Language Acquisition,* Z. Dörnei & R. Schmidt (eds), 1–19. Mānoa HI: Second Language Teaching & Curriculum Center, University of Hawaii.

Gass, S. M. & Selinker, L. 1993a. Introduction. In *Language Transfer in Language Learning* [Language Acquisition and Language Disorders 5], S. M. Gass & L. Selinker (eds), 1–17. Amsterdam: John Benjamins.

Gass, S. M. & Selinker, L. 1993b. Afterword. In *Language Transfer in Language Learning* [Language Acquisition and Language Disorders 5], S. M. Gass & L. Selinker (eds), 233–236. Amsterdam: John Benjamins.

Gee, J. P. 1992. *The Social Mind: Language, Ideology, and Social Practice.* New York NY: Bergin and Garvey.

Gee, J. P. 1996. *Social Linguistics and Literacies: Ideology in Discourses.* Bristol PA: Falmer Press.

Genesee, F. 2003. Rethinking bilingual acquisition. In *Bilingualism Beyond Basic Principles,* J.-M. Dewaele, A. Housen & L. Wei (eds), 204–228. Clevedon: Multilingual Matters.

Gossett, T. F. 1963. *Race: The History of an Idea in America.* Dallas TX: Southern Methodist University Press.

Gould, S. J. 1981. *The Mismeasure of Man.* New York NY: Norton & Company.

Griswold del Castillo, R. 1990. *The Treaty of Guadalupe Hidalgo: A Legacy of Conflict.* Norman OK: University of Oklahoma Press.

Grosjean, F. 1995. A psycholinguistic approach to code-switching: The recognition of guest words by bilinguals. In *One Speaker, Two Languages: Cross-disciplinary Perspectives on Code-switching,* L. Milroy & P. Muysken (eds), 259–275. Cambridge: CUP.

Grosjean, F. 2006. Studying bilinguals: Methodological and conceptual issues. In *The Handbook of Bilingualism,* T. K. Bhatia & W. C. Ritchie (eds), 33–63. Malden MA: Blackwell.

Gumperz, J. & Levinson, S. 1996. *Rethinking Linguistic Relativity.* Cambridge: CUP.

Gumperz, J. J. 1982. *Discourse Strategies.* Cambridge: CUP.

Hakuta, K. 1986. *Mirror of Language: The Debate on Bilingualism.* New York NY: Basic Books.

Haugen, E. 1950. The analysis of linguistic borrowing. *Language* 26: 210–231.

Haugen, E. 1953[1969]. *The Norwegian Language in America: A Study in Bilingual Behavior.* Philadelphia PA: University of Pennsylvania Press & Bloomington IN: Indiana University Press.

Heller, M. 1982. Negotiations of language choice in Montreal. *In Language and Social Identity*, J. Gumperz (ed.), 108–118. Cambridge: CUP.

Hinkel, E. 2002. *Second Language Writers' Text: Linguistic and Rhetorical Features*. Mahwah NJ: Lawrence Erlbaum Associates.

Hirsch, E. D. Jr. 1987. *Cultural Literacy: What Every American Needs to Know*. Boston MA: Houghton Mifflin.

Hoff, E. 2009. *Language Development*, 4th edn. Belmont CA: Wadsworth Cengage Learning.

Hoffmann, C. 1991. *An Introduction to Bilingualism*. London: Longman.

Holm, J. 1988. *Pidgins and Creoles*, Vol. 1: *Theory and Structure*. Cambridge: CUP.

Hornberger, N. 2003. Continua of biliteracy. In *Continua of Biliteracy: An Ecological Framework for Educational Policy, Research, and Practice in Multilingual Settings*, N. Hornberger (ed.), 3–34. Clevedon: Multilingual Matters.

Hornberger, N. & Skilton-Sylvester, E. 2003. Revisiting continua of biliteracy: International and critical perspectives. In *Continua of Biliteracy: An Ecological Framework for Educational Policy, Research, and Practice in Multilingual Settings*, N. Hornberger (ed.), 35–67. Clevedon: Multilingual Matters.

Huffines, M. L. 1989. Case usage among the Pennsylvania German sectarians and nonsectarians. In *Investigating Obsolescence: Studies in Language Contraction and Death*, N. C. Dorian (ed.), 211–226. Cambridge: CUP.

Hymes, D. 1974. *Foundations in Sociolinguistics: An Ethnographic Approach*. Philadelphia PA: University of Pennsylvania Press.

J. Cook-Gumperz. 2006. *The Social Construction of Literacy*. Cambridge: CUP.

Jackson, R. L. & Richardson, E. (eds.). 2003. *Understanding African American Rhetoric: Classical Origins to Contemporary Innovations*. New York, N.Y.: Routledge.

Joergensen, J. N. & Quist, P. 2009. Bilingual children in monolingual schools. In *Handbook of Multilingualism and Multicultural Communication*, P. Auer & L. Wei (eds), 155–173. Berlin: Mouton de Gruyter.

Johanson, L. 1992. *Strukturelle Faktoren in tuerkischen Sprachkontakten*. Stuttgart: F. Steiner.

Johnson, J. S. & Newport, E. L. 1989. Critical period effects in second language learning: The influence of maturational state on the acquisition of English as a second language. *Cognitive Psychology* 21: 60–99.

Kaplan, R. 1966. Cultural thought patterns in intercultural education. *Language Learning* 16: 1–20.

Krashen, S. 1985. *The Input Hypothesis: Issues and Implications*. London: Longman.

Kroll, J & de Groot, A. M. 1997. Lexical and conceptual memory in the bilingual: Mapping form to meaning in two languages. In *Tutorials in Bilingualism: Psycholinguistic Perspectives*, J. Kroll & A. M. de Groot (eds), 169–199. Mahwah, NJ: Lawrence Erlbaum Associates.

Labov, W. 1972. *Sociolinguistic Patterns*. Philadelphia PA: University of Pennsylvania Press.

Labov, W. 1982. Objectivity and commitment in linguistic science: The case of the Black English trial in Ann Arbor. *Language in Society* 11: 165–202.

Labov, W. 2006. *The Social Stratification of English in New York City*, 2nd ed. Cambridge: CUP.

Ladefoged, P. 1975. *A Course in Phonetics*. New York NY: Harcourt Brace Jovanovich.

Lakoff, G. 1987. *Women, Fire, and Dangerous Things: What Categories Reveal about the Mind*. Chicago IL: University of Chicago Press.

Lakoff, R. 1975. *Language and Woman's Place*. New York NY: Harper and Row.

Larsen-Freeman, D. & Long, M. H. 1991. *An Introduction to Second Language Acquisition Research*. London: Longman.

Lehmann, W. P. 1992. *Historical Linguistics, An Introduction*. New York NY: Holt, Rinehart and Winston.

Lewis, M. P. (ed.). 2009. *Ethnologue: Languages of the World*. Dallas TX: SIL.

Lightbown, P. & Spada, N. 2008. *How Languages are Learned*. Oxford: OUP.

Lindfors, J. W. 1980. *Children's Language and Learning*. Englewood Cliffs, NJ: Prentice-Hall, Inc.

Linton, A. & Franklin, R. 2010. Bilingualism for the children: Dual-language programs under restrictive language policies. In *Forbidden Language: English Learners and Restrictive Language Policies*, P. Gándara & M. Hopkins (eds), 175–191. New York NY: Teachers College Press.

Lippi-Green, R. 2004. Language ideology and language prejudice. In *Language in the USA: Themes for the Twenty-first Century*, E. Finegan & J. Rickford (eds), 289–304. Cambridge: CUP.

Lucas, T., Henze, R. C. & Donato, R. 1990. Promoting the success of Latino language-minority students: And exploratory study of six high schools. *Harvard Educational Review* 60(3): 315–340.

Lucy, J. A. 1992. *Language Diversity and Thought: A Reformulation of the Linguistic Relativity Hypothesis*. Cambridge: CUP.

Lux, P. 1991. Discourse Styles of Anglo and Latin American College Student Writers. PhD dissertation, Arizona State University.

Makgamatha, P. M. 1999. Narration as art in the Northern Soth narrative: From oral to written. In *African Mosaic: Festschrift for J. A. Louw*, R. Finlayson (ed.), 1–13. Pretoria: University of South Africa.

Martin-Jones, M. & Jones, K. 2000. Introduction: Multilingual literacies. In *Multilingual Literacies* [Studies in Written Language and Literarcy 10], M. Martin-Jones and K. Jones (eds), 1–15. Amsterdam: John Benjamins.

Matras, Y. 2000. How predictable is contact-induced change in grammar. In *Time Depth in Historical Linguistics*, Vol. 2., C. Renfrew, A. McMahon & L. Trask (eds), 563–583. Cambridge: Oxbow Books.

McLaughlin, B. 1978. *Second Language Acquisition in Childhood*. Hillsdale NJ: Lawrence Erlbaum Associates.

Meisel, J. 2006. The bilingual child. In *The Handbook of Bilingualism*, T. K. Bhatia & W. C. Ritchie (eds.), 91–113. Malden: Blackwell

Menn, L. 1989. Some people who don't talk right: Universal and particular in child language, aphasias, and language obsolescence. In *Investigating Obsolescence: Studies in Language Contraction and Death*, N. C. Dorian (ed.), 335–345. Cambridge: CUP.

Metcalf, A. 1974. The study of California Chicano English. *Linguistics* 128: 53–58.

Meyer, M. C., Sherman, W. L. & Deeds, S. 1999. *The Course of Mexican History*. Oxford: OUP.

Michael, E. & Gollan, T. 2005. Being and becoming bilingual: Individual differences and consequences for language production. In *Handbook of Bilingualism: Psycholinguistic Approaches*, J. Kroll & A. de Groot (eds), 389–407. Oxford: OUP.

Moll, L. & Ruiz, R. 2002. The schooling of Latino children. In *Latinos: Remaking America*, M. M. Suárez-Orozco & M. M. Páez (eds), 362–374. Berkeley CA: University of California Press.

Montaño-Harmon, M. 1991. Discourse features of written Mexican Spanish: Current research in contrastive rhetoric and its implications. *Hispania* 74: 417–425.

Moore, J. & Vigil, J. 1993. Barrios in transition. In *the Barrios: Latinos and the Underclass Debate*, J. Moore & R. Pinderhughes (eds), 27–49. New York NY: Russell Sage Foundation.

Moore, J. & Pachon, H. 1985. *Hispanics in the United States*. Englewood Cliffs NJ: Prentice-Hall.

Mougeon, R. & Beniak, E. 1989. Language contraction and linguistic change: The case of Welland French. In *Investigating Obsolescence: Studies in Language Contraction and Death*, N. C. Dorian (ed.), 287–312. Cambridge: CUP.

Mous, M. 2003. *The Making of a Mixed Language: The Case of Ma'a/Mbugu* [Creole Language Library 26]. Amsterdam: John Benjamins.

Mufwene, S. 2001. *The Ecology of Language Evolution*. Cambridge: CUP.

Muysken, P. 2000. *Bilingual Speech: A Typology of Code-Mixing*. Cambridge: CUP.

Myers-Scotton, C. 1993a. *Duelling Languages: Grammatical Structure in Codeswitching*. Oxford: OUP.

Myers-Scotton, C. 1993b. *Social Motivations for Codeswitching*. Oxford: OUP.

Myers-Scotton, C. 2002. *Contact Linguistics: Bilingual Encounters and Grammatical Outcomes*. Oxford: OUP.

Myers-Scotton, C. 2006. *Multiple Voices: An Introduction to Bilingualism.* Oxford: Blackwell.

Nash, G. B., Jeffrey, J., Howe, J., Frederick, P., Davis, A. & Winkler, A. 1990. *The American People: Creating a Nation and a Society,* Vol. 1, 2nd edn. New York NY: Harper Collins.

Nation, I. S. P. 1990. *Teaching and Learning Vocabulary.* Boston MA: Heinle and Heinle.

National Virtual Translation Center. <http://www.nvtc.gov/lotw/languageStudy.html> (July 11, 2009).

Oakes, J. 1985. *Keeping Track: How Schools Structure Equality.* New Haven CT: Yale University Press.

Ogbu, J. 1987. Variability in minority responses to schooling: Nonimmigrants vs. immigrants. In *Interpretive Ethnography of Education: At Home and Abroad,* G. Spindler & L. Spindler (eds), 255–278. Hillsdale NJ: Lawrence Erlbaum Associates.

Pearson, B. Z. 2002. Bilingual infants: Mapping the research agenda. In *Latinos: Remaking America,* M. M. Suárez-Orozco & M. M. Páez (eds), 306–320. Berkeley CA: University of California Press.

Pearson, B., Fernandez, S. C. & Oller, D. K. 1995. Cross-language synonyms in the lexicons of bilingual infants: One language or two? *Journal of Child Language* 22: 345–368.

Peñalosa, F. 1980. *Chicano Sociolinguistics: A Brief Introduction.* Rowley MA: Newbury House.

Penfield, J. 1984. The vernacular base of literacy development in Chicano English. In *Form and Function in Chicano English,* J. Ornstein-Galicia (ed.), 71–81. Malabar FL: Robert E. Krieger.

Penfield, J. & Ornstein-Galicia, J. L. 1985. *Chicano English: An Ethnic Contact Dialect* [Varieties of English around the World G7]. Amsterdam: John Benjamins.

Pienemann, M. 1998. *Language Processing and Second Language Development: Processability Theory* [Studies in Bilingualism 15]. Amsterdam: John Benjamins.

Pienemann, M. 2000. Psycholinguistic mechanisms in the development of English as a second language. In *Language Use, Language Acquisition, and Language History: (Mostly) Empirical Studies in Honour of Rüdiger Zimmerman,* I. Plag & K. P. Schneider (eds). Trier: Wissenshaftlicher Verlag Trier.

Pinker, S. 1994. *The Language Instinct.* New York NY: Harper Collins.

Poplack, S. & Meecham, M. 1995. Patterns of language mixture: Nominal structure on Wolof-French and Fongbe-French bilingual discourse. In *One Speaker, Two Languages: Cross-disciplinary Perspectives on Code-switching,* L. Milroy & P. Muysken (eds), 199–232. Cambridge: CUP.

Ramírez, M. & Castañeda, A. 1974. *Cultural Democracy, Biocognitive Development, and Education.* Orlando FL: Academic Press.

Reid, J. 1988. Quantitative differences in English Prose Written by Arabic, Chinese, Spanish, and English Students. PhD dissertation, Colorado State University.

Resnick, D. P. & Resnick, L. B. 1988. The nature of literacy: A historical exploration. In *Perspectives on Literacy,* E. R. Kintgen, B. M. Kroll & M. Rose (eds). Carbondale IL: Southern Illinois University Press.

Reymer, J. 1992. Policies towards American Indian languages: A historical sketch. In *Language Loyalties: A Source Book on the Official English Controversy,* J. Crawford (ed.), 41–47. Chicago IL: University of Chicago Press.

Rickford, J. R. & Rickford, R. J. 2000. *Spoken Soul: The Story of Black English.* New York NY: John Wiley & Sons.

Rivera, T. 1967. *Y no se lo trago la tierra.* Berkeley CA: Quinto Sol Publications.

Rodriguez, L. J. 1993. *Always Running: La Vida Loca, Gang Days in L.A.* Willimantic CT: Curbstone Press.

Romaine, S. 1989. Pidgins, creoles, immigrant, and dying languages". In *Investigating Obsolescence: Studies in Language Contraction and Death,* N. C. Dorian (ed.), 369–383. Cambridge: CUP.

Romaine, S. 1995. *Bilingualism,* 2nd edn [Language in Society 13]. Cambridge MA: Blackwell.

Romo, R. 1983. *East Los Angeles: History of a Barrio.* Austin TX: University of Texas Press.

Rothman, J. & Rell, A. B. 2005. A linguistic analysis of Spanglish: Relating language to identity. *Linguistics and the Human Sciences* V(1.3): 515–536.

Rumberger, R. W. & Tran, L. 2010. State language policies, school language practices, and the English Learner Achievement gap. In *Forbidden Language: English Learners and Restrictive Language Policies*, P. Gándara & M. Hopkins (eds), 86–101. New York NY: Teachers College Press.

Santa Ana, O. 1991. Phonetic Simplification Processes in the English of the Barrio: A Cross-generational Study of the Chicanos of Los Angeles. PhD dissertation, University of Pennsylvania.

Santa Ana, O. & Bayley, R. 2004. Chicano English phonology. In *A Handbook of Varieties of English*, Vol. 1: *Phonology*, E.W. Schneider, B. Kortmann, K. Burridge, R. Mesthrie & C. Upton (eds), 407–424. Berlin: Mouton de Gruyter.

Sapir, E. 1921. *Language: An Introduction to the Study of Speech*. New York NY: Harcourt Brace Jovanovich.

Seelye, H. N. 1994. *Teaching Culture: Strategies for Intercultural Communication*. Lincolnwood IL: National Textbook Company.

Serros, M. 1994. *Chicana Falsa and Other Stories of Death, Identity and Oxnard*. Valencia CA: Lalo Press.

Serros, M. 2000. *How to Be a Chicana Role Model*. New York NY: Riverhead Books.

Silva-Corvalán, C. 1994. *Language Contact and Change: Spanish in Los Angeles*. Oxford: OUP.

Skutnab-Kangas, T. & Toukomaa, P. 1976. *Teaching Migrant Children's Mother Tongue and Learning the Language of the Host Country in the Context of the Sociocultural Situation of the Migrant Family*. Helsinki: Finnish National Commission for UNESCO.

Skutnab-Kangas, T. & Toukomaa, P. 1976. *Teaching Migrant Children's Mother Tongue and Learning the Language of the Host Country in the Context of the Sociocultural Situation of the Migrant Family*. Helsinki: Finnish National Commission for UNESCO.

Skutnabb-Kangas, T. 1981. *Bilingualism or Not? The Education of Minority Children*. Clevedon: Multilingual Matters.

Smitherman. G. 1978. *Talkin and Testifyin: The Language of Black America*. Detroit: Wayne State University Press.

Soto, G. 1976. *The Elements of San Joaquin*. Pittsburgh PA: University of Pittsburgh Press.

Soto, G. 1978. *The Tale of Sunlight*. Pittsburgh PA: University of Pittsburg Press.

Spindler, G. & Spindler, L. (eds). 1987. *Interpretive Ethnography of Education: At Home and Abroad*. Hillsdale NJ: Lawrence Erlbaum Associates.

Spolsky, B. 1988. Bilingualism. In *Linguistics: The Cambridge Survey*, Vol. IV: *Language: The Socio-cultural Context*, F. J. Newmeyer (ed.), 100–118. Cambridge: CUP.

Steele, R. 2008. Mexican Americans in 1940: Perceptions and conditions. In *World War II and Mexican American Civil Rights*, R. Griswold del Castillo (ed.), 7–18. Austin TX: University of Texas Press.

Street, B. 2001. Literacy events and literacy practices: Theory and practice in the New Literacy Studies. In *Multilingual Literacies* [Studies in Written Language and Literacy 10], M. Martin-Jones & K. Jones (eds), 17–29. Amsterdam: John Benjamins.

Suárez-Orozco, M. M. & Páez, M. M. 2002. Introduction. In *Latinos: Remaking America*, M. M. Suárez-Orozco & M. M. Páez (eds), 1–37. Berkeley CA: University of California Press.

Thomason, S. G. 1997. Introduction. In *Contact Languages: A Wider Perspective* [Creole Language Library 17], S. G.Thomason (ed.), 1–8. Amsterdam: John Benjamins.

Thomason, S. G. 2001. *Language Contact: An Introduction*. Washington DC: Georgetown University Press.

Thomason, S. G. & Kaufman, T. 1988. *Language Contact, Creolization, and Genetic Linguistics*. Berkeley CA: University of California Press.

Trudgill, P. 1999. *The Dialects of England*. Oxford: Blackwell.

Tsitsipis, L. 1989. Skewed performance and full performance in language obsolescence: The case of an Albanian variety. In *Investigating Obsolescence: Studies in Language Contraction and Death*, N. C. Dorian (ed.), 117–138. Cambridge: CUP.

US Census Bureau. Language use and English-speaking ability: 2000. Issued October 2003. <http://www.census.gov/prod/2003pubs/c2kbr-29.pdf> (August 28, 2009).

US Census Bureau. Robert Bernstein, May 17, 2007. <http://www.census.gov/Press-Release/www/releases/archives/population/010048.html> (August 28, 2009).

Valdés, G. 1998. The world outside and inside school: Language and immigrant children. *Educational Researcher* 27 (6), 4–18.

Van Coetsem, F. 2000. *A General and Unified Theory of the Transmission Process in Language Contact*. Heidelberg: C. Winter.

Vigil, J. 1988. *Barrio Gangs: Street Life and Identity in Southern California*. Austin TX: University of Texas Press.

Vigil, J. 2007. *The Projects: Gang and Non-gang Families in East Los Angeles*. Austin: TX: University of Texas Press.

Vigil, J. D. 1980. *From Indians to Chicanos: The Dynamics of Mexican American Culture*. Prospect Heights IL: Waveland Press.

Villarreal, J. A. 1959. *Pocho*. Garden City NY: Doubleday and Company.

Wald, B. 1984. The status of Chicano English as a dialect of American English. In *Form and Function in Chicano English,* J. Ornstein-Galicia (ed.), 14–31. Malabar FL: Robert E. Krieger.

Wardhaugh, R. 2006. *An Introduction to Sociolinguistics*. New York NY: Blackwell.

Weinreich, U. 1953 [1968]. *Languages in Contact*. The Hague: Mouton.

Weltens, B. & Grendel, M. 1993. Attrition of vocabulary knowledge. In *The Bilingual Lexicon* [Studies in Bilingualism 6], R. Schreuder & B. Weltens (eds), 135–156. Amsterdam: John Benjamins.

Wentworth, L., Pellegrin, N., Thomson, K. & Hakuta, K. 2010. Proposition 227 in California: A long-term appraisal of its impact on English Learner student achievement. In *Forbidden Language: English Learners and Restrictive Language Policies*, P. Gándara & M. Hopkins (eds), 37–49. New York NY: Teachers College Press.

Wiley, T. G. 1988. Literacy, Biliteracy, and Educational Achievement among the Mexican-origin Population in the United States. PhD dissertation, University of Southern California.

Wiley, T. G. 2005. *Literacy and Language Diversity in the United States*. Washington DC: Center for Applied Linguistics.

Wiley, T. G. 2007. Immigrant language minorities in the United States. In *Handbooks of Applied Linguistics*, Vol. 9: *Language and communication: Diversity and change*. Berlin: Mouton de Gruyter.

Wolfram, W. 1969. *A Linguistic Description of Detroit Negro Speech*. Washington DC: Center for Applied Linguistics.

Wolfram, W. & Fasold, R. 1974. *The Study of Social Dialects in American English*. Englewood Cliffs NJ: Prentice-Hall.

Wolfram, W. 1985. Variability in tense marking: A case for the obvious. *Language Learning* 35, 229–253.

Wolfram, W. 1989. Systematic variability in second-language tense marking. In *The Dynamic Interlanguage: Empirical Studies in Second Language Variation*, M. R. Eisenstein (ed.), 187–197. New York and London: Plenum Press.

Wolfram, W., & Hatfield, D. 1986. Interlanguage fads and linguistic reality: The case of tense marking. In *Languages and Linguistics: The Interdependence of Theory, Data, and Application*, D. Tannen & J. E. Alatis (eds.), 17–34. Washington, D.C.: Georgetown University Press.

Wolfram, W., & Thomas, E. R. 2002. *The Development of African American English*. Malden, MA: Blackwell.

Wolfram, W., D. Christian, & D. Hatfield. 1986. The English of adolescent and young adult Vietnamese refugees in the United States. *World Englishes* 5 (1): 47–60.

Woolard, K. A. 1989. Language convergence and language death as social processes. In *Investigating Obsolescence: Studies in Language Contraction and Death*, N. C. Dorian (ed.), 355–368. Cambridge: CUP.

Yip, V. & Matthews, S. 2007. *The Bilingual Child: Early Development and Language Contact*. Cambridge: CUP.

Zentella, A. C. 1997. *Growing Up Bilingual: Puerto Rican Children in New York*. Oxford: Blackwell.

Zentella, A. C. 2002. Latin@ languages and identities. In *Latinos: Remaking America*, M. M. Suárez-Orozco & M. M. Páez (eds), 321–338. Berkeley CA: University of California Press.

Zentella, A. C. 2005. Introduction: Perspectives on language and literacy in Latino families and communities. In *Building on Strength: Language and Literacy in Latino families and Community*, A. C. Zentella (ed.), 1–12. New York NY: Teachers College Press & Covina CA: California Association of Bilingual Education (CABE).

Index